DECEPTION

by

Charles R. Smith

Deception

Published by:

Main Headquarters:

The Pine Lake Media Group
208 Pine Lake Avenue, Suite #200
La Porte, IN 46350-3032

Sales, Inquires:

The Pine Lake Media Group
P.O. Box 211054
Columbus, OH 43221-1054

Phone: (614) 275-0830
Fax: (614) 275-0829

Website: http://www.pinelakemedia.com
E-Mail: sales@pinelakemedia.com

Author: Charles R. Smith
Cover Art by: Anonymous
Proof by: Keith W. Kimmel

Printed and Assembled in the United States of America.

ISBN: 0-9761168-0-4

CONTENTS

DECEPTION

INTRODUCTION

There are those who claim that the Clinton administration only lied to the world about sex. The claims are wrong because I was a witness to the smashing of the biggest lie, the arming of communist China.

I am not a lawyer but I have won three out of four cases brought before a Federal Court. The wins were against the best lawyers that the government could buy. The victories also came at a cost, not to me, but to the credibility of the U.S. government and the Clinton presidency.

The first and most damaging lie that the Clinton lawyers made was that a Chinese commissioner, named Shen, was a civilian representative of the communist government, and not a member of the People's Liberation Army. This claim, and the accompanying claim of personal and business privacy, was made before a Federal Judge. The claim was part of an elaborate effort to deny access to over 1,000 pages of information dealing with Shen and his so-called civilian organization, the Commission of Science, Technology and Industry for National Defense (COSTIND).

When the Clinton lawyers finished I, in turn, dropped a complete bio of General Shen on the desk of Federal Judge Robert Payne. The dossier on General Shen included his current military status and details about COSTIND the military unit he was in. Shen was not only second in charge of COSTIND but the unit itself is run entirely by and for the Chinese Army under the command of General Ding Henggao.

To say that Judge Payne was upset is an understatement. While many Judges facing Clinton administration lawyers took lying for granted, Judge Payne threatened to lock all of the U.S. government attorneys up and throw away the key if he did not have the 1,000 pages of withheld materials on his desk in 48 hours. This book, in part, is based on that hard won material.

It took some risk and a great deal of effort on my part to win back the Freedom of Information that was ours to begin with. Death threats and various probes of personal and private information are common now. The cost, personally and professionally, has been great.

The price of documenting the success of General Shen and his commander General Ding is small when compared to what the Chinese Army obtained from the Clinton administration.

In a span of eight years the PLA moved from a second rate peasant army to a first class global fighting force. That great leap forward came from the incredible success of General Shen, General Ding and others like them who won the first information war. The Chinese Army took the Clinton White House armed only with a checkbook.

DECEPTION

1

LORAL AND HUGHES

All war is based on deception…
Sun Tzu - The Art of War

In 1989 China faced a military crisis. China was about to become an ex-super power. In 1989, Major General Yang Huan, Chinese Deputy Commander of the Second Artillery (Strategic Rocket Forces), wrote a paper in the National Defense review. Yang admitted that China had to rapidly improve the red nuclear missile force or face third rank global status.

General Yang outlined three areas absolutely necessary for China to "improve" its aging "first generation" of nuclear missiles. General Yang's three goals were to improve "the survivability… the striking ability… [And] the penetration technology of strategic weapons." According to Yang, "accuracy and power are chief factors used to judge weapon striking power."

Yang wrote in 1989 that China's strategic missiles were cumbersome, inaccurate and unreliable. Yang predicted that in the near future American anti-missile defenses would halt any Chinese missile attack.

According to Yang, "strategic weapons can be used in actual fighting only when they can penetrate enemy defenses and reach and strike the target a necessary condition to protect itself and destroy a target."

Yang's fear was that America would deploy a "STAR WARS" system large enough to neutralize China's nuclear missile force but small enough to not threaten Russia. The U.S./Iraq Gulf war that followed Yang's article was filled with nightly battles between Patriot and SCUD. The results from the Iraq war accelerated the military view that anti-missile systems could neutralize Chinese rocket forces.

In 1994, General Ding Henggao served as Chairman, Commission on Science, Technology and National Defense Industry (COSTIND). General Ding solved China's nuclear strategic problems.

In 1994, General Ding wrote a small article titled REFORMING DEFENSE SCIENCE, TECHNOLOGY, AND INDUSTRY that appeared in China Military Science.

Ding wrote "in a future anti-aggression war, our country will uphold the concept of active defense. It means that active defense is not just defensive, it is offensive as well. Our air-defense weapons system and even the whole

1

weapons system should have two capabilities. It could greatly help overall quality and effectiveness if we possess one or two effective weapons that can assume the offensive."

In 1994, Chinese Army General Ding Henggao, and his team of two sub-commanders, Lt. General Shen Rongjun and Lt. General Huai Guomo, led the most spectacular raid of U.S. military technology since the 1949 atomic espionage by Soviet spies, Ethel and Julius Rosenberg.

Secret documents forced from the Commerce Dept. by a Federal lawsuit prove that the Clinton administration sought direct military exports to China. The documents detail Commerce Dept. contacts with a Chinese Army unit called COSTIND.

COSTIND, according to the General Accounting Office, "oversees development of China's weapon systems and is responsible for identifying and acquiring telecommunications technology applicable for military use."

In 1994 COSTIND took the offensive - target USA. COSTIND Vice Minister, Lt. General Shen met and consummated a series of satellite deals with Bernard Schwartz the CEO of Loral. The technology obtained from the COSTIND/Loral deals saved China billions in missile R&D and turned the Second Corps into a deadly force of thermonuclear war.

In 1994 Bernard Schwartz, CEO of Loral Aerospace, went to China with Commerce Secretary Ron Brown. Bernard Schwartz, by co-incidence, also donated just over a million dollars to the DNC.

Before moving to Commerce, Brown headed the Democratic National Committee. The Federal Election Commission fined the DNC in 2002 for "knowingly and willingly" accepting donations from Chinese army sources.

When Mr. Schwartz flew to China he hoped to make a sale or two. For example, Loral manufactures satellites, radars, global navigation and world-wide secure communications systems. All the fine things a "wannabe" super-power would desire.

In 1994, just prior to traveling with Brown, Mr. Schwartz had his LORAL staff prepare a shopping list for the Chinese and Ron Brown. This list, complete with very big pictures, would make Loral's large ticket items easier to understand and digest at Ron Brown's (executive) level. However, the same list would also make anyone familiar with military equipment go bananas.

On that day Ron Brown stopped being Secretary of Commerce and started his new career as an international arms dealer. The items LORAL carried to the meeting with Ron Brown resemble a JANE'S Defense catalog of high tech weapons.

Some of the Loral suggested "red" ticket items up for sale included "Airborne Reconnaissance Cameras, Weapon Delivery, Target Acquisition, Missile Guidance, Shipboard Target Acquisition, Radar Warning, Missile Warning, RF Jamming, IR Jamming..." and so on.

Please note - Anything that starts with "weapon", "missile" or "target acquisition" does NOT qualify as a civilian application.

During the August 1994 trade trip to China, Schwartz met with Liu Ju-Yuan the minister of China Aerospace Corporation. China Aerospace makes both the civilian Long March rocket and the nuclear tipped CSS missile for the Chinese Army Second Artillery Corps.

Minister Liu is also the official boss of Chinese Army Colonel Liu Chao Ying who contributed thousands of dollars to the DNC through convicted

China-Gate figure Johnny Chung. Colonel Liu's real boss, however, turned out to be General Ji, the Military Intelligence Director of the People's Liberation Army.

Schwartz also met directly with a Chinese General at his own request. In 1994, Chinese Army Lieutenant General Shen Rougjun was second in command at COSTIND - the Chinese Commission for Science, Technology and Industry for National Defense. In 1994, COSTIND General Shen attended several business meetings with Hughes and Loral.

In August 1994, Lt. General Shen met and consummated a series of satellite deals with Bernard Schwartz, the CEO of Loral. The Beijing meeting was requested by Schwartz arranged by President Clinton and included Commerce Secretary Ron Brown. The technology obtained from Loral included advanced rocket guidance and encrypted satellite telemetry systems.

Loral's CEO says the company never sought special treatment but the facts and documents differ from his assertion. The August 1994 meeting with General Shen was at the request of Loral CEO Bernard Schwartz. President Clinton personally approved the request.

Furthermore, in June of 1994, presidential aide and Democrat Party fundraiser Mark Middleton received a letter from Loral Chairman Bernard Schwartz.

Schwartz, a million dollar donor to the Democrat Party and a donor to Mrs. Clinton's New York Senate bid, thanked Middleton for a 1994 meeting at the White House with another top Clinton aide "Mr. McLarty." The letter was obtained from the U.S. Commerce Department by using the Freedom of Information Act.

The meeting, according to a Loral attachment, was to ask Russia to change their "GLONASS" navigation satellite system to another radio frequency. According to Loral, "international aviation interests are considering using GLONASS for position-location, navigation and precision landing of civil aircraft, either alone or in conjunction with the U.S. GPS system."

The "problem" was that the U.S. GPS system "could interfere with the receipt of GLONASS signals used by aircraft for precision landings.... The Russian administration is very interested in the use of GLONASS by the aviation community as part of a Global Navigation Satellite System (GNSS) which would utilize both the U.S. GPS system and GLONASS."

"Russia has stated it is willing to consider such a frequency shift over the next few years. It is critical that the Russians make a commitment that the frequency shift will occur, and provide a timetable for implementation of this change."

And what of the joint U.S./Russian system pushed by Schwartz? The shared Russian GLONASS and U.S. GPS system sought by Schwartz succeeded. Russia moved their satellite frequencies and a whole new line of avionics were developed for the market. The global military market.

It is not civilian airliners that guide themselves for "precision landings". Instead, both U.S. and Russian military forces depend on accurate GPS and GLONASS satellite signals for weapons. The most accurate U.S. bombs that fell on Serbia used GPS satellite to land within inches of their intended targets. Russian made GLONASS guided bombs also continue to fall inside Chechnya with devastating accuracy.

3

Still, the largest buyer of dual GLONASS/GPS guided weapons is China. Ashtech, a maker of GPS (Global Positioning Satellite) receivers, gave Chinese Army Air Force officers a demonstration in Sunnyvale California. The briefing for the Chinese Air Force and Chinese Navy states, "Ashtech produces a receiver that uses both the U.S. GPS signals and the Russian GLONASS signals resulting in significantly greater availability and integrity."

According to a 1997 Rand Corp. report on the Chinese Defense Industry, "more accurate GPS systems would enhance the PLA's ability to carry out attacks against Taiwan's military and industrial facilities, potentially reducing the ability of the Taiwanese military to defend itself against PRC coercive diplomacy."

"The use of GPS to enhance the accuracy of long-range Chinese cruise missiles, coupled with long-range sensors, would raise serious concerns for the U.S. Seventh Fleet in the Pacific, and possibly circumscribe their ability to provide an effective deterrent in a crisis over Taiwan," concluded the Rand report.

In February 1996, a Chinese Long March rocket carrying a Loral Intelsat satellite failed and crashed on lift-off. The Loral Intelsat payload was also destroyed. The Chinese intended to launch the Loral satellite into deep space as they had been paid to do by Mr. Schwartz.

However, it was discovered that a vital computer control board was missing from the satellite. The satellite would have failed in orbit. The missing board from the Loral Intelsat satellite is no mystery. Chinese engineers removed it and kept the board for examination. The stolen Loral electronics consist of radiation hardened, encrypted, telemetry chips, stored in a hardened flight control box similar to those found on airliners.

The Chinese operation was the perfect crime. China could blame American engineers when the satellite failed to function. The sabotaged satellite would be given up as space junk and lost forever. The U.S. could not recover the satellite to discover the real cause of the failure without great expense.

However, fate took a twisted path, and so did the Chinese rocket. The Long March rocket failed on launch and crashed into a nearby Chinese village, killing over 200 innocent civilians. The failure of the Long March allowed the U.S. to recover the sealed satellite guidance box that revealed the control board of radiation-hardened chips was missing.

Loral and Chinese engineers worked together to determine the reason for the Long March vehicle failure. The investigation led by General Shen of COSTIND revealed the many flaws in Chinese missile guidance and control systems.

Improvements in rocket electronics design and guidance system assembly obtained directly from Loral were quickly applied to the Second Artillery's force of CSS strategic missiles. Loral engineers eagerly improved Chinese nuclear missile accuracy and reliability to near state of the art.

Previous flight test results indicated that almost half of the CSS class missile force would fail due to bad guidance. Today, China operates with the verified results from Long March test flights funded by U.S. satellite launches.

The Chinese missile force will perform flawlessly, dropping nuclear payloads within yards of any target on Earth. The Second Artillery has a reliable global reach with powerful accuracy thanks to the successful COSTIND operation with Loral.

Loral provided more than accurate navigation and control systems to the Chinese Army. A 1996 State Department report contradicts Clinton administration claims that advanced communications exports to China were for "civilian" projects. The report states that the Chinese Army was keenly interested in obtaining Loral Globalstar satellite technology. Loral Globalstar satellite cellular phones use a unique communications technology originally built for the U.S. military called Code Division Multiple Access (CDMA).

Ambassador to China and former Tennessee Senator, James Sasser wrote the 1996 Department report. Sasser was the target of a Dept. of Justice investigation that resulted in 47 indictments against a million dollar Democratic donor and Sasser associate, Franklin Haney.

The 1996 State Department report was obtained using the Freedom of Information Act (FOIA). In addition, the State Department refused to release another document on Clinton sponsored exports to China, claiming to do so would threaten the "national defense".

The report states "The PLA has for some time been discussing with the MPT (Ministry of Posts and Telecommunications) the possibility of using frequencies allocated to the PLA for establishing a mobile phone network based on CODE DIVISION MULTIPLE ACCESS (CDMA) technology."

A secret 1996 White House memo shows that Loral requested that President Clinton delay a pending waiver for a satellite export. The delay also came at a time when Loral was under secret investigation by the FBI for sending advanced satellite technology to China without a waiver.

According to the July 1, 1996 action memo for Presidential National Security Advisor Anthony Lake, "In mid-June, Globalstar's parent company, Loral requested that we temporarily delay evaluation of their request for a national interest waiver for this project. The company has now asked us to resume processing of their application, and State has confirmed its support for approval of the license."

"The Dept. of State, with the concurrence of the Departments of Commerce and Defense and the Officer of Science and Technology Policy, recommends that the President report to Congress that it

is in the national interest to waive the Tiananmen Square sanctions in order to allow the licensing of communications satellites and related equipment for export to China," states the memo.

In July 1996, President Clinton signed the waiver for Loral immediately after the memo to Lake. Loral was then under investigation for the loss of an encryption control board from a Loral Intelsat satellite that crashed in China. The missing board prompted an investigation by the FBI.

The Clinton waiver allowed Loral to sell CDMA communications and a secure telemetry control ground station to China for the Loral Globalstar satellites. The station was built just outside of Beijing.

Loral's CDMA technology has already been adapted by the Chinese Army for battlefield use in both short range and global command links. Loral's Globalstar technology can be adapted by the PLA to use as a secure radio for local data and voice links in a "walkie talkie" mode as well as global mode from anywhere on the Earth.

The first twelve Globalstar satellites were destroyed in July 1998, during a failed Russian Zenit rocket launch. Loral contracted the Russian Space

Agency to launch replacement satellites in the hopes of making Globalstar operational by the end of 1998.

According to documents obtained from the U.S. Commerce Department, Loral was aware that the exported satellite systems were developed from American military equipment. Loral documents obtained from the files of Ron Brown included a folder labeled "for Secy. Brown" with a page titled "Commercial Applications Of DoD Technology".

The Loral document lists "Intelsat", "Cellular - Globalstar" and "Direct Broadcast Satellite" technology along with a variety of other products developed from "DoD" projects.

The Globalstar venture never paid off for Loral. By the beginning of 2003, Loral and other investors sold their stake in the $4 billion dollar satellite phone venture Globalstar LLP for $55 million. New Valley Corp., an investment group headed by Bennet LeBow, offered to pay $20 million up front and the remaining $35 million when Globalstar completes its Chapter 11 restructuring.

The space phone venture, the brainchild of Loral CEO Bernard Schwartz, failed to take off because of large and expensive phones (up to $5000 each) and costly service ($35 to $50 a minute). Globalstar's international partners such as China's Great Wall Industries were never able to convince local governments that the space phone system was worth the price.

Loral satellites, however, were not the only U.S. technology on the Chinese shopping list. In 1996 Ron Brown, Loral and China were all very interested in the export of an advanced military technology called synthetic aperture radar or SAR.

A letter discovered in the previously unreleased files of Ron Brown shows that Loral Defense Systems President, Jerald A. Lindfelt, wrote Brown in March of 1996. Lindfelt sought Brown's help in the export of military grade radar technology to China's State Science and Technology Commission.

Lindfelt's appeal also included a direct request for Ron Brown to over rule the Department of Defense, the State Department and even Brown's own Commerce Department which had all previously denied SAR radar export to China.

"We've worked hard trying to resolve these problems with the Department of State, the Department of Commerce and the Defense Technology Security Administration (DTSA)," Loral's Lindfelt wrote to Brown.

"But someone in these organizations always manages to block our participation... Over the years we have found that this type of obstacle often comes from lower levels of management rather than by people willing to look at the bigger picture. Could you help us by identifying someone in the Commerce Department high enough in the organization to help us resolve these issues and open this marketplace..."

Of course, Lindfelt knew he was writing to someone "high enough" in the Commerce Department who could appreciate Loral's plight. Brown had already established a long working relationship to Lindfelt's boss, Bernard Schwartz, from his DNC fundraising days. Lindfelt's letter was not the first from Loral to Brown seeking help from friends.

Loral's Lindfelt also had his own contacts inside the Chinese government. Lindfelt attached a letter for Brown from Mrs. Zheng Lizhong, Deputy Director of the National Remote Sensing Center for the State Science and Technology

Commission of China.

Mrs. Zheng wrote Frank Kelly, Loral's Defense Systems Director in November of 1995. Loral Defense is located in Arizona and specializes in military radar and infrared systems. Please note - again "Defense" means military NOT commercial products.

Mrs. Zheng requested that Loral Defense help China upgrade old 1982 SAR radar sold to the PRC during the Reagan administration. The SAR radars were installed on "highly modified" U.S. made business jets and, according to Mrs. Zheng were used to "give our officials up to date news" on flooding in areas of China.

To compare the 1982 model to the current SAR systems sold by Loral Defense is about equal to comparing a 1982 Personal Computer to a present day super fast desktop PC.

Mrs. Zheng said China could use an upgraded SAR system for other things rather than just predicting floods. Her list included "countering illegal immigration, drug interdiction... and illegal deforestation".

Left unsaid is the fact that SAR radars are used to find targets and attack them in any weather. Furthermore, according to a recently declassified document on Chinese laser technology, the "Institute of Remote Sensing" is actually a front for the Chinese Army missile laboratories.

The Institute of Remote Sensing is "a developer of optical precision and photoelectric guidance systems for surface-to-air missiles". Li Hue, the Director of the Beijing Institute of Remote Sensing Equipment, runs the Chinese missile electronics design bureau. Director Li Hui recently stated that "laser technology as the only effective means to counter cruise missiles."

What Mrs. Zheng neglected to mention was that SAR would also give the Chinese Ministry of State Security the ability to monitor, track and target dissidents driving across China's remote borders. SAR could help MSS track the movements of Tibetan refugees fleeing the Chinese occupation. In fact, U.S. SAR technology will enable the Chinese government to see deep inside India and Taiwan to watch military movements.

However, Mrs. Zheng had to have the SAR radar. She also knew exactly where the problem was. It was not Loral Defense but the US State Department that blocked the export of the new 1990s SAR radar because of the Tiananmen Square massacre.

"Since 1989 the US Government has with held any support for the equipment installed in our aircraft," Mrs. Zheng wrote Loral's Kelly.

"Your company has been very helpful in trying to solve the problems and release the equipment from the embargo, but so far have been unable to achieve a result. According to your manufacturers because of the function of the equipment can be classed as military and civilian the US State Department continues to block any moves to put the products in the control of the Commerce Department".

Thus, here is direct evidence the Chinese military was seeking to neutralize State Department regulations. The Chinese were very much in favor of removing U.S. "defense" controls from State. The letter makes it clear that PRC Generals were aware enough to even single out the Ron Brown controlled Commerce Department as more being friendly toward exporting SAR radar technology.

One of the most important technologies to emerge from the Gulf war was

Synthetic Aperture Radar (SAR) employed on J-STARS. The E-8 (J-STARS) aircraft to the non-technical is a highly modified Boeing 707 packed with powerful computers and a special ground tracking radar.

Most people associate radar with airplanes or missiles in the sky. J-STARS is designed to look down, tracking cars, trucks and tanks on the ground. The flying combination of Synthetic Aperture Radar (SAR) and high speed computing power enabled our desert warriors to watch Iraqi tanks moving hundreds of miles away. In war fighting terms this is known as "God's Eye View" or the "Bigger Picture".

J-STARS and SAR radar paid off big in the Gulf war. The ability to get the big picture allowed us to see deep behind enemy lines. J-STARS alerted allied commanders to the Iraqi attack centered on Hafji, a small Saudi border town, just as the Iraqi tanks began to move south. J-STARS and the special radar immediately guided U.S. and allied aircraft to the columns of Iraqi tanks in Kuwait. The result was Saddam's big offensive was stopped cold in its tracks.

In 1996, then-President Clinton moved control for advanced technology exports to the Commerce Department. The Chinese National Remote Sensing Center quickly won approval for the radar export the Clinton Commerce Department, and the Chinese army currently operates the system on a U.S.-made Gulfstream jet.

In a September 1994 memo to Clinton, Harold Ickes, then White House chief of staff, informed him that Schwartz could be used to raise campaign donations "in order to raise an additional $3,000,000 to permit the Democratic National Committee to produce and air generic TV/radio spots as soon as Congress adjourns."

Ickes then urged Clinton to invite Schwartz to the White House "to impress [him] with the need to raise $3,000,000 within the next two weeks." In another memo, Ickes informed Clinton that Schwartz "is prepared to do anything he can for the administration."

Between October 1995 and March 1996, as Clinton mulled over whether to ignore the State, Justice, and Defense Departments' reasons against granting Loral waivers to export advanced technology to China, Loral Chairman Bernard Schwartz injected more than $150,000 into the DNC's coffers.

After Clinton's decision to lift the ban in Loral's case and to allow the exportation of the company's technology to the Chinese military, Loral CEO Schwartz handed over an additional $300,000 to the DNC.

COSTIND General Shen did not focus all his efforts on Loral. Instead, General Shen also played U.S. high-tech contractors against each other. For example, General Shen also led the successful penetration of Hughes in the purchase of satellites.

Again, through a series of meetings with Brown and U.S. Commerce officials, Shen and his operatives in front companies secured whole satellites from Hughes. The Hughes satellites provide the Chinese Army with secure communications that are invulnerable to earth combat and highly accurate all weather navigation for strike bombers and missiles.

Shen did obtain help from the Clinton White House by pressuring Hughes with satellite contracts. Hughes CEO Michael Armstrong wrote President Clinton in 1993, threatening to pull support for Clinton if he did not allow the space technology transfers to China. In 1994, Clinton approved a waiver for Hughes to transfer advanced satellite encryption systems to China.

In 1995, Armstrong wrote Clinton National Security Advisor Anthony Lake, seeking to transfer satellite export authority from the State Department to the Commerce Department.

"The USG [U.S. government] does not require Congressional approval to remove commercial satellites from the United States Munitions List (USML), which is under State Department jurisdiction, and placing them on the Commerce Control List (CCL), which is under Commerce Department jurisdiction," wrote Armstrong.

"It is my understanding that State has resisted vigorously Commerce attempts to do just that. For the national good, this situation must change. A commercial communications satellite is not a defense item. State Department control of satellites is not required for national security. Continued State Department control is damaging to the U.S. satellite industry and is not warranted."

In 1996, President Clinton moved the oversight of satellite exports from the State and Defense Departments to the Commerce Department. In response, Armstrong and his counterparts wrote a thank-you letter to Clinton.

In a May 3, 1996, letter signed by the CEOs of Hughes, Lockheed and Loral, the three executives expressed their thanks directly to Bill Clinton.

"In October of last year we wrote to you asking you to complete the transfer of responsibility for commercial satellite export licensing to the Department of Commerce. Your administration recently announced its intention to do just that.

"We greatly appreciate this action which demonstrates again your strong commitment to reforming the U.S. export control system," states a letter signed by Hughes CEO Armstrong, Lockheed CEO Norman Augustine and Loral CEO Bernard Schwartz.

The Commerce Department was ill-equipped to deal with satellite exports to China. The resulting fiasco at Commerce allowed the Chinese army to obtain a vast array of advanced missile, satellite and space technology. In fact, in 1998 the Defense Department charged that the Commerce Department exceeded its legal authority by authorizing export transfers to a foreign military.

The alleged improper export by Hughes of satellite technology was cited as a key reason when Clinton's secretary of state, Warren Christopher, rejected a plan to give the Commerce Department full authority to control satellite exports.

According to a Sept. 22, 1995, memorandum, Christopher rejected plans to give Commerce the authority to approve satellite exports after an interagency study noted that "significant" military and intelligence capabilities could be lost.

The memorandum stated the Pentagon and U.S. intelligence agencies strongly opposed the policy change because Hughes exported two satellites with sensitive cryptographic technology without first getting a State Department munitions license. Cryptographic technology is used to scramble communications sent to satellites to prevent unauthorized access.

President Clinton, who transferred the power to regulate sensitive satellites to Commerce, under Commerce Secretary Ron Brown, ultimately overruled Christopher.

A newly released document from the U.S. State Department reveals that the most successful Chinese espionage operation in recent history occurred during the Clinton administration. The document accuses Hughes Space and Communications Company of violating U.S. national security 123 times by knowingly sending detailed missile and space technology directly to the Chinese army.

According to the State Department, the most serious violations occurred when Hughes gave the Chinese army information that supported its analyses of the investigation of the January 1995 failure of the launch of a China Long March 2E (LM-2E) rocket carrying the Hughes-manufactured ASTAR II commercial communications satellite.

On Jan. 26, 1995, approximately 52 seconds into flight, a Chinese LM-2E carrying the Hughes APSTAR II communications satellite failed. This was the LM-2E's second failure. The first failure of the LM-2E in December 1992 involved an attempted launch of the Hughes OPTUS B-2 commercial communications satellite.

"Respondents decided to form and direct a launch failure investigation beginning in January 1995 and continuing throughout much of that year. The investigation involved the formation of several groups of leading technical experts from China and the U.S., which throughout the investigation engaged in an extensive exchange of technical data and analysis, producing a wide range of unauthorized technology transfers," noted the State Department charge document.

"At no time did the Respondents seek or receive a license or other written approval concerning the conduct of their APSTAR II failure investigation with PRC authorities," states the charge document.

According to the State Department, "this strategy was further influenced by Respondents' business interests in securing future contracts with the PRC and with Asian satellite companies in which PRC influence figured prominently, and concern that U.S. Government policy constraints on technology transfer as administered by ODTC were an impediment to achieving these interests."

According to a 1998 Defense Department investigation, the reason for Hughes passing the technical information to China was because the Chinese army blamed Hughes for the rocket failure.

"Following the APSTAR II failure, there was disagreement between Hughes and the Chinese about whether the principal cause of the failure was the launch vehicle or the satellite. The subsequent joint Hughes-Chinese failure investigation was apparently intended, at least in part, to resolve this dispute," states the 1998 Defense Department report.

"According to the Hughes/Apstar materials, the disagreement between Hughes and the Chinese focused on two views of the cause of the launch failure: (1) the Chinese claim that the satellite was defective as evidenced by satellite fuel igniting; and (2) Hughes' claim that the satellite was a contributing factor only after the launch vehicle fairing had failed which exposed the satellite to catastrophic conditions."

Video of the launch examined by Hughes and the Chinese early in the investigation showed that there was a noticeable glow observed coming from the payload fairing or shroud as the LM-2E launch vehicle ascended. The video also showed that fire was visibly streaming down the side of the Chinese rocket.

When the stream of fire reached the LM-2E main engines the rocket blew up. The Chinese asserted that the glow indicated that the satellite fuel tanks had ruptured, spilling and then igniting the satellite fuel.

However, telemetry from the Chinese launch vehicle indicated that there was a breakwire failure, which Hughes interpreted as an indication of the likely loss of the rocket fairing prior to the destruction of the U.S. satellite.

The fairing is part of the launch vehicle. It is the nose-cone cover sitting atop the rocket that houses the satellite. The Chinese Long March fairing consisted of two sections or halves and a two-section dome. It was designed and manufactured by the Chinese rocket maker to protect the Hughes satellite during the first portion of its flight.

"The fairing must be designed as an integral part of the launch vehicle system as determine the success of the launch. The breakwire is a continuity wire across the fairing which, when broken, indicates a separation of the halves of the fairing," noted the Defense Department report.

"According to the Hughes/Apstar materials, the disagreement between Hughes and the Chinese focused on two views of the cause of the launch failure: (1) the Chinese claim that the satellite was defective as evidenced by satellite fuel igniting; and (2) Hughes' claim that the satellite was a contributing factor only after the launch vehicle fairing had failed which exposed the satellite to catastrophic conditions. Because of the disagreement, the failure investigation undertook to examine in a very thorough and methodical manner all of the potential causes of the launch failure, including the two hypotheses offered by the Chinese and Hughes."

"Hughes' satellite and fairing debris analysis, much of which was shared with the Chinese, determined that the satellite fuel tanks had ruptured in a manner that suggested the satellite structure had collapsed on its fuel tanks. Thus, the satellite appeared to have experienced a significant load or stress condition," stated the Defense report.

"The investigation also examined the fairing and the loss of the breakwire telemetry signal. Upon examination of the fairing debris, Hughes found scratches and wear on the fairing dome that indicated the dome may have collapsed on itself. Loss of the fairing breakwire signal could indicate a loss of fairing integrity, either due to the fiberglass dome of the fairing or a zipper (which holds the two halves of the fairing together) failure. Hughes created a detailed timeline of events based on data gathered both from visual and LM-2E telemetry. From this timeline, it was observed that the breakwire failure came before the fairing glow and while the spacecraft was still intact."

Information contained in the Hughes/Apstar materials obtained by the Defense Department showed that Hughes learned that the Chinese "Coupled Loads Analysis" was deficient. Specifically, the Chinese had not performed an analysis of the loads from the satellite payload stack to the fairing and had no real idea of the true forces at play on the rocket from wind shear and aerodynamic buffeting.

"Hughes then worked with the Chinese, presumably to correct the Finite Elements Model of the LM-2E and performed a Coupled Loads Analysis that more accurately characterized the loads actually experienced by the fairing during the failed launch. Hughes also presented the results of the analysis to show the Chinese that the launch vehicle and satellite were designed to comfortably withstand the flight loads, but that the oversimplified Chinese Coupled Loads Analysis failed to account for- windshear and buffeting loads on the fairing," noted the Defense Department report.

"DoD assesses that a thorough Coupled Loads Analysis was central to Hughes' effort to prove that the Chinese failed to account for (1) the high winds aloft and buffeting, and (2) the resultant LM-2E non-zero angle of attack (i.e., the LM-2E's guidance System failure to compensate for the upper level winds). These factors combined to produce stresses that exceeded the rivet shear strength along the fairing zipper and/or collapsed the fairing fiberglass dome."

"DoD believes it is reasonable to infer that, during the close collaboration between Hughes and Chinese engineers, Hughes imparted to the Chinese sufficient know-how to correct the overall deficiencies," noted the Defense report.

"The conclusions outlined in the Hughes/Apstar materials provided to the Chinese (and reviewed by DoD for this assessment) were sufficiently specific to inform the Chinese of the kinds of launch vehicle design or operational changes that would make the LM-2E (and perhaps other launch vehicles as well) more reliable."

"The provision of technical assistance in connection with the failure investigation to the Chinese by Hughes in the design, engineering, and operation of the Chinese launch vehicle and the Hughes satellite constitutes a 'defense service' within the meaning of the State Department's International Traffic in Arms Regulations (ITAR) under the Arms Export Control Act (AECA). This was clearly beyond the scope of Commerce export control jurisdiction because only the Department of State is authorized to issue licenses for defense services," states the Defense report.

"The Commerce license issued for APSTAR II covered only the export of the satellite and very limited technical data. There was no reasonable basis to conclude that a launch vehicle failure investigation of the scope evidenced in the documents would not be subject to State Department export control jurisdiction."

"The Hughes/Apstar materials reviewed by DoD reveal that the Chinese were provided with technical data and assistance from Hughes' failure investigation that enabled the Chinese launch manufacturer and launch service provider to make design and/or operational adjustments that improved launch vehicle reliability. They also reveal that the Chinese were provided practical insight into a diagnostic and failure analysis technique for identifying and isolating the, cause of a launch failure," noted the 1998 Defense Department report.

"DoD believes that the scope and content of the launch failure investigation conducted by Hughes with the Chinese following the January 1995 APSTAR II failure raises national security concerns both with regard to violating those standards and to potentially contributing to China's missile capabilities," concluded the Defense Department report.

Why would Hughes risk passing vital missile design information on a satellite crash investigation? Hughes, according to the State Department, was willing to risk illegal transfers in order to continue their profitable relationship with General Shen.

The 2002 State Department letter makes it clear that they believe Gen. Shen led the successful penetration of the Clinton administration and Hughes. According to a Sept. 20, 1995, memorandum, Hughes regarded Gen. Shen as "the most important Chinese space official."

"On February 22, 1996, Respondents' Chairman at the Board wrote to Chinese General Shen Rongjun (then Deputy Director of the Commission for Science, Technology, and Industry for National Defense 'COSTIND') and asked 'if there is anything we at Hughes Space and Communications can do to support your investigation into the cause of the loss (i.e., LM 3B and INTELSAT 708).'"

"The next day, February 23, 1996, Respondents' Chairman wrote to Major General Hu Shixiang, Director of the Xichang Satellite Launch Center, to assure him of his 'personal support and that of my company as you investigate the causes for the loss.'"

The Hughes documents went further, noting that the effort was undertaken in order to "not to rock the boat" while an export license application for yet another satellite export involving China was undergoing review by the U.S. government.

"In light of Respondents' assumption that SS/L's chairmanship would act as a 'buffer' for it e.g... an April 9, 1996 response to Herron from Steinhauer opines that 'it is in HSC advantage to stay engaged. An outside consultant may buffer HSC somewhat relative to the technology transfer issue.'"

"Also, a May 6, 1996, message to SS/L from Steinhauer referring to 'detailed suggestions for specific testing in the controls laboratory, for specific fixes to the iMU (inertial measurement unit) single point wire solder joint failure' notes that 'the committee could be approaching the border of technology transfer, i.e., how to improve the launch vehicle' and asks 'will SS/L be the filter for tech transfer issues?'"

On May 8, 1998, Hughes announced that they had concluded a contract with Asia Pacific Mobile Telecommunications Satellite (APMT); a company sponsored by Chinese and Singapore partners, for a satellite based mobile phone system. The turnkey system was to include two satellites to be launched from China on the Long March 3B SLV.

In addition, the deal included five gateways, one network operations center, one satellite operations center and an initial purchase of 70,000 user terminals, with the ground network equipment and handsets to be provided by HUGHES NETWORK SYSTEMS.

The APMT satellite was equipped with a unique 40-foot antenna and would have provided Asia-Pacific mobile telecom with 16,000 secure voice channels, using man portable phones and radios. The APMT satellite can be used not only to provide secure military communications but the spacecraft also has "Passive ELINT interception capacity" - or the ability to listen in on wide variety of earth signals, including military communications.

What escaped the notice of U.S. Commerce Department officials was the fact that APMT is also owned and operated by COSTIND. The very same COSTIND, a Chinese military unit, under the command of General Ding and his able assistant General Shen.

The Chinese army penetration of Hughes was so successful that Gen. Shen managed to get his son, Shen Jun, a job at Hughes as the lead software engineer for all Chinese satellites. According to Hughes, Shen Jun had access to "proprietary" satellite source code.

"The record indicates that Shen Jun's role for Respondents went well beyond that of an interpreter/translator and more closely resembled that of an intermediary with his father, General Shen, and other PRC space authorities, in order to cultivate their support in various matters of interest to Hughes, including the handling of the APSTAR II launch failure investigation and the APMT contract," noted the 2002 State Department charge letter.

"On July 9, 1996, Respondents submitted a munitions export license application to ODTC seeking authorization for one of its employees, Shen Jun, described as a dual Canadian Chinese national, in order to provide Chinese-English language translation and interpretation support for the preliminary design phase of the APMT satellite project," states the 2002 charge letter.

"In no place in that submission nor otherwise did HUGHES SPACE AND COMMUNICATIONS COMPANY inform ODTC that this individual was, in fact, the son of PLA General and COSTIND Deputy Director Shen Rongjun, which fact was material to the U.S. Government's consideration of whether the license application should be approved or denied."

"The record indicates that Shen Jun's role for Respondents went well beyond that of an interpreter/translator and more closely resembled that of an intermediary with his father, General Shen, and other PRC space authorities, in order to cultivate their support in various matters of interest to Hughes, including the handling of the APSTAR II launch failure investigation and the APMT contract," noted the State Department 2002 charge letter.

According to the State Department, Hughes contends that it followed the law with regard to hiring Gen. Shen's son.

"Respondents have maintained as of December 3, 2002, that this information was not material and that its omission was proper because there is no place in the munitions license application for them to disclose father-son relationships between General officers at the People's Liberation Army who are overseeing a project they are working on and their foreign national employees working in U.S. facilities on the same project."

An August 8, 1995, memorandum from Bruce Elbert reports on APMT related activities by Shen Jun: "in a telephone conversation last night with Jun he provided the following information after having talked to important people involved with APMT ... Lockheed Martin has sweetened their bid with technology transfers on launch vehicles and changed their price... These points were reiterated by the highest official he interfaced with Jun has the worry that if it goes wrong in Munich (an apparent reference to an APSTAR II launch failure briefing to insurance providers) we open the door for Lockheed Martin and their unique proposal for technology transfer on the launch vehicle. This could result in our not getting into the final round of APMT negotiations."

The memo goes on to report that Shen Jun has been asked, "to make a proposal to CASC and CGWIC that they describe their redesign of the LM-2E fairing and that Hughes discuss what it will do only if we use the LM-2E again."

Ironically, at the same time General Shen had his son gain employment with Hughes, another shadowy figure appeared inside the Clinton White House. Macao hotel/casino owner Ng Lapseng frequently visited the Clinton White House with his good friend Charlie "Yah Lin" Trie, the Arkansas restaurant owner and alleged member of the 14K Triads. Ng reportedly stayed overnight at the White House as a guest of the Clintons.

Further proof of Ng Lapseng's association with the Bill and Hillary Clinton comes in the form of photographs. There is the 1995 photo of Ng Lapseng and the Clintons taken in front of a DNC symbol. The photo of Ng Lapseng is very telling in that both Bill and Hillary Clinton were certainly aware that Ng is the owner of the Macao-based Fortuna Hotel.

The Fortuna hotel is more than just a casino and resort in Macao. According to the Fortuna advertisements, children under 12 can stay free at the hotel. However, according to the Fortuna brochure, for a fee beautiful young hostesses from various countries can also entertain businessmen.

Ng also has a very interesting connection to the Hughes violations of national security. According to the 123 national security violations filed against Hughes Satellite Corporation, a Fortuna based company was involved in some questionable events.

The Sino-Canada Telecommunications and Investment Management Company were incorporated in Macao, "having its principal place of business at the Hotel Fortuna."

According to the State Department charges, the Sino-Canada Telecommunications Company also had contracted with Hughes for a large part of the APMT satellite contract then destined for China in 1995. In fact, Sino-Canada paid Hughes $5 million up front that was not reported to the State Department.

"Sino-Canada's managing director, Suen Yan Kwong, was the founder of Chung Kiu Telecommunication, which had invested in cellular telecommunications for use under special network by China's People's Liberation Army (PLA) in military districts along the coastal provinces," noted the December 2002 State Department charge letter.

It is amazing that a company based inside a Macao hotel owned by Ng Lapseng would contract with a U.S.-based satellite company when its owner was then also in business supplying communications to the Chinese army. Even more amazing is the Clinton's silence on Ng Lapseng and the money that somehow slipped out of his pockets into DNC coffers at the same time.

Clinton's transfer allowed the Chinese army to acquire advanced U.S. technology for military purposes. Hughes satellites currently provide the Chinese army with secure communications that are invulnerable to earth combat and highly accurate all-weather navigation for strike bombers and missiles.

Hughes satellites purchased by Shen also provide direct TV and cable TV broadcasts to most of Asia. Thus, cable and pay-per-view services help pay for the Chinese army satellite communications. The brilliant planning and logistics mean that Chinese military communications pay for themselves.

Hughes CEO Armstrong's contention that "a commercial communications satellite is not a defense item" is simply false. In fact, Hughes executives admitted that the satellites sold to China were military items. Ironically, the admission came when the company tried to sell a former Chinese satellite to the U.S. military.

AsiaSat, a company founded in 1988 in part by the Chinese army, made a March 1996 satellite purchase from Hughes to build the AsiaSat-3 with a $220 million loan from a consortium of banks.

DECEPTION

Asiasat-3 was placed into an incorrect orbit by a Russian Proton booster rocket launched from Baikonur in 1997. In 1998, space insurance companies paid off the satellite loss and transferred ownership to Hughes.

AsiaSat-3, a "commercial" satellite sold to China, was more than just a $220 million piece of orbiting junk. Hughes recovered the satellite, using a special lunar orbit technique to bring it back into a useable position around the earth.

Hughes then offered the recovered satellite to the U.S. Navy for military purposes. Mark J. Schwene, Hughes Global Services vice president, was quoted in Aviation Week and Space Technology making the offer.

"Possible markets for the satellite (AsiaSat-3) include providing capacity over ocean regions for the Navy as well as providing sufficient communications services in times of crisis to meet military communications surge requirements," stated the Hughes VP.

The very same Hughes "commercial" satellite sold to China was offered to the U.S. Navy to serve in times of crisis to meet American military requirements. Of course, it never occurred to C. Michael Armstrong that the Chinese army might use Hughes satellites for "military communications."

The satellite and missile technology obtained from Hughes by the Chinese army is critical for the design and manufacture of missile nose cones and electronic missile control systems. The technology clearly helped the Chinese army field a new generation of ICBMS, including the Dong Feng 31 missile, which can drop three nuclear warheads on any city in the U.S.

The success of General Shen is a story of espionage, missiles, politics and greed. Gen. Shen succeeded in using Loral, Hughes and President Clinton as valuable tools to obtain weapons that are now pointed at the United States.

C C 44447

LORAL

Defense Systems–Arizona

P.O. Box 85
Litchfield Park, AZ 85340-0085
(602) 925-6380

Jerald A. Lindfelt
President

March 15, 1996

Ron Brown, Secretary of Commerce
United States Department of Commerce
14th Street & Constitution Avenue, NW
Washington, DC 20230

Dear Secretary Brown:

Your recent keynote speech at the Arizona Association of Industries' luncheon in Phoenix was interesting and informative. I was particularly pleased with your offer to have the Commerce Department assist us with work issues in foreign countries. We have a problem in our Division regarding dealings with the Peoples Republic of China and I would appreciate your assistance in resolving these complex issues.

Several years ago our division sold two radar systems to the Peoples Republic of China for use in geological surveys. Since that time the U.S. trade relations with the Peoples Republic of China have been such that we have not been allowed to pursue additional business in that country. The systems we sold them are in need of an upgrade. Since we are not eligible to perform the work, a foreign company simply modifies our equipment. This results not only in lost follow-on business, but also the loss of numerous new opportunities emerging in China that we would like to pursue.

Attached is a copy of a letter from the National Remote Sensing Center in Beijing that outlines a few of the problems we have encountered. We've worked hard trying to resolve these problems with the Department of State, the Department of Commerce and the Defense Technology Security Administration (DTSA), but someone in these organizations always manage to block our participation.

The Synthetic Aperture Radar System is dated technology and can be offered to China by a number of countries. It seems foolish to allow other countries to market their similar products while our efforts are blocked. Over the years we have found that this type of obstacle often comes from lower levels of management rather than by people willing to look at the bigger picture. Could you help us by identifying someone in the Commerce Department high enough in the organization to help us resolve these issues and open this marketplace to our participation.

We have representatives scheduled to travel to Beijing in April and it would be very helpful if we had a contact identified who could assist us in making this visit a success.

Respectfully yours,

J. A. Lindfelt,
President

jvb

Attachment

17

中华人民共和国国家科学技术委员会国家遥感中心
NATIONAL REMOTE SENSING CENTER
STATE SCIENCE AND TECHNOLOGY COMMISSION OF CHINA
15B, Fuxing Road, Beijing 100861, China

TELEX: 22349 SSTCC CN   TELEPHONE: (+86-10) 8512081
FAX: (+86-10) 8512081

To: Mr. Frank K. Kelly
       Loral Defense Systems-Arizona
       P.O.Box 85
       Lichfield Park, AZ85340-0085

Fm: Mrs. Zheng Lizhong
       Deputy Director,
       National Remote Sensing Centre,
       State Sciences & Technology Commission of China

Date: Nov. 29, 1995

Dear Sir:

It is with great pleasure for me to write the letter to you. Please find a brief introduction of National Remote Sensing Centre herewith. If it is possible, would you please to assist us in resolving some issues on the Equipment's of First Department of Aerial Remote Sensing of NRSC, which were imported from your country.

In 1982 the US Government approved the sale of Learjet aircraft to China which are now based at Nanyuan Airport near Beijing. These aircraft were highly modified in that they were fitted with the best available equipment for flood relief missions. For example the aircraft had installed Synthetic Aperture Radar (SAR) made by your manufacturer.

The SAR systems allowed us to monitor the floods that happened in various regions of China every year. The SAR systems can take mapping images through dust, cloud and heavy precipitation making it the perfect medium to give our officials up to date news of the floods, thereby allowing many life saving activities to be carried out. The pre-warning given to us by the airborne equipment enables us to build levy banks, evacuate town and villages and close flood gates thus saving many lives during the flood season.

This year again the loss of human life during the typhoons and floods caused great suffering and many deaths in China and had moved me to contact you asking for your help. Since 1989 the US Government has with held any support for the equipment installed in our aircraft. These include the return of out own spare parts now in the USA for repair, the selling of new spare parts, the updating and overhaul of the equipment, and support of the manufacturer's technical staff to assist in problem solving.

Your company has been very helpful in trying to solve the problems and release the equipment from the embargo, but so far have been unable to achieve a result.

According to your manufacturers because the function of the equipment can be classed as military and civilian the US State Department continues to block any moves to put the products in the control of the Commerce Department. There are many uses for this type of equipment all over the world in non-military areas that help people in need. Most of countries in the developed world are using the same technology for mineral exploration, countering illegal immigration, drug interdiction, monitoring of natural disasters, monitoring of ice flow movement and illegal deforestation. All these uses are non-military and vital important to the countries concerned.

In summary, Mr. Kelly, I implore you on behalf of NRSC, State Science and Technology Commission and all the individuals who will be affected by future natural disasters in this country to assist us in obtaining your government support to release from embargo the vital airborne equipment needed so importantly for our work in saving lives.

If you have any suggestion, don't hesitate to contact us directly.

With Best Regards.

Sincerely Yours

Zheng Lizhong

Zheng Lizhong

No objectionable release (4?)

Corporate Offices
P.O. Box 80028, Los Angeles, CA 90080 0028
7200 Hughes Terrace, Los Angeles, CA 90045 0066
(310) 568 6117
FAX (310) 417 2840

GMH
GM HUGHES
ELECTRONICS

C. Michael Armstrong Chairman and Chief Executive Officer

March 13, 1995

Mr. Anthony Lake
Assistant to the President
for National Security Affairs
National Security Council
Washington, D.C. 20506

Dear Mr. Lake:

Fifteen years ago, the United States (US) was the absolute leader in the manufacture and sale of commercial communications satellites. Now, it is facing a major challenge from Europe and Japan.

Given our economy and technology at the time, the United States Government (USG) had little direct involvement in the development of the commercial communications satellite industry. By contrast, foreign government involvement in supporting and guiding the communications satellite industry was considerable and continues to be commonplace. Whereas the USG currently treats many commercial communications satellites as defense items, making their export more difficult, the foreign governments aggressively pursue trade opportunities. Increasingly, our foreign competitors promote the view that because of the USG's restrictive export policies, US satellite manufacturers are uncertain and unreliable suppliers.

I request your help in turning this situation around. The USG does not require Congressional approval to remove commercial communications satellites from the United States Munitions List (USML), which is under State Department jurisdiction, and placing them on the Commerce Control List (CCL), which is under Commerce Department jurisdiction. It is my understanding that State has resisted vigorously Commerce attempts to do just that. For the national good, this situation must change. A commercial communications satellite is not a defense item. State Department control of satellites is not required for national security. Continued State Department control is damaging to the US satellite industry and is not warranted.

As pointed out in the attached White Paper, the technology keeping our satellites on the USML is no more sensitive than comparable technology on a Boeing 747 aircraft or a 600 MTOP computer, both of which are on the CCL. Unlike the 747 or the 600 MTOP computer, however, our satellites are placed in orbit where there is neither the risk nor the possibility of technology transfer. We need to quickly right this situation and move all commercial communications satellites to the CCL.

Sincerely,

C. Michael Armstrong

cc: R. H. Brown
W. Christopher
W. J. Perry

99KA3315

20

- **Crosslinks** (ie. intersatellite data relay communication links that do not involve a ground relay terminal). The use of crosslinks is another example of readily available technology that has led to new commercial applications, such as Motorola's IRIDIUM and Hughes' SPACEWAY. Similar systems are being developed in Europe and Japan and will have wide spread commercial applications.

- **Baseband Processing** (ie. spaceborne baseband processing that uses any technique other than frequency translation and which can be changed several times a day on a channel-by-channel basis among previously assigned fixed frequencies). The uses of on-board processing for commercial applications are many, particularly for the rapidly-emerging mobile commercial communications marketplace. Its applications range from routine sorting and routing of incoming calls to maintaining compliance with prescribed frequency spectrum management.

- **Encryption devices.** Satellites traditionally have been used for the transmission of sensitive financial and business data that require absolute integrity and privacy. The encryption device is a relatively sophisticated equipment item, but is manufactured for commercial use and, in the case of commercial communications satellites, it generally is employed to scramble/unscrambling video and audio programming in order to protect this data. Once it is embedded in the satellite, the encryption device has no military significance.

- **Radiation Hardening.** Commercial communications satellites daily operate in a natural radiation environment harmful to electronic circuits. Hence, they need protection from the environment in which they operate. This protection comes from radiation hardened devices embedded in the satellite.

- **Perigee Kick Motors.** The perigee kick motor is of a type routinely used to deliver commercial communications satellites to their proper orbital slots. Using foreign manufactured perigee kick motors on US-manufactured satellites might work and alleviate problems associated with

11-03-95 01:34PM   FROM SS/L MGT LIAISON CMT   TO 912024823345   P001/001

OCT. -27'95(FRI) 13:30   LORAL LEGISLATIVE   TEL:703 416 5537   *stuff*
                                                                                        P. 002

To: GENE CHRISTIANSEN - DOC
FROM: D. REYNARD - SS/L

- October 6, 1995

The President
The White House
Washington, D.C. 20500

Dear Mr. President:

Your Administration can take justifiable pride in its effort to promote U.S. aerospace exports. We understand you may soon be issuing an Executive Order intended to make further improvements to the process for reviewing export license applications. We would like to voice our strong support for this important initiative.

We have been engaged in a very constructive dialogue with the State and Commerce Departments concerning issues related to licensing export of U.S. commercial communications satellite technologies. In particular, we have highlighted the fact that these technologies are now widely used in the civilian marketplace, both here and abroad. Continuing to license exports of these technologies under the more stringent and cumbersome Munitions List places American companies at a distinct disadvantage in global markets. If we are to remain globally competitive in this key industry sector, licensing procedures and requirements must permit U.S. companies to have the same flexibility as their global competitors.

The most effective way to accomplish this objective would be to complete the transfer of all responsibility for commercial satellite export licensing to the Commerce Department. Under the proposed Executive Order, all interested agencies, including State, DOD and NSA, will be able to review and object to licenses for commercial satellites. With this review mechanism in place, there should be no remaining arguments against moving commercial communications satellites from State's Munitions List to Commerce's Commodity Control List.

During a recent meeting involving Vice President Gore and representatives of the satellite industry discussing national/global information infrastructure, this was one of several issues raised. We clearly appreciate your administration's strong commitment to reforming the U.S. export control system, but we respectfully request your personal support for establishing the Commerce Department's jurisdiction over the export of all commercial communications satellites.

C. Michael Armstrong
Chairman & CEO
Hughes Electronics Corporation

Bernard L. Schwartz
Chairman & CEO
Loral Corporation

Daniel M. Tellep
Chairman & CEO
Lockheed Martin Corporation

Release [?]

May 3, 1996

The Honorable William J. Clinton
President of the United States
The White House
1600 Pennsylvania Avenue, NW
Washington, DC 20500

Dear Mr. President:

In October of last year we wrote to you asking you to complete the transfer of responsibility for commercial satellite export licensing to the Department of Commerce. Your Administration recently announced its intention to do just that. We greatly appreciate this action which demonstrates again your strong commitment to reforming the US export control system.

The press release announcing your decision indicated that regulations implementing the transfer would be developed within 30 days. We sincerely hope that this process, and that of providing any necessary Congressional notifications, will be completed as quickly as possible.

We also hope that your decision is implemented broadly so that the US satellite industry will be able to realize the full benefit of your decision. By making possible real "one stop shopping" for all export authorizations related to commercial communications satellite systems, your decision will greatly enhance the ability of US manufacturers to retain our global competitiveness.

On behalf of the thousands of dedicated American workers at our companies, we thank you again for this important decision.

C. Michael Armstrong	Norman R. Augustine	Bernard L. Schwartz
Chairman and CEO	President and CEO	Chairman and CEO
Hughes Electronics Corporation	Lockheed Martin Corporation	Loral Space and
		Communications Limited

99KA0069

Post-it™ brand fax transmittal memo 7671 # of pages ▶ 3
To Bill Reinsch   From B. Kjarland
Co.   Co.
Dept.   Phone 703-284-4283
Fax # 202-482-2387   Fax #

2

TIGER SONG

*Therefore no one in the armed forces is treated as familiarly as are
spies, no one is given rewards as rich as those given to spies,
and no matter is more secret than espionage.*
Sun Tzu - The Art of War

In 1994, General Ding Henggao served as Chairman, Commission on
Science, Technology and National Defense Industry (COSTIND).

COSTIND, according to the GAO "oversees development of China's
weapon systems and is responsible for identifying and acquiring telecommunications technology applicable for military use."

General Ding knew the Chinese Army had a big problem dealing with the
potential threat of advanced U.S. military technology. COSTIND General
Ding spearheaded penetrations of American military technology, using the
officers under his command, his own relatives and a Chinese "defector", missile scientist Hua Di.

The real truth about Chinese missile scientist Hua Di remains unpublished
by the mass media. What on the surface appears to be a foolish defector
arrested by the Chinese government is actually a cover for espionage. Hua
Di was the self-described "matchmaker" in a Clinton administration high tech
deal for the Chinese Army.

Hua Di was born into a family of prominent Communist officials. He stud-
ied missiles in Russia and worked in China's missile program for 24 years.
In 1984, Hua went to work for the China
International Trust and Investment Co. (CITIC) a firm part owned by the
Chinese Army.

In 1989, Hua became a defector, leaving China after the Tiananmen
Square crackdown on student democracy demonstrators. Hua went to work
as a researcher at Stanford's Center for International Security and Arms
Control, whose co-directors are former Secretary of Defense William Perry
and Stanford Political Science Professor John Lewis.

In December 1997, I tried to contact Chinese missile expert Hua Di at
Stanford University in California. In 1996, Hua had given Aviation Week and
Space Technology detailed information on the Chinese Dong Feng - 15 mis-
sile (DF-15), the weapon China used during the 1996 Taiwan crisis. Hua had

24

published nothing really new about the DF-15 but I wanted his personal comments as the "official source".

Curiously, Hua Di would not grant an interview. In fact, immediately after my call, Hua Di suddenly decided to return to China.

In late October 1998, it was announced that Hua Di had returned to China. He met with Chinese security officials in late 1997 and was assured that he would not be prosecuted. On December 31, 1997 Hua returned to China.

On Jan. 6, 1998 Hua was arrested and charged with passing state secrets to U.S. officials. Stanford officials and John Lewis have written to the Chinese government appealing for Hua's release.

Condoleezza Rice, then the Provost for Stanford University, said Professor John Lewis "had provided evidence to the fact that the source materials for publications written by him and Mr. Hua were provided by approved Chinese authorities or already were available through the Stanford University library."

Hua Di and John Lewis shared more than an academic career. In 1992, Chinese Commission of Science, Technology, and Industry for National Defense (COSTIND) Lt. General Huai Guomo contacted Hua Di to start a joint venture called Galaxy New Technology.

"Lewis and I were matchmakers," recalled Hua about Galaxy New Technology in 1996. "(General) Huai is my good friend."

In 1994 Secretary of Defense William Perry was also a close friend with the mastermind of the Galaxy New Technology deal, Professor John Lewis from Stanford.

SCM/Brooks Communications purchased large quantities of secure communications gear for sale to a so-called "civilian" Chinese firm, Galaxy New Technology, including real-time, encrypted, fiber-optic video systems.

The Galaxy New Technology fiber-optic communication system is providing the General Logistics Division of the People's Liberation Army with secure communications. The Hua Mei system is safe from nuclear attack and secure from prying U.S. intelligence monitoring.

John Lewis and Hua Di worked together in 1994 on the Hua Mei project using SCM/Brooks. Hua Di located Ms. Nie Li to run the project as the Chinese co-chair. Dr. Lewis located Aldai Stevenson III, the former Democratic Senator from Ohio, to lead the American side.

Documents obtained from the Department of Defense using the Freedom of Information Act (FOIA) shows Mr. Lewis was being paid by the Chinese Army for Hua Mei while serving on the U.S. Defense Policy Board and working for DoD as a contractor.

In 1994, Dr. Lewis was officially listed on the U.S. Defense Dept. payroll as Defense Secretary William Perry's personal "consultant". Dr. Lewis traveled to Beijing with Secretary Perry to meet with General Ding and his subordinate, General Huai Guomo as a consultant to Secretary Perry.

It was no co-incidence that the Chinese Galaxy New Technology head Madam Nie Lie was also the wife of Chinese Army General Ding Henggao. In 1994, General Ding Henggao was both the director of COSTIND and the boss of Lt. General Huai Guomo, the PLA contact for Hua Di.

According to the Far Eastern Economic Review, Lewis had his friend Perry write a letter on his behalf to U.S. government officials, favoring the fiber-optic export to China.

Lewis located Adlai Stevenson III, the former Democratic senator from

Illinois, to lead the American side of the joint venture.

SCM/Brooks contracted AT&T to ship advanced, secure, communication systems directly to the Chinese Army. AT&T officials who sold most of the equipment and software to SCM/Brooks were adamant that there was no need to check the Chinese firm, Galaxy New Technology, since Ms. Nie Lie led it.

Lewis then contracted AT&T to ship the secure communication system directly to a Chinese army unit using Galaxy New Technology as a front.

The export took place through Ron Brown's Commerce Department, using a special license waiver that had never been issued before and has never been issued since.

However, the so-called civilian firm Hua Mei was actually packed with Chinese army officers and experts. Madam Nie Lie was not only the wife of Gen. Ding Henggao; Madam Nie was actually Lt. General Nie Lie of the Chinese army.

The so-called "civilian" firm was heavily packed with Chinese Army officers and experts. One member of Galaxy New Technology management, according to the Defense document, was Director and President "Mr. Deng Changru". Mr. Deng Changru is also Lt. Colonel Deng Changru of the People's Liberation Army, head of the PLA communications corps.

Another Chinese Army officer in the Galaxy New Technology staff is co-General Manager "Mr. Xie Zhichao" who is really Lt. Colonel Xie Zhichao, Director of the COSTIND Electronics Design Bureau.

The Galaxy New Technology deal went public in 1996, drawing a GAO report and the DoD document cited here. It also drew far too much public attention to Hua Di and John Lewis.

In 1997, John Lewis was charged with using Stanford University funding to set up the profitable Hua Mei deal. Lewis faced an investigation from the Stanford University administration because he has used University stationery for his Hua Mei business.

In the 1997 investigation, Provost Condoleezza Rice said, "we'll follow what is a normal process under these circumstances,"

"Similar issues arise quite frequently," Rice added. "It's not all that unusual that issues arise concerning conflict of interest," she said.

Lewis was charged but no actions were taken against him despite the Stanford Policy on Conflict of Commitment and Interest.

Janet Reno, however, needed to be publicly scolded in order to invoke some action. In 1997, Congressman Hyde wrote Attorney General Reno a letter outlining his concerns about Galaxy New Technology.

According to Congressman Hyde's letter to Reno, "In 1994, sophisticated telecommunications technology was transferred to a U.S.-Chinese joint venture called HUA MEI, in which the Chinese partner is an entity controlled by the Chinese military. This particular transfer included fiber-optic communications equipment, which is used for high-speed, secure communications over long distances. Also included in the package was advanced encryption software."

In 1997, Janet Reno quickly responded to the threat to U.S. national security. Reno held back the FBI investigation of the Hua Mei deal until the "matchmaker" Hua Di could skip America. Reno neatly dodged a major scandal linked to her boss, Bill Clinton by doing nothing.

Tiger Song

The Clinton Department of Justice, led by the inept Attorney General Janet Reno, refused to investigate the Hua Mei deal despite repeated protests from Congress and the Defense Department.

Instead, the General Accounting Office (GAO) wrote a scathing report noting the military links of the Hua Mei deal and of the failures of the Clinton administration.

"The equipment was exported to Hua Mei without Commerce review, even though the company was partially controlled by several high-level members of the Chinese military," states the GAO report.

In addition, the GAO clearly noted the military value of the Hua Mei deal included, "sharing of intelligence, imagery and video between several locations, command and control of military operations using video-conferencing, and medical support and telemedicine between the battlefield and remote hospitals."

"When used in a military application, both types of equipment requires encryption devices to protect communications from interception," stated the GAO report.

In Feb. 2001 U.S. warplanes struck a new Iraqi air defense system installed around Baghdad. Pentagon officials were mum in naming the country that sold the new air defense missile system to Saddam Hussein.

The Washington Post revealed that China was assisting Iraqi air defense, an allegation promptly denied by Iraq. According to the Post article, Chinese engineers were helping Iraq to install a network of fiber-optic communications and computers designed to track and destroy U.S. warplanes. The export violated U.N. weapons embargoes against Saddam.

President Bush's national security advisor, Condoleezza Rice, confirmed that Chinese engineers were indeed helping Iraq.

The Chinese army's Electronics Design Bureau modified the American fiber-optic communication system, changing it into a secure air-defense system. The Chinese army then exported the newly modified system to Iraq.

The Iraqi air defense network, NATO code-named "Tiger Song," is made of U.S. and French fiber-optic parts modified by the People's Liberation Army.

The Tiger Song system is best described as an Internet for surface-to-air missiles. Previous generations of air defense systems had to directly link radar sites to missile batteries.

The classic pattern of Soviet style air defense missile sites took the form of a six-pointed star. Each point of the star contained one missile launcher and the radar itself was located at the center along with the command control unit.

However, using the Tiger Song fiber optic communications system, Iraqi air defense missile sites were able to spread out, becoming mobile and difficult to detect. Missile launchers, radars and command centers were placed anywhere as long as they could hook up to the fiber-optic network. Radars, computers, and missiles shared the whole picture carried live over the Tiger Song network.

Allied war fighters had a difficult time with Tiger Song. The system allowed radars that were previously associated with a specific missile or gun system to trade information. Radar sites for anti-aircraft guns that could not reach high flying allied planes passed target information to large missile launchers which can reach altitudes over 80,000 feet.

In addition, the Chinese network allowed Iraqi missile batteries to move quickly. The network had many hidden prepared positions, ready to be hooked up to waiting radar, command center or missile launcher. The units were then able to move from position to position, hooking up to the network when necessary.

The ultimate irony is that the Tiger Song system is made from U.S. manufactured parts and equipment exported to China during the Clinton administration. In 1994, Chinese General Ding Henggao obtained the advanced fiber-optic system through his contacts inside the Clinton administration.

Chinese military engineers from 2nd and 4th Signals Corps of the Chinese Army Headquarters repaired the damaged Iraqi air defense system under a contract with Saddam.

The story of Hua Di does not end in the desert of Iraq. Hua Di also served his masters in Beijing by passing false information to the west.

In 1992, Hua Di claimed the new "DONG FENG" (East Wind) DF-25 missile was too expensive to be deployed. Hua documented that the DF-25 is a mobile two-stage missile capable of hurling a conventional 4,000-pound warhead over 1,000 miles. However, Hua also documented its failure.

According to the co-author of "Red Dragon Rising", William Triplett, in August 1999 Clinton administration officials were shocked by Chinese communist press announcements declaring the DF-25 to be fully operational and tipped with multiple nuclear warheads. Triplett's book has put the White House on the defensive, trying to explain their acceptance of the Chinese defector and his DF-25 dis-information.

Chinese defector Hua Di is not in prison. Hua was most likely given a medal for serving the Chinese Army through his espionage in America. His involvement with Secretary of Defense Perry and the payment he received as an advisor on the Chinese Army "Hua Mei" project all remain unanswered questions.

Hua Di passed false information to the west, obtained secure communications for the Chinese Army and penetrated into the Clinton White House through the U.S. Secretary of Defense. Hua Di served his party, and comrade General Ding. Hua Di returned home to a hero's welcome.

Hua Di was no fool - nor was he a dissident. Hua Di was one of many in a network of spies run by Chinese mastermind General Ding. It is no surprise that General Ding and COSTIND won the top honors of the Chinese communist party.

The spectacular success of this single Chinese army unit turned China into a regional power that dominates Asia and a world power capable of flexing military force anywhere on earth.

In early October 1998, Vice Premiere Zhu Rongji selected COSTIND over the Chinese Army Central Military Command (CMC) to run all space programs, including manned space flight.

COSTIND won out over the older regular Army staff officers in the CMC for an obvious reason. General Ding is the most successful Chinese military commander since Mao.

Mao took Mainland China in 1949 after fighting a twenty-year war against both the warlords and the Imperial Japanese Army. General Ding turned the Second Artillery Corps - the Chinese strategic missile force - into a feared world power and defeated America without firing a shot in the short span of six years.

General Ding and COSTIND celebrated the 50th anniversary of Mao's revolution with a Chinese Army space rocket launch. China plans to orbit a manned spacecraft in 2003 thanks in part to the efforts of General Ding.

The Shenzhou spacecraft will be under the command of COSTIND and a tribute to Ding. The new space powers granted to COSTIND are a reward to Vice Minister General Shen and Minister General Ding for their brilliant and successful penetration of the Clinton White House.

General Ding had his admirers here in the U.S. Unfortunately, they were also key officials of the Clinton administration. One key document previously withheld from public view is a 1995 letter from Defense Secretary William Perry to General Ding Henggao of COSTIND.

"On behalf of the United States Department of Defense," wrote Secretary Perry in July 1995. "I extend my regard to the officers and soldiers of the People's Liberation Army's Commission on Science, Technology and Industry for National Defense on the 46th Anniversary of the founding of the People's Republic of China."

"Advancing the military relationship between our two nations remains an objective which we agree serves the long-term interests of peace and stability the Asia-Pacific Region," wrote Perry.

"In the area of air traffic control. We have accomplished Step 5 of the Eight Point Air Traffic Control Initiative, and are prepared to carry our Step 6 by sending a delegation to China at any mutually agreed upon time in the future. Upon completion of Step 6, we would welcome a combined civil-military air traffic control delegation from China to the United States which will mark Step 7 of the Eight Point Plan."

"Let me close by again conveying my respects to you on your National Day," wrote Perry. "And by reiterating my support for our bilateral military relationship."

In 1998, the Commerce Dept. denied access to all China-Gate documents, citing national security, on the grounds that they could "neither confirm nor deny" their existence. In response, this reporter filed suit in Federal Court, located in Richmond, Virginia, seeking the withheld information.

Previously released information, forced from the Clinton administration using the Freedom of Information Act (FOIA), clearly showed meetings between Commerce officials and COSTIND. For example, one document described an August 1994 meeting in Beijing that included COSTIND General Shen, Commerce Secretary Ron Brown, and Loral CEO, Bernard Schwartz.

The evidence showed that the Commerce Dept. was withholding details on "military" exports directly to the Chinese Army. The Commerce Dept. is not authorized to issue export licenses to military end-users.

Clearly, the Commerce Dept.'s vain attempt in 1998 to dispute the fact COSTIND was not a Chinese Army unit was another White House spin effort that failed. COSTIND, to Defense Secretary Perry, was indeed a military unit, commanded by General Ding and manned by "officers and soldiers" of the PLA.

The recently released information on the PLA Generals was withheld from the American public until Federal Judge Robert Payne ordered the materials to be released in a ruling issued on June 29, 1999.

The documents underscore the Clinton administration's attempt to form a political/military alliance with communist China. U.S. Defense Perry could not help but include direct references to a "bilateral" military relationship.

The Clinton/China military relationship included the "Eight Point Plan" to transfer a state-of-the-art air defense system directly to the People's Liberation Army Air Force (PLAAF). The air defense technology transfer to the PLAAF, according to 1998 GAO testimony on U.S. military sales to China, required a waiver signed by President Clinton.

The declassified documents from the Clinton administration reveal that a civil airline modernization program for China was actually a program to train and equip the People's Liberation Army Air Force (PLAAF).

Other documents, forced from the Federal Aviation Administration (FAA) by the Freedom of Information Act (FOIA), are official USAF, Commerce and FAA reports on Chinese military contacts.

According to the FAA documents, PLAAF officers toured Edwards Air Force Base in May 1999 for military purposes. The PLAAF officers were given training on USAF combat missions, including "bombing and strafing" and "combat readiness."

In 1994, then Secretary of Defense William Perry began a "Joint Defense" conversion project with Chinese General Ding Henggao. General Ding was the commander of the Chinese Army Unit "COSTIND" (Commission on Science, Technology and Industry for National Defense). One part of the U.S./China project was to modernize the communist civil "Air Traffic Control" (ATC) system.

The documented meetings show that the Clinton administration attempted to conceal the military background of the Chinese representatives from everyone, including FAA officials. In 1993, a Chinese military delegation visited America. Yet, according the FAA, which sponsored the visit, the entire delegation was civilian.

The 1993 FAA delegation list includes a "Mr. Kui Fulin" who toured FAA Headquarters in Washington, Andrews AFB in Maryland, and Boeing aircraft Corporation in Washington state. "Mr. Kui Fulin" was actually General Kui Fulin, Chinese Army Deputy Chief of the General Staff.

The 1993 FAA list states "Mr. Li Yongtai" was the Commissioner of the Air Traffic Control Commission of China. According to hand written notes taken by the FAA, Mr. Li Yongtai was actually "Lt. General" Li Yongtai of the Chinese Air Force.

In fact, FAA officials who attending the meeting wrote "military" next to the names of seven members of the 1993 "China Air Traffic Control" delegation in an apparent effort to track the Chinese Army officers. Another example shows that a "Mr. Li Zhongli" was part of a Chinese civilian delegation visit in 1997 to San Francisco that was sponsored by Stanford University. "Mr. Li Zhongli" was actually Colonel Li Zhongli of the PLAAF.

In 1999, the Clinton administration offered the PLAAF the latest in advanced "mobile radars", command and control systems, GPS navigation, and "Surveillance Avionics" such as "Air to Air", "Air to Ground" and "surface Area Movement" surveillance radars.

According to a U.S. Air Force May 1999 report, the PLAAF was given details on USAF "Special Airspace" areas inside America used for military training, research and national security zones. The details include Edwards

Air Force base and a mapped tour of the facility. Edwards AFB is a test center for USAF, and NASA research aircraft, including the space shuttle.

The newly released materials also includes training manuals from the USAF 334th Training Squadron in both English and Chinese. The documents show Clinton administration officials proposed to train PLAAF military air controllers.

The USAF documents show PLAAF officers were given a "simulated" training mission. The training included a "two ship formation of F-16s from Luke AFB, Arizona" on a "bombing" and over flight mission in a training area, code-named "Baghdad", northwest of Prescott Arizona. The simulated exercise also included "in-flight refueling" with a tanker aircraft under control of a USAF AWACs plane.

The USAF "AWACS" (airborne warning and control system) is a flying radar plane manned by Air Force radar controllers. The Boeing E-3 Sentry AWACS aircraft provided cover and control for thousands of allied aircraft during the Gulf war and again during the operation in Kosovo. AWACs aircraft are expensive and only a few Boeing E-3 Sentry aircraft have been exported to Saudi Arabia and NATO.

The PLAAF is not currently equipped with an airborne radar control plane or an airborne refueling tanker aircraft. The Chinese Air Force did recently purchase Sukhoi twin seat SU-30 variant super-sonic bombers, which are equipped with a retractable air-refueling probe, giving them virtually unlimited range. The Sukhoi bombers are nuclear-strike capable.

The Chinese Air Force has tried to by an Israeli made Phalcon airborne radar system. However, the PLAAF radar plane deal from Israel was fell apart when it was revealed the aircraft was actually a former U.S. made Boeing 707 airliner refitted with the airborne electronics, violating U.S. export laws. The Israelis tried to modify the Phalcon system using a Russian airframe from Antonov. However, U.S. Congressional objections finally killed the program outright.

One 1995 meeting document from the Commerce Dept. also includes several names familiar to China-Gate and found in the Cox Report. In 1995, FAA, Commerce and USAF officials staged a meeting with officers from the Chinese Army Unit COSTIND (Commission for Science, Technology and Industry for National Defense). An all-star cast including Lt. General Huai Guomo, Maj. General Deng Yousheng, and Major General Wang Shouyun represented COSTIND.

In 1999, Softwar obtained the full bio, in Chinese and English, of COSTIND Lt. General Huai after winning a Freedom of Information lawsuit against the Commerce Dept. The official White House spin is that COSTIND was not a Chinese military unit but a "civilian" agency. According to a November, 1997 report, written for the Commerce Dept. by "think-tank" company SAIC, COSTIND was neither civilian nor engaged in purely commercial activities:

"COSTIND supervises virtually all of China's military research, development and production. It is a military organization, staffed largely by active duty officers... COSTIND also coordinates certain activities with the China National Nuclear Corporation (CNNC), which produces, stores, and controls all fissile material for civilian as well as military applications. COSTIND approves licenses for the use of nuclear materials for military purposes."

The Commerce Dept. claimed in August 1999 that it had complied with the orders of Federal Judge Robert Payne and turned over all documents on the Chinese Army unit COSTIND.

However, the newly released Commerce Dept. documents dealing with COSTIND were found by the FAA, not the Commerce Dept. The documents were turned over by the FAA in response to a FOIA request for Chinese military contacts.

None of the newly released Commerce documents were given to Judge Payne in response to his Court order. Thus, the new documents show the Commerce Dept. did not fully comply with Federal Judge Payne's order.

The Chinese Army unit COSTIND and the Chinese Air Force control "civilian" assets inside China. According to the Clinton administration, the PLAAF controls all air traffic in China, civil and military. PLAAF officers and enlisted personnel man all air control (ATC) facilities in red China. The ATC system and the PLAAF controllers are directly connected to the Chinese integrated air defense network of surface-to-air missiles (SAMs) and fighter-interceptors.

The PLAAF also owns several businesses. According to a 1994 report by the U.S. Army defense attaché in Beijing, "the major enterprise subordinate to the PLA Air Force is the China Lantian (Blue Sky) Industrial Corp. Also affiliated to Lantian is the Tian Ma (Sky Horse) Brand of vehicles and vehicle repair parts and facilities. China United Airlines (CUA) is a commercial entity of the PLA Air Force."

China United Airlines is a unique case of a military company operating inside the United States. China United Airlines is one of nearly 2,000 Chinese army-owned companies doing business in America. China United Airlines also operates U.S.-made civilian jet as military aircraft.

According to Seattle-based Boeing Aircraft Corp., the Chinese army air force company obtained 10 civil 737-300 jet transports in 2000 through a purchase by China United Airlines. U.S defense officials confirmed that the Chinese Air Force is operating the 10 Boeing civil airliners as military jet transports.

"If PLA commandos capture a Taiwan airfield, there will be scores of U.S. made transports bringing in troops and weapons to make it secure," stated Richard Fisher, a defense analyst and fellow at the Jamestown Foundation.

"There are several PRC airlines that are either owned or linked to the PLAAF (People's Liberation Army Air Force)," noted Fisher.

"They mostly fly Boeing craft, though some Russian airliners as well. I assume that most airliners in PRC airlines are subject to mobilization if necessary. Both Boeing and McDonnell Douglas aircraft were used to move a division of the 15th Airborne Army to Beijing for use in Tiananmen Square."

According to it's own website, the PLAAF owned China United Airlines also operates a small fleet of Russian made Ilyushin IL-76 jet transports. The IL-76 four-engine jet is the current front-line PLAAF military transport and the Chinese civil version is frequently armed with a cannon located in a rear turret.

In addition, PLAAF IL-76 transports dropped paratroopers, tanks and artillery directly on to the battlefield during the fall 2000 Chinese military exercises.

The Clinton administration also approved the sale of a used Delta Airlines

Boeing 767 to China United. The Boeing 767 was intended to become Chinese President Jiang Zemin's personal plane. The 767 was refitted at a Texas airport with sophisticated American made electronics, including satellite communications and navigation systems.

Ironically, the aircraft was also fitted with a series of covert eavesdropping devices, including bugs placed inside President Jiang's airborne bedroom, bathroom and secure telephone systems.

The 767-bugging incident led to the arrest of China United head Major General Liu Taichi. Maj. Gen. Liu Taichi is the air force officer in charge of air travel for Chinese leaders and the Chairman of China United Airlines, a military-owned commercial airline that buys the leadership's planes.

The youngest son of a revolutionary marshal, Gen. Liu is also the deputy head of the Chinese Army Air Force equipment department. General Lui often traveled to the United States as a civilian using his position at China United as a cover. General Liu also became a familiar face inside U.S. aviation companies such as Boeing. During the Clinton years, Gen. Liu bought six Boeing planes for use as VIP aircraft.

"He (General Liu) was one of Boeing's best customers," said a former business associate of the PLAAF commander in a recent article published by the Wall Street Journal.

The Washington Times reported that President Jiang suspected former Chinese Premier Li Peng was behind the bugging incident because of corruption charges against Li's wife and children. Li later disputed reports that he was behind the bugging of Jiang's airplane during a press conference in Macao.

General Liu's arrest re-enforced reports from intelligence sources that the U.S. had little if anything to do with the eavesdropping devices found on Jiang's airplane. Instead of publicly blaming the United States for the bugging incident, Chinese authorities have quietly tried to cover-up the entire affair.

Another incident highlights the difference between U.S. and Chinese airborne surveillance techniques. For example, U.S. Navy Aircraft PR-32, the Lockheed EP-3E Aries II that was captured by China after colliding with a PLAAF F-8 fighter jet, was clearly marked as a U.S. military plane.

The markings on the huge four-engine reconnaissance plane include large black block letters and brightly painted stars against battleship gray, identifying it as property of the United States Navy.

In contrast, China United Airlines aircraft B-4138, a Russian-made TU-154M three-engine airliner, is also clearly marked. B-4138 is painted in the colors of the communist government-owned airline and flies under an international civilian number as a passenger plane. The markings on B-4138 include large black block letters and a CUA symbol on the tail.

B-4138 is a Chinese spy plane. Defense analysts confirmed that the so-called "civil" aircraft is actually a Chinese air force spy plane equipped with a sophisticated radar and communications equipment. The modified TU-154M airliner is equipped with an array of communications antenna on the rear and a huge radar dome on the bottom of the aircraft.

"The Tu-154M is indeed from China United," stated Richard Fisher.

"It is equipped with a new Synthetic Aperture Radar (SAR) system," noted Fisher, pointing out the characteristic tub like radar dome that dominates the lower half of the Chinese spy plane.

"This Tu-154M is likely involved in research for the development of SAR systems that can be used in a similar fashion to the U.S. JSTARS, which provided unprecedented battlefield awareness to U.S. commanders in the Gulf War. For the PLA, this and future SAR aircraft will help to manage military operations over Taiwan and to find critical targets for air and missile strikes."

"There is no doubt in my mind that they [China United Airlines] operate this type of aircraft," stated Larry Wortzel, senior Asia analyst at the Heritage Foundation.

"I have no doubt they have FLIR [forward-looking infrared] and SAR radar on some U.S made Gulfstreams as well," noted Wortzel.

According to a 1994 U.S. military report, the Clinton administration was aware that the People's Liberation Army Air Force (PLAAF) owns and operates China United Airlines. Documentation obtained using the Freedom of Information act shows that China United Airlines is a known front company operated by PLAAF.

According to the 1997 Rand report on the Chinese Defense Industry, "for those who oppose any subsidization of the PLA, there is thus ample evidence that profits from PLA-affiliated enterprises directly benefit the main-line forces of the Chinese military."

China United is not the only company to operate inside the U.S. The Commerce Department documents also included a detailed bio of COSTIND General Huai Guomo, a personal letter to COSTIND commander, General Ding Henggao, and a letter from U.S. defense contractor, Allied Signal Corporation, seeking help for a jet engine transfer to the Chinese "Harbin" aerospace company.

According to materials sent to Commerce Secretary Ron Brown by Chinese Army General Ding, the Chinese Army owns "HARBIN". Harbin currently manufactures fighters and bombers for the People's Liberation Army Air Force (PLAAF) and for export to Iraq, Syria, Pakistan and Iran.

The detailed documents included two pages of information on Chinese General Huai Guomo in both English and Chinese. Huai Guomo, according to the Clinton administration, is "a career administrator in China's defense industrial complex" and the very model of a modern Chinese General.

General Huai's credits include joining the Chinese communist party in 1953 and working in the PLA "nuclear industry". Huai reportedly "impressed" his U.S. Defense "counterparts" over the years as a "competent, professional as well as a cordial individual to work with."

The details of a 1995 Chinese Army meeting at the Energy Dept. with General Huai are written in a report by the U.S. Commerce Dept. The 1995 Commerce Dept. report is part of over 1,000 pages of materials on meetings with Chinese Army officials obtained from a Federal lawsuit filed in 1998. The documents were forced from the Commerce Dept. in a Feb. 23, 1999 Court order issued by Judge Robert Payne.

According to the Commerce Dept. documentation, Susan Tierney, Assistant Energy Secretary of Policy attended the meeting with the Chinese Army. "She noted that the DOE Secretary visited China last month and that cooperation with China is a high priority," states the Commerce report.

"(Tierney) noted that DOE and the China State Planning Commission have similar goals in the following areas: 1) Science and technology development (especially in energy); 2) Funding of research (such as fusion and fission)".

According to the March 1995 report, Lt. General Huai explained that his unit, COSTIND, had "six specialty areas - 1) Aerospace; 2) Aviation; 3) Electronics; 4) Ground Force Military Equipment; 5) Shipbuilding; 6) Nuclear."

"The business leaders asked for POC's (point of contact) for the 49 projects and Huai suggested they contact Col Xu at the Embassy," states the Commerce Dept. report.

"Barry Carter (Commerce) mentioned the package he was preparing which will include POC info. MGen Deng offered his assistance in COSTIND if any company had difficulty communicating with industries in China. He said there are investment dollars put aside for the 9th five year plan, and they do not have to be limited to the 49 projects... The Chinese said that anyone wanting to make deals should move forward rapidly so that it will be covered in the next 5 year plan which is just being drawn up".

Then, according to the Commerce report, Lt. General Huai asked several questions, concerning the financial and legal aspects of U.S. nuclear power. "LTG Huai asked if the govt takes back its

money when industry develops the final product...Does the business keep tech patent rights?"

"At the end of the meeting at Energy," concludes the Commerce document. "The Chinese indicated that they would like to develop cooperation in the nuclear field. They expect to have problems in handling nuclear waste and would like to develop future cooperation in handling such waste. US has no cooperation right now in the nuclear area, but China hopes to have some in the future".

General Huai had good reason to have high hopes for nuclear cooperation with the Clinton administration. The COSTIND operations against the Commerce Dept. also included a vast array of U.S. military nuclear weapons technology. One deadly example, and a specialty of COSTIND General Huai, was the export of U.S. super-computers for Chinese Army nuclear weapons research.

Commerce Dept. documents show that SUN Corp., a U.S. computer maker, sold a super-computer directly to a Chinese Army nuclear weapons lab at Yuanwang Corp. The documents also show that the Clinton administration knew that the Chinese Army operated Yuanwang.

Detailed information was given to the Commerce Dept., including the direct PLA contacts at the Chinese weapons labs prior to the sale by none other than COSTIND General Ding himself. According to the Commerce documents, Yuanwang manufactures test equipment for the Lop Nor nuclear weapons facility in China.

The Bush administration has accused Sun Microsystems Inc. of violating export rules in high-speed computer sales it made to China during the Clinton administration.

According to a letter the company received in February 2002 from the U.S. Commerce Department's Bureau of Industry and Security (BIS), the illegal sales took place in 1997 and 1998. The letter was released on Sept. 30 by Sun in a regulatory filing.

According to the letter, in 1997 Sun sold equipment to a Hong Kong reseller, which later sold the hardware to military organizations in China. Sun officials would not discuss the nature of the equipment.

However, Sun Microsystems has a long history of equipment sales to military users inside China. For example, on Dec. 26, 1996 a Hong Kong reseller for Sun Microsystems, Automated Systems Ltd., sold a supercomputer to the Chinese Scientific Institute, a technical institute under the Chinese Academy of Sciences.

According to documents obtained from the U.S. Commerce Department, the Chinese Scientific Institute is a government laboratory specializing in parallel and distributed processing.

At some point after the sale but before delivery, the computer was sold to Yuanwang Corp. Yuanwang is an entity of the Chinese army unit COSTIND (Commission on Science, Technology, and Industry for National Defense). According to Defense Intelligence Agency (DIA) documents, COSTIND oversees nuclear weapons research and design for the Chinese army.

Sun officials claimed in 1997 that they were unaware of the supercomputer transfer to the Chinese nuclear weapons lab. However, according to the Chinese Foreign Ministry, Sun Microsystems was aware of Yuanwang Corp.'s Chinese military ties.

According to the Cox report, the Chinese Ministry of Foreign Trade and Economic Cooperation (MOFTEC) explained that the actual buyer of the computer was the "Yuanwang Corporation" and that Sun was aware of "this corporation's PRC military ties."

In another case, the Clinton administration approved the export of a Sun supercomputer directly to the Yuanwang Group. The Sun supercomputer was moved to the National Defense Technical Institute in Changsha, part of the Lop Nor nuclear weapons facility, for atomic bomb design.

In 1996 the Sun supercomputer sale came to the attention of Frank Deliberti, then the U.S. Commerce Department's deputy assistant secretary for export enforcement. Deliberti gave the information he obtained to Sun Microsystems, which then initiated efforts to have its computer returned. The computer was returned to the United States on Nov. 6, 1997.

There is ample evidence that Clinton administration officials were aware that Yuanwang was a company owned by the Chinese military. According to the Commerce Department's own documents, official meetings with Chinese army owned companies took place before documented computer transfer to Yuanwang Corp.

The documents include a list of Chinese military owned corporations compiled by Gen. Ding, then commander of COSTIND. The list provides the direct contact phone number of the Chinese army official in charge at Yuanwang Corp.

On April 6, 1994, Defense Intelligence Agency official Col. Blasko sent an unclassified memo to Commerce officials. The memo states that "YUANWANG" Corp. and "GREAT WALL INDUSTRIES" are "significant to the Defense conversion" along with other known PLA-owned companies such as "CHINA NATIONAL NUCLEAR" and "China North" NORINCO.

The Chinese People's Armed Police is also well equipped with Sun-made computer equipment to track, identify and quickly jail any dissidents. Sun Microsystems has a contract with the Chinese version of the Nazi Gestapo, the Public Security Bureau, to make use of instant computer identification of fingerprints.

In 1993, Great Wall, along with nine other PLA controlled companies, sold nuclear tipped M-9 missiles to Pakistan. In response, Great Wall was banned from purchasing U.S. controlled
technology such as computers.

Only a few months later, Great Wall was allowed to buy over $100 million of U.S. computers. Tandem Corp. CEO James Treybig attended an August 1994 Presidential trade mission to Beijing with Ron Brown. A Brown trade mission document states "Tandem and China Great Wall Industry will announce in August their joint venture".

Another document found in the files of former Commerce Secretary Ron Brown states that Treybig "negotiated a $100 million dollar joint venture for Tandem Computers while in China".

The PLA purchase of U.S. computer power was the perfect cap to Chinese nuclear espionage operations against America. The computers that power U.S. atomic weapon labs have evil twins
inside red China. The PLA super-computers can run American nuclear bomb design software and codes with little or no modification. They are identical to the computers at U.S. weapons labs right down to the vendor support.

Yet, the U.S. computer industry could not have made these lucrative export deals without the direct assistance of then-President Bill Clinton. In 1995, Tony Podesta, a powerful Washington lobbyist and brother of John Podesta, then Clinton's White House adviser, had a consortium of top U.S. computer CEOs attend secret meetings inside the White House. The meetings were on computer hardware and software exports to China and Russia.

In 1995, Tony Podesta represented Computer Systems Policy Project. CSPP was a group of computer companies that in 1995 included Apple, AT&T, Compaq, Cray, Data General, Digital Equipment, Hewlett-Packard, IBM, Silicon Graphics, Stratus Computer, Tandem, Unisys and Sun Microsystems.

These major computer corporations, including Sun, sought Clinton's assistance in exporting computers to Russian and Chinese military end users.

According to a May 1995 CSPP document sent to Commerce Secretary Ron Brown, "controls on computer exports to Russia and China for commercial, civil end-users should be eliminated; controls on exports for actual military end-uses may be appropriate until there is greater certainty that neither country poses a threat to U.S. national security."

One 1995 secret meeting inside the White House was attended by CSPP Director Ken Kay, then an employee of Podesta Associates. The meeting with Tony Podesta's employee took place while John Podesta was employed at the White House. John Podesta left the employ of the White House and went directly to work for his brother in July 1995.

The meeting occurred just before Clinton changed supercomputer policy. Within weeks, Russian and Chinese military units were buying hundreds of U.S.-made computers.

Another Commerce Department letter outlined the lack of concern for U.S. national security by the Clinton administration and the CSPP computer makers. The letter includes an e-mail from then Commerce Undersecretary Dave Barram dated Jan. 3, 1996.

According to Undersecretary Barram, "Terrorist activity" was of no concern to the corporate members of CSPP. "They aren't likely to think the risk society avoids for however long offsets the economic risk to American industry."

Unsaid in the memo is the fact that David Barram, former CEO of Cray Corp., then the leading supercomputer maker in America, was also a former member of CSPP.

In 1999, the General Accounting Office released a scathing report critical of Clinton's high-tech export policy. According to the GAO, "the President's July 1999 report to Congress did not fully satisfy the reporting requirements of the Defense Authorization act."

Overall, only 3 percent of all computer licenses were for "sensitive" end-users such as foreign military units. The GAO noted that the Clinton administration issued more than 1,900 licenses for high-speed computers to communist China between November 1997 and August 1999. Of the 1,924 computers licensed for China, 48 computers were to "sensitive end-users or uses," or nearly 2.5 percent of all sales to China.

"The [president's] report did address two of the three requirements," wrote the GAO. "To determine the availability of high performance computers in foreign countries and the potential use of the newly decontrolled computers for significant military use. These applications include advanced aircraft design, anti-submarine warfare sensor development, and radar applications."

Clinton's report "did not, however, assess the impact of such military use on the national security interests of the United States," wrote the GAO. "Instead, the report discussed the economic importance of a strong U.S. computer industry to U.S. national security. The President's report concluded that failure to adjust U.S. export requirements for computers and processors would have a significant negative effect on the U.S. computer industry."

"The [Clinton] report implied that high-performance computers are readily available for foreign sources," states the GAO. "A 1998 study sponsored by DOD [Department of Defense] and Commerce found that the United States dominates the international computer market."

Sun Microsystems says it is now in settlement talks. The Bush administration has given the computer maker until Nov. 1 to respond to the accusations. Sun said it would defend itself against the charges if the settlement talks fail.

"We expect to reach a resolution on this, and it will not have a materially adverse effect on Sun," stated company spokesman Andy Lark.

If Sun is found to have violated the regulations, it could face financial penalties or the loss of its export privileges. America and its allies will not be so lucky as to pay a price in mere money. The Chinese army used U.S.-made computers such as those sold by Sun to help design a new family of lightweight nuclear weapons.

The economic impact of losing sales was far more important to Clinton and his Big Business backers than U.S. national security. As a result, Beijing is deploying nuclear weapons designed and built using American supercomputers.

According to U.S. Naval Institute defense analyst Norman Friedman, "The Chinese obtained the computer programs (codes) Los Alamos uses to simulate what happens inside an exploding nuclear warhead. The software is exactly what a designer of an advanced weapon would need."

"Softened" Clinton-led export regulations, according to Friedman, "made it possible for the Chinese to buy 600 super-computers on which to run that software. Thus, the Chinese have transformed their weapons development capability in a very few years."

According to defense sources, China has already deployed advanced nuclear weapon designs stolen from the United States. The Chinese Army Second Artillery Corps has tested the deadly Dong-Feng (East Wind) 31 missile in celebration of 50th anniversary of the July 1949 take over of China by Mao.

The DF-31 is reported to be able to deliver three, newly developed, lightweight, 90 Kiloton nuclear warheads to any target in America. The Chinese DF-31 is a road mobile, nuclear tipped SCUD like missile, that is nearly impossible to find, much less destroy. It is intended to counter the USAF B-2 bomber in a "limited" nuclear war scenario where China and the U.S. would only kill a few million people on each side.

If deployed in large numbers, the DF-31 could pose a significant first strike threat against stationary military targets inside the U.S. homeland, such as the MX missile fields and the single B-2 bomber base.

In the end, General Ding, General Shen, and General Huai have all retired with the highest rewards from the communist party. Their operations against America were carefully planned and executed. Their meetings were quietly withheld from public view by a U.S. administration seeking to reap the benefits from "military" sales to the People's Liberation Army in the form of political donations.

The Clinton administration assisted China in its efforts to become the next nuclear super-power. The next cold war has begun and with it will come another expensive nuclear arms race.

PARTICIPANTS FROM CHINESE SIDE:

1. Ding Henggao — Head of Chinese Delegation, Minister of COSTIND, Chinese Co-Chairman
2. Huai Guomo — Vice Minister of COSTIND
3. Ma Zhengang — Director of America-Oceanica Department, Ministry of Foreign Affairs
4. Yu Zhonglin — Director of Defense Department, The State Planning Commission
5. Tang Xinmin — Director of Department of Science and Technology Achievements, The State Science and Technology Commission
6. Jiang Xiaopei — Deputy Director of Technical Renovation Department, The State Economy and Trade Commission
7. Maj. Gen. Hou Gang — Deputy Director of the Intelligence Department, Headquaters of General Staff of the Chinese PLA
8. Deng Yousheng — Deirector of Foreign Affairs Department, COSTIND
9. Yao Wenping — Devision Chief, Science and Technology Department Ministry of Foreign Trade and Economic Cooperation
10. Ju Jian — Executive Secretary, Division Chief, Foreign Affairs Department, COSTIND
11. Feng Hui — Business Liaison, Foreign Affairs Department, COSTIND
12. Maj. Gen. Fu Jiaping — Director of Foreign Affairs Bureau, Ministry of Defense
13. Maj. Gen. Chen Kaizeng — PRC DATT
14. Liu Xiaomin — Councilor, America-Oceanica Department, Ministry of Foreign Affairs
15. Su Xuguang — Division Chief, General Office, COSTIND
16. Sr. Col. Du Xingtian — Division Chief, FAB, Ministry of Defense
17. Su Wenli — Deputy Division Chief, Budget and Planning Department, COSTIND
18. Liu Yongen — Deputy General Secretary, CAPUMIT
19. Sr. Col. Ge Yunsong — FAB, Ministry of Defense
20. Col. Qian Lihua — FAB, Ministry of Defense
21. Col. Yuan Xiaocheng — Chief of Security, Ministry of Defense
22. Zou Yijun — Interpreter, Ministry of Foreign Affairs
23. Wang Feng — General Office, COSTIND
24. Lu Yongxin — FAD, COSTIND
25. Cui Yu — FAD, COSTIND

SUPPORTS:

26. Zhang Tongsheng — Photographer, COSTIND

U.S.-CHINA JOINT DEFENSE CONVERSION COMMISSION
MINUTES OF THE FIRST MEETING-BEIJING, OCTOBER 17, 1994

Appendix I

U.S.-CHINA JOINT DEFENSE CONVERSION COMMISSION
NAME LIST OF PARTICIPANTS OF THE FIRST MEETING

PARTICIPANTS FROM U.S. SIDE
1. Dr. William J. Perry — Head of U.S. Delegation, Secretary of Defense, U.S. Co-chairman
2. Barry Carter — Deputy Under Secretary of Commerce
3. Joseph Nye — Assistant Secretary of Defense for International Security Affairs
4. Winston Lord — Assistant Secretary of State for East Asia and Pacific Affairs
5. Stanley Roth — Special Assistant to the President, Senior Director for Asian Affairs
6. Mike Nacht — Assistant Director, ACDA
7. Mitch Wallerstein — Deputy Assistant Secretary of Defense
8. Maj.Gen.David Mcilvoy — Office the Joint Chiefs of Staff, Deputy Director for Politico-Military Affairs
9. Dr. Eden Woon — Executive Secretary, Office of Secretary of Defense
10. Ms. Susan Long — Special Assistant, OSD
11. Thomas Becherer — Business Liaison, ODS
12. Frank Colson — Executive Director, DOD Policy Board on Federal Aviation
13. Major General Paul Kern — Military Aide, Secretary of Defense
14. Bob Hall — Special Assistant to the Secretary of Defense
15. Mr. Bacon — Asst. to Secretary of Defense for Public Affairs
16. Ambassador Stapleton Roy
17. BG Michael T. Byrnes — DATT
18. Ltc. Dennis J. Blasko — ARMA
19. Michael Finegan — Political/Military officer, U.S. Embassy
20. Fred Lee — Senior Representative for the Federal Aviation Administration, U.S. Embassy
21. Jim Brown — U.S. Embassy Interpreter

OBSERVERS:
22. Mr. Richard Collins — Senate Staff
23. Mr. Steven Cortese — Senate Staff
24. Ms. Margaret Sullivan — Assistant for White House Affairs
25. Dr. John Lewis — Stanford University, Civilian Consultant to SECDEF

SUPPORTS:
26. Col. Joe Shaffer — Trip Coordinator
27. Helene Stikkel — Photographer
28. Mr. Roland Jackson — Security
29. Mr. Christopher Olvera — Secutity

335

THE CHINA DESK
OFFICE OF THE SECRETARY OF DEFENSE
(INTERNATIONAL SECURITY AFFAIRS)
ASIAN AND PACIFIC AFFAIRS
ROOM 4C840, THE PENTAGON • WASHINGTON, D.C. 20301-2400
OFC: (703)697-7757 AV 227-7757 FAX: (703) 695-8222 AV 225-8222

NUMBER OF PAGES (INCLUDING COVER)	DATE
3	October 4, 1995
FROM	**OFFICE TELEPHONE**
Don Rogers	(703) 697-3027
TO	**OFFICE**
Ms. Terri Dawson	DOC/BXA
OFFICE TELEPHONE	**FAX NUMBER**
(202)482-1455	(202)482-2387

REMARKS:

Terri:

Attached is the text of the Perry letter to Ding.

Thanks,

Don

R023

General Ding Henggao
Commission on Science, Technology and Industry
  for National Defense
People's Republic of China

Dear General Ding,

On behalf of the United States Department of Defense, I extend my regards to the officers and soldiers of the People's Liberation Army's Commission on Science, Technology and Industry for National Defense on the 46th Anniversary of the founding of the People's Republic of China.

Advancing the military relationship between our two nations remains an objective which we agree serves the long-term interests of peace and stability the Asia-Pacific Region. In this regard, I am hopeful in the months ahead we will move forward in the important area of defense conversion cooperation. We have already made significant progress on our Sino-American Joint Defense Conversion Commission work plan. I believe we must now concentrate on sustaining the momentum achieved to date.

Let me briefly review the status of our Joint Commission's projects. As you know, together with the United States Department of Commerce, we have published the *China Defense Industry Directory* and *U.S. Industry Directory*.

In the area of air traffic control, we have accomplished Step 5 of the Eight-Point Air Traffic Control Initiative, and are prepared to carry out Step 6 by sending a delegation to China at any mutually agreed upon time in the future. Upon completion of Step 6, we would welcome a combined civil-military air traffic control delegation from China to the United States which will mark Step 7 of the Eight Point Plan.

We have also responded positively to your list of 49 defense conversion projects for potential cooperation with U.S. industry. Beyond publication of the *China Defense Industry Directory* , we are making arrangements for the visit of a delegation of Chinese defense managers to the United States in the near future. This group will be hosted by the Departments of Defense and Commerce, as well as by U.S. industries. At the same time, we are exploring the possibility of providing assistance in facilitating intern programs for defense conversion specialists.

R24

Lastly, there are arrangements being made by our Department of Commerce and your Ministry of Foreign Trade and Economic Cooperation to include defense conversion as a topic for discussion at the upcoming Joint Committee on Commerce and Trade (JCCT) meeting in Beijing next month. From my perspective, it will be very useful to establish informal linkage between the Joint Defense Conversion Commission and the JCCT since on our side the Department of Commerce plays such an active role in bilateral defense conversion activities. Your support would be most appreciated in pursuing this initiative.

Clearly, while much has been accomplished, we must renew our efforts if the objectives we established at our Joint Defense Conversion Commission's First Plenary Session in Beijing last October are to be accomplished. I suggest that both sides carefully examine the various ongoing Joint Defense Conversion Commission projects and work together to achieve concrete results. At the point we have achieved sufficient progress, I propose we explore the possibility of convening the Joint Defense Conversion Commission Second Plenary Session in Washington, D.C., hopefully at some time in the coming year.

Let me close by again conveying my respects to you on your National Day, and by reiterating my support for our bilateral military relationship, in which defense conversion plays a prominent role. I hope to see you again at the earliest opportunity.

Sincerely,

44

The following individuals will be visiting Washington, D.C., 26-19 March 1995 as part of the Sino-U.S. Joint Defense Conversion Commission/Chinese Air Traffice Control/Aviation Delegation Visit to U.S. 14-29 March 1995:

LTG Huai Guomo, Vice Minister, State Commission for Science, Technology & Industry for National Defense (COSTIND)

MG Deng Yousheng, Director of Foreign Affairs Bureau (FAB), COSTIND

Mr Cheng Dedi, State Planning Commission

Lt Col Wang Feng, COSTIND Central Office, Special Assistant to LTG Huai

Maj Feng Hui, Staff Officer, COSTIND Foreign Affairs Bureau

Mr Liu Luhong, COSTIND Planning Commission

E055

45

EXECUTIVE SUMMARY

GENERAL ((HUAI)) GUOMO

COSTIND DEPUTY DIRECTOR

GENERAL HUAI IS A CAREER ADMINISTRATOR IN CHINA'S DEFENSE INDUSTRIAL COMPLEX. HE HAS A LONG BACKGROUND ON COOPERATION WITH THE U.S. AND IS A KEY FIGURE IN CHINA'S DEFENSE CONVERSION EFFORTS. GENERAL HUAI HAS BEEN COSTIND DEPUTY DIRECTOR SINCE APR 1988.

BORN IN ZHEJIANG IN 1932, GENERAL HUAI GRADUATED FROM SHANGHAI'S JIAOTONG UNIVERSITY IN 1952. HE JOINED THE CHINESE COMMUNIST PARTY IN 1953. UPON GRADUATION, HUAI BEGAN HIS CAREER AS SECRETARY OF THE STEEL BUREAU, MINISTRY OF METALLURGICAL INDUSTRY. HE LATER SERVED AS A TECHNICIAN OF A CHEMICAL FACTORY IN NANJING. HE THEN BECAME INVOLVED IN THE NUCLEAR INDUSTRY, JOINING THE SECOND MINISTRY OF MACHINE BUILDING INDUSTRY AS AN ENGINEER OF ITS PLANNING BUREAU. HE NEXT ENTERED THE STATE COUNCIL'S NATIONAL DEFENSE INDUSTRIES OFFICE (NDIO) AS A STAFF OFFICER OF THE SECOND BUREAU, DEPARTMENT DIRECTOR OF THE SECOND DIVISION, AND DEPARTMENT DIRECTOR OF THE PRODUCTION BUREAU.

IN 1982 THE NDIO WAS MERGED WITH THE NATIONAL DEFENSE SCIENCE AND TECHNOLOGY COMMISSION TO FORM THE PRESENT-DAY COSTIND. GENERAL HUAI BECAME DEPUTY DIRECTOR AND THEN DIRECTOR OF COSTIND'S DEPARTMENT OF COMPREHENSIVE PLANNING, IN CHARGE OF BOTH BUDGET AND PLANNING. GENERAL HUAI WAS PROMOTED TO COSTIND DEPUTY DIRECTOR IN SPRING 1988 AND WAS MADE A MAJOR GENERAL IN THE FALL.

GENERAL HUAI SEEMS TO BE AN EXPERT ON THE CONVERSION OF MILITARY TO CIVILIAN PRODUCTION. IN AUGUST 1990, HE ATTENDED A U.N. MEETING ON THE SUBJECT HELD IN MOSCOW. IN OCTOBER 1991, HE WAS IDENTIFIED AS HONORARY PRESIDENT OF THE CHINA ASSOCIATION FOR PEACEFUL USE OF MILITARY INDUSTRIAL TECHNOLOGIES. IN FEBRUARY 1992, HE HEADED A DELEGATION TO GERMANY TO ATTEND ANOTHER U.N.-SPONSORED CONFERENCE ON MILITARY TECHNOLOGY FOR CIVILIAN USE. HE HAS ALSO PUBLISHED ARTICLES AND SPOKEN ON THE SUBJECT. GENERAL HUAI'S PREVIOUS MEETINGS WITH U.S. VISITORS IN THE POST TIANANMEN PERIOD INCLUDE ASSISTANT DEFENSE SECRETARY FREEMAN IN NOV 1993 AND DEPUTY DEFENSE SECRETARY WISNER IN MAR 1994.

BEFORE TIANANMEN, LTG HUAI WAS DEEPLY INVOLVED IN THE DEVELOPMENT OF THE U.S.-PRC TECHNOLOGY COOPERATION RELATIONSHIP DURING THE 1984-88 TIME FRAME. AS PLANNING DIRECTOR, HE TRAVELLED TO THE U.S. AND HOSTED U.S. MILITARY DELEGATIONS WORKING THE AREA OF QUALITY ASSURANCE AMONG OTHER ISSUES. HE IMPRESSED U.S. COUNTERPARTS AS COMPETENT, PROFESSIONAL AS WELL AS A CORDIAL INDIVIDUAL TO WORK WITH.

E053

怀国模
中华人民共和国国防科学技术工业委员会副主任。中将。

1932年12月生。浙江嘉兴人。1952年交通大学毕业。1953年加入中国共产党。历任鞍山钢铁厂技术员、冶金工业部钢铁局秘书、南京永利宁化工厂技术员，第二机械工业部计划局工程师，国务院国防工业办公室二局参谋、二处副处长、生产局副局长、国防科工委综合计划部副部长、部长。1988年起任国防科工委副主任。同年被授予少将军衔。1993年晋为中将。

Huai Guomo (b. Dec 1932) Native of Jiaxing, Zhejiang

Vice-minister in charge of Commission of Science, Technology and Industry for National Defence; *lieutenant general*

Graduated from Jiaotong University in Shanghai, 1952. Joined CPC, 1953. Served as technician of Anshan Iron and Steel Works; secretary of Steel Bureau, Ministry of Metallurgical Industry, 1952-54; technician of Yonglining Chemical Factory in Nanjing, 1957-58; engineer of Planning Bureau, 2nd Ministry of Machine-Building Industry, 1958-64; staff officer of 2nd Bureau, deputy director of 2nd Division and deputy director of Production Bureau under Office of National Defence Industries of State Council, 1964-82; deputy chief and chief of Comprehensive Planning Department under Commission of Science, Technology and Industry for National Defence under State Council, 1982-88; vice-minister in charge of Commission of Science, Technology and Industry for National Defence, 1988.

Granted rank of major general, 1988; lieutenant general, 1993.

E054

47

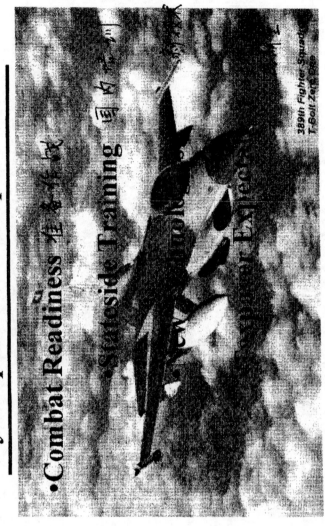

怎什么需要特别用途空域？
Why Is Special Use Airspace Needed?

- Combat Readiness 准备作战

Stateside Training 国内训练

389th Fighter Squadron
T-Bolt Zone

CHINA AIR TRAFFIC CONTROL SURVEY DELEGATION

Chief Delegate:

01. Mr. Wang Shuming   Deputy Secretary-General,
                             the State Council of China

Deputy Chief Delegates:

02. Mr. Jiang Zhuping   Director General,
                             the Civil Aviation Administration
                             of China (CAAC)

03. Mr. Kui Fulin   Commissioner,
    Deputy Chief of general   the Air Traffic Control Commission   *MILITAR*
    Staff, PLA   of China

04. Mr. Li Yongtai   Commissioner,
    Lt. general, PLAF   the Air Traffic Control Commission   *MILITARy*
                             of China

Delegates:

05. Mr. Qu Yongxiu   Official,   *MILITARy*
                             the Air Traffic Control Office,
                             the Air Traffic Control Commission
                             of China

06. Mr. Fu Youyun   Official,
                             the Air Traffic Control Office,   *MILITARY*
                             the Air Traffic Control Commission
                             of China

07. Mr. Chen Xuhua   Deputy Director,
                             Department of Flight Operations,
                             CAAC

08. Mr. Li Keli   Deputy Director,
                             Department of International Affairs,
                             CAAC

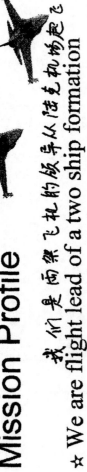

任务轮廓
Mission Profile

我们是两架飞机的领导人/这是机场起飞

☆ We are flight lead of a two ship formation of F-16's from Luke AFB, Arizona.

☆ Today's mission will be 任务

→ low level training flight to a bombing range 低空飞行到/轰炸范围

→ an in-flight refueling 空中加油

→ a cross country flight to a MOA, 越国家飞到/军事行动区

→ IFR practice approaches at a civilian airport 仪表飞行/到/民用机场

→ return home for VFR pattern work
以目视飞行回家

Phase Three 第三节

☆ We enter and fly low level training route VR-231 under VFR rules while ABQ monitors our progress
我们进入依空目视目视地区 VR-231，ABQ 监控我们的情况
我们飞 坐VR-231

☆ We exit VR-231 as we enter the restricted area (R-2301) and we conduct our training bombing and strafing runs
飞入限制地区 R-2301完成轰炸 和扫射任务

☆ We remain under VFR rules for our time in R-2301
我们 仍 依照 目视 飞行 规则 在 R-2301内

51

3

SUNBURN

*Ask yourself which political leadership - your own or that of your
enemy - is able to reject flatterers and draw close to the wise.*
Du Mu - The Art of War

In 1995, Vice President Al Gore traveled to Moscow and cut a secret deal
with Russian Prime Minister Chernomyrdin. Part of that deal allowed the
U.S. military to purchase Russian made weapons in a series of test programs.

In August 2000, the Navy released documents showing the Clinton administration declined a 1995 offer from Russia to purchase the advanced SS-N-
22, NATO code name Sunburn, supersonic cruise missile. The documents
were obtained from the Clinton administration using the Freedom of
Information Act.

According to the recently released documentation, the effort started under
a secret U.S. Navy project code-named "Ballerina." In September 1993 the
Point Mugu California Naval Warfare Center prepared a report titled "22-
Surrogate Targets Program (STP) SS-N-22 'Sunburn' Launch Integration and
Firing Demonstration."

The document shows that the U.S. Navy had previously acquired and test
fired older "Styx" anti-ship missiles from Russia. The document also shows
that as early as 1993 the U.S. Navy had tendered offers to Russia for the
more advanced Sunburn cruise missile.

"Recently, the Navy has acquired approximately 175 SS-N-2D (Styx) Anti-
Ship Cruise Missiles (ASCMs) with documentation, spares, support equipment, and portable launch platforms," states the Sunburn Navy document.

"As of August 1993, four Styx have been flown from the NAECWPNS San
Nicholas Island (SNI) facility to demonstrate capacity. The ASCMs were
operated in their original configuration with exception of some minor modifications for operating on the Sea range. These included warhead removal,
addition of a radar tracking beacon, redundant flight termination system, and
a Global Positioning System receiver with low-volume telemetry transmitter."

The documents show that the U.S. Navy planned to test Sunburn missiles
as early as 1993. The 1993 plan includes detailed maps of proposed
Sunburn test flights from the Navy missile range located at Point Mugu,

California.

"The Navy is ... proposing to conduct flight demonstrations of the modern SS-N-22 supersonic ASM," notes the Navy 1993 report.

"To perform the pilot phase of flight demonstrations, there is a need for complete documentation, support equipment, launch control systems and foreign technical assistance. The later will consist of foreign trained SS-N-22 weapon systems specialists that can provide training/instruction on handling, maintenance and operation of the system."

Another document, a 1995 status report prepared for the Navy, states that U.S. defense contractor Vector Microwave had "reached a basic agreement with the Russian manufacturer of the SS-N-22 (Arsenjev Aviation Company 'Progress') on the concept of acquiring the SS-N-22 missiles as targets."

The 1995 document notes that the contractor planned to obtain as many as 100 Sunburn missiles directly from the Russian Navy inventory. The missiles including "active and dummy warheads" complete with the current Russian made electronics such as the radar seeker, navigation systems and radio altimeter.

A July 1995 status report written for the Navy noted that the Russians had agreed to the Sunburn sale and that a "letter of 'bona fides' from the U.S. government would be necessary" in order to enter into formal negotiations.

The status report noted that a major incentive for the sale was money. In fact, Russian missile maker Arsenjev was so hard pressed for cash that it had to make "titanium golf clubs" for sale in South Korea. The 1995 report also warned "the Russians felt that strict confidentiality of such an acquisition program should be maintained."

The documents show the U.S. Navy responded two months later. In September 1995, U.S. Navy Principal Deputy Vice Admiral W.C. Bowes sent a letter to Admiral Felix Gromov, then Commander-in-Chief of the Russian Navy, advising the Admiral of the possible sale.

"I appreciate the opportunity to convey to you the United States Navy's interest in acquiring all variants of the SS-N-22 'Sunburn' Anti-Ship Supersonic Ship-to-ship missile for test and evaluation," wrote U.S. Admiral Bowes.

Russian Embassy Press officer Mikhail Shugalian did not deny the "authenticity" of the documents in an interview from his office in Washington D.C. The Russian military attaché in Washington D.C. was unavailable for comment. Russia has sold Sunburns to China and eight nuclear tipped SS-N-22 missiles reportedly arm an advanced Russian made now operated by the Chinese Navy.

"I can provide no comment," stated Shugalian.

The documents set off a firestorm inside Capitol Hill, threatening to start an investigation on a scale similar to the Cox Committee Report.

"Outrageous," responded Representative Curt Weldon, R. Pa. "This is outrageous. I am going to demand a full official inquiry into the way this was handled."

Representative Curt Weldon is a ranking member of the House National Security Committee and Chairman of the Military Research and Development Subcommittee. Representative Weldon was given a copy of the U.S. Navy documents for the interview. Weldon currently oversees key U.S. military weapons programs

"This is simply unbelievable," stated Weldon. "The Sunburn is the greatest threat today against the U.S. Navy."

"Any U.S. Navy officers that participated in this can expect short careers," noted one retired Navy missile engineer. "Rank officers have to go in front of the Senate for promotion."

Weldon is not alone in his evaluation of the Russian Sunburn. In July 1999, Jamestown Foundation defense analyst Richard Fisher wrote an evaluation of the Russian built Sunburn missile being sold to China. According to Fisher, the U.S. Navy cannot stop the Sunburn.

"The Sunburn anti-ship missile is perhaps the most lethal anti-ship missile in the world," wrote Fisher in a review of the Chinese Navy.

"The Sunburn combines a Mach 2.5 speed with a very low-level flight pattern that uses violent end maneuvers to throw off defenses. After detecting the Sunburn, the U.S. Navy Phalanx point defense system may have only 2.5 seconds to calculate a fire solution - not enough time before the devastating impact of a 750 lb. warhead."

According to the newly released U.S. Navy documentation, each SS-N-22 Sunburn missile can be armed with a "nuclear" warhead equal to over 200,000 tons of TNT. News reports of nuclear warheads on Sunburn missiles sold to China were first published in 1999.

William Triplett, co-author of Red Dragon Rising, stated that the new Chinese Sovremenny class destroyer is equipped with eight nuclear-tipped Russian made Sunburn anti-ship missiles. China is expected to purchase as many as eight more nuclear-armed Sovremenny destroyers from Russia.

The Clinton administration's failure to take advantage of the 1995 Russian offer was re-enforced by the U.S. Navy. On August 11, 2000 the U.S. Navy again issued a proposal to "evaluate the feasibility of obtaining" the Russian Sunburn. The proposal, prepared by the Naval Air Systems Command, is titled "SS-N-22 Concept, Exploration and Definition Analysis."

According to the August 2000 Navy contract proposal, "the Russian SS-N-22 missile (North Atlantic Treaty Organization (NATO) designator ('Sunburn')) is manufactured in and by the Republic of Russia. The Russian Federation is the only known source for this system... The (U.S.) Contractor would have sole responsibility for acquiring and importing the SS-N-22 assets and coordinating all attendant license and clearance necessities with the U.S. and foreign governments."

Representative Weldon, however, was not pleased with the renewed Navy effort to purchase the deadly Russian missile. Weldon is considered Capitol Hill's leading expert in Russian studies.

"This entire affair is a further indication of the absolute bankruptcy of the Clinton/Gore administration's foreign policy," concluded Weldon.

Amazingly, the 1995 Russian Sunburn offer was turned down by the U.S. Defense Department run by then Secretary William Perry. According to one Pentagon source, the administration balked at the Sunburn price of nearly "a million dollars" per missile.

The American failure to take advantage of this extraordinary offer forced the then bankrupt Moscow defense regime to sell the deadly missiles to Beijing. Without the 1995 U.S. Navy sale, the hard-pressed Russian contractor cut a deal with Beijing twelve months later, agreeing to supply the inventory of Sunburn missiles to China.

The Sunburn sale came after the Clinton administration denied the sale of Aegis missile ships to Taiwan. The Clinton administration denial of the Aegis missile system left Taiwan with no defense against the Sunburn-armed Sovremenny 956A warships now being deployed by China.

In 1996, China purchased the Russian Sovremenny destroyer Yekaterinburg and another warship named the Alexandr Nevskiy. China took possession of the Yekaterinburg in November 1999.

The Chinese Navy acquired the second warship, the Alexandr Nevskiy, in December 2000. A July article published in Janes Defense contained photographs taken by German Navy of the new warship on its shakedown cruise in the Baltic Sea. China has signed a deal with Russia to purchase up to eight Sovremenny destroyers armed with Sunburn cruise missiles.

Each Chinese warship is armed with eight nuclear tipped Sunburn missiles. Official Navy documentation notes that the Sovremenny Sunburn missiles are armed with a "nuclear" warhead equal to over 200,000 tons of TNT.

The SS-N-22 Sunburn weighs over 8,000 pounds and carries a nuclear punch ten times as powerful as the atomic bomb used on Hiroshima. The Sunburn also flies to its target at over 1,500 miles an hour, as fast as a rifle bullet, skimming the water at only a few feet over the surface.

"It is our judgment that in the event of hostilities over Taiwan, China will declare these ships to be 'Strategic Nuclear Assets' in defense of their homeland," concluded Timperlake and Triplett.

"The Russians should not be selling the Sunburn to anyone," stated Al Santoli, former national security advisor to Rep. Dana Rohrabacher, R. - California.

"This is an example of the criminal abandonment of essential military research and development by the Clinton administration," he said.

"The Clinton administration is responsible for this lapse in critical research. We have known about the Sunburn for years. We could have, and should have, developed a counter before this."

"The Sunburn sales are most damaging to the U.S./Russian relations," added Santoli. "As long as communist China is the Clinton administration's 'strategic partner,' the Sunburn missiles will continue to be a threat."

Santoli also noted that Rep. Rohrabacher had introduced a bill that would withhold debt re-scheduling with Russia unless the Russian military discontinues sales of the Sunburn missile to China. The bill was stalled by a threat of a Clinton veto.

"We have to be very concerned about the new Russian bi-polar turn toward China," said Santoli.

"We urgently need to develop a defense against these deadly missiles. If the Navy purchase helps develop a defense, then so much the better," he said.

"If the communist Chinese launch an invasion of Taiwan, then the number one threat to our aircraft carriers is the Sunburn."

Santoli is not the only defense analyst who is concerned about the new Sunburn missile. According to two top China experts, the Sunburn missiles and the new Russian destroyers are a significant threat to the U.S. Navy.

"Recently, the PLA Navy took delivery of its initial Russian Sovremenny-class destroyer," said Edward Timperlake and William C. Triplett, in an article published in the Washington Times.

Triplett, a former China analyst at the CIA, and Edward Timperlake, a former Republican foreign policy aide in Congress, teamed up to write two books, "Year of the Rat" and "Red Dragon Rising."

"These ships were designed to be aircraft carrier 'killers,' as the PLA's principal newspaper. More ominously, the PLA's paper quietly confirmed that the SS-N-22 missiles carried aboard the Sovremenny can be 'nuclear capable,'" noted Timperlake and Triplett.

"The U.S. Navy has no defense against this missile system," stated Red Dragon author William Triplett. "One nuclear tipped SS-N-22 (Moskit) will kill thousands of American sailors, airmen and marines. The message to the U.S. Navy is clear: Stay away or die."

According to official Chinese Army statements published by the Chinese news agency Jiefang Ribao, the Internet version of daily newspaper of the Shanghai Municipal Communist Committee, the new weapon is specifically designed to attack American aircraft carriers.

"As an aircraft carrier fleet is apt to come under saturation attacks by satellite-guided missiles, its entire combat effectiveness can be paralyzed by paralyzing its electronic equipment, which is its central nervous system," states the Feb. 12 article by Chinese military analyst Ye Jian, "Armchair Strategy: Using a Bomb to Deal With Aircraft Carrier".

"If the central nervous system of an aircraft carrier is paralyzed, even a comparatively backward naval vessel or aircraft (like a Jian-6) will be able to aim at the aircraft carrier as a conventional target, thereby thoroughly changing the balance between the strong and the weak," noted the Chinese military analyst.

"The strong magnetic field and electromagnetic pulse caused by an explosion can destroy all important integrated circuits and IC chips of the electronic equipment within the demolition scope, thus paralyzing the radar and telecommunication system of the aircraft carrier and vessels around it as well as the ship-mounted missiles and aircraft."

"An electromagnetic pulse bomb has a good anti-interception function. It does not have to hit the aircraft carrier but only needs to explode within dozens of kilometers around the aircraft carrier," states the Chinese military article.

"The success rate of its saturation attacks is high. It will perform better if mounted on a Moskit (Sunburn) ship-to-ship or air-to-ship missile. As long as an electromagnetic pulse bomb can successfully explode, an aircraft carrier will be paralyzed."

Despite the threats, claims and concerns - the Clinton administration elected to ignore the Chinese purchase of the Sunburn and the advanced Russian warships. In 1999, the Clinton State Department spokesman James Rubin denied that the Sunburn equipped warship is a problem.

"We don't believe that the purchase by China of the ship poses a significant threat to the U.S. military posture in Asia," said Rubin.

The fact remains that the Clinton/Gore administration could have purchased the entire active inventory of deadly Sunburn missiles in 1995 for a few million dollars, ending forever a deadly threat to our allies and U.S. Navy warships.

Today, Chinese Sunburn missiles are deployed within striking distance of the U.S. Seventh fleet, Japan, Korea and Taiwan. Instead of turning their swords into plowshares, the Russians continue to make the best weapons in the world with our help.

There is evidence supporting the allegations that the U.S. Navy cannot stop the Sunburn. The only U.S. missile capable of duplicating the Sunburn's blistering low-level performance was the Allied Signal Vandal. Vandal target drones reportedly penetrated U.S. Navy Aegis air defenses during trials. The Vandal program was eventually canceled by the Clinton administration.

The U.S. Navy Aegis warships are reported to be unable to defend themselves against the latest Russian super-sonic cruise missiles, the SS-N-22 Sunburn and the SS-N-26 Yahont.

Both Russian cruise missiles are huge, weighing nearly five tons each, and both can fly only a few feet over the surface at over twice the speed of sound - faster than a rifle bullet.

U.S. Navy Aegis warships are vulnerable to the Moskit. The Navy Aegis system failed to defend itself in live fire tests against a similar U.S. made super- sonic target missile called the Vandal. Vandal target drones, flying as low as ten feet over the ground at speeds of over 1,500 miles per hour, defeated the Aegis defenses and scored direct hits on simulated Navy targets.

The American Vandal is a rebuilt version of the U.S. Navy Talos ramjet powered missile. Honeywell, formerly Allied Signal, modified the Talos missiles into target drones at its Indiana facility located at Mishawaka.

Talos was deployed as the number one surface-to-air defense (SAM) missile for the Navy during the early Cold war years. Defense Department inventory records show that the Navy ran out of Talos missiles in 2001. With no more missiles, the U.S. Navy is now facing a missile shortage.

The only U.S. made missile capable of simulating the Moskit, an updated Talos called the Sea Snake, was canceled by the Clinton administration in September 1999. The U.S. Navy SSST or Super-Sonic Sea Skimming Target project ended eight years of study without a selection, leaving the service without a means to test the multi-billion dollar Aegis missile air defense system. The Mishawaka facilities closed permanently.

According to an internal memo from Navy defense contractor Logicon the Clinton cancellation of the Sea Snake "will have significant impact upon future SSST testing."

Logicon is the U.S. Navy contractor responsible testing the Aegis warship air defenses. The Logicon Corp. memo also noted that Russia benefited from the move. The Clinton administration cancellation of Sea Snake allowed the Navy to close a deal with Russian missile maker Zvezda for a new target drone. Russia provided the U.S. Navy a supersonic target missile - the Zvezda MA-31 Krypton.

According to the Logicon memo the Navy "plans to procure 37 additional (Russian Zvezda) MA- 31 targets in FY00, providing politics does not stop the procurement." The MA-31 is a target version of the Zvezda Kh-31A, NATO code-named AS-17 Krypton, supersonic missile.

The sales of the Ma-31 to the U.S. Boeing Company are part of an ongoing deal between Boeing and Zvezda-Strela State Scientific-Industrial Centre to deliver two hundred Ma-31 missiles over a 10-year period for the U.S. Navy.

Russia has decided to sell this deadly cruise missile to China. Moscow's decision to sell the Kh-31, NATO code-named AS-17 Krypton, missile was reported in the Washington Times as part of a secret multibillion-dollar package of arms destined for Beijing.

However, what has not been reported is the fact that Moscow could not sell the Krypton if it were not for Bill Clinton and Al Gore. During the 1990s, the Clinton administration made direct payments to Russia for the Krypton missile program and provided direct assistance to Russian engineers developing the weapon for sale.

In 1995, Vice President Al Gore traveled to Moscow and cut a secret deal with Russian Prime Minister Chernomyrdin. According to Gore, Russia agreed not to export advanced weapons in exchange for U.S. assistance.

In 1995, Russian missile maker Zvezda-Strela was on the verge of collapse. The Russian weapons company could not sell its missiles to the bankrupt ex-Soviet military, and many of its newest weapons were not ready to be exported. One such untested weapon was the Zvezda Kh-31 Krypton.

In 1995, the U.S. Navy needed a special missile target supersonic drone. The drone would replicate the anticipated threat of ex-Soviet missiles entering the international market, such as the massive SS-N-22 Sunburn missile purchased by China.

The Clinton administration found a solution that it thought would kill two birds with one stone, turning to Russia for the Navy supersonic drone program and as a way to assist the Russian weapons maker Zvezda in finding peaceful markets for its lethal products.

The Zvezda missile deal with Moscow was decidedly flawed. Official U.S. Navy sources noted the 1,100-pound Ma-31 does not replicate the massive 9,920-pound Moskit threat and the missile does not carry any Russian electronics.

Documents obtained by using the Freedom of Information Act (FOIA) from the U.S. Navy show that the missile did not meet the original range requirements. According to the U.S. Navy "Foreign Comparative Testing Contract" published in 1995, the Russian MA-31 "will be capable of meeting the following range requirements... 25 nmi (nautical miles) at an altitude of 30 ft and at full throttle."

The Zvezda target had a very limited range. According to official U.S. Navy statements, the Ma-31 missile can fly "only 16 miles on the deck" and cannot duplicate the Moskit's performance of over 50 miles at low level.

The documentation also showed the Russian target drone being equipped with U.S. made radio beacons to assist the Aegis missile system.

In 1997 the U.S. Navy test fired four kerosene ramjet powered MA-31 missiles with a blistering Mach 2.7 performance at 30 feet over the sea. Three of the MA-31 target drones were test fired to verify performance - which according to the manufacturer was over 1700 miles an hour at sea level and over Mach 3.5 at altitude.

The fourth MA-31 drone was flown in a live fire exercise in which the Navy was reportedly unable to shoot it down. The Navy was so impressed with the MA-31 they have requested and obtained permission from the Clinton administration to purchase nine more of the cruise missiles from the Russian Zvezda-Strela missile design bureau.

"Russian personnel were involved," states the official response prepared on Dec. 17, 1999 by Navy Freedom of Information officers George W. Griffith and Cole Cartledge.

According to the prepared U.S. Navy response, Russians were involved in obtaining the required "approvals to negotiate, engineer, and modify Russian equipment for use on U.S. Navy ranges as part of the Foreign Comparative Test program."

"No Russian engineering support for the MA-31 follow-on procurement is currently anticipated," stated the Navy response.

"U.S. Navy contacts with Russian nationals is very limited since all MA-31 procurement actions are with the McDonnell Douglas Corporation."

According to Janes Defense, each U.S purchase also includes a 28% "fee" given directly to Russian Generals. Navy documents show that each MA-31 missile costs $910,000. The extremely high price for the MA-31 is almost twice the price of current U.S. weapons. In addition, the 28% fee amounts to over a quarter million dollars per missile paid directly to the Russian Generals.

Under pressure from a Freedom of Information (FOIA) request, U.S. Navy managers denied any knowledge of allegations of corruption regarding kick-backs in the payments for the Russian missiles.

"We send the money to the Russians," stated Mr. G. Hotze, the Navy MA-31 program manager in 1999. "What they do with it is their business."

"The prime contractor with McDonnell Douglas, now a wholly owned subsidiary of The Boeing Company, does not include, and is not required to include any clauses specifically addressing the Foreign Corrupt Practices Act," states the Navy response.

"Should we become aware of any credible evidence of a violation of U.S. law by the prime contractor during the course of, and related to, performance of its contract, we will report such potential violations to the appropriate investigative organizations."

"Weapons system deployment issues such as this are not under the purview of the Navy's Aerial Targets Program Office," states the U.S. Navy response.

"The Boeing Company obtains the basic MA-31 target vehicles via sub-contracts with Rosvoorouzhenie, a Russian State corporation specifically chartered to deal with foreign military sales. It is recommended that you contact that organization if there are questions on how it distributes the funds."

"The (Allied Signal) Vandal and MA-31 targets are used to represent two different threats identified in the Supersonic Sea Skimming Target (SSST) Operational Requirements Document," states a December 1999 U.S. Navy response.

"The SSST "C" target will eventually replace both targets. Until the SSST "C" is fielded, requirements for SSST targets will be satisfied through the use of the existing inventory of Vandal targets and limited procurement of the MA-31 targets. This plan is a result of the date for the fielding the SSST "C" slipping over the years," states the reply from the Naval Air Systems Command.

Boeing spokesman Bob Alarotti confirmed the U.S. Navy deal with Boeing and Russian contractor Zvezda to supply MA-31 target missiles.

"We have an active contract with the Navy to supply MA-31 targets from Russia," stated Alarotti. "There have been a whole series of tests done against the MA-31 missile since the mid-1990s."

The limited range of the MA-31 places the launching Navy pilot and aircraft in great danger of being shot down instead of the MA-31 target drone. U.S. Navy officials confirmed that the Russian missile would have to be fired from "un-manned" radio controlled jet fighters in future target practice.

"The MA-31 is currently launched from manned QF-4 aircraft," states the official Navy response. "The capability to launch from unmanned QF-4s and improved launch capacity will be demonstrated in 2000."

"Increasing the range of the MA-31 is an operational consideration from a range safety standpoint," states the Navy response. "Extending the operational capacity by allowing the target to glide longer prior to booster ignition is planned for demonstration in 2000. This approach will allow more time for the launch aircraft to exit the hazard area."

Since the MA-31 could not replicate the actual threat from the Russian Sunburn cruise missile the Clinton administration elected to co-operate with Russian missile maker Zvezda Strella in jointly developing "pre-planned product improvements (P3I)" for the Kh-31 Krypton missile.

The declassified documents show that the U.S gave improvements for the Krypton missile to Russia in 1995 and 1996. Defense contractor McDonnell Douglas, which is now part of the Boeing Corporation. The documents were obtained from the Clinton administration using the Freedom of Information Act.

The improvements to the Russian Krypton, including design and fuel changes for "extended range", were given directly to the Russian missile contractor in a joint U.S./Russian "Foreign Technology Comparison Test" and as part of an effort to win a low altitude supersonic target contract from the U.S. Navy.

According to the U.S. Navy documentation, the American program to improve the Russian Krypton missile was intended to provide the U.S. Navy with a super-sonic target drone. Defense contractor McDonnell Douglas wrote one 1995 document, titled "MA-31 FOREIGN TECHNOLOGY COMPARISON TEST (FCT) PROGRAM REVIEW HIGHLIGHTS", for the U.S. Navy.

"The MA-31 target will need (pre-planned product improvements) P3I in order to meet the range and ground/surface launch requirements for the Supersonic Sea Skimming Target program (SSST). The range of the MA-31 target in its FCT configuration is approximately 15 nm (nautical miles) at low altitude," states the review document.

According to the 1995 McDonnell Douglas review, one "extended range option" given to the Russian contractor "adds an auxiliary fuel tank, a reduced drag nose cone, changes the fuel to JP-10 (which has a higher specific energy content than the Russian fuel), and modifies the ramjet nozzle. The extended range modification is intended to increase range to approximately 42 nm (nautical miles) at 10m (meter) altitude."

Another more crucial design improvement given to Russia, involved "Ground Jettison Testing" done by the U.S. defense contractor against the Russian missile. According to the 1995 program review document, the Russian built AKY-58M missile launcher for the MA-31 was fatally flawed and could destroy the firing plane.

"Two jettisons were planned; four completed," states the 1995 review document. "An anomaly was encountered during testing of the emergency jettison sequence. The lanyard which, during normal launch, remains with the launch rail and pulls the Booster Safe/Arm Plug which arms the booster for ignition, is supposed to remain with the target during Emergency Jettison. In three emergency jettison tests, the lanyard stayed with the launch rail instead of with the target. In all cases the booster would have been armed, and ignition could have occurred for any of several reasons."

"(McDonnell Douglas) MDAC has determined that use of a longer lanyard and slower separation velocity would allow proper operation of the emergency jettison sequence. The problem has been turned over to the Russians for resolution," states the 1995 review document.

According to one Russian source, the Krypton missiles supplied to the U.S. Navy are a little more than a "hollow target shell."

The 1995 review document notes that the MA-31 missiles supplied by Russia do not include the all-important radar "seeker" and the on board guidance electronics from the Kh-31 weapon version. Thus, the Russian MA-31 target missiles cannot be used to test U.S. Navy warship electronic defenses and anti-missile counter-measures.

"Removal of the seeker will preclude use of the MA-31 for testing the effectiveness of soft-kill EW (electronic warfare) systems and decoys," states the 1995 report.

Boeing spokesman Bob Alarotti confirmed that the Russian MA-31 missiles did not include the electronics and "seeker" head.

"The Russians supply the basic MA-31 vehicle only," stated Alarotti. "No Russian electronics. No radar seeker."

The MA-31 is derived from the Russian ramjet powered Kh-31 cruise missile. The titanium Kh-31 was built in 1988 by Zvezda-Strela for the former Soviet Union as an anti-ship cruise missile. Normally the MiG-29 Fulcrum or Su-27 Flanker fighters carry the Kh-31. The Kh-31 is currently being offered for export equipped with either an active or passive RF seeker.

The Kh-31 has also appeared under the MiG-31 in an anti-air role, using the passive R/F seeker to home in on U.S. radar planes such as the E-2 Hawkeye or E-3 Sentry.

Possible customers for the Kh-31 include India, Syria, Libya, Iran and China. In September 1999, the Navy SSST super-sonic target project ended after eight years of study without a selection, leaving America without a means to test the multi-billion dollar AEGIS missile air defense system.

The Navy noted that an American target drone, the Vandal, outperformed the Russian missile. Unfortunately, since the U.S. drone is launched from a land base, most of the extra range is wasted.

"The (Allied Signal) Vandal target has a range of 43 - 45 miles in a sea skimming role. Much of this range is used to get the target into position for the user from the land based launcher," states the Navy reply.

However, the U.S. Navy allegedly solved the position problem in 1996. In Oct. 1996, the U.S. Navy purchased an expensive robot warship designed to fire Allied Vandal target missiles from any location. The new warship is not designed to fire the Russian MA-31 missile.

The Aerial Target Launch Ship (ATLS) cost $3.6 million and was built by Halter Marine Industries in Mississippi. The ATLS is currently stationed at Point Mugu, California. According to the ship's designer, Jeffrey Blume, head of the Surface Targets Division at Point Mugu, the ATLS warship allows for the launch from undisclosed sites of aerial targets.

"It's called 'video game syndrome,'" explained Blume. "If your kid plays video games long enough he'll know when the bad guy is going to pop out on the screen. That's what can happen on ranges. One of the advantages of remotely launching an aerial target is that you can launch it anywhere on the range and the shooters just know that there's a threat out there, they don't know where it's coming from."

Videogames aside, the Navy claims the Russian missile is a realistic threat.

In September 1999, the U.S. Navy decided not to purchase the 8,000-pound Allied-Signal Sea Snake super-sonic cruise missile. The reason, according to the Navy Undersecretary Buchanan, was the Sea Snake was "too large" to represent the 9,000 pound Sunburn missile.

"The MA-31 replicates a threat with higher speeds, higher g maneuvers and g onset rates, and smaller in size. The MA-31 also provides a very challenging and representative anti-radiation missile profile," asserted the official Navy reply.

Meanwhile, the U.S. Navy is also suffering from a glut of old missiles that could serve as target drones. Many early versions of the Navy Standard and Sparrow missiles are now retired, and several thousand are scheduled to be destroyed at great taxpayer expense. In addition, the U.S. Navy F-14 Tomcat fighter jet is also scheduled to be retired along with hundreds of long-range AIM-54 Phoenix missiles.

Could a U.S. Navy missile from existing stocks match the MA-31 performance?

"We have not precluded industry from considering either Sparrow or Phoenix (or any other missile) as a potential to our SSST requirements," states the Navy reply.

Ironically, China and Russia have entered into a joint venture to produce a deadly new version of the same Zvezda Krypton missile. Jane's Defense Weekly reported that China purchased second batch of 40 Sukhoi Su-30MKK super-sonic strike-fighters to supplement its initial order for 40 aircraft, which was concluded in August 1999. The SU-30MKK sale includes air-to-air missiles, laser-guided bombs, and large numbers of the Zvezda Kh-31P mod-2 super-sonic cruise missile.

The new Zvezda Kh-31P mod-2 being sold to China is designed specifically to attack U.S. Navy Aegis warships and U.S. Army Patriot radar batteries. The missile being sold to China is reported to have a range of 125 miles - over seven times farther than the older version of the Krypton supplied to America.

According to defense analyst, Richard Fisher, the American assistance was invaluable for a major Russian arms sale to China.

"China has recently signed a deal with Russia to co-produce an extended range version of the Krypton," said Jamestown Foundation fellow Richard Fisher.

"The Chinese intend to produce the KR-1 their own version of the Kh-31p improved Krypton. The recent sale of Russian Sukhoi SU-30MK supersonic strike bombers to the Chinese Air Force also includes the Kh-31 missile."

The Navy supersonic cruise missile development was ignored by the Clinton administration. With cancellation of the Sea Snake, the American military arsenal has no weapon to match Yahont or the Sunburn.

The U.S. Air Force ALCM, and the U.S. Navy Tomahawk missiles fly at low sub-sonic speeds. Both U.S. cruise missiles are no longer armed with nuclear warheads, and both missiles have been shot down by conventional anti-aircraft fire in Iraq and Serbia.

"We need a Mach three Tomahawk to over come new surface-to-air defenses. Kosovo and the recent deployment of advanced Russian air defenses like the SA-10 Grumble showed that we need a hypersonic replacement for our cruise missiles," stated Jamestown Foundation defense analyst Richard Fisher.

"Such a hyper-sonic missile would be used against high value or heavily defended targets," noted Fisher. "It would not need to carry a large conventional warhead because the high velocity alone can penetrate even the most heavily fortified underground bunker.

The USAF nearly ran out of smart weapons during the air war over Kosovo. The Air Force "JASSM" stealthy cruise missile is not slated to begin production and costs nearly a million dollars a copy. The shortage of sub-sonic cruise missiles and smart bombs   drove the Air Force to seek alternative solutions to strike   heavily defended targets deep inside enemy territory.

Newly developed Russian air defense missile such as the SA-10C Grumble are capable of defeating Tomahawk and ALCM attacks. The Russian maker of the SA-10C states that it has a kill ratio ranging from 0.8 to 0.98 against Tomahawk-class cruise missiles.

USAF officials evaluated the export of advanced Russian air defense systems and modern warships after the war in Kosovo. In September 1999, USAF officials openly expressed fear that the latest C version of the Russian SA-10 Grumble air defense missile will soon be exported to Iran, Iraq, Libya and Serbia. China currently fields their own version of the SA-10 and also plans to upgrade with purchases of the SA-10C.

In response, Air Force bomber crews expressed a need for a heavyweight, high speed, surface- skimming missile that could defeat the best air defenses. Allied engineers noted the Sea Snake meets the USAF requirements and could exceed them with little or no modification.

An Allied Signal engineer commented that a single weapon version of the Sea Snake would "obliterate" an SA-10 site. According to the Allied Signal source, a minor change in the Sea Snake fin system might be required. This is because, at a speed of over 2,000 miles an hour, air friction will melt its current aluminum control surfaces. The Allied proposal was intended to upgrade the Sea Snake with stainless steel or composite fins.

When asked if a USAF B-52 could drop the huge four-ton missile, the engineer noted, "No problem. You can drop a kitchen sink from a B-52."

The weapon version of the Sea Snake, called Talos, is already a battle proven missile. Talos had a long and successful career filling Navy air defense needs until it was retired from service in the late 1980s. Allied Signal Director for New Business Development Mike Boies noted that the Talos story did not end with its retirement from active service.

"When Talos was retired we modified and successfully fired over 500 missiles as Navy target drones called Vandal," stated Boies.

Allied Signal claimed that Vandal was merely "successful" are modest indeed. The Vandal/Talos is so fast and maneuverable that it frequently outperforms the Navy Aegis anti-missile defenses intended to replace it. During the Vietnam War a single Talos destroyed two MiGs at a distance of over 65 miles. Talos was also used to strike North Vietnamese radar sites on the ground over 75 miles inland.

The missile threat from Russia did not end with the Sunburn. Russian missile makers are now offering China the very latest in super-sonic killing technology, the NPO Mashinostroyenya Yahont. The Yahont ramjet missile is nearly 30 feet long, over 2 feet in diameter, and weighs in at 8,598 pounds.

The Russian SS-N-26 was put on sale in August 1999, during an air-show, as the primary anti-ship weapon for the Sukhoi SU-30 strike fighter variant of the SU-27 Flanker. The Yahont is being offered to China, India, and Vietnam. Other potential customers include Iraq, Iran and Libya.

The Yahont missile was described as an integral kerosene fueled ramjet with a top speed of Mach 2.6 at 45,000 feet and a range of 180 miles. The SS-N-26 appears to be almost a duplicate of the Allied Signal developed Sea Snake, which was rejected as "too large" by U.S. Navy Undersecretary Buchanan.

The Yahont guidance system is provided by an inertial system with the missile descending to a sea- skimming mode 33 feet (10 meters) for its terminal phase of active/passive radar homing. The Yahont is reported to deliver a 440-pound warhead at an impact velocity of 2,460 feet per second - faster than a rifle bullet.

"The Yahont is fast, compact, and lethal," stated defense analyst Richard Fisher. "You can place a large number of them on a very small platform."

An air breathing ramjet engine powers the Yahont giving it a top speed of Mach 2.6 at 45,000 feet and a range of 180 miles. The Yahont is reported to deliver a 440-pound warhead at an impact velocity of 2,460 feet per second - faster than a rifle bullet.

According to a defense intelligence source, Russia is offering to sell China up to eight more super-Sovremenny destroyers armed with eight nuclear tipped Moskit missiles each. In addition, the super-Sovremenny will also be armed with Yahont missiles and a naval version of the SA-10C, NATO code-named "Grumble", advanced surface-to-air defense missile.

Gerbert Yefremov, General Designer for Mashinostroyenya, clearly documented that his Yahont missile is intended for export.

"We have good undertakings for the future and all reason to believe that the Yahont anti-ship missile system will appear on the foreign market," states the official Yahont documentation from Moscow based Mashinostroyenya. "In addition to the well-known inclined and vertical installation methods applied to submarine-and ground-based anti-ship missiles, some innovative basing and launching methods have emerged for which Yahont is quite suitable."

U.S. defense analysis indicates that Yahont comes in a nuclear tipped land attack version, enabling it to strike ground targets such as U.S. cities. Each Yahont is produced in a sealed launch canister, enabling the missile to be fired from simple and low cost platforms such as a diesel submarine or a common truck.

Defense sources confirmed that Russia is also offering to upgrade Chinese Kilo diesel class submarines, arming them with vertically mounted Yahont missiles in a hull plug.

The cruise missile fiasco was part of a political deal made by the Clinton/Gore administration with Russia. The troubled Navy SSST project became a political plum that Clinton and Gore gave to corrupt Russian Generals.

The only real threat, new heavy Russian missiles, are now being offered in Beijing, Tehran, Baghdad and Tripoli by the same Generals who cut the MA-31 deal with the Clinton/Gore administration.

According to a July 2000 General Accounting Office report, "unless the Navy can improve the self-defense capabilities of its surface ships, these ships will be increasingly vulnerable to cruise missile threats."

"The threat to surface ships from sophisticated anti-ship cruise missiles is increasing," states the General Accounting Office report, titled "Comprehensive Strategy Needed to Improve Ship Cruise Missile Defense."

"Nearly 70 nations have deployed sea- and land-launched cruise missiles, and 20 nations have air-launched cruise missiles. Current anti-ship cruise missiles are faster, stealthier, and can fly at lower altitudes than the missiles that hit the U.S.S. Stark in 1987, killing 37 sailors. The next generation of anti-ship cruise missiles -- most of which are now expected to be fielded by 2007 -- will be equipped with advanced target seekers and stealthy design. These features will make them even more difficult to detect and defeat."

The 1995 trip to Moscow by Al Gore was supposed to be an effort to buy Russia's advanced weapon systems. The idea was to study the former Soviet weapons and stop the Russian arms industry from selling these systems to nations such as China and Iran.

The main U.S. competitor was forced out of business by the lack of a Clinton administration selection. In the end, the missile manufacturing facility in Mishawaka, Ind., was closed and all the U.S. engineers laid off.

In contrast, Russian missile-maker Zvezda was able to use the American money given to it by the Clinton administration to improve its manufacturing facility at Kaliningrad. Today, Zvezda is selling the advanced version of the Krypton around the world, with the Chinese Army Air Force being the latest buyer.

The Clinton/Gore administration used these weapons to as a means to pass money to the bankrupt Russian arms makers, keeping them in business. The effort also allowed the Clinton/Gore administration to close down U.S. facilities and lay off American engineers. The Clinton/Gore administration created a missile gap.

The Clinton/Gore missile gap closed an important U.S. defense industrial center and forced American engineers into the unemployment line. The Clinton/Gore missile gap left U.S. Navy warships with untested defenses, untrained crews and no domestic source for realistic target missiles. Thanks to Bill Clinton and Al Gore, our Navy will now sail into harm's way unprepared and vulnerable.

The troubled Navy supersonic drone project became a political plum that Clinton and Gore gave to corrupt Russian generals. We must face the real Clinton legacy: advanced weapons, financed by the U.S. taxpayer, pointed directly at America.

**MA-31 FOREIGN TECHNOLOGY COMPARISON TEST (FCT)
PROGRAM REVIEW HIGHLIGHTS
31 OCT - 1 NOV 1995
McDonnell Douglas Aerospace Corp. (MDAC), St. Louis MO**

1. BACKGROUND: This was the first program review for the PMA 208/MDAC FCT of the Russian AS-17 (KRYPTON) missile modified into a target proposed for use as a Supersonic Sea Skimming Target (SSST) to satisfy USN DT&E/OT&E and Fleet training requirements. The agenda for this review is contained in Attachment A. A complete List of Attendees is provided in Attachment B. A copy of the handouts of all viewgraphs will be forwarded separately.

Key attendees included:

> CAPT R.T. Moeller, USN (OSD/DOT&E)
> Mr. Tom Blann (OSD/DOT&E)
> Mr. Joe Milligan (Navy International Programs Office (NIPO)/DON FCT Program)
> Ms. Susan Law (CNO N913)
> Dr. W.V. McCanless (PMA 208)
> Mr. G. Hotze (PMA 208B1 (MA-31 Program Manager))
> Chris Kreitlein (COMTHIRDFLT)
> LCDR Mike Gallet (COMNAVSURFLANT AAW Officer)
> OSCM(SW) Rick Dillard (COMNAVSURFPAC (N812A))
> GMC(SW) Eddie McDaniels (COMOPTEVFOR Norfolk)
> Mr. Andy Kristovich (PEO(TAD)-A1)

Highlights of this Program Review will be reported by topic, rather than chronologically.

2. PROGRAM OVERVIEW:

a. CONTRACT: McDonnell Douglas Aerospace Corporation (MDAC) was issued a Firm Fixed Price (FFP) contract on 12 May 1995 in the amount of $4,760,290 for the Basic MA-31 FCT Demonstration. The basic contract calls for the acquisition, modification, and test flights for 3 MA-31 targets from QF-4 aircraft on the NAWCWD Pt. Mugu range. The contract includes FFP options for an additional 3, 12, or 20 targets ($4,386,701, $10,430,401, and $15,241,604 respectively) and launches from unmanned QF-4 aircraft as part of what is called the Expanded Demonstration Test (EDT).

The MDAC contract includes a FFP subcontract to the Russian firm Rosvoorouzhenie for hardware, test and support equipment, data, reports, and field technical support. The basic subcontract is for $1,702,900. The subcontract also contains options for an additional 3 to 20 MA-31 targets ($1,920,000 and $7,050,000 respectively) including field support for launch from an unmanned QF-4 aircraft.

b. PROGRAM OBJECTIVES: (Reference: Master Test Plan)

66

Mr. Kristovich suggested that JTAMS may also be interested in observing the flight tests. MDAC replied that, by law, FCT programs may not be used for exploitation purposes.

e. PRE-PLANNED PRODUCT IMPROVEMENTS (P³I): The MA-31 target will need P³I in order to meet the range and ground/surface launch requirements for the Supersonic Sea Skimming Target program (SSST). The range of the MA-31 target in its FCT configuration is approximately 15 nm at low altitude. In addition, the MA-31 FCT program only addresses launch from the centerline station of a QF-4 aircraft. MDAC briefed the following P3I programs with no timeline or associated costs identified:

> **1) MA-31 EXTENDED RANGE:** This improvement adds an auxiliary fuel tank, a reduced drag nose cone, changes the fuel to JP-10 (which has a higher specific energy content than the Russian fuel), and modifies the ramjet nozzle. The extended range modification is intended to increase range to approximately 42 nm at 10m altitude.

> **2) MA-31 SURFACE LAUNCH:** MACD also proposes to surface/ground launch the MA-31 Extended Range target from the Mk-10 launcher. The surface/ground launch capability will require modification of the existing booster to accommodate a 27% increase in propellant weight. The modified booster will also require the addition of fixed stabilization fins.

3. TARGET CONVERSION: Several modifications are being made to convert the Russian X-31A missile into the FCT version of the MA-31. The modifications are summarized in Table 1. The extent of the required modifications, particularly in the guidance and autopilot interface areas, poses the question of whether or not the MA-31 FCT configuration is truly a Commercial Off-the Shelf (COTS) item. (Note: Removal of the seeker will preclude use of the MA-31 for testing the effectiveness of soft-kill EW systems and decoys.)

ITEM	CONFIGURATION	RESPONSIBILITY
AIRFRAME	New Nose Cone. Modified Payload compartment.	OEM
PROPULSION	Unmodified.	

GUIDANCE	Modified. Seeker removed. INS guidance installed. New autopilot interface computer. (Note 1)	OEM/MDAC
ALTIMETER	New.	OEM
AUTOPILOT	Unknown. May require modification to be compatible with new interface computer. (Note 1)	OEM
PAYLOAD	New. Warhead removed. Includes range integration equipment (Flight Termination System, Tracking Beacon, and Telemetry).	MDAC

Note 1: It appears that the flight control algorithms may be under development. JHU/APL is using a 6 Degree-of-Freedom (6 DOF) simulator and Russian provided algorithms to model MA-31 flight characteristics. All simulations to date have resulted in failure. When advised of the results and queried about the algorithms used, the Russians have, in each instance, provided a new algorithm.

Table 1 - X-31A FCT Modifications

4. AIRCRAFT INTEGRATION: MDAC is integrating the MA-31 with QF-4 airborne launch capability. The integration requires installation of GPS, a Control Display Unit and MA-31 Control Panel assembly in the QF-4 cockpit, Inertial Navigation Systems (2) in the nose avionics bay, and a cockpit launch computer, a 36 VAC 1000 Hz inverter and a power/discrete control panel in the Door 19 avionics bay.

MDAC has received the Russian AKY-58M launcher, and the launcher adapter has been fabricated. MDAC is fabricating a Vehicle Integration Test Set (VITS) to simulate the launch aircraft to the target and vice versa. MDAC is also developing software for the VITS and an Operational Flight Program for the Cockpit Launch Computer.

MDAC has completed wind tunnel testing on 5% scale models of the QF-4 and the MA-31 in the CALSPAN 8' Transonic Wind Tunnel. Results were as expected, and the resultant data will be used to validate separation simulation.

Ground Jettison Testing was performed at NAWCWD Pt. Mugu on 9/30/95. Two jettisons were planned; four completed. An anomaly was encountered during testing of the emergency jettison sequence. The lanyard which, during normal launch, remains with the launch rail and pulls the Booster Safe/Arm Plug which arms the booster for ignition, is supposed to remain with the target during Emergency Jettison. In three emergency jettison tests, the lanyard stayed with the launch rail instead of with the target. In all cases the booster would have been armed, and ignition could have occurred for any of several reasons. MDAC has determined that use of a longer lanyard and slower separation velocity would allow proper operation of the emergency jettison sequence. The problem has been turned over to the Russians for resolution.

(Note: There may be a problem with QF-4 availability to support the aircraft integration efforts and the flight testing. Ms. Law (N913) stated that the Navy only has 10 QF-4

N00019-95-R-0003
Attachment (4)

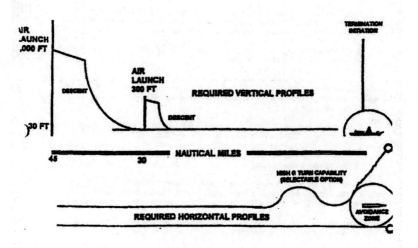

FIGURE 2   X(M)-31 FLIGHT PROFILES

10

LETTER OF INTENT AND AGREEMENT

Date: 25 February 1995   Arsenjev

The parties of the Seller, Arsenjev Aviation Company "Progress", in the person of its Director-General V. I. Manoilenko on one side, and the Buyer, Vector Microwave Research Corporation in the person of Executive Vice President and General Manager Milferd E. Barnett on the other side, have agreed to the following:

1. The Seller intends to enter into a contract [Draft Contract (95-SC-031)] with the Buyer for the following products and support services:

    a) 3M-80E (SS-N-22 variant) missiles and associated launch/control systems, ground support equipment, depot level test equipment, spare parts, technical documentation, factory training, performance warranty, and on-site field support at U.S. Navy ranges.

    b) Conversion of missiles for use on U.S. Navy ranges through incorporation of Buyer supplied Range Augmentation Equipment.

2. The Buyer intends to enter into a contract with the U.S. Government for the above goods and services. Then, the Buyer agrees to enter into a contract [Draft Contract (95-SC-031)] with the Seller for:

    a) Purchase of an initial quantity of twenty-five (25) missiles with annual options for up to twenty-five (25) additional units to a maximum of 100 units.

    b) Provide Range Augmentation Systems and engineering support for converting the missiles for use on the test range.

3. The Buyer shall act as the Seller's sole and exclusive representative for the sale of the missiles and associated materials and documentation to the U.S. Government until completion of the intended Contract (95-SC-031). (This paragraph only concerns the USA)

4. The Buyer agrees to treat this entire acquisition and implementation contract with the utmost confidentiality and request that the U.S. Government do likewise.

5. Due to unreadiness of the boat 1242.1 (tropical version) it is recommended that for the initial period to consider the question of leasing the boat 1242.1.

MILFERD E. BARNETT
Executive Vice President
Vector Microwave Research Corporation

V. I. MANOILENKO
Director-General
Arsenjev Aviation Company

70

SYSTEMS ENGINEERING
DESIGN REQUIREMENTS DOCUMENT
for
22-SURROGATE TARGETS PROGRAM (STP)

SS-N-22 "SUNBURN"
LAUNCH INTEGRATION
and
FIRING DEMONSTRATION

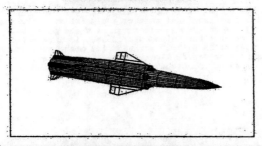

NAVAL AIR WARFARE CENTER WEAPONS DIVISION
THREAT SIMULATION DIRECTORATE
TARGET SYSTEMS DEPARTMENT
SYSTEMS ENGINEERING BRANCH - CODE P3821
POINT MUGU, CALIFORNIA

20 September 1993

DEPARTMENT OF THE NAVY
OFFICE OF THE ASSISTANT SECRETARY
(Research, Development and Acquisition)
WASHINGTON, D.C. 20350-1000

SEP 25 1995

Admiral Felix N. Gromov
Russian Navy
Commander-in-Chief

Dear Admiral Gromov:

I appreciate the opportunity to convey to you the United States Navy's interest in acquiring all variants of the SS-N-22 "Sunburn" Anti-ship Supersonic Ship-to-Ship missile for test and evaluation.

Vector Microwave Research Corporation has advised the United States Navy that it is negotiating for the purchase of SS-N-22 missiles and associated support equipment from Arsenjev Aviation Company, the Russian manufacturer of these missiles. This is to advise you that the United States Navy is interested in purchasing these SS-N-22 missiles and associated support equipment from Vector Microwave Research Corporation if agreement can be reached on acceptable terms and conditions.

Sincerely,

W. C. Bowes
Vice Admiral, U.S. Navy
Principal Deputy

4

MOTOROLA

Folly consists not in committing folly, but in nothiding it when committed.
Balthasar Gracian - The Art of Worldly Wisdom

Dr. Richard Barth was a former National Security Council (NSC) Director of Nonproliferation and Export Controls under President Bush and President Clinton. Mr. Barth's story is typical of the Washington musical chairs game of bureaucrat to politician to lobbyist and back again.

In 1991 Mr. Barth was writing TOP SECRET encryption papers inside the conservative Republican Bush White House for the National Security Council. Dr. Barth appears to be the perfect bureaucrat because little things like ideology and politics have had no effect on his career.

When Clinton was elected in 1992 Dr. Barth made a smooth transition into a liberal Democratic White House. Still, by July of 1993, Barth would leave the Clintons for a much higher paying job at Motorola.

On June 17, 1993 Barth wrote a secret memo covering export controls on encryption. Inside this memo he expressed his concerns that big bucks were at stake selling crypto behind the bamboo curtain.

"With the rapid decentralized growth of manufacturing in advanced telecommunications systems, other markets such as the PRC may be lost to US exporters due to export control restrictions," wrote Barth. "Recent evidence from AT&T seems to indicate that indigenous PRC production and availability of advanced switches from Israel are costing US exporters millions in lost sales."

Barth's friendship with current CIA Director, George Tenet, can be described as close because of email Tenet sent to Barth during their joint 1993 term inside the White House. At one point, in a humorous attempt to convince Barth not to leave the Clinton administration, Tenet offered Barth some very unusual perks.

"Can you shoot me a copy of the paper going to principals regarding telecommunications sales and the Russkies. I have some equities in this fight and should be up to speed, particularly with your departure being as imminent as it is. When can I take you to lunch by the way? When can you spare an hour to debrief me on exports/encryption? Why are you leaving me? Do you want my job? my wife? My 1974 Camaro? This place will suck eggs without you to keep me sane," wrote Tenet.

It may be ironic that the future Clinton CIA Director offered his "wife" as an incentive to stay, however it is a safe assumption that Mr. Tenet and Mr. Barth were close friends.

Mr. Barth replied that HIS (Barth's) wife would be out of town the following week...

However, Barth's real job seemed to be maintaining the inside contacts at the White House. On Aug. 16, 1993, George Tenet wrote an email to another NSC member, William Clements titled "export issues and encryption". Inside this email Tenet would write about the ex-NSC member Barth and how much he was needed.

"I had previously asked Barth to get Commerce to provide us with a dispassionate assessment of the world's encryption market place. I called him. He says he is seeing a woman tonight who should know where this study is. In addition, we had tasked CIA to study the issue as well. They have a paper in draft which will be coming along shortly.... I am trying to set up a meeting with you, Barth and myself in the next day or two."

And on Aug. 17, 1993, David Kelly of the NSC would also write to William Clements about Barth.

"George Tenet and I would like to review the bidding on the export policy aspects of the encryption issue with you and Rich Barth. Are you available to get together in George's office at 9:00 tomorrow, following the weekly status meeting? I've contacted Rich and will clear him into the building."

I find it odd that someone who had already been inside the White House since 1991 had to be "cleared" again. That is, of course, unless he no longer worked for the White House. By August of 1993, Dr. Barth was now working for Motorola.

On Aug. 18, 1993, George Tenet would write up the results of the 9:00 meeting, titled "Next Steps on Encryption". Tenet wrote, "I am baffled by Ray Kammer's announcement that someone has to ask RON BROWN to be a key escrow holder.... Ray Kammer has been asked to put together a status report... Please ensure that Clements and Barth have provided a thoughtful export piece for Kammer."

How extraordinary. Motorola's Barth was writing policy for the Clinton administration - after he had left government service.

In March 1994, Melissa Moss Director Office of Business Liaison for Ron Brown at the U.S. Commerce Department wrote to Barth at his new job as Assistant Director, International Trade Relations for Motorola.

"In preparation for Secretary Brown's Presidential Business Development Mission to Russia, in which your President of European Affairs will be participating, I would like to invite you to a briefing at the Department of Commerce to be held on Wednesday, March 16, at 9:30 a.m. in Room 5430," wrote Moss.

"The purpose of this meeting will be to give you an overview of the trip's objectives, to go over the schedule for the mission, as well as to answer any questions you may have about the trip. The briefing will be conducted by myself and other senior Department of Commerce officials."

In early 1994, Barth wrote his own memos to Commerce official Sally Painter. Barth sent the U.S. Commerce Department a Motorola company objective paper for a trade trip to Russia and the bio of Motorola Executive Vice President James Norling. Norling had accepted the Commerce Department's offer to travel with Ron Brown to Russia in April 1994.

Clearly, Barth knew the administration's position, since he helped write it only a few days before. Barth, however, was paid by Motorola to apply his knowledge and influence. The Motorola position paper sent by Barth noted that the company was anxious to end Cold War restrictions (COCOM) on advanced technology trade with Russia.

"The outlook for Motorola in Russia is strong. The communications infrastructure is inadequate for competing in a free market economy on a global scale. Wireless communication offers competitive, immediate and-lasting solutions to these problems," noted Barth in his letter to Painter.

"Our participation in the mission is a further demonstration of our seriousness and great interest in the Russian market. We look forward to a very positive outcome of the presidential level talks leading to abolishing of COCOM restrictions on communications products, and the streamlining of procedures within the Russian Government."

Barth's close relationship with the Clinton administration went so far as to invite him back to the White House to make policy - even if that policy he was making directly affected his employer - Motorola. Yet, Motorola was paying him to influence the Clinton administration.

On November 23, 1994, Barth wrote the State Department a letter addressed for Theodore McNamara in the Bureau of Political-Military Affairs. His detailed letter sought a special waiver for Motorola to export advanced, encrypted, radios and cellular phones to China. Barth's level of detail extended beyond the general and he named names.

"This is to request that your office initiate action to obtain a waiver from requirement for individual export license notifications to Congress for wireless mobile communications systems containing encryption for China. Such a waiver was issued by the President in September of this year for civilian satellite systems and encrypted products for use by American firms operating in China," wrote Barth.

"The cellular phone market highlights the problem that also exists for other telecommunications providers. European firms, including Nokia, Ericsson, Alcatel and Siemens, have for a number of months been able to market and sell GSM cellular systems with A5-2 encryption in China as a result of a decision taken by the UK intelligence agency, GCHQ. I understand that our National Security Agency is aware of this change in GCHQ's position and would support our request for a change in US requirements for export licenses for China. The NSA has agreed that there should be a "level playing field" in regard to China and would concur with allowing US firms to supply A5-2 GSM systems to that market."

On December 2, 1994, State's McNamara replied to Barth, noting the diplomatic and human rights issues that State reviewed along with Motorola's November request.

McNamara wrote to Barth, "As you know, there are important issues that must be considered carefully, in light of the post-Tiananmen sanctions. The President recently renewed the Administration's commitment to these sanctions when he de-linked MFN and human rights issues. Government policies regarding exports of US Munitions List items are covered by these Congressionally mandated sanctions. We shall of course take into account the new information you have provided regarding the recent decision in

Europe to allow the export of A5-2 encrypted GSM cellular systems as we continue to review our policies toward China."

Alas, human rights and diplomatic sanctions did not stand between Motorola and China. To Motorola the real enemy was the State Department, citing such non-profit items as human rights and sanctions. Thus, additional Motorola pressure was required.

Now the question of influence peddling inside the Clinton administration by China and Motorola involves more than just Richard Barth. Motorola blamed the British intelligence agency GCHQ for it's lost exports to China and demands a level playing field. Barth's trusted source is a quote from the NSA.

What ordinary citizen can write to friends inside the White House, citing quotes about "level playing fields" for exports to China from the NSA?

To illustrate my point, the NSA is so secret about themselves that they once refused to tell this author if they even had a fax machine.

The issue leaves many unanswered questions about the dark work of the intelligence listening agency located at Ft. Meade Maryland. What is the NSA doing issuing Motorola such a blanket statement? Why would the NSA, an agency tasked by law with intelligence activities, not commerce, help Motorola? Why was this not made public and Motorola competitors given the same opportunity?

Yet, besides being unfair to ordinary U.S. businesses there is a decidedly dangerous edge to this. In 1993, after the Soviet Empire fell, China was facing a military radio crisis. Chinese military communications were then based on aging Russian radios. Radios we defeated in the Gulf war.

In addition, satellite photo, communications, navigations, radio intercept and warning systems helped the U.S. win big. Simply put, an army without satellites and secure radios is blind, deaf, dumb and lost on the modern battlefield.

Encryption radio communications with satellites means secure worldwide communications for military and commerce. Secure voice communications was demonstrated to America by Tom Cruise in the recent film "Mission Impossible". Cruise simply slipped a special microphone into a pay telephone and said, "Go secure".

Modern radio systems used in jet fighters, such as the F-15 Eagle, are also digitally ciphered. These radios use special codes and high speed chips so anyone without the code hears nothing but garbage.

Chinese officials sought the Motorola communications technology to call from anywhere on the globe and "Go secure" just like the IMF team.

The Motorola sale has an even darker edge than simply providing secure military communications. China has begun a new round of imprisoning dissidents. The enforcer of the brutal red policy of oppression and murder is the People's Armed Police.

Chinese Police orders to arrest, torture and kill are being given out over radios made in the U.S.A. by Motorola. The $100 million in radios "tied up" in U.S. red tape were destine for the Chinese People's Armed Police.

The State Department objected to the Motorola sale to the Chinese Police for diplomatic reasons. After all, the linking of human rights and high tech exports dated back to Roosevelt policy on Nazi Germany in the 1930s and continued right through the war against apartheid in South Africa during the

1980s.

The State Department had good reason to distrust the red Gestapo with advanced U.S. technology. The Chinese Police run the "Lao Gai" prison camps - slave labor factories where beating, torture and starvation are a matter of policy. The red Gestapo is funded by slave labor factory products produced in the Lao Gai slave labor camps.

The Chinese Police execute dissidents - they are the red sword of justice against anyone opposing the party. The most gruesome PAP policy is to sell the organs of executed prisoners for hard cash. Some of those executed were guilty of no more than speaking out against the Communists.

According to Congressional testimony, PAP officers drag pregnant women out of their homes and take them to forced abortion clinics. No license - no baby. Many women are also forcibly sterilized as part of China's one child per couple program. The State Department knows this and so does Congress. It is the stuff of equal to Nazi war crimes.

However, delays in U.S. government approval because of murdering dissidents and violating human rights ran up against the Motorola corporate bottom line. Human rights are an expense, a cost that threatened to kill a lucrative Chinese export deal for Motorola.

By early 1995, Motorola was quickly growing impatient with the delay over human rights and their proposed sale to red China. In February 1995, Motorola's CEO wrote Ron Brown an angry letter detailing his objections.

"Even more critical to Motorola, however, is the system of controlling exports of products containing encryption. I do not- wish to get involved in the debate regarding which U.S. agency controls these exports, but the simple fact remains that the controls are administered in a manner that causes us serious competitive harm," wrote Motorola CEO Tooker.

According to Tooker, Brown needed to "Delegate to the export control officer appropriate authority for reviewing certain classes of controls, e.g., encryption... Export controls administered by the State Department at the behest of the National Security Agency (NSA) should NOT be referred for endless delay to the human rights bureau and myriad others in State."

Motorola applied more pressure against the diplomats at State in another 1995 Motorola document, a fax letter from Richard Barth which was cc'd to various players such as current CIA Director George Tenet, who was then inside the White House National Security Council (NSC).

Barth wrote to his White House, and Commerce friends, "Please forgive the informality of this note, but I want to move the process along here and not stand on formalities. As you can see from the attached, Motorola has been trying to clarify the policy regarding sales to China of telecom systems containing encryption for several months now. We currently have about $100 million worth of two way radio business tied up by the lack of a waiver for China and face losing a market of about $500 million in GSM infrastructure sales alone over the next five years if we cannot sell systems that GCHQ in the UK has already approved last summer for export from Europe. On top of that are hundreds of millions worth of cellular phone sales that could be lost."

Barth's plea for an export waiver for China not only covered encrypted radios and cellular phones but for satellite controls as well.

Barth wrote, "While we now are not yet applying for licenses for encrypted systems for satellite system positioning, we may within months be applying for such licenses for our Iridium systems."

Barth made it clear in his March 1995 memo that Motorola was being held up by the State Department. Furthermore, Barth also noted how close he was with the Commerce Department and the White House by citing a previously unreported agreement on the Motorola export in question. Despite the State Department objections - this was already a done deal.

"The bottom line is that getting a waiver through the system today, as we requested on November 23, 1994, for "all commercial cellular, PCS (personal communications systems) and other telecommunications system hardware and software," is realistic and appropriate for today's markets and those in the immediate future. However, we are getting quite anxious about getting this waiver through asap because of the risk of lost business, so if this request for the broadest possible waiver will further slow down the process, I urge you to get in writing to the State Department asap language that seeks a waiver for "cellular, PCS and two way radio systems," as recently agreed. Then we can start all over again for the additional waiver coverage," wrote Barth.

Motorola's CEO Tooker wrote a letter on May 10, 1995 to Secretary of State Warren Christopher. Richard Barth would copy that letter to Ron Brown at Commerce, Admiral McConnell Director of the National Security Agency, Ted McNamara at the State Department and Sue Eckert at the Commerce Department.

Tooker wrote in his letter to Christopher, "In November, we asked for relief for these kind of exports in a letter to Assistant Secretary McNamara. To date the requested waiver has not been granted, despite the fact that we had already ascertained in October last year that NSA is supportive of this change."

Tooter's 1995 letter to the Secretary of State also made it clear what Motorola had at stake. Tooker wrote, "Encryption export controls are increasingly causing lost and seriously delayed sales as the marketplace demands security and privacy in these systems. In this case, we estimate that Motorola's China market for these products will exceed $750 million through the end of this decade... Resolving the overall problem must be addressed, this waiver for China is a particularly acute issue for Motorola and I hope you can help resolve it. I ask that you promptly provide the White House with proposed telecommunications encryption waiver language so that this situation can be rectified."

In July 1995, Motorola got the waiver. Clinton over-rode the objections of his diplomats and approved the export with his signature. The CEO of Motorola, Gary Tooker, wrote a personal note to Ron Brown, expressing his gratitude for Clinton's signature.

"Dear RON," wrote Tooker to Brown.

"I am writing to thank you and some key members of the Commerce Department for your assistance in obtaining the Presidential waiver for encryption export sales to China. Motorola was facing a contract deadline and a potentially long-term loss of a major market when we requested urgent help to expedite our pending waiver request. Fortunately, Maureen Tucker and Sue Eckert, of the Bureau of Export Administration, were responsive to our request and helped work-out the complicated details of this issue. These individuals are the front line in responding to industry's efforts to ensure a level playing field when exports are subjected to national security controls, and they should be commended."

"The outcome of this waiver is good both for U.S. economic security as well as our broader national security interests. Losing sales to companies located in Europe and Japan would have been a double loss, averted only by the President's action to waive the sanctions," wrote Tooker.

Motorola's sale to the red Police came at a very high cost. During a 1998 interview, Chinese dissident Harry Wu told of his failed attempt to enter China through the remote border with Kazakhstan. Wu was quickly identified by the Chinese State Security and arrested by the People's Armed Police (PAP). After his arrest, the PAP officers escorted him to prison, taking their orders over brand new Motorola encrypted radios.

Democrat Representative Nancy Pelosi backs up Wu's observation that the Chinese police are equipped with Motorola radios from California. PAP thugs in Beijing too roughed her up along with her husband while trying to meet Chinese dissidents. According to Pelosi, the PAP officers took their orders over Motorola radios.

Motorola's Barth, rightly, asserted that perhaps the Europeans could have sold a similar system to the Chinese police. That may be true but Motorola is not thy brother's keeper. Motorola is a soulless corporation with a cash bottom line.

Motorola made the sale to the red Gestapo, a sure sign of strong customer product support. Nokia, Ericsson, Alcatel and Siemens lost out. Why not brag about it? Why not tell the whole world? Why does Motorola want to cover it all up?

Would you brag about a deal with the Devil?

Clearly, if the Chinese Police need more Motorola equipment then all they have to do is cut-up another dissident. No one will ask where the money came from.

Do nine out of ten murdering red Gestapo agents prefer Motorola over the next leading brand? Maybe not but there is considerable documentation that Motorola and Bill Clinton tried very hard to make it at least eight out of ten.

Even more dangerous was Barth's request to export encrypted satellite positioning systems to China. Encryption for "satellite positioning" is used to secure the radio commands sent to satellites to move, or change functions. Secure satellite control is considered an even more sensitive technology than "Mission Impossible" cell phones as such systems also control nuclear-tipped missiles.

Motorola's Iridium satellites gave the Chinese Army a wide spectrum of advanced military technology. According to the GAO, in 1995 Motorola had already obtained waivers from President Clinton to export their IRIDIUM satellites to China.

Once blessed with a Presidential "waiver", Motorola and Chinese engineers worked closely to develop a method of placing two satellites into orbit on top of the PRC "Long March" space rocket.

Satellite phones such as Iridium are nothing more than glorified cellular phones where the cell-tower is on a satellite in low earth orbit (LEO). Iridium deployment requires that both the lower and upper satellite be dropped into accurate orbits. The satellites are carried on a large, maneuvering, space-bus and deployed in groups of two.

Unfortunately, the Chinese Long March space-bus could only deploy one satellite and it often did not work. Motorola helped China fix the bus and launch two Iridium satellites from a single bus successfully.

The Motorola Iridium satellite bus has other uses. The same system has been adapted into a Multiple Re-entry Vehicle (MIRV) bus by the Chinese Second Artillery Corps - the Chinese nuclear missile force. The new missile bus is capable of deploying satellites or nuclear warheads into orbit with great accuracy. Warheads, of course, would be deployed in a rapid decay orbit to land at a pre-designated target.

According to Henry Sokolski, Executive Director at the Nonproliferation Policy Education Center, the Iridium sale "helped China master the technology needed to develop its own multiple independently targetable re-entry vehicles for the new solid rocket intercontinental ballistic missile it is trying to derive from SS-25 missile technology with the Russians".

"Validated Chinese upper stage separation technology, vibrational and load coupling analysis, attitude control, and payload mounting. Two Motorola communication satellites were to be delivered with a kick motor and new satellite dispenser of Chinese design. To assure successful launch, the contractor demanded that the Chinese prove that the Chinese systems would work properly and do the job. Concerns included the properly timed release of the satellites, the mounting of the satellites in the delivery bus (would the two satellites break from their moorings due to improper vibrational and load coupling analysis), would the delivery bus's attitude control be destabilized by the release of the fast satellite, and would the kick motor generate too little or too much thrust at the wrong time."

Not all of the Motorola Iridium technology fell directly into Chinese Army hands without some breakage. For example, in 1999 an Iridium satellite was "compromised" while waiting to be launched in China, forcing Motorola return the $200 million satellite to the U.S.

Aviation Week & Space Technology published the "compromise". The satellite was found in the open, unsecured, at the PRC space facility, with it's plastic wrapping torn open. The satellite was exposed to a shower during the event so there was extensive damage to the onboard systems.

The Department Of Defense officer attached to the satellite, by a Congressional mandate, made the discovery. The satellite was returned to America to be fixed.

During its short life span, Iridium managed to sign up only fraction of the customer base required to keep the project alive. The Iridium project fell into disarray in late 1999 after Motorola threatened to cease financial support unless the other international partners shared in the losses. Finally, Motorola and Chase Manhattan bank pulled the plug, declaring Chapter 11 bankruptcy protection.

The multi-billion dollar satellite phone venture floundered after sales dropped to near zero. Nine months after it's debut, Iridium went bankrupt. At one point, the space-based phone system planned to deorbit and destroy the chain of 66 operational satellites.

"Iridium was one of the more colossal screw ups in history. The magnitude of the damage is not yet fully realized," stated Douglas Humphrey, head of Cidera Inc., a satellite based Internet routing company.

"Iridium seriously damaged Wall Street perceptions of satellites," said

Humphrey.

Motorola blames poor market analysis but some investors disagree. Chinese espionage led to accusations that Motorola passed military technology to the People's Liberation Army (PLA). China Great Wall Industries, a PLA owned missile manufacturer, was a major Iridium partner. Virtually all of the Iridium satellites have been put into orbit using the Great Wall LONG MARCH space rocket.

The Chinese Army unit COSTIND, working with the Ministry of Posts, China Great Wall Industries and China Aerospace, also penetrated Motorola using satellite orbit contracts as paying bait for Iridium spacecraft. Motorola scientists eagerly modified, tested and verified a Long March satellite orbit bus that is capable of deploying two Iridium satellites.

In September 1998, the CIA testified before the Senate National Security Committee that the Motorola technology is being modified by China to double the number of nuclear warheads on the CSS strategic missile. The Motorola transfer also allowed China to upgrade their DF-15 (DONG FENG - Maoist slogan "East Wind") missile with maneuvering warheads that can avoid American anti-missile defenses.

Motorola transfers significantly upgraded the nuclear firepower and accuracy of Chinese weapons. Motorola technology transfers mean that Chinese warheads can now "penetrate enemy defenses".

President Clinton wrote the waivers for Motorola. President Clinton paraded many of the projects as part of his golden era of economic expansion. President Clinton should also shared the blame that the Motorola technology transfer is now pointed in the form of nuclear weaponry at the United States.

In addition, testimony taken in a successful lawsuit by Judicial Watch, an independent government watchdog group, revealed deeper links between buyer and seller. These links involve Motorola, China, the DNC and the Commerce Department. Commerce officials testified during Judicial Watch depositions that they removed sensitive documents involving satellites and encryption exports to China after Ron Brown died.

Commerce employee Ira Sockowitz removed highly classified documents without permission, including secret materials on China, satellites and encryption. President Clinton appointed Sockowitz, a former DNC fundraiser involved with John Huang, to his position. In 1996 Sockowitz left Commerce for a new job at the Small Business Administration, taking over 2,000 pages of classified materials with him.

NSA Chief of External Affairs Jon Goldsmith testified during the lawsuit that disclosure of one document removed by Sockowitz would "result in foreign governments taking countermeasures and the US being denied valuable intelligence information".

The documents, according to Goldsmith, were based on information provided to NSA by the intelligence services of US allies around the world. The nations and services named by Goldsmith include the GCHQ - UK, the Defense Signals Directorate (DSD) - Australia, Bundesnachrichtendienst (BND) Germany, Canada, Israel, Italy, Spain, Denmark, Sweden, the Netherlands and Norway. The report is a military-industrial goldmine that would be of great value to, for example, China, North Korea, Russia, Iran, Nokia, Ericsson, Alcatel, Siemens or Motorola.

In addition to illegally removed documents, the Judicial Watch lawsuit also reveals that an ex-Motorola employee, and another close friend of John Huang, Hoyt Zia, was in charge of Commerce exports to China during 1995. Chief Legal Counsel of the Commerce Department Bureau of Export Affairs (BXA), Hoyt Zia was charged with overseeing sensitive exports such as Iridium satellites and encrypted radios for China when Richard Barth wrote his 1995 letter to Tenet.

Zia previously spent over six years at Motorola specializing in cellular and radio exports to Asia prior to taking his job in the Commerce Department. Zia stated under oath during a Judicial Watch deposition that he had contact with Motorola official, and ex-Commerce employee, Charlotte Kee on more than one occasion.

Yet, Zia also worked at the DNC with John Huang, Melinda Yee and Charlie Trie during the 1996 campaign. Zia admitted under oath that he called John Huang when US Marshals were seeking Huang. Zia, the top Commerce official for exports, knew where Huang was hiding when Huang was being sought for questioning by Federal authorities.

Zia abruptly ended his testimony after he admitted seeing Huang's testimony about himself (Zia), contradicting previous statements he made under oath. Zia has since refused to submit any further testimony.

Further insiders included several former Clinton administration officials who later took high paying jobs with Motorola or Iridium. For example, Zia's Motorola contact Charlotte Kee and Iridium's Laura Fitz Pedgado. Ms. Pedgado was also a close associate of the late Ron Brown and tripped with him to China.

Pedgado, who was employed at Iridium, admitted under oath during a Judicial Watch deposition that she has little knowledge of satellite technology. All this was uncovered by Tim Maier in his article "Commerce-ial Espionage" published in the INSIGHT Magazine Sept. 1, 1997 issue.

Motorola's CEO flew with Ron Brown on a Far East trade mission in 1994. Motorola's Hong Kong VP had coffee in the White House in 1996 with President Clinton. In fact, Motorola's CEO had dinner with Chinese President Jiang Zemin and President Clinton in the White House.

No small company could match this. Not the high paying lobby jobs, the Commerce trips to China, the White House coffees nor the state dinners. We have a game of musical chairs, with the players occasionally changing titles on six figure jobs as they rotate from industry to bureaucracy to political staff and back again.

Despite all the information, Attorney General Janet Reno refused to open an investigation. Even the Republican Congress was reluctant to question Motorola officials because of the relationship between President Bush and Richard Barth.

However, a host of other U.S allies were involved in the Motorola scramble for Chinese Army money. Will GCHQ, DSD, or the BND answer U.S. questions so easily in the future? I doubt it. The damage already extends beyond our shores and threatens the security of many countries. Damage soon to be measured in lost alliances or, perhaps, lost lives.

Motorola technology also played a key role in the production of advanced weaponry for the Chinese Army. U.S. semiconductor chips sold by Motorola to China for "civilian" purposes such as car alarms and smoke detectors have been diverted into a massive inventory of advanced microchip driven land mines.

The Motorola chips are the heart of China's latest electronic anti-personnel land mine, an updated version of the popular "bouncing betty". The new chip driven Chinese mine is virtually impossible to detect, impossible to defuse, sensitive enough to detonate when someone steps close to it (instead of on-top) and can kill out to a radius of 20 yards.

The question of U.S. chips controlling Chinese land mines also has far reaching consequences. China will not sign an anti-land mine treaty banning such weapons. China is one of the largest sellers of anti-personnel mines in the world.

The new land mines are a very profitable business for the People's Liberation Army (PLA). Not only does the Chinese Army deploy the advanced microchip land mines but they have also sold large quantities to North Korea, Cambodia, Iran, Pakistan and Cuba. Thus, Chinese mines equipped with U.S. chips are proliferating and killing around the world.

Gary L. Tooker
Vice Chairman of the Board

Chief Executive Officer

July 5, 1995

The Honorable Ronald H. Brown
Secretary
U.S. Department of Commerce
14th Street and Constitution Avenue, NW
Washington, DC 20230

Dear Secretary Brown;

I am writing to thank you and some key members of the Commerce Department for your assistance in obtaining the Presidential waiver for encryption export sales to China. Motorola was facing a contract deadline and a potentially long-term loss of a major market when we requested urgent help to expedite our pending waiver request. Fortunately, Maureen Tucker and Sue Eckert, of the Bureau of Export Administration, were responsive to our request and helped work out the complicated details of this issue. These individuals are the front line in responding to industry's efforts to ensure a level playing field when exports are subjected to national security controls, and they should be commended.

The outcome of this waiver is good both for U.S. economic security as well as our broader national security interests. Losing sales to companies located in Europe and Japan would have been a double loss, averted only by the President's action to waive the sanctions.

Again, thank you for helping ensure that America stays competitive in the global marketplace.

Sincerely,

Gary Tooker
Gary Tooker

Motorola

NATIONAL SECURITY COUNCIL

01-Jul-1993 09:23 EDT

MEMORANDUM FOR:
George J. Tenet   (TENET)

FROM: Richard C. Barth
(BARTH)

SUBJECT: meeting, etc.

I'd be happy to brief you up on the export control stuff.

My wife is out of town next week and my schedule is therefore more open. Let's
set something up on Tuesday after the holiday.

Thanks

CC: Records   (RECORDS)

Additional Header Information Follows

Date Created: 01-Jul-1993 09:22
Deletable Flag: Y
DOCNUM: 010812
VMS Filename: OA$SHARE23:ZUTEDEVSB.WPL
A1 Folder: JUL93
Message Format:
Message Status: READ
Date Modified: 01-Jul-1993 09:22
Forward Flag: YES
Read-Receipt Requested: NO
Delivery-Receipt Requested: NO
Message Priority: FIRST_CLASS

NATIONAL SECURITY COUNCIL

29-Jun-1993 14:30 EDT

SECRET

MEMORANDUM FOR:
Richard C. Barth   (BARTH)

FROM: George J. Tenet
(TENET)

SUBJECT: PAPER FOR PRINCIPALS

Declassified/Released on 6/7/96
under provisions of E.O. 12:53
by J. Saunders, National Security Council

DOC # 52

85

CC: Records   (RECORDS)

BARTHMAN:

Can you shoot me a copy of the paper going to principals
regarding telecommunications sales and the Russkies. I have
some equities in this fight and should be up to speed,
particularly with your departure being as imminent as it is.
When can I take you to lunch by the way?
When can you spare an hour to debrief me on
exports/encryption?
Why are you leaving me?
Do you want my job? my wife? my 1974 Camaro?
This place will suck eggs without you to keep me sane.

GJT

CC: GEORGE

FAX COVER SHEET
1350 I Street, N.W.
Suite 400
Washington, DC 20005
OFFICE Number: 202-371-6900
FAX Number: 202-842-3578

To: Sue Eckert   482-3911
        Charlotte Kuepper   301-688-8183
        Julie Kavanaugh   647-4232
        George Tenent   456-9340
        Ron Lee   301-688-4546

From: Richard Barth
        Motorola - Washington, DC

Re: See Attached

You should receive 6 pages *including this cover sheet*. If you do not
receive all the pages, please contact Shannon Ibey on 202 371-6919.

Check appropriate POPI classification of information being sent:

Motorola General Business Information   X
Motorola Internal Use Only
Motorola Confidential Proprietary

Declassified Released on 6/6/96
under provisions of E.O. 12358
by J. Saunders, National Security Council

Pages: 6 (including cover sheet)

Doc # 35

March 22, 1995

Note for Julie Kavanaugh
        Charlotte Knepper

Please forgive the informality of this note, but I want to move the process along here and not stand on formalities. As you can see from the attached, Motorola has been trying to clarify the policy regarding sales to China of telecom systems containing encryption for several months now. We currently have about $100 million worth of two way radio business tied up by the lack of a waiver for China and face losing a market of about $500 million in GSM infrastructure sales alone over the next five years if we cannot sell systems that GCHQ in the UK has already approved last summer for export from Europe. On top of that are hundreds of millions worth of cellular phone sales that could be lost.

You requested a brief summary of why Motorola was requesting broad waiver authority. First, such a waiver would not reduce NSA's oversight over all encryption containing exports to China. Current controls remain, only the need to notify Congress of each sale is removed.

Second, we only request a level playing field. This does not now exist when our key competition, Ericsson, Siemens, Alcatel, etc., are able to sell two way radios, cellular and PCS systems to China and we are denied that ability by current U.S. policy.

Third, as you well know, this technology is not standing still. While we NOW are only at risk of losing perhaps a billion worth of sales, the future systems that may be announced in a month or a year or more may require going back for a new waiver. Why waste all that time applying for waivers for that which is in the U.S. Government's best interest.

Finally, while we now are not yet applying for licenses for encrypted systems for satellite system positioning, we may within months be applying for such licenses for our Iridium systems.

The bottom line is that getting a waiver through the system today, as we requested on November 23, 1994, for "all commercial cellular, PCS (personal communications systems) and other telecommunications systemhardware and software," is realistic and appropriate for today's markets and those in the immediate future. However, we are getting quite anxious about getting this waiver through asap because of the risk of lost business, so if this request for the broadest possible waiver will further slow down the process, I urge you to get in writing to the State Department asap language that seeks a waiver for "cellular, PCS and two-way radio systems," as recently agreed. Then we can start all over again for the additional waiver coverage...

Thanks and please call me if there are any further data I can provide.

Rich

Rich Barth
Assistant Director, International Trade Relations

cc: Sue Eckert
      George Tenent
      Ron Lee

Charlotte / Julie
I hope this can be
moved more quickly now.
Rich

United States Department of State

*Assistant Secretary of State
for Political-Military Affairs*

Washington, D.C. 20520
December 2, 1994

Dr. Richard C. Barth
Assistant Director, International Trade Relations
Government Relations Division
Motorola
1350 I Street, N.W., Suite 400
Washington, DC 20005-3305

Dear Dr. Barth:

I am replying to your letter of November 23, in which you
requested that my office initiate action to obtain a waiver of
the requirement for individual export license notifications to
Congress for exports to China of wireless mobile communications
systems containing encryption.

As you know, there are important issues that must be
considered carefully, in light of the post-Tiananmen
sanctions. The President recently renewed the Administration's
commitment to these sanctions when he de-linked MFN and human
rights issues. Government policies regarding exports of U.S.
Munitions List items are covered by these Congressionally
mandated sanctions. We shall of course take into account the
new information you have provided regarding the recent decision
in Europe to allow the export of A5-2 encrypted GSM cellular
systems as we continue to review our policies toward China.

We have begun consulting within State and with other
concerned agencies on various aspects of this issue. We may
need to contact you for additional information as we continue
these consultations.

If you wish to have further discussions on the issue, I
suggest that you contact Dr. Martha Harris, the Deputy
Assistant Secretary of State who is directly responsible for
our work in this area. Dr. Harris can be contacted here in the
Bureau of Political-Military affairs at (202) 647-6977 (FAX:
(202) 647-4232). Alternatively, you may contact Cesare Rosati,
the action officer in the Bureau for encryption policy, at
(202) 647-0397 (FAX: (202) 647-4232).

Sincerely,

Thomas E. McNamara

90

November 23, 1994

Theodore McNamara
Assistant Secretary of State
Bureau of Political-Military Affairs
Department of State
2201 C Street, N.W.
Washington, DC 20520

Dear Mr. McNamara:

This is to request that your office initiate action to obtain a waiver from requirements for individual export license notifications to Congress for wireless mobile communications systems containing encryption for China. Such a waiver was issued by the President in September of this year for civilian satellite systems and encrypted products for use by American firms operating in China.

The commercial/consumer telecommunications industry has become a truly global arena, and China represents a large potential market. The major suppliers of wireless systems, offering comparable or identical technologies, are engaged in a constant struggle to capture and retain market share. Currently, U.S. companies are at a significant competitive disadvantage in the marketing and selling of digital communications systems with encryption in China because our competitors are allowed to market and sell such systems while U.S. manufacturers are prohibited from doing so.

The cellular phone market highlights the problem that also exists for other telecommunications providers. European firms, including Nokia, Ericsson, Alcatel and Siemens, have for a number of months been able to market and sell GSM cellular systems with the A5-2 encryption in China as a result of a decision taken by the U.K. intelligence agency, GCHQ. I understand that our National Security Agency is aware of this change in GCHQ's position and would support our request for a change in U.S. requirements for export licenses for China. The NSA has agreed that there should be a "level playing field" in regard to China and would concur with

Government Relations

91

allowing U.S. firms to supply A5-2 GSM systems to that market.

All such export transactions in China involving encryption would continue to be subject to the usual strict compliance requirements of the State Department's ITAR regulations, and NSA would continue their participation in the license review process. The only change we are requesting is from the requirement for Congressional notification for each and every export of these technologies.

We request waiver authority for "all commercial cellular, PCS (personal communications systems) and other telecommunications system hardware and software."

Please let me know if I can provide further information on this subject. Because of the competitive disadvantage suffered by Motorola under the current export control constraints, I request your urgent attention to this matter.

Sincerely,

Richard C. Barth, Ph.D.
Assistant Director, International Trade Relations

cc:　Assistant Secretary Dan Tarullo
　　　Deputy Assistant Secretary Martha Harris
　　　Lou Giles
　　　Bill Clements
　　　Will Lowell
　　　Karen Hopkinson
　　　Ray Mislock

5

JOHN HUANG

*For living spies, it is imperative to choose those who are inwardly
bright but outwardly appear to be stupid.*
Du Mu - The Art of War

Bill Clinton's personal choice for the Commerce Department was former
Lippo banker John Huang. In 1993, John Huang was very close to the
Clintons, having worked with both Bill and Hillary during the Arkansas years
at the part Indonesian owned Worthen Bank.

Indonesian billionaire Moctar Riady and James Riady paid Huang very
well at Lippo Bank, much more than any income he could legally earn at the
Commerce Department.

While in Arkansas, Huang also got to know Arkansas billionaire, and Lippo
partner, Jackson Stephens. When Huang left Lippo for the Clinton administration, he bravely took a major cut in pay and a secret clearance.

In 1993, before Bill Clinton was sworn into office, Lippobank Vice
Chairman John Huang sought out DNC chairman Ron Brown. John Huang,
a major Riady backed Clinton fundraiser, sought to leave his six-figure job at
Lippo to work as an underpaid U.S. government employee under Brown.

In a Jan. 1993 letter addressed to DNC headquarters, John Huang wrote
to Brown for a meeting with Lippo CEO Moctar Riady. The letter was
obtained from the U.S. Commerce Department using the Freedom of
Information Act.

"Daer Ron," wrote Huang in a poorly written letter filled with broken
English. "Congratulations for great performance during yesterday Senate
hearing. I was watching it in the Senate Russell Building and came away
with the strong feeling that you will do an outstanding job as the Secretary of
the Department of Commerce in the coming years."

"I was trying to reach you. But there were too many people there and I
was not successful to do it," noted Huang. "What I really want to do is to
identify a convenient time in the coming week to arrange a meeting between
you and Dr. Moctar Riady, our Group Chairman."

Huang met with the President and others at the White House ten times
between June 21 and June 27, 1994. Right after the June meetings, Webb
Hubbell, who was about to be indicted by a Federal grand jury, received
$100,000 from the Lippo Group.

Two weeks after this possible hush money was given to Hubbell, Huang got a job over at the Commerce Department as Assistant Secretary of the Commerce Department.

Just what did ex-banker turned-patriot Huang do at the Commerce Department?

Huang was no ordinary former-banker. The documents found in Huang's Commerce Department office show that the Clinton appointee met with American defense contractor Raytheon in an effort to sell the Patriot anti-missile system to South Korea. The documents were obtained from the Clinton Commerce Department using the Freedom of Information Act.

Judicial Watch obtained the documents, part of a cache of over 200 boxes of material, a Washington based political watchdog group. Huang, a Clinton appointee to the Commerce Department, pled guilty to campaign finance violations in August 1999.

In an Oct. 1994 letter, Richard Elliot of the legal offices of Paul, Weiss, Rifkin, Wharton and Garrison, noted that Raytheon requested and obtained the meeting with Huang.

"Thank you for agreeing to host a meeting with representatives of Raytheon at 2:30 pm next Thursday, November 3," wrote Elliot.

"As we discussed, the purpose of the meeting is to brief you and other Commerce Department officials concerning Raytheon's efforts to sell the Patriot missile system to South Korea. Needless to say, we would like to request Commerce Department support for these efforts - - and, in particular, for accelerated South Korean procurement of the Patriot."

Raytheon gave Huang, the ex-Lippo banker, detailed information on the Patriot missile and South Korean missile defenses. Huang obtained both "Coalition" military tactical information on North Korean offensive missiles" and a "U.S. Army analysis" of South Korean defenses. According to a Raytheon attachment sent to Huang, titled "Modernization of South Korean Air Defense", South Korea has no defense against a North Korean missile attack.

"The North Korean threat consists of primarily of high performance aircraft, cruise missiles and an extensive family of tactical ballistic missiles," states the Raytheon documentation given to Huang. "The SCUD tactical ballistic missiles deployed by North Korea are a serious threat to all populated areas and industrial areas and military forces in South Korea."

"Rapid reinforcement of South Korea by Coalition nations cannot occur until air superiority is established following the outbreak of hostilities. Given the close proximity of Seoul to the North Korean threat, this air superiority must be in place prior to the conflict, air lifts of reinforcements can begin immediately and available friendly air power can be freed to place maximum effort on interdiction of attacking land forces."

"An all weather, day and night Patriot Missile defense of South Korea is essential to establishing a credible long term deterrence to the North Korean aircraft, cruise and tactical ballistic missile threats and is key to the United States objectives for regional stability," states the document.

"The destabilizing influence of North Korea's tactical ballistic missile program must be countered with a defensive capability that can deny the use of these missile as weapons of terror against the people of South Korea."

"Korea is currently considering a minimum Patriot acquisition program of five Patriot Fire Units four tactical and one training. U.S. Army analysis presented to the Government of Korea in May 1993 assessed that this minimum program can be deployed as an integrated air defense with existing HAWK and other air defense assets and effectively defend the populated areas of Seoul and Inchon against the full range of North Korean high performance aircraft, cruise missiles and SCUD tactical ballistic missiles," states the Raytheon documentation.

"North Korea, as a leading developer and exporter of these weapons, will continue to increase the accuracy of its tactical ballistic missiles which raises the specter of selective destruction of key industrial assets such as nuclear power facilities. A Patriot defense can counter this growing threat and preclude the use of this threat as a future means of coercion," states the Raytheon document.

"At the request of the Ministry of Defense planners, the proposed program includes four tactical Fire Units with six launchers each, a training fire unit with two launchers, and a total of 196 Patriot missiles; intended for the defense of the Seoul/Inchon metropolitan area," states the Raytheon document.

"An all weather, day and night Patriot Missile defense of South Korea is essential to establishing a credible long term deterrence to the North Korean aircraft, cruise and tactical ballistic missile threats and is key to the United States objectives for regional stability," states the document.

The U.S. Army currently deploys the Patriot to protect over 37,000 U.S. troops stationed in South Korea against North Korean ballistic missiles. The Patriot system has also been sold to Japan and Taiwan for missile defense against communist China. South Korea has not elected to buy the Patriot but Korean defense forces are reported to be considering a future purchase.

Investigators inside Congress requested and obtained copies of the Huang documents. According to the investigators, Huang never mentioned working on the Patriot missile sale during his Congressional testimony.

"We were not aware that Mr. Huang had dealings with weapons for South Korea," stated the source inside Congress who requested not to be identified.

"The only known ties Huang had with South Korea was a two hundred and fifty thousand dollar donation to the DNC from Cheong Am company," stated the Capitol Hill source.

While few knew of Huang's work on the Patriot missiles for South Korea, the Federal Election Commission and Congress knew of the South Korean Cheong Am Company paid meetings with Bill Clinton. Five Cheong Am executives gave Huang "an envelope with a corporate check for $250,000 made out to the DNC," reported the FEC. The DNC was forced to return the money.

Yet, Huang worked on other contracts for Raytheon, lobbying the United Arab Emirates (UAE) to purchase the advanced surface-to-air missile. However, according to the Commerce documents, Raytheon faced stiff competition for the UAE air defense contract from Russian made SA-10 and SA-12 systems and the French made Aster missile system.

"Raytheon reports that Russian Prime Minister Chernomyrdin and Defense Minister Grachev as well as French Defense Minister Leotard have advocated on this program," notes the Commerce document.

"The UAE currently has the Raytheon HAWK missile system so a Patriot purchase would provide interoperability and a common missile/air defense architecture. The French system is still in development and while the Russian system is reputed to be technically excellent, the support structure is very poor," notes the Commerce report.

One time event? According to more documents discovered at the U.S. Commerce Department, convicted John Huang also obtained detailed information about Chinese and American artillery sales to the Middle East.

In 1995, Kuwait allocated $1.3 billion to upgrade its field artillery. Included in this new program was an intense competition between U.S. based United Defense and China North Industries, or "Norinco" to win the contract.

The documents in Huang's files note that there was "heavy pressure from the Chinese Government" on Kuwait "to select Norinco."

"China also remains the only member of the UN Security Council that has not been awarded a large military contract from Kuwait. It is understood that the Chinese are pressing this issue with the Kuwait Government," notes the Commerce document from Huang's files.

Huang's file on the Kuwaiti howitzer purchase also contains detailed weapon information of great value to the Chinese military.

"The Chinese offer is of particular concern in that its howitzer has been recently modernized and configured to NATO standards for ammunition interoperability," states the Commerce Department document.

According to documents discovered at the U.S. Commerce Department, convicted China-Gate figure John Huang possessed detailed information about Chinese and American weapons sales to the Middle East. The documents were obtained from the Commerce Department using the Freedom of Information Act.

The documents also contain detailed price and negotiation information considered invaluable to the Chinese military.

According to United Defense officials, Kuwait selected the American made M109A6 Paladin. The M109A6 Paladin is the latest in 155mm self-propelled artillery, including advanced onboard electronics for navigation and fire control. The tank like mobile howitzer has both a Kevlar-lined chassis and a pressurized crew compartment to guard against ballistic, nuclear, biological, and chemical threats.

The American firm that won the artillery contract also noted that the Kuwait government has not approved the money for the purchase.

"The project is still in limbo. The money just has not been released," said a United Defense director for international marketing.

"We did not know that John Huang was involved," stated the United Defense director.

The fact that Huang knew of Norinco while other members of the Commerce Department were in the dark about the Chinese arms firm is curious but not unexpected. Huang's work on an artillery contract in Kuwait was clearly something that Norinco and its Chinese Army owners would be interested in. Yet, Huang also worked on other high-tech weapons for sale to the Middle East.

In 2001, the Bush administration released a batch of Freedom of Information documents after initially refusing to do so. The batch of documents details the export of advanced F-16 fighter jets to the United Arab Emirates. In an Aug. 5, 2002, letter, the Department of Commerce defended its "advocacy" of U.S. arms but failed to explain the role of convicted Chinagate figure and DNC fund-raiser John Huang in the sales of such weapons.

In fact, the Commerce Department's written defense of its role inside global arms sales appear confused and contradicts the documented evidence.

"BIS [Bureau of Industry and Security] advocates on behalf of U.S. companies involved in foreign procurements of defense articles, including arms. This advocacy only occurs after the United States government had decided to approve an arms export if the U.S. company wins the foreign procurement," states the August 2002 Commerce Freedom of Information reply letter.

"DOC [Department of Commerce] plays no role in the approval of any defense articles or services under either the Department of State's arms licensing process or the Department of Defense's FMS [Foreign Military Sales] program," states the 2002 Commerce reply.

One document released by the Commerce Department illustrates the role of the Clinton administration in an F-16 fighter jet sale to the United Arab Emirates. According to a 2000 memo for Commerce Secretary Daley, the department appears to have had a great deal to do with the sale of jet fighters to the U.A.E.

"On 12 May 1998 President Clinton, Vice President Gore, His Highness UAE Crown Prince Khalifa, and Secretary Daley participated in a White House ceremony announcing the selection of Lockheed Martin as the winner of the UAE combat fighter competition. The award was for up to 80 F-16 fighter aircraft and is worth $6 billion," notes the 2000 memo for Commerce Secretary Daley.

While the Commerce Department claims that the fighter jet sale was already approved, the Commerce 2000 memo notes quite clearly that the arms deal was far from being final. In fact, in 1999 the U.S. government had not approved the F-16 sale to the UAE.

"However, although the UAE agreed to buy the fighters, a final contract has not yet been signed largely because of U.S. national disclosure policy on some of the key software involved in the electronic warfare systems of the aircraft," states the memo to Commerce Secretary Daley.

"U.S. policy has consistently denied the release of the software to any foreign nation. Government to government discussion on disclosure of these key codes are ongoing. In early September 1999 most technology release issues were resolved although contract negotiations continue," noted the memo.

According to Commerce Department documents, the export issues involved in selling advanced jet fighter were not resolved before Commerce Secretary Daley helped His Highness UAE Crown Prince Khalifa sign on the dotted line. One document found in the office of John Huang explains quite clearly what was holding the final approval of the arms sale to the UAE.

"There are potential obstacles in the selection of a U.S. aircraft due to technology transfer/releasability concerns. As with the export of any sophisticated defense article, countries seek to leverage maximum technology transfer from the U.S. The U.S. also seeks to maintain a qualitative technological edge over any product that is exported by the U.S.," states a 1995 memo found in the convicted China-gate figure's office.

"Accordingly, the UAE is seeking aircraft sub-systems in the areas of electronic warfare systems, communications equipment, and weapons that are not releasable at this point. This is due to regional stability (maintaining the qualitative military advantage of Israel) and national disclosure policy (systems and equipment which is to be utilized by the U.S. only)," noted Huang's document.

The UAE contract is worth up to $6.4 billion and includes 55 single seat and 25 two-seat versions of the Block 60 F-16. The F-16 fighters for the UAE are designed to counter Russian made SA-10 and SA-12 surface-to-air missiles now being offered to Middle East customers.

U.S. Air Force and Navy officials admit that the Falcons sold to the UAE are more advanced than any aircraft currently operated by American armed forces. Deliveries of the advanced strike aircraft to the UAE are scheduled to begin in 2004.

Huang's work at the Commerce Department also included work on a proposed sale of U.S. made missile warships to the UAE. One document found in Huang's vast files on weapons noted that the personal advocacy of Ron Brown was required to sell missile frigates to the UAE.

In 1994 Commerce Secretary Ron Brown wrote a letter addressed to Lt. General Shaykh Mohammed bin Zyed Al-Nahyyan, Chief of Staff of the United Arab Emirates Arms Forces. In the letter, Brown pressed the Commander of the UAE Armed Forces to purchase advanced U.S. made missile warships.

"I am confident that Newport News Shipbuilding's frigate FF-21 will be judged to be superior based on price, performance, and logistical support. The selection of U.S. manufactured frigates will also ensure the great interoperability with U.S. naval forces stationed in the Gulf and Arabian Sea," wrote Brown.

"In this regard, the provision of two leased Oliver Hazard Perry Class frigates (FFG-7) will provide excellent substitutes while you await the delivery of your new ships," noted Brown.

The Commerce documents show exactly how far the agency went to help the UAE obtain the warships. The Bureau of Export Administration (BXA), the section of the Commerce Department that authorizes foreign sales of aircraft, computers and commercial security software to civilian end users, pressed Congress to sell the warships to the UAE Navy.

"Related to this competition, is that until the new ships are constructed and delivered, the UAE Navy will require leased frigates to provide a bridge during the interim period," notes a Commerce Department advocacy document.

"The UAE has requested that the USN provide used leased Oliver Hazard Perry class (FFG-7) ships, this require approval from Congress. BXA working with the DOD and the Department of State through our role in the review of excess defense articles (EDA) sought to expedite the FFG-7 frigate allocation process. After an extensive review of this project and intensive lobbying by BXA on the need to provide these vessels, the USG (U.S. Government) approved the allocates of two FFG-7 frigates to the UAE."

How Huang obtained these documents and why he was involved in arms sales remains unanswered, but it is clear that U.S. defense contractors sought Commerce Department help with foreign sales prior to any approval by the Defense Department or State Department.

Huang's assignment to weapon systems is more than just a curious series of events. The U.S. Commerce Department is not authorized to conduct the business of warfare. Things that kill like bombs, bullets, missiles and cannons are by law under the Defense Department and the State Department.

Huang was briefed on many of the arms sales to Kuwait, UAE and South Korea. Immediately after such briefings, Huang would walk across the street from the Commerce Department to a firm owned by Jackson Stephens, an old Arkansas friend of President Clinton, and place long distance calls back to Indonesia and the Lippo Group.

"Huang took the Fifth Amendment more than two thousand times when asked by Judicial Watch if he had ties to Chinese intelligence," stated author and Asian Defense analyst William Triplett.

According to Triplett, co-author of "Red Dragon Rising", the Commerce Department has no authority over weapon sales.

"Commerce doesn't do weapons," stated Triplett flatly.

Still, the ex-banker did manage to put in some time covering the secret financial art-works of the Clinton administration. According to an August 1994 "TPCC" or "Trade Policy Coordinating Committee" document, John Huang and the CIA discussed pay-offs to Indonesian dictator Suharto.

The Central Intelligence Agency provided convicted China-Gate figure John Huang with information on corrupt trade deals with Indonesia. In an apparent breach of U.S. national security, the documents released from Huang's files also included the names and phone numbers of CIA agents.

The original documents that identified the CIA agents were heavily blacked out and marked as being withheld for "national security" reasons. However, the Clinton administration officials accidentally included a second un-blacked out copy, revealing the CIA contacts with Huang.

Judicial Watch, a Washington based political watchdog group, obtained documentation on the CIA meetings with Huang as part of a cache of over 200 boxes of materials from the U.S. Commerce Department.

John Huang met 37 times with the CIA for secret briefings. Documents from the U.S. Commerce Department show that in 1994 agents from the Central Intelligence Agency met with John Huang and representatives from the U.S. Export-Import Bank and the Overseas Private Investment Corporation.

According to the documents, CIA agents Bob Beamer, Chris Crosby, Lia Fidas and Nancy Goldcamp attended an August 1994 "TPCC" or "Trade Policy Coordinating Committee" meeting with Huang on Indonesian. The subject of the meeting was U.S. government financed trade deals that contained "first family involvement" or payments to relatives of then Indonesian dictator Suharto.

The subject of the meeting was U.S. government financed trade deals that contained "first family involvement" or illegal payments to relatives of then Indonesian dictator Suharto.

The 1994 meeting between the CIA and Huang provided detailed information on a now-invalid $2.6 billion U.S. sponsored electric power plant for Indonesia. A 1994 Commerce Department report found in Huang's files noted that the Indonesian "Paiton" power plant had encountered difficulties with financing because the "Asian Development Bank (ADB)" knew it contained money for a Suharto family member.

"ADB had raised concern about first family involvement during its consideration of the $50 million financial portion," states the Paiton Project document found in Huang's files.

Another document found at the Commerce Department states, "Ambassador Barry stated that the project is facing two problems (i)   the ADB financing may cave in and (ii) EXIM financing.

Regarding ADB, technical questions have been satisfied, but ADB is skiddish about involvement of Indonesia's first family (a minority shareholder is married to Pres. Suharto's daughter)."

In 1999, an Indonesian government audit revealed that the Paiton power plant has accumulated losses of over $280 million. PLN, the Indonesian power company, estimated that it had lost over $18 billion in total to Suharto corruption inside various power plant contracts.

After the CIA meeting on Indonesian corruption, Huang immediately left the Commerce Department and went to an office owned by Arkansas billionaire Jackson Stephens where Huang made a very long phone call to his former Indonesian employer - the Lippo Group.

The Cox report detailed that some very interesting parties helped John Huang stay in touch with his boss, Moctar Riady. According to the Cox report, "Huang maintained contact with representatives of the Lippo Group while he was at the Department of Commerce."

"During the 18 months that he was at Commerce," states the report. "Huang called Lippo Bank 232 times, in addition to 29 calls or faxes to Lippo Headquarters in Indonesia. Huang also contacted Lippo consultant Maeley Tom on 61 occasions during the same period. Huang's records show 72 calls to Lippo joint venture partner C. Joseph Giroir."

The one key fact missing from the Cox report is that "Maeley Tom" is also an employee of the powerful beltway lobbyist company, Cassidy Associates. In 1994, Cassidy Associates sent DNC donor Maeley Tom to Indonesia on a Ron Brown trade mission. The same mission included DNC donors Charlie Trie, Pauline Kanchanalak and Nora Lum.

Why no mention of the D.C. lobbyists? The answer may be that Cassidy Associates also made hundreds of thousands of dollars in political donations to both Republicans and Democrats. In fact, Cassidy Associates made a total of over 2,500 political contributions between 1991 and 1998, nearly one donation every two days.

Exactly how much corruption remains hidden inside the U.S. energy bill may never be known. Even the largest energy producers, such as Exxon were not above paying off Suharto.

According to the documents found in John Huang's office, Exxon's $34 billion dollar Natuna sea gas deal with Indonesia was laced with "first family involvement". A 2001 Freedom of Information response from the U.S. Commerce Department noted that the exact amount of money that Exxon paid to the Suharto regime must remain secret.

In 2002, the CIA refused to release any of the documents obtained by Huang on the corruption inside Indonesia. According to the CIA denial letter, the agency "can neither confirm nor deny the existence or non existence" of records concerning Huang's meetings.

"Unless officially acknowledged, such information would be classified for reasons of national security," wrote Karthryn Dyer, the CIA Coordinator for

Information and Privacy.

When the facts about John Huang became public the official investigation began. Huang, at one point, disappeared while being sought to testify about illegal donations to the DNC and his unofficial work at the Commerce Department.

One close friend of John Huang, Hoyt Zia, was in charge of Commerce exports to China during 1995. Chief Legal Counsel of the Commerce Department Bureau of Export Affairs (BXA), Hoyt Zia was charged with overseeing sensitive exports such as Iridium satellites and encrypted radios for. Zia previously spent over six years at Motorola specializing in cellular and radio exports to Asia prior to taking his job in the Commerce Department.

Zia stated under oath during a Judicial Watch deposition that he had contact with Motorola official, and ex-Commerce employee, Charlotte Kee on more than one occasion.

Yet, Zia also worked at the DNC with John Huang, Melinda Yee and Charlie Trie during the 1996 campaign. When Huang sought by U.S. Marshals, Zia admitted under oath that he called John Huang. Zia, the top Commerce official for exports, knew where Huang was hiding when Huang was being sought for questioning by Federal authorities. Zia abruptly ended his testimony after he admitted seeing Huang's testimony about himself (Zia), contradicting previous statements he made under oath. Zia later refused to submit any further testimony but continued to hold his key government position at the Commerce Department.

It is a fact that Bill and Hillary Clinton share a close financial relationship with John Huang and Moctar Riady, the Indonesian billionaire owner of the Lippo Group. Mrs. Clinton reportedly insisted that John Huang be given a position at the U.S. Commerce Department under Ron Brown. Mrs. Clinton has not made any public comment on her relationship with Huang's employer, Indonesian billionaire Moctar Riady.

In addition, the Indonesian billionaire Moctar Riady has been accused of passing illegal monies to the 1992 and 1996 Clinton/Gore campaigns. In 1996, Arief and Soraya Wiriadinata were closely connected to the Riadys when they passed a check to Bill Clinton. Arief was a gardener living in Virginia. Arief earned about $25,000 a year but he and his wife somehow managed to donate $450,000 to the DNC in a single contribution.

Just by coincidence, Soraya's father, Hashim Ning, was a business partner of Mochtar Riady and the Lippo Group in Indonesia. Hashim wired $500,000 that the Wiriadinatas used to make the $450,000 contribution. For their troubles, the Wiriadinatas kept $50,000 but the bulk of the money was obviously laundered from Indonesia through the Wiriadinatas into the Democrat National Committee.

Ironically, the CIA also accused Riady of working for Chinese military intelligence. According to a 1998 CIA report presented to Senator Thompson (R. Tenn.), "James and Moctar Riady have had a long term relationship with a Chinese intelligence agency. The relationship is based on mutual benefit with the Riadys receiving assistance in finding business opportunities in exchange for large sums of money and other help."

"The Chinese intelligence agency seeks to locate and develop relationships with information collectors, particularly with close association to the U.S. government," states the CIA report on Riady.

According to the testimony before Sen. Fred Thompson, the Lippo Group is in fact a joint venture of China Resources, a trading and holding company "wholly owned" by the Chinese communist government and used as a front for espionage operations.

One such Chinese Army operation involved an airliner part owned by Riady with a live missile stuffed in its belly.

In 1996 China obtained the most advanced Russian air-to-air missile, NATO code-named the AA-11 ARCHER. According to the Cox Report, in 1996, Hong Kong Customs officials removed a fully operational AA-11 missile from the cargo hold of a Chinese Dragonair L-1011 airliner stuffed with paying passengers.

"In 1996, Hong Kong Customs officials intercepted air-to-air missile parts being shipped by (China National Aerotechnology Import and Export Company) CATIC aboard a commercial air carrier, Dragonair. Dragonair is owned by China International Trade and Investment Company (CITIC), the most powerful and visible PRC-controlled conglomerate, and the Civil Aviation Administration of China," states the Cox report.

It was Aviation Week and Space Technology that carried the full story. Aviation Week reported that the missile was in a box labeled, as "Machine Parts" and the Chinese government and Clinton buddy-billionaire Moctar Riady then owned that Dragonair jointly. According to intelligence sources, the Chinese missile was bound for Israel for an upgrade with stolen U.S. Sidewinder technology.

Dragonair was fined for carrying the Chinese missile in the cargo bay of a L-1011 airliner full of paying passengers. According to Aviation Week & Space Technology (AW&ST), the missile was found by accident. Both the volatile solid fuel rocket motor and the deadly explosive warhead were intact and fully operational.

What the Cox report left out was that in 1996, the Chinese government owned only 36% of Dragonair. Indonesian billionaire Moctar Riady then owned the remaining 64% lion-share of the Hong Kong based carrier.

Dragonair was fined for carrying the Chinese missile in the cargo bay of a L-1011 airliner full of paying passengers. According to Aviation Week & Space Technology (AW&ST), the missile was bound for Israel, enclosed in a mislabeled box, partially dismantled, and only found by accident. Both the volatile solid fuel rocket motor and the deadly explosive warhead were intact and fully operational.

Missiles and airliners full of people should not be mixed. There is an old U.S. Marine axiom: "Never load munitions and troops on the same ship." PLA owned airliners, however, do not operate along the same rules with or without illegal loads of munitions.

The Dragonair incident may shed light on unexplained civil airline accidents such as TWA-800. For example, in the 1980s, a South African 747 blew up over the Indian Ocean while carrying a load of artillery shells along with the paying passengers. The illegal load of cannon shells exploded over the Indian Ocean, killing everyone onboard.

What remains unanswered is the role Israel played in the Dragonair case - a U.S. ally anxious to obtain a copy of an enemy missile or a willing aerospace contractor eager to upgrade a weapon for a paying customer with stolen U.S. Sidewinder technology?

Why is there no mention of the ever-popular Moctar Riady, the foreign billionaire, and major contributor to Bill Clinton?

Another issue left unresolved by the Dragonair incident is the relationship between the Chinese Army and Moctar Riady, owner of the Lippo Group.

In 1999, John Huang pled guilty to Federal charges of making illegal political contributions to the Clinton/Gore campaign. In September 2002, the Federal Election Commission fined John Huang $95,000 for illegal contributions to the 1996 re-election campaign of Clinton and Gore.

To this day, Huang remains silent on his work for the Chinese Army.

LIPPOBANK

Formerly BANK OF TRADE

January 7, 1993

Mr. Ronald H. Brown
Chairman
Democratic National Committee
430 South Capital Street, S.E.
Washington, D.C. 20203

Dear Ron,

Congratulations for great performance during yesterday Senate hearing. I was watching it in the Senate Russell Building and came away with the strong feeling that you will do an outstanding job as the Secretary of the Department of Commerce in the coming years.

I was trying to reach you. But there were too many people there and I was not successful to do it.

What I really want to do is to identify a convenient time in the coming week to arrange a meeting between you and Dr. Mochtar Riady, our Group Chairman. Dr. Riady will be coming to the States. I firmly believe such a meeting will be quite beneficial and valuable given Dr. Riady's many years experience in the business arena. In fact, he is so good that he has been named as advisor to two of largest Japanese Banks (Tokai Bank and Daiwa Bank). Dealing with Japan and other Asian matters will be all of our important agenda.

Please if possible give me (if you are busy, please ask Bill Morton or your other assistant) a call at my office at (213) 625-1888 x668 or at my home at (818) 244-5089 so that I can quickly finalize this matter.

Thanking you in advance for taking a little moment on this matter. I know you're extremely busy. But I think this matter is also important as well.

Again, congratulations and looking forward to hearing from you soon.

Sincerely yours,

John Huang
Vice Chairman

JH/dt

John Huang

UNITED STATES DEPARTMENT OF COMMERCE
International Trade Administration
Washington, D.C. 20230

03BA2646

TASKER

October 31, 1994

MEMORANDUM FOR DAS NANCY LINN-PATTON

From: Stacey Moore

Subject: Meeting with Raytheon on November 3

PDAS John Huang and Assistant Secretary for Export Administration Sue Eckert will be hosting a meeting with Raytheon Representatives at 2:30pm on Thursday, November 3.

Attached are briefing materials sent to A/S Eckert regarding the Raytheon meeting, please review and provide your thoughts on the materials as soon as possible or no later than 12:00noon on Thursday, November 3 to Stacey Moore or Janice Stewart.

Thank you!

cc: JS

TASKER

IMMEDIATE ATTENTION

105

PAUL, WEISS, RIFKIND, WHARTON & GARRISON

1615 L STREET, NW   WASHINGTON, DC 20036-5694
TELEPHONE (202) 223-7300   FACSIMILE (202) 223-7420   TELEX 248237 PWA UR

1285 AVENUE OF THE AMERICAS
NEW YORK, NY 10019-6064
TELEPHONE (212) 373-3000
FACSIMILE (212) 757-3990
TELEX WUI 666-843

199, BOULEVARD SAINT-GERMAIN
75007 PARIS, FRANCE
TELEPHONE (33-1) 45.48.32.85
FACSIMILE (33-1) 42.22.64.38
TELEX 203178F

AKASAKA TWIN TOWER
17-22, AKASAKA 2-CHOME
MINATO-KU, TOKYO 107, JAPAN
TELEPHONE (81-3) 3505-0291
FACSIMILE (81-3) 3505-4540
TELEX 02425120 PWRWGT

BEIJING OFFICE
SUITE 1910 SCITE TOWER
22 JIANGUOMENWAI DAJIE
BEIJING, 100004
PEOPLE'S REPUBLIC OF CHINA
TELEPHONE (86-1) 5123628-30
FACSIMILE (86-1) 5123631

WRITER'S DIRECT DIAL NUMBER
(202) 223-7324

03BA2646

October 28, 1994

The Honorable Sue E. Eckert
Assistant Secretary for Export Administration
U.S. Department of Commerce, Rm. 3886C
14th Street & Constitution Avenue, N.W.
Washington, DC 20230

Re: Meeting with Raytheon on November 3

Dear Ms. Eckert:

Thank you for agreeing to host a meeting with
representatives of Raytheon at 2:30 pm next Thursday,
November 3. As we discussed, the purpose of the meeting is
to brief you and other Commerce Department officials
concerning Raytheon's efforts to sell the Patriot missile
system to South Korea. Needless to say, we would like to
request Commerce Department support for these efforts --
and, in particular, for accelerated South Korean procurement
of the Patriot.

The Raytheon attendees at the meeting will be as
follows:

Raytheon

(1)   Stephen R. Stanvick, Vice President and Manager of Air
      Defense Programs, Raytheon Missile Systems Division

(2)   John J. Lavoie, Director for Far East Development, Air
      Defense Programs, Raytheon Missile Systems Division

(3)   Robert C. Johnson, Deputy Director for International
      Programs, Washington Operations, Raytheon Company

Paul, Weiss

(1)   Lionel H. Olmer

(2)   myself

— What do we have to give up
on our program currently in
negotiation w/ S. Korea?

Doc #:EC2:15137.1 DC-1323A

106

PAUL, WEISS, RIFKIND, WHARTON B GARRISON

03BA2646

As you requested, I am enclosing some background materials. In addition to discussing the overall status of the Patriot program and the Patriot's technical capabilities, these materials provide an overview of the specific economic and security benefits associated with a Patriot sale to South Korea.

Please let me know if you have any questions in advance of the meeting.

Sincerely,

Richard S. Elliott

cc:

Commerce Department

Raymond E. Vickery, Jr.
Assistant Secretary for Trade Development

John Huang
Deputy Assistant Secretary for International
 Economic Policy

John A. Richards
Deputy Assistant Secretary for Industrial
 Resources Administration

Raytheon

Stephen R. Stanvick
Vice President, Missile Systems Division

Paul, Weiss

Lionel H. Olmer

VIA HAND DELIVERY

Doc #:DC1:15137.1 DC-1323A

DECEPTION

03BA2646

Subject: Status of Korea's Consideration of Patriot Procurement

Background: Korea's Air Defense Forces currently deploy the HAWK and NIKE-Hercules Air Defense Systems. Modernization of the HAWK Systems to the Phase II configuration will be completed during early 1995. Further modernization of HAWK systems to the Phase III configuration is under consideration. The aging NIKE-Hercules system is based on early-1950's technology, not effective against current regional threats and cannot be effectively maintained or upgraded. As a result, the Korean Government has programmed funds in its five year defense plan beginning in 1998 to replace the NIKE system. The Patriot Air Defense System is the leading replacement candidate. A decision on the acquisition method and designation of the replacement system is the next milestone in the Korean system acquisition process.

Threat Requirements: The North Korean threat consists primarily of high performance aircraft, cruise missiles and an extensive family of tactical ballistic missiles. The "Scud" tactical ballistic missiles deployed by North Korea are a serious threat to all populated and industrial areas and military forces in South Korea.

US Government Patriot Deployments: The United States deployed Patriot Fire Units to Korea in early 1994 to protect selected United States military warfighting assets against the North Korean Scud missile threat. Other military assets and Korean populated areas and national assets, including the Seoul capitol area, remain exposed to the Scud missile threat.

Korean Patriot Program: Korea is currently considering a minimum Patriot acquisition program of five Patriot Fire Units, four tactical and one training. U.S. Army analysis presented to the Government of Korea in May 1993 assessed that this minimum program can be deployed as an integrated air defense with existing HAWK and other air defense assets and effectively defend the populated areas of Seoul and Inchon against the full range of North Korean high performance aircraft, cruise missiles and Scud tactical ballistic missiles.

Current Status: Korean procurement of new major weapons system has been essentially suspended since the new Korean Government assumed office in March 1993. Extensive investigation of the Korean defense modernization process has resulted in widespread replacement of military and civilian defense officials. Recent escalation of tensions over the North Korean nuclear program may soon result in decisions to proceed with some defense modernization. Patriot is a leading candidate for early procurement to counter the Scud tactical ballistic missile threat and modernize Korean and Combined Forces Command, Korea air defense forces.

John Huang

Subject: Modernization of South Korean Air Defense with the Patriot Air
            Defense System

South Korea should be encouraged to proceed as soon as possible with the
modernization of its air defense forces. South Korea today relies on the
aging Nike-Hercules system for long range and high altitude air defense.
This system is ineffective against modern high performance aircraft, cruise
and tactical ballistic missile threats. The Korean Government should be
encouraged to procure the Patriot Air Defense System to establish an
effective integrated air defense capability.

An all weather, day and night Patriot Missile defense of South Korea is
essential to establishing a credible long term deterrence to the North
Korean aircraft, cruise and tactical ballistic missile threats and is key to
United States objectives for regional stability. Rapid reinforcement of South
Korea by Coalition nations cannot occur until air superiority is established
following the outbreak of hostilities. Given the close proximity of Seoul to
the North Korean threat, this air superiority must be in place prior to the
conflict so that reinforcements can be immediately air lifted and arrive in
time to impact the defense of the capital area. With a Patriot air defense in
place prior to hostilities, air lifts of reinforcements can begin immediately
and available friendly air power can be freed to place maximum effort on
interdiction of attacking land forces. The need for a Patriot defense, in
place with its assured air superiority, will be a decisive consideration to any
future reductions in U.S. deployed forces on the peninsula. Such reductions
will make assured, rapid reinforcement of the peninsula one of the highest
military priorities.

The destabilizing influence of North Korea's tactical ballistic missile
program must be countered with a defensive capability that can deny the
use of these missiles as weapons of terror against the people of South
Korea. North Korea, as a leading developer and exporter of these
weapons, will continue to increase the accuracy of its tactical ballistic
missiles which raises the specter of selective destruction of key industrial
assets such as nuclear power facilities. A Patriot defense can counter this
growing threat and preclude the use of this threat as a future means of
coercion.

Patriot is a purely defensive weapon and its acquisition should not upset
current efforts to achieve a lasting peace. Air defense of Korea should be a
Korean host nation responsibility and investment in defense.

7/8/94

109

03BA2646

━━━━━━━━ **FACT SHEET** ━━━━━━━━

Patriot for Korea

PATRIOT

- Is a surface-to-air missile air defense

- It is all weather, low to high altitude and long range;

- It effectively counters enemy aircraft, helicopters, cruise missiles and tactical ballistic missiles in the most severe electronic countermeasures and natural environments;

- The U.S. Government has and continues to invest in Patriot enhancements to maintain its effectiveness well into the next century. This advanced Patriot now available to Korea;

- The threat to South Korea requires a balanced air defense combining aircraft (F-16's) and surface-to-air missiles (Patriot). Aircraft cannot counter TBMs or modern low altitude cruise missiles;

- As deployed today, Patriot interoperates with the Hawk Air Defense System providing a layered defense. Hawk is medium altitude and medium range; Patriot reaches to high altitude and very long range;

- Patriot is an integral part of Theater Missile Defense (TMD). It counters short to medium range TBMs as well as current cruise missiles. When THAAD (Theatre High Altitude Area Defense) becomes available, Patriot will protect THAAD against aircraft and cruise missiles and engage TBM leakers.

Raytheon Company
Missile Systems Division

PATRIOT FOR KOREA

- Five (5) Fire Units (4 tactical, 1 training) are recommended for the defense of Seoul/Inchon area;

- Each Fire Unit consists of:

1	Radar Set (RS)
1	Engagement Control Station (ECS)
6	Launching Stations (LS)
1	Battery Maintenance Group (BMG)
1	Electric Power Plant (EPP)
1	Guided Missile Transporter (GMT)
1	Small Repair Parts Transporter (SRPT)
1	Large Repair Parts Transporter (LRPT)

- Each launcher contains four ready to fire Patriot missiles. Additional missiles are provided for reload;

- Additional equipment is provided for communications and battalion level command and control;

- A 1994 Patriot Procurement can yield a first unit deployed capability in 1997;

- A Patriot deployment interoperating with Hawk and F-16 command and control is recommended;

- Korea will receive the latest Patriot production configuration (PAC-2+) which incorporates enhancements since Desert Storm.

October 26, 1993

110

03BA2646

FACT SHEET

Patriot for Korea

(Cont'd.)

PRODUCTION IN KOREA

- GoldStar Precision Company is teamed with Raytheon Company (the Patriot Producer);

- Technology transfer will be conducted for Korean Industry to produce parts of the Patriot System, accomplish end item integration and provide logistics support (training, maintenance, depot operations);

- Parts of the Patriot system are likely to be produced in Seoul, Kumi, Taegu and Kwangju;

- Direct industrial participation provides long term, high technology jobs to Korean workers.

SUMMARY

- Patriot is required for defense of the Seoul/Inchon population areas;

- Patriot defeats the SCUD threat;

- Patriot protects against a cruise missile attack;

- Patriot provides the Korean Air Force with the means for increasing aircraft assigned to interdiction and force projection missions;

- Any Patriots purchased today will be an integral part of a future TBM system.

Raytheon Company
Missile Systems Division

October 26, 1993

Distribution List

Bob LaRussa/DOC
John Huang/DOC
Clyde Robinson/DOC
Jay Brandes/DOC
Chris Crosby/CIA Liasion
Kelly Rouleau/CIA
Lia Fidas/CIA
Nancy Goldcamp/CIA
Bob Beamer/ CIA
Kay Thomson/DOE
Yasamin Al-Askari/EXIM
Richard Greenberg/OPIC
Fred Eberhart/TDA
Evans Wiley/DOT
Mary Tarnowka/State
Bob Lee/DOC

U.S. & Foreign Commercial Service
Office of the Director General
U.S. Department of Commerce
Washington, DC 20230
Tel #: (202) 482-5025
Fax #: (202) 482-5013

Date: August 25, 1994

To: TPCC Indonesia Advocacy-Finance Working Group
(See attached distribution list)

From: Stephan Kanlian

# of Pages: 4

Comments:

Attached are the minutes from our last meeting. Please submit any comments or revisions to me via fax at 482-5013.

The DOC Advocacy Center is preparing a matrix of the priority projects agreed upon by the group at the last meeting. We should have the matrix to each of you by early next week for your comments, additions and identification of agency contacts for each project. We are working to include all information possible to make the matrix complete. However, any additional or new information you have on these projects can be added to the matrix after your review. We will set a date for the next meeting as soon as Bob LaRussa returns from Asia next week.

Thanks you for your assistance. Best regards.

10C00646
40CD0948

Memorandum For: TPCC Finance/Advocacy Subgroup
From: Stephan Kanlian
Subject: Minutes from Aug. 17th meeting

Attached please find a list of attendees from the August 17th meeting. What follows are highlights of the meeting:

Clyde Robinson opened the meeting by outlining what needed to be accomplished in this session. The group agreed on three key areas vital to further cooperation:

1. Consensus on a Major Projects list, based on interagency input and priorities.
2. Mechanism for dissemination of Pre- and Post-Award information to potential suppliers.
3. Travel Information for Senior Officials that could serve as tool for interagency advocacy.

Discussion ensued among the group regarding each agency's prioritized list of projects. Information on insurance application/registration was provided by OPIC, financing details were provided by Ex-Im Bank and grants awarded for feasibility studies by OPIC were discussed in relation to each project. The final list of projects the group decided upon numbered 18 projects, 16 of which have potential as deliverables for the APEC meeting in November. The other two projects are important, but have timelines which are long-term.

Bob Beamer suggested that any primary competitors known to the group for these projects should be included as background information. Clyde Robinson suggested that Commerce devise a matrix by late this week which identifies the key information for each project on the interagency list. The group agreed that the matrix should be for Official Use Only.

The group next tackled the issue of informing suppliers both pre- and post-awarding of projects, to allow them to compete for sub-contracts on major awards. Several members of the group expressed concern with this issue. Fred Eberhart of TDA felt that it would be better to promote the mix of small companies among suppliers by asking the project awardee to provide us with their supplier list and include number of employees for each firm. Bob Lee of DOC also pointed out that pre-award dissemination of information might tip off an awardee's competitors, which would be objectionable to the firms we are advocating for.

Clyde Robinson briefly outlined his ideas for a central database of Senior Level Official travel that could be a tool for advocacy efforts on an interagency level.

Next Meeting will be in early September, date and time to be determined.

40CD0646
40CD0948

114

TPCC ADVOCACY/FINANCE MEETING
August 17, 1994

Name	Agency	Phone	Fax
Salim Akhtar	DOE	586-8672	586-3588
Evans Wiley	DOT	366-9527	366-7417
Bob Beamer	CIA	(703) 482-9125	(703) 790-5736
Fred Eberhart	TDA	(703) 875-4357	(703) 875-4009
Bob Lee	Commerce	482-3277	482-5702
Yasamin Al-Askari	EXIM	535-9456	566-7524
Richard Greenberg	OPIC	336-8616	408-5155
Clyde Robinson	Commerce	482-1464	482-5697
Chris Crosby Lia Fidas Nancy Goldcamp	O/IL	482-2516	482-0187 Call first
John Huang	Commerce	482-2993	482-5444
Mary Tarnowka	State	647-1625	647-5713

40CD0646
40CD0948

6

CORRUPT POWER SUPPLY

If you let the troops plunder at will - they will get out of hand.
Wang Xi - The Art of War

Critics have often accused former U.S. President Clinton and former Indonesian President Suharto of being corrupt. In fact, declassified documents show that both Presidents joined to form an alliance of global corruption, collusion and nepotism.

In 1994, President Clinton signed a trade agreement to supply Indonesia with electric power using U.S. taxpayer loans. The trade agreement was worth billions to U.S. corporations such as Mission Energy and General Electric.

"As markets expand, as information flows, the roots of an open society will grow and strengthen and contribute to stability," stated President Clinton during the 1994 signing.

Until the discoveries made by this author, no one outside of the Clinton administration knew of the illegal payments. No one would have known until a mistake led to the crime. In 1998, the Commerce Department returned a "blacked-out" version of a document that it had previously sent in full.

The mistakenly released document from the Commerce Department titled "Indonesia Advocacy Projects", contained information on the privately held east Java Paiton Power Plant.

"Ambassador Barry stated that the project is facing two problems," noted Commerce officials on the Paiton project status document. "(i) the ADB financing may cave in and (ii) EXIM financing. Regarding ADB, technical questions have been satisfied, but ADB is skiddish about involvement of Indonesia's first family (a minority shareholder is married to Pres. Suharto's daughter)."

The November 1994 Commerce Department advocacy document shows the Indonesian Paiton project encountered difficulties with financing because the Asian Development Bank (ADB) knew it also contained a Suharto family kick-back. Suharto's son-in-law, according to the U.S. government advocacy document, was known to be a shareholder in P.T. Batu.

In 1994, Ron Brown was aware of a crime in progress. Brown knew that Indonesian Dictator Suharto had cut his son-in-law into a kickback scheme, involving U.S. tax money. The documents show that Brown was not only aware of Suharto's corrupt activities but also quietly co-operated by seeking

U.S. backed financial aid for the project.

The public side of the joint agreement between Clinton and Suharto hid a far more insidious scheme. According to an August 1994 "TPCC" or "Trade Policy Coordinating Committee" document, John Huang and the CIA discussed pay-offs to Indonesian dictator Suharto.

John Huang met 37 times with the CIA for secret briefings. Documents from the U.S. Commerce Department show that in 1994 agents from the Central Intelligence Agency met with John Huang and representatives from the U.S. Export-Import Bank and the Overseas Private Investment Corporation.

According to the documents, CIA agents Bob Beamer, Chris Crosby, Lia Fidas and Nancy Goldcamp attended an August 1994 "TPCC" or "Trade Policy Coordinating Committee" meeting with Huang on Indonesian. The subject of the meeting was U.S. government financed trade deals that contained "first family involvement" or illegal payments to relatives of then Indonesian dictator Suharto.

The 1994 meeting between the CIA and Huang provided detailed information on a now-invalid $2.6 billion U.S. sponsored electric power plant for Indonesia. A 1994 Commerce Department report found in Huang's files noted that the Indonesian "Paiton" power plant had encountered difficulties with financing because the "Asian Development Bank (ADB)" knew it contained money for a Suharto family member.

"ADB had raised concern about first family involvement during its consideration of the $50 million financial portion," states the Paiton Project document found in Huang's files.

"Huang clearly had access to commercial information that would have been of keen interest to the Riadys," noted Asian Defense specialist, and co-author of YEAR OF THE RAT, William Triplett. "That very night Huang called Lippo in Jakarta."

"Huang took the Fifth Amendment more than two thousand times when asked by Judicial Watch if he had ties to Chinese intelligence," stated Triplett.

The Clinton Commerce Department tried to conceal evidence and hide the facts. On June 7, 1999, the Commerce Department refused to release all the information on the Indonesian "Paiton" power plant, citing "commercial" privacy. Many of the documents released by the Clinton administration contained whole sections blacked out for "privacy" reasons.

However, more mistakes were made. Once again, the complete copy of a document previously blacked out as secret by the Clinton administration was provided in full. The critical section blacked out by Commerce officials matched the secret documents that John Huang obtained from the CIA.

"First Family Involvement: ADB had raised concern about first family involvement during its consideration of the $50 million."

The 1999 Commerce Department attempts to black out evidence clearly demonstrated that the Clinton administration feared the truth. The documents show a premeditated effort to conceal the criminal activity.

Commercial members of the corrupt projects did not view the illegal payments as favorable for future business. The reluctance to participate in an illegal pay-off led GE and Mission Energy to seek Clinton help.

"Although the ADB financing is only $50 million, GE views the ADB component to be important because it has a long-term interest in having a multinational bank support the project. Furthermore, if ADB rejected financing, EXIM and the commercial banks involved in the deal would ask questions," states a GE document obtained from the Commerce Department files.

Obviously asking questions would not be good for any project with a built in $50 million kickback for the local dictator. The documents show that Edison officials were aware of the $50 million destine for Suharto's daughter. The released documents also show that Edison Chairman John Bryson actually pressed Commerce Secretary Ron Brown to support the $50 no-pay back loan.

Federal Election Commission records show that Mission Energy CEO John Bryson donated money to the Clinton/Gore campaign and contributed money to President Clinton's legal defense fund. In 1994, Bryson also wrote a personal letter to Brown, pressing for quick approval of the $50 million U.S. government backed loan.

Dear Ron," wrote John Bryson, then Chairman of Southern California Edison.

"I am writing to request your support of the application of the Paiton Private Power Project in Indonesia for funding by the Asian Development Bank (ADB). The Project, which is described in the attached background sheet, is a $2.6 billion power project being developed by Mission Energy Company (a subsidiary of SCEcorp) together with its partners General Electric Company, Mitsui & Co., Ltd., and Batu Perkasa of Indonesia."

"We have applied to the ADB for $50 million of funding as part of a $1.9 billion financing package. The bulk of the funds will come from a group of commercial banks, the U. S. Export Import Bank and Japan Ex-Im," noted Edison CEO Bryson.

"I would greatly appreciate it if you would indicate your support for ADB funding of this project. With that in mind, enclosed is a draft letter to Ambassador Linda Tsao Yang, U.S. Executive. Director of ADB, for your consideration."

The CEO of Mission Energy took it upon himself to write a letter from Ron Brown to Linda Yang, the Director of the Asian Development Bank, directing his total support for a $50 million loan to the Suharto family. According to Bryson, Brown had to convince the Asian Development Bank (ADB) that the so-called loan was legal and had U.S. government support.

"Dear Ambassador," wrote Bryson for Brown. "I understand that an application for funds is currently before the Asian Development Bank (ADB) for the Paiton Private Power Project in Indonesia. By way of this letter, I am conveying to you and ADB my support for this very important power project."

"The project, as you know, represents a major step toward the development of private power in Asia, thereby enhancing sustainable economic development. The United States Government strongly supports the participation of the private sector in this critical industry and believes that such participation will help the development of all nations. This project, being developed by a consortium of leading companies from the United States, Japan, and Indonesia with financing from the United States, Japan and Europe, is an outstanding example of the success of private power."

"Moveover, the project expects to purchase between $500 million and $900 million of equipment, goods and services from U.S. based companies. As many as 5,000 U.S. jobs will be created over the four year construction/procurement period," noted Bryson in his letter for Brown. "I hope that the ADB will act favorably on the application," wrote Bryson. In 1995, the entire $2.6 billion dollar project was on the brink of failure because the Asian Development Bank would not make the $50 million "loan" to the Suharto regime. In the end, the Suharto corruption quietly killed the $50 million financing and the Asian Development Bank refused to make the instant loan to Suharto's daughter.

However, the project was certainly not dead but funding the $50 million for the Suharto family had to be found elsewhere. Thus, Lippo partner Edison Mission Energy convinced the Clinton administration to financially back the project. In 1995, the Brown led Commerce Department found financing for the power plant through the U.S. taxpayer.

In April 1995, $1.82 billion in limited recourse project debt was provided to Paiton by the Export-Import Bank of Japan, the Export-Import Bank of the United States, the Overseas Private Investment Corporation ("OPIC") of the United States, and eight commercial banks. According to State Department cable's, the financial support by OPIC was not without risk.

According to a July 1998, State Dept. cable written by Ambassador Roy, "OPIC was concerned that PLN payment problems and inaction on suspended IPP projects may result in expropriation claims under OPIC political risk insurance polices... OPIC's combined exposure in Indonesia is close to USD 1 billion, or 5 percent of OPIC's global exposure, all in the electric power sector. As such, resolution of potential insurance claims and/or actions could result in 'an adverse material impact' on OPIC finances."

Obviously, the Indonesian power sector failure threatened an OPIC collapse with it. If OPIC failed then it would be audited, along with the U.S. Export-Import Bank, the World Bank and various other commercial investors. Thus, the intense fear inside the Clinton/Gore White House was that the "corruption, collusion and nepotism (KKN)" would be uncovered and prosecuted.

The partners in the Paiton I consortium included Edison Mission Energy, Mitsui & Co., Ltd. of Japan, General Electric Capital Corporation, and P.T. Batu Hitam Perkasa. Suharto's youngest daughter, Titek Prabowo and her brother-in-law, Hashim Djojohadikusumo, own PT Batu.

Mr. Hashim is closely tied to the former dictator of Indonesia, President Suharto. Mr. Hashim's brother is married to Suharto's youngest daughter, Ms. Prabowo. Ms. Prabowo is also a part owner of the Paiton power plant. Hashim's father was also a close friend of Suharto and a former economic minister to the Indonesian strongman.

Mission Energy is also a partner of Indonesia's Lippo group, a consortium part-owned by Indonesian billionaire Moctar Riady and the Chinese Army CITIC (China International Trust and Investment Corporation) bank. Moctar Riady was accused of illegally donated money to the Clinton/Gore political campaigns.

Paiton I was billed as the first "private" electric plant in Indonesia. However, private ownership in Indonesia actually meant privately owned and operated by the Suharto "First Family." The Indonesian company that owned, operated and fueled the Paiton I plant under a 30 year, no-cut, contract is PT Batu Hitam Perkasa.

Prawabo's brother-in-law, Hashim, also received an exclusive, no bid, no-cut contract to supply coal for the power plant. The State Dept. characterized the over-priced coal contract with Hashim as "the Achilles Heel" of Paiton Swasta I.

The payments, along with a cut for "brother-in-law" Hashim and various other Suharto relatives, was provided up front, in cash, in the form of a $50 million loan. The $50 million loan was to be paid back by the profits (dividends) returned from the $2.6 billion Paiton project. Since there are no profits, there is no pay back.

According to the Commerce Dept., ".75%" of the Paiton project was reserved for Suharto's daughter Prabowo. Prabowo's cut amounted to an instant $15 million.

PLN electric officials, fearing for their lives, are pointing fingers at Suharto. Ex-PLN President Djteng Marsudi has repeatedly stated he was forced to sign unfairly priced contracts, including Paiton.

In August 1998, the Indonesian meltdown caused Mission Energy to panic and again seek aid from the Clinton administration. Declassified documents from the Clinton administration included a briefing of current Secretary of Commerce William Daley for a meeting with Mission Energy CEO Edward Muller.

"Mr. Muller will raise his concerns about developments in Asia in general and about the Paiton project in particular. He will probably attempt to enlist your support for the Paiton project. Given competing interest by other U.S. firms, we cannot commit to this particular project."

Translation: Ron Brown is long dead and Bill Clinton is not anxious to cuddle up to the Suharto family for fear of raising questions about donations from Indonesian billionaire Moctar Riady.

"Ex-Im (Export Import Bank) is the guarantor for $540 million in the pre-completion phase. OPIC is the senior lender (provides guarantees for banks to lend) and insurance provider for the post-completion phase ($200 million). (Mission did not take out political risk insurance from OPIC or Ex-Im.)"

Translation: Mission Energy's mistake in not seeking the "political" insurance was a calculated risk that will cost stockholders and customers. Corporate losses overseas will have to be made up with lower profits at home and higher rates for CalEdison customers.

In fact, according to the Commerce Dept., there were U.S. companies with contracts inside Indonesia who have an interest in the failure of the Paiton power plant:

"Both Ex-Im and OPIC confirmed that if the 1200 MW Paiton project were to go on line, it would most likely wipe out any further GOI (Government of Indonesia) need for other power plants. Thus, several other major U.S. power developers with other projects, in varying stages of completion, are potential competitors with Edison for power purchase agreements."

According an October 1998 State Dept. cable from the U.S. Ambassador to Indonesia, J. Stapleton Roy, Clinton administration officials met with Indonesian Director General of Electricity Endro Utomo Notodisoerjo:

"Commenting on corruption, collusion and nepotism (KKN), Endro said that in the past there was no separation between 'power' (not electric but former first family power) and business. 'All the IPP's have a relation with power, and it is still going on,' added Endro."

On August 19, 1999, the U.S. State Department declassified 26 documents on corruption in American financed electric power projects inside

Indonesia. In addition, the State Dept. also elected to withhold parts of 15 documents and three full documents "in the interest of national security or foreign relations."

All of the withheld documents concern U.S. financed electric power plant projects inside Indonesia. One declassified November 1998 State Dept. cable dedicates an entire section on "DEALING WITH UNWANTED PARTNERS."

According to the State Dept., U.S. electric power manufacturer El Paso International entered into the Sengkang power project with Suharto's second daughter "Tutut". In an effort to deal with the "unwanted" Suharto partner, El Paso tried to buy Tutut out of the Sengkang project.

"Tutut holds two and one half percent in PT Triahsra Sarana, which has a 5 percent share in PT Energi Sengkang. According to Sengkang, Tutut does not intend to divest from the project at this time."

The "Unwanted Partners" section also reveals yet-another kickback, this time for a Suharto "crony" instead of a relative.

"Unocal executives told resources officer that the firm is close to reaching a deal with its partner, PT Nusamba (controlled by former President Soeharto crony Bob Hasan) to sever ties in two production sharing contracts (PSC) in east Kalmantan and East Java."

Each of the 26 documents has some sort of allegation of corrupt activities between U.S. power manufacturers and the Suharto government. In fact, the warnings of corruption came as early as 1996.

In April 1996, Ambassador Barry in Jakarta wrote, "Java Power Company has obtained a USD 1.7 billion financing package for its 2 X 610 coal fired Paiton Swasta II power plant... Java Power Company is 50 percent owned by Siemens Power, 35 percent Powergen PLC of the UK and 15 percent by PT Bumiperitwi Tatapradipta. The latter is a subsidiary of the Bimantara Group controlled by Bambang Trihatmodjo, President Soeharto's second son."

However, a bribe for Suharto's second son was really nothing new to the Clinton administration in 1996. Previously released documents from the U.S. Commerce Dept. clearly show that the crown jewel of Indonesian power, the Paiton Swasta I project, is actually filled with Suharto corruption.

The declassified State Dept. documents highlight that the Paiton I electric project was of extreme importance to the former member of the Clinton administration. The U.S. Commerce Dept. documents also state that "Warren Christopher is on Edison Mission's board of directors."

"Paiton Energy President Ronald Landry provided the IPP's (independent power producers) with an overview of former Secretary of State Warren Christopher's visit to Indonesia," states a U.S. embassy cable from 1998.

"Mr. Christopher, representing Edison International's board, was here to launch a proposal."

According to Paiton CEO Landry, Christopher "spoke on behalf of the IPP's" when he said that any solution reached with Indonesia must:

"-Be a 'Win-Win' solution and not 'embarrass' Indonesia; --

Protect the USG, other government agencies and the financial community; -- Maintain debt coverage and the sanctity of the contract-Focus on financial rather than legal issues."

In 1998, the Indonesian power company PLN lost almost a billion dollars.

PLN announced it would pay the independent power producers, not in dollars as originally contracted, but in the poorly valued Indonesian Rupiah. The total amount of foreign investments sunk into the Indonesian power sector was over $10 billion.

Moreover, the question of whether Indonesia can pay for Clinton and Suharto corruption is an invalid one. According to the State Dept., "The current selling price is U.S. 2 cents per kwh and it needs to be increased to U.S. 9 cents per kwh just to break even... (World Bank advisors now estimate that nothing less than a 200 percent tariff increase is needed)."

In addition, there are serious issues to consider other than corruption, collusion and nepotism or "KKN". The Dieng Indonesian geothermal project, being constructed by CALENERGY, is also a serious environmental problem.

In July 1998, Calenergy CEO Don O'Shei told State Dept. officials that some wells at the "Dieng" geothermal power project "are temporarily plugged" and "would have to be permanently sealed to prevent environmental problems."

Indonesian geothermal power is based on super-heated steam from volcanic activity underground much like "Old Faithful" in Yellowstone National Park. The steam is tapped by drilling a series of wells into the geyser.

However, that steam also contains high amounts of deadly sulfuric acid which can pollute the air and water. At the Deing power plant many of the wells needed to be plugged. The cable also noted that Calenergy CEO O'Shei said, "this is a costly procedure."

O'Shei also had a long statement on corruption. Curiously, the State Dept. blacked out O'Shei's comments on "KKN" (corruption, collusion and nepotism) involving "Calenergy's partner in Dieng." Thus, Calenergy's information on "KKN" with their "partner" was withheld for "national security" or "foreign relations" reasons.

Inronically, the partners of Calenergy turned out to be a group of ex-Indonesian military officers. Again, connections to the Suharto dictatoship played a key role in the construction of a U.S. backed power plant. Moreover, Calenergy was not above more direct access to the Suharto regime. For example, documents previously obtained from the U.S. Commerce Dept. state "Sigit" Harjojudato, Suharto's oldest son, was Calenergy's partner in the Bali geothermal plant.

In a December 1998 article published in the Wall Street Journal, Calenergy officials denied they knew that Suharto's son was their partner. Yet, Mr. O'Shei's comments on "KKN" with their "partner" in July 1998, prior to the blanket denial in December 1998, illustrates that at least the Calenergy CEO was aware of Sigit's slice of Dieng.

The documents show that both Indonesia and America have been the victims of a Clinton sponsored crime wave. The surreal comments on one "crony" after another becoming "unwanted partners" while doing dirty deals, were complied by two U.S. ambassadors to Indonesia; former Ambassador Barry and Clinton appointee, J. Stapleton Roy.

The State Dept. documents tell a offensive, scandalous and ugly story of greed and corruption. They also tell the unvarished truth, an accurate self-portrait painted by the Clinton/Gore administration.

According to the Indonesian Financial Control and Development Agency (BPKP), the Clinton administration documents detail "corruption, collusion and nepotism" at the Power Generating Project Paiton I (PLTU), located in East Java.

The Executive Director of the Indonesian state power company PT PLN confirmed that a report was prepared by the Indonesian government on the criminal activity.

"Yes, it's true," stated Director Tung Gono. "We have asked BPKP to look into two items. First, concerning a cluster of 27 private power projects, second, concerning 27 project implementations. The report has just come in."

Some 14 officials, who handled the agreement at the time, are now suspected of facilitating or providing special treatment to an economic unit connected to the power plant.

Despite the overwhelming evidence of criminal activity, according to Paiton's president Ronald Landry, the U.S. controlled power company preferred to resolve the issue through negotiation.

"Unfortunately, it has become clear to us by PLN's pursuit of this undeserving suit that PLN is not sincerely interested in negotiation," said Landry in a December 1999 press announcement.

The announcement of a criminal investigation into the Paiton project came after the Central Jakarta district court ruled that it had jurisdiction to examine the legality of the purchase contract between state electricity company PT PLN and independent power producer PT Paiton Energy.

The Indonesian court turned down Paiton's proposition that the court did not have the right to examine the case, and that international arbitration should settle the matter. Paiton had argued that the purchase agreements signed by both parties in 1994 required all disputes be resolved through international arbitration in Stockholm.

Indonesian legal counsel, Adnan Buyung Nasution, argued that the contract was void ab initio or "void from the beginning."

Buyung stated that the contracts were invalid and based on the "corrupt, collusive and nepotistic practices associated with the administration of former president Suharto."

Buyung said that despite the stipulation that all disputes would be resolved through an arbitration court, the contract contained the requirement that Paiton was subject to Indonesian laws.

The Paiton company began the arbitration litigation after the Indonesian state run electric company PLN filed suit in the Central Jakarta court in 1999. Paiton dropped the proceedings after the court ordered it to desist from pursuing the litigation. The Indonesian court threatened Paiton with a $600 million penalty if it did not comply with the ruling.

Paiton's lawyer, Frans Hendra Winarta, said the court's ruling would discourage foreign investors from investing in the country.

"Paiton Energy is deeply disappointed by the decision," Frans said in a statement for the press.

However, not everyone was disappointed in the court's decision.

"It is a landmark decision," stated PLN president Adhi Satriya.

The connection between Paiton and Moctar Riady, a major figure in the DNC campaign finance scandals, are clearly documented through PT bank LIPPO. The leader of the U.S. project in the Paiton power plant, Mission Energy, was a partner of Indonesia's Lippo group. The Lippo group is a consortium, part owned by billionaire Moctar Riady.

PT Lippo also provided financing to "bother-in-law" Hashim for his coal mining company that supplies Paiton. Hashim is himself a key figure. While serving as the minister for mines under Suharto, Hashim also managed to purchase the world's only "low sulfur" coal mine. His financial backers include Moctar Riady's PT Lippo and, his sister-in-law, Prawabo.

Hashim and Moctar Riady both found themselves with a global monopoly thanks to Bill Clinton's executive order for the 1.7 million-acre Grand Staircase-Escalante National Monument in Utah, over the only other known "low sulfur" deposit.

In an April 2000 response to the legal request, the Export-Import Bank refused to release much of their documentation on the grounds of "confidential business information" and "internal government communications."

One document that was partially released by the Export-Import Bank is a heavily blacked out 1997 email on an Indonesian "tax holiday", titled "TPPI Briefing."

"The granting of this tax holiday does not represent a 'special' government support," states the email. "But is a standard support available for capital intensive projects in priority sectors of development," states the email.

Another document withheld in part is a letter from Takaya Naito, Director of the Export-Import Bank of Japan.

"I would like to inform you that we have issued a letter supporting the project to P.T. Paiton Energy," wrote Naito to several U.S. and Indonesian backers of the power project.

The Export-Import Bank materials are based on a November 1994 meeting in Jakarta Indonesia, attended by President Clinton and Commerce Secretary Ron Brown. The 1994 meeting ended with the signing of several U.S. power contracts that included Indonesian President Suharto and his relatives as business partners.

Billions of U.S. tax dollars were poured into twenty-six different electric power projects by the Clinton administration. Unfortunately, even the Clinton administration noted that Indonesia only needed one power plant.

One partly blacked out cable from the State Department is titled "on power projects, corruption, draft laws." The December 1998 cable, a discussion between Ambassador Roy and an individual whose name was withheld, states that the individual "stressed that solutions to the problem must be simple to convince 'the people' that corruption, collusion and nepotism ('KKN') are being dealt with properly."

Curiously, many secrets still surround the Edison coal fired power plant in east Java. The U.S. State Department maintains that some information on Pation must remain classified.

"The information in the one document withheld in full and in the deleted portions of the sixteen other documents withheld in part is properly classified in accordance with Executive Order 12958 (National Security Information) despite the passage of time. It's release reasonably could be expected to cause damage to the national security of the United States," wrote Ambassador Francis McNamara in November 2000.

The corrupt power deals did not end with Edison International and the Paiton Power project. The ongoing investigation into the failure of Enron has led directly to Indonesia and the corrupt Clinton administration.

One such Enron deal pushed by the Clinton White House was an exclusive power plant project with the son of Indonesian dictator Suharto - Bambang Trihatmodjo.

Bambang is Suharto's second son and at one point he was worth over $3 billion. The 48-year-old Bambang also owns an $8 million penthouse in Singapore and a $12 million mansion in an exclusive neighborhood of Los Angeles, two doors down from rock star Rod Stewart.

Starting in 1994, Enron invested $25 million into a deal for the first natural gas-fired power plant in Pasuruan, East Java. According to Commerce Dept. documents, Enron's partner in the planned $525 million project was Bambang Trihatmodjo.

P.T. East Java Power Corp., which was then 50.1 percent owned by Enron, wanted to conclude a deal for a 500 megawatt power plant in East Java, Indonesia. The 20-year deal was later signed by Enron with P.T. PLN Persero (PLN), Indonesia's state-owned electric utility, which agreed to purchase the power from the natural-gas-fired plant.

According to Enron, the natural gas for the project was to be provided by Pertamina, Indonesia's state-owned oil and gas company. Commerce Department documents noted that Pertamina stalled the project with excessive demands for gas prices.

"Enron is now engaged with Pertamina over access to natural gas. These discussions may prove difficult," states a 1994 Commerce Department advocacy document.

"Enron is registered for OPIC (Overseas Private Investment Corporation) insurance," states the document, noting that the giant corporation obtained U.S. taxpayer-backed insurance if the Indonesian deal fell apart.

Despite the clear evidence of Suharto corruption, Ron Brown personally sought approval for the Enron electric power plant. According to a personal letter directed to the Indonesian Minister for Trade and Industry, Brown endorsed Enron deals for two gas fired power plants with the corrupt Suharto regime.

"Enron power, a world renowned private power developer, is in the final stages of negotiating two combined cycle, gas turbine power projects," wrote Brown in his 1995 letter.

"The first, a 500 MW plant in East Java, should begin commercial power generation by the end of 1997 if it can promptly negotiate a gas supply Memorandum of Understanding with Pertamina. The other project, a smaller plant in East Kalimantan, also awaits a gas supply agreement."

"I urge you to give full consideration to the proposals," concluded Brown to the Indonesian minister. In October 1995, Brown wrote another letter, this time to Hartarto Sastrosurarto, Indonesia's Coordinating Minister for Trade and Industry, pressing him to conclude Enron's power plant deal.

"I would like to bring to your attention a number of projects involving American companies which seem to be stalled, including several independent power projects. These projects include the Tarahan power project, which involves Southern Electric; the gas powered projects in East Java and East Kalimantan, which involves Enron," wrote Brown.

"Your support for prompt resolution of the remaining issues associated with each of these projects would be most appreciated," concluded Brown.

In addition, the Clinton administration enlisted the State Department to strong arm the Indonesians to accept the power plant deal. In a March 1995 memo from the American embassy in Jakarta, U.S. officials pressed the Indonesians to conclude the contracts for Enron.

"Enron Corp. continues to negotiate with the relevant authorities regarding availability and price of gas supply," states the embassy memo. "Embassy continues to raise the issue of deregulation of the gas supply system with Pertamina."

By September 1997, Enron announced the Indonesian power deal was nearly complete. According to Enron, it had signed an agreement to acquire natural gas for its 500-megawatt power plant under development in East Java Indonesia. The 20-year supply agreement was signed with Pertamina, Indonesia's state owned oil and gas company.

"This is one of the last critical steps before the East Java project can achieve financial close and commence construction," said Rebecca P. Mark, chairman and CEO of Enron International.

"We expect the power plant to be operational in early 2000," said Mark.

On Nov. 18, 1996, Enron CEO Ken Lay announced that the deal with Suharto was complete. According to Enron's public statement, the U.S.-led energy company had finally won the East Java Power project.

"Enron is extremely pleased to reach this crucial step in this project," stated Kenneth L. Lay on the successful conclusion of the Java power deal, Enron chairman and CEO.

"Enron's strong experience in developing natural gas-fired plants makes this project ideal for Enron, our partners and our customer."

Although, Enron's partner in East Java was Suharto's son, the gas supply contract points directly toward Beijing. The gas sold by Pertamina was to be produced under a contract with Mobil Madura Strait Inc. and Husky Oil Ltd. from the Madura field offshore of East Java in the Madura Strait.

Canadian based Husky Oil is part owned by Chinese billionaire Li Kashing. Billionaire Li Kashing is currently in business with the Chinese army and reportedly has very close links to Beijing's military intelligence.

By 1997 the Indonesian economy collapsed and Suharto was over-thrown. The resulting economic mess forced Indonesia to default on its payments for the Enron power plants. These developments caused Standard & Poor's to downgrade Enron's ratings to triple "B" minus.

The Enron power project was suspended in September 1997, after the power purchase agreement had been signed and the gas contract was completed with the state owned gas supplier Pertamina. Enron officials objected to the suspension because the final financial close on the power plant was reported to be only days away.

PLN, the state owned Indonesian electric utility, said that the project was no longer viable because electricity demand did not justify it and the tariffs were unrealistically high.

Despite the loss, the U.S. taxpayer using its insurance obtained through the World Bank Multilateral Investment Guarantee Agency paid off Enron.

"In June of this year, MIGA paid $15 million to Enron Java Power Co. for its investment in P.T. East Java Power Corporation in Indonesia," states the 2000 official public release from the World Bank.

"The venture was one of many suspended by the presidential decree of September 20, 1997, issued in response to the country's economic crisis," noted MIGA officials.

However, after heavy World Bank pressure, the Indonesian government agreed to pay the $15 million back to MIGA. Initially the World Bank suspended further guarantees of investments in the country until the government agreed to reimburse MIGA the amount paid to Enron. Discussions on the payout took more than a year, and the amount represented compensation for Enron's preparatory work done on the project, which was cancelled before construction began. Enron reportedly paid Suharto's son Bambang the $25 million in order to lay the groundwork for the project.

According to documents obtained from the U.S. Commerce Dept., the Clinton administration was keenly aware that Suharto's son was being cut in on various U.S. backed power deals including Enron's Pasuruan gas plant. In fact, the warnings of corruption came directly from the U.S. Ambassador in Jakarta.

"Java Power Company has obtained a USD 1.7 billion financing package for its 2 X 610 coal fired Paiton Swasta II power plant," states a 1996 cable from then U.S. ambassador Barry.

"Java Power Company is 50 percent owned by Siemens Power, 35 percent Powergen PLC of the UK and 15 percent by PT Bumiperitwi Tatapradipta. The latter is a subsidiary of the Bimantara Group controlled by Bambang Trihatmodjo, President Soeharto's second son."

Bambang was not only in business with Siemens and Enron but also had an exclusive multi-million power plant deal with Duke Energy Corp., a no-cut satellite contract with Hughes Space and an Indonesian government enforced monopoly trash contract with Waste Management. Bambang's corruption is so well known that even the U.S. Federal Reserve has published information on him.

"Shareholders of the 16 insolvent banks scheduled to be closed in December in Indonesia included several members of the former Royal family, relatives of the President, the brother of an industrialist convicted of bank fraud, and the former head of the state oil company, Pertamina, who was dismissed for unauthorized borrowing of $10 billion," noted a Federal Reserve report on bank fraud.

"Bambang Trihatmodjo, second son of Suharto, the President of Indonesia, admitted that his bank had broken the legal lending limit with loans to the Chandra Asri petrochemical plant, which he and other shareholders owned. He said 'We admit we broke the legal lending limit.... But to be fair 90% of other Indonesian banks did the same.'"

The Clinton administration pursued Indonesia even after Suharto left office. Suharto's hand picked replacement was his Vice President B.J. Habibie. According to his official Clinton White House intelligence report, Indonesian President B.J. Habibie was "the type of official needed today in developing countries."

The declassified documents show Habibie specifically requested to see "Vice President Gore, Secretary of State Christopher, Secretary of Energy O'Leary, National Economic Council Chairman Rubin and the White House Director of Science Technology Policy Gibbons."

The reports are part of a series of documents obtained from the U.S. Commerce Department using the Freedom of Information Act.

The documents include allegations that Clinton officials knew of "corruption, collusion and nepotism" inside U.S. funded projects for Indonesia. The documents show that U.S. taxpayer dollars were used to bribe Suharto relatives and "crony" officials to obtain contracts.

The newly declassified intelligence reports include full details on Habibie's life before he took over Indonesia as Suharto's hand picked successor. The documents were included in a 1993
briefing package given to Mission Energy Corp.

Habibie's intelligence report reveals that he worked as an engineer in Germany for Messerschmitt, and as Indonesian Technology Minister, wanted to produce "7,000 megawatts of
commercial nuclear power by the early 21st century."

Furthermore, the intelligence report noted "A brother, Jusuf Effendy (J.E.) Habibie, heads the Communications Ministry's directorate general for sea communications".

Habibie's report is identical in format to the official Clinton White House reports on the entire communist Chinese leadership which were provided by an unspecified "intelligence agency". In
order to obtain the intelligence reports, this reporter had to take the Commerce Dept. to Federal Court for illegally withholding the documents.

The intelligence reports were given by the Clinton White House to corporate heads who accompanied Ron Brown on trade missions to the far east. The CEOs who received the intelligence reports included DNC donors such as Loral CEO Bernard Schwartz, Hughes CEO Michael Armstrong, investment banker Sanford Robertson and Mission Energy CEO John Bryson.

According to the official U.S. intelligence report, Bacharuddin Jusuf Habibie was picked by Suharto to be President and Director of the "Indonesian Aircraft Industry."

Habibie also headed Suharto's "Agency for Strategic Industries", placing him in charge "10 state-owned industrial firms", including state owned PT Telkon, Indonesia's satellite TV system.

In 1994 the U.S. and France were competing to orbit the Indonesian Palapa C TV satellite. A previously released, November 1, 1994 Dept. of Commerce report accuses France of bribing the Suharto government in the fierce trade war between the U.S. and France over satellite launches for Indonesia.

The Commerce document noted, "There are also allegations that the French have paid 'incentive money' to the Indonesians, but this cannot be confirmed."

The Commerce document states "General Dynamics is bidding to provide launch services for the
new Palapa C satellite. The package to build and launch the third generation satellite is worth
$300 million."

"The French Government in an effort to break a 20 year American monopoly on Indonesian launches, has been quite open in the support for the Ariannespace launch program. Last month several high level French Government officials called on GOI officials to press their case."

The document, a 1993 briefing memo for a Commerce Dept. meeting with Indonesian advisor William Hollinger, includes allegations the French were also attempting to bribe the Suharto regime. Suharto, however, had other ideas for the satellite.

According to the Commerce document, "Hughes and General Electric both submitted bids ... Hughes now appears to have the edge, but is dependent upon an earlier EXIM financing commitment, which was given while the satellite was solely owned by the GOI (Government of Indonesia). In the past month the project was spun off into a new public/private venture."

The Palapa C deal concerned the Clinton administration since Michael Armstrong, Hughes CEO, was close to President Clinton and donated money to the DNC.

"The General Dynamics Atlas launch vehicle appears to have the technical and cost edge over Ariane," states the memo. "But the Europeans hope to gain the advantage through political pressure, 'FREEBIES' and financing."

The Clinton administration knew of the French "freebies" and "incentive money". Furthermore, they also knew about Suharto's real plan for the Palapa C satellite.

"We may have trouble coming up with a better financing offer through EXIM since the State owned PT Telkon has just transferred the satellite business to a new public/private joint
venture, PT Satelindo. The majority private interest in Satelindo is controlled by Bimantara, a 'FIRST FAMILY FIRM'."

In 1993, Habibie transferred control from the Indonesian government to the new "private" venture. "Private", of course, meant privately owned by Suharto and his "first family". Thus,
the Indonesian dictator stole an entire satellite.

Yet, Clinton officials did not stand idly by while Suharto raided the space-based assets of his impoverished nation. The Clinton/Gore administration acted quickly to the allegations that the French were bribing Suharto by upping the ante with U.S. taxpayer money and a letter backing the deal from Ron Brown.

"Commerce strongly endorses the application," states the 1993 memo. "And at the request of the Indonesia desk, IEP and TD/Aerospace are drafting a Secretarial letter of support for General Dynamics. Underscore USG interest in General Dynamics winning the rights to build and launch Indonesia's Palapa C satellite."

In the end, Clinton got the donations from Hughes CEO Armstrong, while the governments of Indonesia, France and the United States grew a little more corrupt and Suharto got his satellite,
complete with CNN and pay-per-view TV.

Of course, one would think the Clinton/Gore connection to Habibie and Suharto should make the news. However, you will not see this story on CNN nor read about it in Time magazine... And
the reason for such poor news coverage may surprise you.

According to a recently discovered letter from the personal files of Ron Brown, Time-Warner sought and obtained Secretary Brown's help in an exclusive "recording" deal with Indonesia.

In 1995, Ron Brown wrote a letter to Hartarto Sastrosurarto, Indonesian Minister for Trade and Industry, "we would welcome the conclusion of the negotiations on phase II of the auxiliary
dredging equipment project with Ellicott Machine Corporation and on Time Warner's investment in Indonesia's recording sector."

Clearly, CNN reporting the truth might affect Ted Turner's bottom line more than his politics. It is no surprise that CNN has picked up the White House spin, portraying Habibie, a powerful Suharto "crony", as an innocent bystander in the East Timor genocide.

Much has been said recently about "the truth" from former Clinton officials. The truth is that Clinton quietly considered Habibie to be "the type of official needed today in developing countries." The truth about Bill Clinton is a ugly story of "corruption, collusion and nepotism."

PAITON PROJECT

U.S. Supplier:	Mission Energy Co.
Purchaser:	P.T. Paiton Energy Co.
Guaranteed Lender:	Mission Energy, GE and Mitsui Equity; loans from Eximbank, ADB, commercial banks
Total amount of Contract:	$2.5 billion
Amount of U.S. Content:	$800 million
Amount of Exim Financing:	$500-800 million
Description of Project:	2x600 MW coal-fired, base-load, Build-Own-Operate power plant
Description of U.S. content:	Flour Daniel will lead construction, GE will supply turbines and boilers.
Location of Plant from which sourced:	Both will source their inputs in - U.S. content will be the United States,
Status of Project in Exim:	
Obstacles to Project Completion:	Uncertainty of obtaining the Eximbank financing.
Type of document to be signed:	MOU, which mentions a draft contract and is subject to financial closing and agreement on commercial themes of individual equipment contract.
First Family Involvement:	ADB had raised concern about first family involvement during its consideration of the $50 million financial portion.
Environmental Concerns:	
Labor check:	OGC is conducting
Congressional Concern:	

2x600 MW, coal-fired, base load, Build-Own Operate Power plant proposed by a consortium comprised of Mission Energy, GE, Mitsui and PT Batu Hitam Perkasa.

1997-1998 time frame. The recently announced "crash program" to construct three 500 MW, gas-fired, combined cycle power plants (granted sans official tenders) has caused some to doubt that either the concept of IPP per se or the Mission Energy consortium will be successful. Negotiations are apparently set to resume in September.
Groundbreaking ceremonies were held in September.

It has been reported that the ADB has some reservations about the project. The project has yet to be presented to ADB's board for approval.
OPIC has committed $200 million in insurance.

9/30 - Ambassador Barry stated that the project is facing two problems; (i) the ADB financing may cave-in, and (ii) EXIM financing. Regarding ADB, technical questions have been satisfied, but ADB is skiddish about involvement of Indonesia's first family (a minority shareholder is married to Pres. Suharto's daughter). Ambassador Barry has been working with Executive Director Linda Yang, at the ADB who is "doing all she can". Regarding Exim, Barry is concerned that Exim has not hired a financial advisor or legal advisor for the project. GE hopes that Exim will immediately select these advisors and allow them to conduct the due diligence review.

Daitan Bank

Several parties are concerned with the fate of this project--Amb.
Barry, ███ and Peter Jasek. Amb. Barry stated that the project
is facing a potential collapse because of two problems: (i) the
ADB financing may cave-in, and (ii) EXIM is quite slow.
Regarding ADB, technical questions have been satisfied, but ADB
is skittish about involvement of Indonesia's first family (a
minority shareholder is married to Pres. Suharto's daughter).
Barry has been working with Exec. Dir. Linda Yang, who is "doing
all she can." GE wants to emphasize the role of Mitsui in the
project to ADB's president who is Japanese. Regarding EXIM,
Barry said that he called Ken Brody on 9/27 to discuss the
project because GE is concerned that EXIM has not hired financial
advisors for the project yet (although Barry understands that the
advisors will be appointed on Monday or Tuesday of next week).
Today, Bob LaRussa, Paul Rosenberg and I sent an E-mail to Jeff
Garten, Ray Vickery and Lauri Fitz-Pegado urging Jeff to
communicate to Ken Brody the need for Brody to contact Amb. Barry
on this project immediately. We understand that the financial
advisor is suppose ███████████████████ and the legal advisor is
supposed to be, ███████████████████ hopes that EXIM will let these
advisors go ahead and conduct the due diligence review.

Although the ADB financing is only $50 million, GE views the ADB
component to be important because it has a long-term interest in
having a multinational bank support the project. Furthermore, if
ADB rejected financing, EXIM and the commercial banks involved in

10. (SBU) COMMENTING ON CORRUPTION. COLLUSION AND NEPOTISM (KKN). ENDRO SAID THAT IN THE PAST THERE WAS NO SEPARATION BETWEEN "POWER" (NOT ELECTRIC BUT FORMER FIRST FAMILY POWER) AND BUSINESS. "ALL THE IPP'S HAVE A RELATION WITH POWER. AND IT IS STILL GOING ON." ADDED ENDRO. ENDRO CONTENDED THAT IN ONE CASE CALENERGY IS "VIOLATING PROFESSIONAL ETHICS" BY NOT COMPLYING WITH THE PPA. WHICH CALLS FOR THE INSTALLATION OF SULFUR REMOVAL EQUIPMENT IN THE DIENG GEOTHERMAL PLANT. COMMENT: IN HIS REMARKS ALLEGING CONTINUED OUTSIDE INFLUENCE FROM "POWER" CENTERS. ENDRO APPEARED TO BE REFERRING TO INTENSIFIED IPP LOBBYING WITH GOI OFFICIALS. END COMMENT.

UNCLASSIFIED

(C-10)

? 31 (d)

CONFIDENTIAL   PTQ0129

PAGE 01   JAKART 06365 01 OF 03 141112Z
ACTION EAP-01

INFO   LOG-00   ACDA-08 ACDE-00 AID-00   ACQ-01   CEA-01   CIAE-00
       CTME-00 DINT-00 DODE-00 SRPP-00 DS-00   EB-00   EUR-01
       EXIM-01 E-00   FBIE-00 FRB-00   H-01   TEDE-00 INR-00
       ITC-01   LAB-01   L-01   ADS-00   NSAE-00 NSCE-00 OES-01
       OMB-01   OPIC-01 PM-00   PRS-00   SP-00   SSO-00   SS-00
       STR-00   USIE-00 EPAE-00 PMB-00   DSCC-00 DRL-02   G-00
       NFAT-00 SAS-00   /022W
       ------------------8C71A9 141157Z /38
R 141033Z DEC 98
FM AMEMBASSY JAKARTA
TO SECSTATE WASHDC 5062
INFO OPEC COLLECTIVE
AMEMBASSY LONDON
AMEMBASSY TOKYO
AMEMBASSY SINGAPORE
AMEMBASSY KUALA LUMPUR
AMEMBASSY CANBERRA
DEPTTREAS WASHDC
USDOC WASHDC
USDOE WASHDC

Dept. of State, RPS/IPS, Margaret P. Grafeld, Dir.
( ) Release (X) Excise ( ) Deny (X) Declassify
Date 3/17/05   Exemption _____

C O N F I D E N T I A L SECTION 01 OF 03 JAKARTA 006365

DEPT FOR EAP/PIMPS, EB/IFD, EB/IEP, EB/ESC/ICD, INR/IL,
L, INR/B

TREASURY FOR OASIA/INA-SAEGER AND REDIFER, GI/GELPERN
                   CONFIDENTIAL

PAGE 02   JAKART 06365 01 OF 03 141112Z

COMMERCE FOR 4430/MIKALIS

USDOE FOR PO-72

PASS EXIM FOR IMAN AND O'BOYLE

PASS OPIC FOR MAHAFFEY AND BRACEY

E.O. 12958: DECL: 12/14/16
TAGS: EPET, ENRG, EINV, PINR, ID

UNCLASSIFIED

UNCLASSIFIED

SUBJECT: ON POWER PROJECTS,
CORRUPTION, DRAFT LAWS AND THE NEW DIRECTOR OF PERTAMINA   *B1*

REF: (A) JAKARTA 6338 (PERTAMINA AND CORRUPTION)
        (B) JAKARTA 6318 (NEW HEAD OF PERTAMINA)
        (C) JAKARTA 6164 (DRAFT OIL AND GAS LAW)
        (D) JAKARTA 6043 (MEETING WITH PLN HEAD)

1. (U) CLASSIFIED BY AMB. J. STAPLETON ROY; REASON
1.5(D)

2. (C) SUMMARY: IN A DECEMBER 14 MEETING WITH THE
AMBASSADOR,[   ] SAID   *B1*
THAT NEGOTIATIONS WITH THE INDEPENDENT POWER PRODUCERS
(IPP'S) WILL BEGIN IN EARLY FEBRUARY, AND STRESSED THAT
SOLUTIONS TO THE PROBLEM MUST BE SIMPLE TO CONVINCE "THE
PEOPLE" THAT CORRUPTION, COLLUSION AND NEPOTISM ("KKN")   *B1*
ARE BEING DEALT WITH PROPERLY. [   ] SAID
THAT HE EXPECTS THE DRAFT OIL AND GAS LAW WILL BE
REVIEWED BY THE INDONESIAN PARLIAMENT BY JANUARY. A NEW
                      CONFIDENTIAL

PAGE 03   JAKART 06365 01 OF 03 141112Z
LAW ON REDISTRIBUTING GOVERNMENT REVENUES FROM THE OIL,
GAS AND
MINING SECTORS MAY ALSO BE IMPLEMENTED NEXT YEAR.   *B1*
[   ]
[   ] END SUMMARY.

IPP NEGOTIATIONS: "NOT UNTIL FEBRUARY"
----

3. (C) [   ] SAID THAT NEGOTIATIONS WITH THE   *B1*
IPP'S WILL BEGIN IN FEBRUARY, NOT JANUARY AS EARLIER
STATED BY PLN PRESIDENT DIRECTOR ADHI SATRIYA (REF D).
[   ] STATED THAT THE GOI IS IN THE PROCESS OF   *B1*
DEVELOPING A GENERAL STRATEGY/APPROACH FOR DEALING WITH
ALL THE IPP'S. SPECIFICALLY ON PAITON I,[   ]
[   ] HINTED THAT THE RESCHEDULING PLAN PRESENTED BY   *B1*
EDISON MISSION ENERGY EXECUTIVES WAS "TOO COMPLICATED".
HE ADDED THAT "IT HAS TO BE SIMPLE IN ORDER THAT I CAN
EXPLAIN IT TO THE PEOPLE. THE PUBLIC THINKS THAT ALL
IPP'S ARE LINKED TO KKN, SO I NEED TO HAVE A SIMPLE PLAN
TO SELL TO THEM."

4. (C) ON PLN REDUCED RUPIAH PAYMENTS TO OPERATING

UNCLASSIFIED

P'S UNOCAL AND PT ENERGY SENGKANG (U.S. EL PASO
ENERGY). _____ SAID THAT HE IS NOT DEALING
DIRECTLY WITH PAYMENT PROBLEMS. HE REPEATED PLN
PRESIDENT DIRECTOR SATRIYA'S JUSTIFICATION FOR REDUCED
PAYMENTS -- THAT PLN IS SAVING THE FUNDS BECAUSE IT IS
NOT CERTAIN HOW MUCH IT WILL RECEIVE TO COVER OPERATING
EXPENSES IN THE 1999/2000 STATE BUDGET.

B1

B1

CONFIDENTIAL

PAGE 04   JAKART 06365 01 OF 03 141112Z
[_____] SAID THAT HE HAD BEEN VISITED BY UNOCAL
EXECUTIVES ON THIS MATTER AND THAT A CONFIDENTIAL
SOLUTION WAS BEING DISCUSSED.

B1

5. (C) [_____] SAID THAT HE HAD DISCUSSED WITH
PLN OPIC'S PROPOSAL TO HAVE CALENERGY AND PLN MEET
OUTSIDE OF THE ARBITRATION PROCEEDINGS OVER THE FIRM'S
DIENG AND PATUHA GEOTHERMAL PLANTS. HE SAID, "WE HAVE
TO GIVE A SIGNAL THAT AN OUT-OF-COURT SETTLEMENT IS
PREFERABLE."

B1

KKN: "PUBLIC OPINION IS AGAINST US ON THIS ISSUE"
----

6. (C) [_____] SAID THAT HE DID NOT "HAVE ANY
SPECIAL INFORMATION" ABOUT AMERICAN COMPANY INVOLVEMENT
WITH KKN. HOWEVER, HE DESCRIBED PAITON'S U.S. 8 CENTS
PER KILOWATT TARIFF AS "SUSPICIOUS".
STATED, HOWEVER, THAT HE WILL "BE CAREFUL" WITH
UNSUPPORTED CLAIMS AND INQUIRED ABOUT THE FREEPORT CASE.
_____ SAID, "THE PUBLIC IS AGAINST ME ON THIS
ISSUE (I.E., FREEPORT) SO WE NEED TO RESPOND
TECHNICALLY."

B1

B1

B1

CONFIDENTIAL

<< END OF DOCUMENT >>

CONFIDENTIAL   PTQ0131

PAGE 01   JAKART 06365 02 OF 03 141112Z
ACTION EAP-01

INFO   LOG-00   ACDA-08   ACDE-00   AID-00   ACQ-01   CEA-01   CIAE-00
       CTME-00   DINT-00   DODE-00   SRPP-00   DS-00   EB-00   EUR-01
       EXIM-01   E-00   FBIE-00   FRB-00   H-01   TEDE-00   INR-00
       IO-00   ITC-01   LAB-01   L-01   ADS-00   NSAE-00   NSCE-00

DEALING WITH "UNWANTED" PARTNERS
---

19. (C) SENGKANG SAID THAT A SENIOR EL PASO
INTERNATIONAL EXECUTIVE WAS MISQUOTED IN THE PRESS
RECENTLY SAYING THAT SENGKANG WAS "BUYING OUT" ITS
PARTNER FORMER PRESIDENT SOEHARTO'S DAUGHTER SITI
HARDIYANTI RUKMANA ("TUTUT"). TUTUT HOLDS TWO AND ONE
HALF PERCENT IN PT TRIHASRA SARANA, WHICH HAS A 5
PERCENT SHARE IN PT ENERGI SENGKANG. ACCORDING TO
SENGKANG, TUTUT DOES NOT INTEND TO DIVEST FROM THE
PROJECT AT THIS TIME.

20. (C) UNOCAL EXECUTIVES TOLD RESOURCES OFFICER THAT
THE FIRM IS CLOSE TO REACHING A DEAL WITH ITS PARTNER,
PT NUSAMBA (CONTROLLED BY FORMER PRESIDENT SOEHARTO
CRONY BOB HASAN) TO SEVER TIES IN TWO PRODUCTION SHARING
CONTRACTS (PSC) IN EAST KALIMANTAN AND EAST JAVA. PT
PRAMA GEOPOWER (NUSAMBA) HAS TEN PERCENT SHARES IN THE
GUNUNG SALAK AND SARULLA GEOTHERMAL PROJECTS. AT PLN'S
INSISTENCE, UNOCAL GEOTHERMAL WAS ASKED TO TAKE AN "IN-
COUNTRY" PARTNER IN 1995. ACCORDING TO UNOCAL, NUSAMBA
PUT USD 20 MILLION INTO GUNUNG SALAK, AND IT WOULD BE
DIFFICULT, DUE TO THE FINANCIAL STRUCTURING OF THE DEAL,
TO UNDO THE PARTNERSHIP.
ROY

BT
#5736

7

THE RED BILLIONAIRE

The best victory is when the opponent surrenders of its own accord.
Cao Cao The Art of War

In September 1998, the Commerce Department was forced by legal action to release documents from the late Secretary Ron Brown. The Clinton White House was illegally withholding the documents from public release. The newly released materials include the detailed biographies of the entire Chinese communist leadership.

The detailed dossiers were given to DNC donors LORAL CEO Bernard Schwartz and investment millionaire Sanford Robertson by the Clinton White House just prior to their August 1994 trade trip to China with Brown.

Curiously, the briefing package also included the detailed bio of a civilian who is not even a Chinese citizen - Hong Kong billionaire Li Ka-Shing. According to FORBES, Li Ka-Shing is the fifteenth richest man in the world. Li is not a red Chinese government official nor is Li a member of any military service.

Yet, a detailed dossier on Li Ka-Shing was included along with Chinese President Jiang Zemin, foreign minister Li Peng and other top communist officials.

Li Ka-Shing's publicly traded companies account for business operations of somewhere between one-quarter to one-third of stock market capitalization of the Hong Kong stock market. Li Ka-Shing's rags-to-riches story is summarized in countless books and articles that use his story to explain his phenomenal wealth and power. The Hong Kong press often refers to him as "Superman" and "Mr. Money."

Li came to Hong Kong from Chiu chow as a boy to study. Li's father died soon after the Japanese invasion of Hong Kong, forcing him to leave school in order to support his mother and the rest of the family.

Li started his own career as a plastic comb salesman in the late 1950s. Li actually began building his empire by starting a plastic flower factory.

Today, Li Ka-Shing owns the huge shipping firm Hutchison Whampoa Ltd. and the giant Far East investment firm Cheong Kong Holdings. According to the 1994 Clinton supplied dossier - Li has "significant economic and political ties to China" including investments in a "power station, a highway construction project and a large contribution to Shantou University."

Li Ka-Shing also had legal troubles and a known criminal record. Li, according to the White House documents, was "found guilty of insider trading after a widely publicized trial in 1984; he was not punished by the courts."

According to the White House, Li was also a "member of the boards of directors of the China International Trust and Investment Corporation (CITIC)." In fact, Li helped form CITIC, which he linked to the communist government in Beijing.

In 1979 communist officials in Beijing appointed Li, along with other prominent Hong Kong merchants Henry Fok and Wong Foon Shing to run the CITIC. Li Ka-Shing, and Macau casino shareholder Henry Fok formed CITIC in 1979 with Beijing's blessing. Li started the bank with an initial investment of $5 million. CITIC now has global assets totaling over $21 billion, with 30 subsidiaries in China and around the world including Canada and the U.S.

Li Ka-Shing made CITIC the bank of the People's Liberation Army, providing financing for Chinese Army weapons sales and western technology purchases. CITIC serves as the chief investment arm of China's central government and holds ministry status on the Chinese State Council.

Ron Brown helped CITIC more than once. Brown had the CITIC American representative, Bai Xingji; serve as a panelist/speaker at the 1995 Big Emerging Markets Conference (BEM). Brown arranged for the Chairman of CITIC, Wang Jun, to meet President Clinton.

Wang Jun was not only chairman of CITIC but also President of Poly Technologies, a firm known to be an outlet for Chinese weapon exports. Wang Jun is an international arms dealer known in every major capitol of the world. Wang Jun met with Ron Brown and DNC fundraiser Charlie "Ya-Lin" Trie prior to meeting Bill Clinton and making a large contribution at a White House coffee/fundraiser.

According to a 1997 report prepared by the Rand Corporation, Poly Technologies was founded in 1985 as a subsidiary of CITIC.

"Poly Technologies, Ltd., was founded in 1984, ostensibly as a subsidiary of CITIC, although it was later exposed to be the primary commercial arm of the PLA General Staff Department's Equipment Sub-Department," states the Rand report.

"Throughout the 1980s, Poly sold hundreds of millions of dollars of largely surplus arms around the world, exporting to customers in Thailand, Burma, Iran, Pakistan, and the United States."

In 1996, Poly Technologies was run by international arms dealer Wang Jun and his "princeling" friend, the powerful Maj. Gen. He Ping, son-in-law of Deng Xiaoping. The Rand Corporation noted that "Wang Jung is both director of CITIC and Chairman of Poly Group, the arms trading company of the General Staff Department."

With the help of CITIC-Beijing, General He Ping arranged a billion-dollar sale of Chinese arms that included missiles to Saudi Arabia and C.802 missiles to Iran during the mid-1980s. The government-controlled China Northern Industrial Corp., or Norinco assisted that deal. Norinco came under investigation for selling chemical-weapons materials to Iran for weapons of mass destruction, according to testimony before a Senate Governmental sub panel.

In 1996, Poly Chairman Wang Jun met with President Clinton inside the White House with convicted China-Gate figure Charlie Trie. Charlie Trie donated hundreds of thousands of dollars to the 1996 Clinton/Gore campaign from Chinese sources much of which was later returned by the democrat party. Trie is also alleged to be a member of the "4 Seas" Triad, an organization of underworld lords based inside Hong Kong.

"CITIC does enter into business partnerships with and provide logistical assistance to PLA and defense-industrial companies like Poly," noted the 1997 Rand report.

"Poly's U.S. subsidiaries were abruptly closed in August 1996. Allegedly, Poly's representative, Robert Ma, conspired with China North Industries Corporation's (NORINCO) representative, Richard Chen, and a number of businessmen in California to illegally import 2000 AK-47s into the United States."

"Unfortunately for them," states the Rand report. "Their 'customers' turned out to be undercover U.S. Customs and BATF agents, posing as members of a Miami syndicate. Poly's representative, Robert Ma, fled the country one step ahead of Federal law enforcement officials who had a warrant for his arrest, and his current whereabouts are unknown."

CITIC also owns a controlling interest in the Hong Kong based Asia Satellite Telecom Co. Ltd., or AsiaSat. AsiaSat, a company founded in 1988, operates several communications satellites in the Far East bought from U.S. manufacturers such as Hughes.

Asiasat also signed an exclusive deal with billionaire Li Ka-Shing to carry his STAR television service - 54 channels of premium cable/satellite television including MTV, re-runs of American sitcoms dubbed in various languages, and pay-per-view X rated movies.

Li's efforts in space, combined with the buying power of the Chinese Army, scored with Indonesian Dictator Suharto, arranging for the Palapa satellite purchased from U.S. space giant Hughes to also carry STAR TV.

After helping kick off AsiaSat with big paying customers seeking Far East satellite TV and cable service, Ka-Shing later sold all of his STAR TV holdings in two huge chunks to news magnate Rupert Murdoch for nearly a billion dollars.

AsiaSat and CITIC are also front companies for the People's Liberation Army (PLA). In addition to the direct TV broadcasts of STAR, AsiaSat satellites also regularly carry communications traffic for Chinese military units and Chinese military owned companies. Thus, with Ka-Shing's help the profits from X-rated films and American PAY-TV channels help fund Chinese Army satellite communications.

Interestingly, one area the Chinese communists decided not to crack down on after the 1989 Tianamen square uprising was satellite TV dish ownership. Instead of going against the tide of global communications, China selected both a profitable and pro-Marxist approach.

AsiaSat HK also has an exclusive deal to carry the official TV news, sports and propaganda outlets for the PRC. By allowing private dish ownership, Beijing can spread propaganda to the masses while concealing military satellite operations among the thousands of commercial dishes.

Furthermore, Beijing's military front companies also manufacture satellite dishes and receivers. Chinese Generals earn a sweet profit from commercial dish exports and sales that provide financial support to the hidden military operations in Chinese commercial satellites.

Red satellite TV is not the only deal that Li Ka-Shing managed to score with the assistance of the Chinese armed forces and Bill Clinton. One deal led by Li Ka-Shing nearly added four new ships to the Chinese Navy.

In 1982, the giant civilian container ship Atlantic Conveyor joined the U.K. Royal Navy task force off the Falkland Islands. The civilian container ship was quickly modified for war and it brought Harrier jump jets and helicopters to re-enforce the already badly underpowered Royal Navy. During the course of the south Atlantic combat, the Atlantic Conveyor was struck and sunk by an Argentine EXOCET cruise missile, killing the entire civilian crew.

In January 1997, Bill Clinton authorized four container ships similar to the Atlantic Conveyor for export directly to China. The four container ships were to be constructed for the China Ocean Shipping Company (COSCO) and Li Ka-Shing's Hutchison Whampoa Ltd. by the Alabama Shipyards, Mobile Ala.

The four ships were to be built using $138 million in private loans backed by the U.S. government. The loans have very favorable terms including low interest rates and a 25-year re-payment plan, longer than the expected life of the ships.

The loans were also U.S. backed, so even if the ship and owner disappeared, the Federal Government would still repay the lenders.

COSCO is better known for the recent unsuccessful attempt to purchase the former Long Beach Naval station. COSCO is also part of the Chinese Navy and wholly owned by the Chinese government.

COSCO is the flag carrier for China, hauling official cargoes exported by the Chinese government including weapons. Recent U.S. Navy photos show COSCO cargo ships carrying missile armed patrol boats bound for Iran and tons of depleted uranium tank shells for Pakistan. COSCO ships have carried jet fighters, missile parts and tanks for export to Iran, Iraq, Syria and Libya.

COSCO ships are considered to be part of the Chinese Navy and are frequently armed with guns and missiles during Chinese Army amphibious training exercises. Chinese military officials often refer to COSCO ships as 'zhanjian' or warships.

In 1996, the COSCO ship "Princess Bride" was caught in an attempt to smuggling over 2,000 fully automatic machine guns into the United States.

"COSCO," according to Defense Department intelligence officials "operates a fleet of ELINT (electronic intelligence) trawlers for the PRC government... When China delivers missiles or chemical agents to the Middle East, specially outfitted COSCO ships deliver them."

The COSCO container ship deal fell apart in November 1997 due to "commercial" reasons blamed on the Asian financial crisis. Nevertheless, the Chinese Navy deal to acquire these ships actually started in 1993 when Bill Clinton and the Democrats were starved for donation cash.

The Maritime shipyard-funding program, managed by the Department of Transportation (DOT), was created to finance American built ships sold to U.S. flag companies. In 1993, the Democratic controlled Congress joined President Clinton and altered the program to allow U.S. financing on ships built for export. Li Ka-Shing, COSCO, Ron Brown and Bill Clinton worked to provide the four container ships, including the low cost, 100% U.S. government backed loans, to Hutchison Whampoa and COSCO.

According to the House Task Force on Terrorism and Unconventional Warfare, "Although presented as a commercial entity COSCO is actually an arm of the Chinese military establishment. The Clinton administration has determined that additional information concerning COSCO that appears in the Select Committees classified Final Report cannot be made public."

Li Ka-Shing was not the only one to take advantage of the Clinton sponsored changes in the Maritime finance program. For example, two power barges for export to Indonesia made by Enron Corp., a large contributor to Bill Clinton, were also built through the DOT Maritime-funding program, and backed by $50 million in taxpayer financing. Another questionable ship deal included over $60 million to build a paddlewheel steam boat/casino. Still another deal landed millions in taxpayer-supported loans for two floating combination hotel/casino barges.

Li's role in Chinese maritime power is clearly outlined by the kind of special deals he has struck with the communist government. It is known that Li Ka-Shing played a significant role in the attempted purchase of the Long Beach Naval station for COSCO.

Li Ka-Shing also owns most of the dock space in Hong Kong. Li Ka-Shing and COSCO co-own the ports at both ends of the Panama Canal (Atlantic and Pacific). In fact, Li has over a billion dollars invested in China and an exclusive deal that includes first right of refusal over all PRC ports south of the Yangtze River.

Li Ka-Shing is also major shareholder of the Lippo company involved in the Chinagate scandal. Li Ka-Shing owned at least 11 % of the Lippo company during its attempts to influence the Clinton White House. Senator Fred Thompson of the American government revealed information in 1997 about the Chinese effort to buy political influence using the financial connections to former president Bill Clinton.

According documents obtained from the Commerce Department using the Freedom of Information Act (FOIA) a 1994 August far east trade trip schedule included Mr. Li on the midnight cruise aboard the "Love Boat" (Pacific Princess) from Hong Kong with Brown and a host of other high level guests.

In Hong Kong Li Ka-Shing met with Brown and the entire trade mission of American executives, including LORAL CEO Schwartz and DNC donor Sanford Robertson.

Li Ka-Shing's role as a front man for the Chinese military was well known to the Clinton administration. A 1996 report written by then U.S. Ambassador to China James Sasser alleges that the Chinese Ministry of Posts and Telecommunications (MPT) and Chinese billionaire Li Ka-Shing were both directly involved with the PLA in financing the communications networks for the Chinese army.

According to the report, "Already, foreign companies are interested in the new PLA-backed entity that is likely to emerge over the next year. Recent press reports indicate that Hutchison Whampoa may be involved with the PLA about possible funding options."

The report also states that the PLA was directly involved in the so-called "civilian" Chinese fiber optic communication systems. Sasser's report noted that the PLA actively worked on a Ministry of Posts and Telecommunications (MPT) fiber optic network that the Clinton administration stated was "civil" for the House National Security Committee.

"For example," wrote Sasser, "in laying long distance fiber optic lines for the MPT's telephones and digital data network, the PLA has provided soldiers to do much of the work. The PLA cadres are considered disciplined and hard working. Once the cable has been laid, the MPT typically allocates some of the bandwidth to the PLA."

"The PLA is already involved in telecommunications in a number of other areas," stated Sasser in his report. "The PLA is probably involved in operation of some networks, particularly in southern China."

Commerce Department documents also show that Gore campaign chairman Commerce Secretary William Daley met in October 1997 with Li Ka-Shing and a firm reported to be "an intelligence-collection front for China."

The documents show that Commerce Secretary Daley met with Chinese billionaire Li Ka-Shing during a closed luncheon sponsored by the powerful investment firm Goldman Sachs. Li Ka-Shing's company, Hutchison Whampoa, currently operates the two ports on the Panama Canal, the Pacific port of Balboa and the Atlantic port of Cristobal.

The meeting was held onboard the Goldman Sachs' boat "Monkey's Uncle" as part of an informal "talk" between Secretary Daley, Mr. Li and several "influential business people." The documents show that Daley's meeting onboard the "Monkey's Uncle" included a Mr. Duo from China Resources, a firm reported to be "an agent of espionage - economic, military, and political - for China."

According to a 1996 document from the U.S. Embassy in Panama, China Resources put a $400 million investment into Li Ka-Shing's company as part of a "front" company controlled by Beijing. Commerce documents describe China Resources Enterprises as "the investment arm of China's Foreign Trade ministry."

"Embassy Panama has received information to the effect that HIT (Hutchison International Terminals) is controlled by mainland Chinese perhaps through a Macao front which allegedly recently invested $400 million in HIT," states the cable. "Such control would have security implications and might affect the Panamanian government's views on awarding the port concessions."

Then Secretary Daley refused to comment on the documents found at the Commerce Department. Although, the Commerce Department public affairs officer Joan Bradshaw did issue an official statement concerning Secretary Daley's status. Daley, according to previous Commerce Department press announcements, had not resigned his post and was scheduled to lobby the U.S. Senate for passage of the China Trade bill in July.

"Mr. Daley is no longer Secretary of Commerce," stated Joan Bradshaw from the U.S. Commerce Department Public Affairs office, in conflict with the official press release. "Everything is being done through Nashville now."

Gore 2000 public affairs officials confirmed that the Gore campaign office located in Nashville Tennessee handled all contacts with the Commerce Secretary. The Gore 2000 public affairs officers, who also refused to identify themselves, did not respond to questions about Secretary Daley's meeting in 1997 or his role at the Commerce Department.

Goldman Sachs New York press office also refused to comment on the 1997 meeting onboard the "Monkey's Uncle." The powerful investment firm currently employs former Clinton cabinet member Robert Rubin.

Defense intelligence sources allege that Rubin, while still serving as Treasury Secretary for President Clinton, also attended the 1997 meeting onboard the "Monkey's Uncle." Rubin is not listed on official documents as attending.

China Resources Enterprises has previously been accused of illegal campaign donations to the Clinton/Gore 1996 re-election. Sen. Fred Thompson, R. Tenn., described China Resources Enterprises as "an agent of espionage - economic, military, and political - for China" during the 1997 Senate Governmental Affairs Committee hearings.

According to Senator Thompson, China Resources Enterprises is directly linked to Chinese military espionage and Indonesian billionaire Moctar Riady.

"Lippo group, run by the Riady family which employed (John) Huang, had over the past few years become a major business partner with China Resources, a trading company wholly owned by the Government of the peoples republic of China, and which has reportedly served as an intelligence-collection front for China," noted Senator Thompson during his summary on the China campaign finance scandal.

The Commerce Department documents show that prior to the meeting U.S. law enforcement agencies were very concerned about billionaire Li Ka-Shing and his connections to international smuggling.

A 1995 cable from the American Embassy in Nassau noted that Li Ka-Shing had signed an agreement to build an $88 million container ship terminal in the Grand Bahamas. The U.S. Embassy in Nassau copied the cable to several law enforcement agencies including the U.S. Customs Service and the Drug Enforcement Agency.

"Reftel describes U.S. agencies' security concerns about possible smuggling attempts through the terminal," states the cable from the American Embassy. "Post will request via septel assistance in addressing these concerns while port development plans are still on the drawing board."

Documents discovered by Larry Klayman and Judicial Watch, a Washington based watchdog group, show the U.S. Defense Department focused carefully on Li Ka-Shing and his company Hutchison Whampoa. According to an Oct. 1999 "Intelligence Assessment", prepared by the U.S. military Southern Command, the Hong Kong billionaire is a potential threat to America.

"Hutchison's containerized shipping facilities in the Panama Canal, as well as the Bahamas, could provide a conduit for illegal shipments of technology or prohibited items from the west to the PRC, or facilitate the movement of arms and other prohibited items into the Americas," concluded the U.S. military intelligence report.

Li Ka-Shing's direct business contacts with the Chinese Army were documented in a 1997 Rand Corporation report on the Chinese military industry. According the 1997 Rand report, "Hutchison Whampoa of Hong Kong, controlled by Hong Kong billionaire Li Ka-Shing, is also negotiating for PLA wireless system contracts, which would build upon his equity interest in Poly-owned Yangpu Land Development Company, which is building infrastructure on China's Hainan Island."

In addition, Commerce Secretary Daley's 1997 meeting on the "Monkey's Uncle" included several other firms identified as Chinese Army front companies.

The participants included Zhu Xizohua, Chairman of China Everbright, a firm directly owned by the Chinese Army and Larry Yung, Chairman of CITIC

Pacific, or the China International Trust and Investment Corporation, a firm alleged to be a front for Chinese arms manufacturer Poly Technologies Corporation.

Li Ka-Shing has more than one questionable business contact. In 1994, Li sent K.S. Wu to America. Wu, then the chairman of Pacific Century Group, a foreign-based company partly owned by Li, obtained a seat with Ron Brown to travel back to China for a U.S. trade mission. In fact, Wu met with his boss, Li Ka-Shing, during the 1994 trade trip on the U.S. taxpayers' tab.

Wu traveled to China in August of 1994 with a self-described "close" friend, Democrat West Virginia Governor Gaston Caperton. In 1996, Caperton described K.S. Wu as a "close friend" and a "trusted advisor to Senator Rockefeller."

Today, none dare speak of Mr. Wu. Former Governor Caperton and Democrat Senator Rockefeller both refused to comment on the late K.S. Wu. All questions to the senator's office on K.S. Wu have been greeted by with the same answer, a short and angry "no comment."

However, Mr. Wu and Li Ka-Shing shared more than just a single trade trip to China in 1994. Wu's attendance at such high-level events becomes less of a mystery when he and his so-called America investment company come into focus. Wu, according to the official Commerce Department information sheet, was chairman of Pacific Century Group, an investment firm working to finance electric power plants inside China with U.S. money.

In 1996 Senator Rockefeller led a delegation of Asian investors to Martinsburg, West Virginia. According to Governor Caperton, K.S. Wu was instrumental in helping Rockefeller bring the Asian investors to West Virginia.

In fact, these investors were so special that Rockefeller ran a VIP train to transport them to West Virginia from Washington, D.C. The joint U.S./Sino delegation broke ground for a new aircraft plant now located at the Martinsburg airport under a project called "Sino-Swearingen SJ-30".

The Sino-Swearingen plant in West Virginia is a joint project between Texas based Swearingen aircraft, the AFL-CIO, and Sino-Aerospace Investment Corporation. The joint interests of PRC billionaire Li Ka-Shing, a big U.S. union, and Senator Rockefeller were teamed up to manufacture business jets in the remote mountains of rural West Virginia.

The so-called SJ-30 "business" jet is state-of-the-art. The SJ-30 can travel 2,500 miles at nearly the speed of sound and is rated to cruise at 49,000 feet. The SJ-30 is considered to be the leading edge of U.S. commercial aerospace technology and includes all the latest in avionics such as GPS navigation.

The immense speed, range and altitude capability of the SJ-30 can be attributed to the twin Rolls Royce/Williams FJ-44 turbofans that power it. The Williams FJ-44 is also used in the Swedish SK-60 military attack trainer and powered the USAF DarkStar stealth robot spy plane. Williams is best known for making the jet engines for U.S. Tomahawk and ALCM cruise missiles.

The Sino-Swearingen facility is located at the Martinsburg airport just south of the town along U.S. Rt. 81. Martinsburg is a key point in the West Virginia hills, located only 50 miles from downtown D.C. The narrow valley is a major north/south and east/west crossing for U.S. microwave and fiber-optic telecommunications. The Martinsburg airport is supported by the U.S. taxpayer via the National Guard facilities and the airport ground facilities, such as fire and rescue.

In 1996, a host of the Asian officials attending the ground-breaking included Dr. Shih-Chein Yang of Taiwan Aerospace and Benjamin Lu of the Taipei Economic office. In fact, the entire ground breaking ceremony at Martinsburg was covered in detail on Senator Rockefeller's web page, including a wonderful photograph of Rockefeller and several Asian businessmen with shovels in hand.

Pacific Century, according to sources on Capitol Hill, is actually a front company partly owned by Li Ka-Shing and Macau prostitution drug lord Ng Lapseng. The U.S.-based business, run by Wu, was actually then owned Li and a major organized crime boss. The Ng family dominance of Far East heroin, and oriental female love slaves in California, Oregon and Washington is well known to law enforcement at both the state and federal levels.

In fact, the CEO of Pacific Century, K.S. "Wu," was related to Ng. Ng, also a major donor to the DNC, often introduced himself as "Mister Wu." K.S. Wu was a cousin of Ng Lapseng.

Crime lord Ng actually entered Clinton's inner circle by introducing large amounts of cash to the DNC. Proof of this can be seen in a wonderful photograph of Mr. Ng with Mr. and Mrs. Clinton at a DNC fund-raising event.

K.S. Wu died in late 1995. No one will comment on his death. No one will comment on his life. No information is available on how, when or even if Mr. Wu died.

K.S. Wu's information sheet included several different phone numbers for the Pacific Century Group. Attempts to seek more information from Mr. Wu's company were fruitless.

It should shock no one to find that repeated calls to the Pacific Century Group about ex-chairman K.S. Wu were not returned. No Pacific Century official would comment on the departed CEO, the deals in China or their relationship with the Democratic Party.

However, Li Ka-Shing knows. Li Ka-Shing appointed his son Richard Li to take over Pacific Century after K.S. Wu's mysterious death.

Li Ka-Shing's role as point man for the Chinese Army continued even after Bill Clinton left office. However, Li has not been as successful in swaying the Bush administration.

In 2002 Chinese billionaire Li Ka-Shing put together a $750 million dollar offer to buyout the bankrupt telecom giant Global Crossing. However, the plan by the close associate of Chinese President Jiang Zemin came under fire from inside Congress and from Global Crossing's creditors.

Li Ka-Shing faces competitive bids for Global Crossing made by AT&T and New York-based KAB Group, LLC, which has filed an alternative plan on behalf of the shareholders that proposes to raise $5.5 billion over the next three years.

The financial competition over Global Crossing was overshadowed by the U.S. national security concerns posed by the sale to the Chinese billionaire.

Rep. Dana Rohrabacher, R - Calif., sent an urgent letter to Defense Secretary Donald Rumsfeld, expressing his opposition to the proposed sale of the telecom giant to Li Ka-Shing and seeking a "full investigation" by the Defense Dept. into the sale.

The concern was that Global Crossing currently holds contracts over secure Defense Dept. communications and that the sale to the Chinese billionaire may compromise the U.S. military. Rep. Rohrabacher expressed his concern directly to Defense Secretary Rumsfeld, noting that a U.S. military contract "under a company owned by Li Ka-Shing would be a national security nightmare."

It is a fact that Global Crossing's favorite proposal came from Li Ka-Shing, along with an 8 percent cut for Global executives if Li was successful in the takeover bid.

Although, the U.S. Defense Department opposed the sale of the fiber-optic giant Global Crossing to Hutcheson Whampoa, Li Ka-Shing fought back. In a frantic attempt to salvage the deal, Bush defense advisor Richard Perle was hired to advise Global Crossing.

According to an editorial by columnist Maureen Dowd, Mr. Perle had a conflict of interest in that he was a member of the Defense Advisory Board.

"Absolutely, categorically untrue," stated Mr. Perle emphatically.

"Mareen Dowd's view of this is very misleading. Ms. Dowd's recent editorial suggested that I was retained to 'help overcome Pentagon resistance' to the proposed sale of Global Crossing to Hutcheson Whampoa. That is not why I was retained," asserted Mr. Perle.

"I have not been retained by Hutcheson Whampoa nor have I been retained by Global Crossing to represent them in any way with the U.S. government. I have been retained by Global Crossing to help them put together a security arrangement that is acceptable to the U.S. government," stated Perle.

"I don't believe there is a conflict because I am not representing the company to the U.S. government," said Perle.

Mr. Perle did concede that the Chinese Army is in business with Hutcheson Whampoa providing military communications for the PRC and that China has provided fiber-optic systems to Iraq.

"I am not surprised," he stated. "I do not trust the Chinese government on these matters. They have sold dangerous things to Iraq and other nations."

"It was very clear that the previous Global Crossing proposal was not going to meet U.S. government requirements. The U.S. government is concerned that the Hutcheson ownership will give them the ability to do injury to U.S. national security. Hutcheson Whampoa will now end up with 20% ownership. I have been retained to help Global Crossing find a structure to protect U.S. national security," said Mr. Perle.

Clearly, the Global Crossing negotiations with the Committee on Foreign Investment in the United States, or CFIUS, had run into a snag. According to reports, FBI officials voiced opposition to a Li Ka-Shing buyout of Global Crossing.

In the end, the Bush administration denied the sale of sensitive U.S. fiber-optic systems to China. The Defense Department opposed the sale of Global Crossing to Chinese billionaire Li Ka-Shing and his Hutcheson Whampoa company for obvious national security reasons.

U.S. and allied forces engaged and destroyed a Clinton-era mistake made in 1994 allowing U.S. fiber-optic systems to be sold to China. The same fiber optic system sent the commands of the Iraqi military to fight our soldiers during operation Iraqi Freedom.

The Chinese Army would love to get its hands on Global Crossing. It is clear from previous sales of such U.S. made systems to Li Ka-Shing that the Chinese Army will benefit from that technology. It is just as clear that - if given the opportunity - the Chinese Army will use Global Crossing technology and assets against the national interests of the United States.

The Clinton supplied documents clearly provide the answer to why civilian/billionaire Ka-Shing was included with communist leader President Jiang Zemin. Li Ka-Shing is really part of the Chinese government.

Li Ka-Shing's partnership with the red Chinese military has been a very profitable story of symbiotic business deals with great financial benefit to both Li and the communists. Without Li Ka-Shing the Chinese army would have to find some other billionaire front man to run their western business dealings.

Li Ka-Shing willingly provided his services for a piece of the action. Li Ka-Shing cashed in on his co-existence with the Chinese military to the tune of billions in his pocket.

Li Ka-Shing bought his way into the Clinton administration through Ron Brown and the DNC. There is no question that Li Ka-Shing's contributions to Chinese Naval power projection should earn him the title "Commodore" in the People's Liberation Navy - if not a more official rank of red Admiral.

LI Ka-Shing
(Phonetic: lee)

Chairman, Hutchison Whampoa, Ltd.
(since January 1981)

Addressed as: Mr. Li

Li Ka-Shing, one of Hong Kong's most visible billionaires, controls several of the colony's largest companies, including Hutchison Whampoa, Ltd., and Cheong Kong Holdings. He has significant economic and political ties to China; his investments there include a joint-venture power station, a highway construction project, and a large contribution to Shantou University in Guangzhou. A member of the Basic Law Drafting Committee, Li has met with Deng Xiaoping and other senior Chinese leaders; their discussions on China's future and its relationship with Hong Kong after 1997 received wide press attention. Li's substantial overseas investments, particularly his energy and property holdings in Canada, have led to press speculation that he may leave Hong Kong after Beijing regains control of the colony.

Li was born on 13 June 1928 in Guangzhou. He went to Hong Kong in 1940 and began his career by manufacturing plastic flowers. He made his fortune in Hong Kong real estate purchased when prices fell during the chaos of the Cultural Revolution. Li is a member of the boards of directors of the China International Trust and Investment Corporation and the Hong Kong and Shanghai Banking Corporation. He also sits on several civic advisory councils. Although the Hong Kong press has described Li as honest and hard working, he was found guilty of insider trading after a widely publicized trial in 1984; he was not punished by the courts.

12 July 1990

150

JIANG Zemin
(Phonetic: jeeyahng)
(3068/3419/3046)

CHINA

*President (since March 1993); General
Secretary, Chinese Communist Party
(CCP); Member, Standing Committee,
Politburo, CCP; Chairman, Military
Affairs Commission (MAC), CCP
(since 1989)*

Addressed as: Mr. President

Jiang Zemin formally heads the three major
sectors of the Chinese political system: the
government, the military, and the CCP. Hong Kong
media reports indicate that, although he has in the
past acted largely as a spokesman for other
policymakers, he has recently taken on more
substantive responsibilities and has improved his
status among his colleagues. According to the press,
Jiang has ties to senior party leaders, including
Deng Xiaoping and economic planner Chen Yun.

Jiang has endorsed the ruling elders' views on
political dissent and pushed for greater political
indoctrination and tougher social controls. He has
long fought political opposition and was among the
first leaders to support Deng's editorial calling for a
crackdown on student protesters in 1989. More
recently, he has played a prominent role in an
ongoing campaign to identify and punish corrupt
government and party officials.

Although Jiang has backed Deng's open-door
policy and has actively courted Western investors,
he is generally not regarded as an ardent market
reformer and has not pushed specific economic
initiatives. Since Deng began his latest reform drive
in January 1992, Jiang has publicly expressed his
backing for the reform agenda.

Jiang has spent most of his career in China's
heavy industry sector. He earned a degree in
electrical engineering in 1947 from Shanghai
Jiaotong University. Chinese press reports indicate
that he held factory posts in China during 1950-54.
In 1955 he began a year of training at the Stalin

Automobile Factory in Moscow. Jiang held a series
of engineering posts after returning to China. By
1964 he was a vice manager of the Shanghai
Electrical Apparatus Company. In the 1970s Jiang
moved to the central government bureaucracy.
From 1971 until 1979 he served in the First
Ministry of Machine Building, which was
responsible for developing heavy industry. During
1980-82 he was a vice minister of the State
Council's Foreign Investment Control and Import-
Export Commissions. Jiang joined the Ministry of
Electronics Industry as a vice minister in 1982; he
became Minister a year later. During 1985-86 he
was a deputy head of the Electronics Industry
Invigoration Leading Group. A member of the CCP
Central Committee since 1982, he was elected to
the Politburo in 1987. Jiang served in Shanghai as
party secretary from 1985 until 1989; he was mayor
from 1985 until 1988.

Jiang was born on 10 July 1926. He joined the
CCP at 20 to oppose Chiang Kai-shek. Jiang speaks
English and Russian and can read French, Japanese,
and Romanian. He is fond of literature and of
Western classical music. He has visited the United
States three times, most recently in 1987. Married,
he has two sons.

7 October 1993

LI Peng
(Phonetic: lee)
(2621/7720)

*Premier, State Council (since 1988);
Member, Standing Committee, Politburo,
Chinese Communist Party (CCP)
(since 1987)*

Addressed as: Mr. Premier

Widely considered one of the most powerful members of his generation of leaders, Li Peng began a second term as Premier in March 1993. He dropped from public view shortly after that, and although official Chinese press statements attributed his absence to a cold, Li later publicly stated that he had suffered from a heart ailment. He resumed a normal schedule of meetings and public appearances in late August 1993, noting that he had fully recovered.

Although Li has long been identified with hardline economic policies, he has publicly expressed support for paramount leader Deng Xiaoping's latest reform drive, which began in early 1992. He has claimed credit for the success of that renewed reform effort and endorsed price and tax reform and the creation of Shanghai's Pudong development zone. Nonetheless, Li has publicly stressed China's continued adherence to socialism, stating that a multiparty system would be inappropriate for China. In the months before his illness, Li published several speeches castigating Hong Kong Governor Chris Patten's proposed reforms, which he characterized as a threat to Chinese sovereignty and stability.

Li was born on 20 October 1928. In 1931 his father, an early Communist leader, was killed by the Kuomintang, and Li came under the protection of

Zhou Enlai, who became Premier under Mao Zedong. At 18, Li joined an elite group of Chinese students studying in the Soviet Union, where he remained for seven years. He worked with Soviet advisers during the early part of his 26-year career in the electric power industry. Because he was under Zhou's protection, he was not purged during the Cultural Revolution. Li launched his national career as a vice minister of electric power in 1980 and became Minister the following year. In 1983 he leapfrogged several more senior leaders to become a vice premier.

Li's wife, Zhu Lin, graduated from the Harbin Foreign Language College and has spent her career in the electrical sector; she now heads the Beijing office overseeing the Daya Bay nuclear power plant near Hong Kong. The couple has a daughter, two sons, and three grandchildren.

26 November 1993

SENT BY: AMEMBASSY ECON NAS;   /- 9-90 3:41PM; 1 809 328 3495 =>   22/1984;   #2/6

1057

UNCLASSIFIED
PROG 04/11/95
CHARGE: JSFORD
ECON: AMCOOPER   EXT. 227
1.POL/ECON: MEEARL, 2.NAU: MBKAPLAN
ECON

AMEMBASSY NASSAU
SECSTATE WASHDC
INFO USDOC WASHDC
AMEMBASSY LONDON
AMEMBASSY SANTO DOMINGO
AMEMBASSY BRIDGETOWN
AMEMBASSY KINGSTON
AMEMBASSY PORT AU PRINCE
AMEMBASSY PORT OF SPAIN
USCUSTOMS SERVICE MIAMI FL//SAC//
USCUSTOMS SERVICE AOCE MIAMI FL//DIR/OPS//
DEA FIELD DIVISION MIAMI
DEAHQS WASHDC
USCUSTOMS WASHDC

STATE PASS TO ARA/CAR (IMWOLD) AND INL/ICJ, EB
USDOC FOR 4322/ITA/IEP/WH/OMCB/MSIEGELMAN
LONDON FOR ECON
SANTO DOMINGO FOR USFCS AND ECON
BRIDGETOWN FOR ECON
KINGSTON FOR ECON
PORT AU PRINCE FOR ECON
PORT OF SPAIN FOR ECON

E.O.: 12356 N/A
TAGS: BEXP, KTNV, ELET, DGOV, DTND, DDET, CMAR, DP
SUBJECT: BAHAMAS PLANS FOR NEW PORT FACILITY

REF: NASSAU 999 (NOTAL)

1. THE GRAND BAHAMA PORT AUTHORITY SIGNED APRIL 7 AN
AGREEMENT WITH HUTCHISON INTERNATIONAL PORT HOLDINGS LIMITED
OF THE UNITED KINGDOM FOR THE CONSTRUCTION OF THE FIRST PHASE
OF A $88 MILLION CONTAINER TRANSSHIPMENT PORT AND FREE TRADE
ZONE AT FREEPORT HARBOR. AN ADDITIONAL INVESTMENT OF $40
MILLION WILL BE INJECTED FOR THE SECOND PHASE OF THE PROJECT
MAKING FREEPORT HARBOR THE LARGEST MAN-MADE HARBOR IN THE
REGION.
THE PORT WOULD BE A TRANSSHIPMENT FACILITY SPECIALIZING IN
CARGO TRANSFERS BETWEEN LATIN AMERICA, EUROPE, THE MIDDLE
EAST AND NORTH AMERICA.

AMEBASSY ECON NAS;   7- 9-96 3:42PM; 1 809 328 3495 =>   2271964;

2. HUTCHINSON INTERNATIONAL PORT HOLDINGS WILL ACQUIRE 50
PERCENT SHARE HOLDINGS OF THE FREEPORT HARBOR COMPANY FOR $10
MILLION. THE REMAINING 50 PERCENT WILL BE HELD BY THE
PRIVATELY-HELD GRAND BAHAMA PORT AUTHORITY. THE GOVERNMENT
PLANS TO AMEND THE CUSTOMS MANAGEMENT ACT REGULATIONS TO
ENSURE THAT THE CONTAINER TERMINAL IS COMPETITIVE WITH OTHER
PORTS IN THE REGION. THE GOVERNMENT ALSO AGREED FOR THE PORT
AUTHORITY TO RE-IMPLEMENT A $3 HEAD TAX ON PASSENGERS LEAVING
FREEPORT HARBOR, AND THE PROCEEDS WILL GO TOWARDS THE
CONSTRUCTION OF THE TERMINAL.

4. THE NEW PORT TERMINAL IS EXPECTED TO CREATE SOME 150
PERMANENT JOBS AND AN ADDITIONAL 750 TO 1,000 SPIN-OFF JOBS.
THE TERMINAL WILL EMPLOY 12 ADDITIONAL BAHAMIAN CUSTOMS
OFFICERS TO FACILITATE THE SMOOTH RUNNING OF THE TERMINAL
WITHOUT THE NEED FOR EXCESSIVE OVERTIME BY CUSTOMS OFFICERS.
WHEN FULLY OPERATIONAL, THE TERMINAL IS EXPECTED TO ATTRACT
AT LEAST THREE MORE MAJOR NEW INVESTORS IN THE INDUSTRIAL
AREA WHO SHOULD PROVIDE SUBSTANTIAL INVESTMENT AND CREATE
MANY MORE JOBS IN THE NEAR FUTURE.

5. COMMENT: IF SUCCESSFUL, THIS INVESTMENT WILL PROVIDE A
MAJOR BOOST TO THE LAGGING FREEPORT ECONOMY THE LAST
SIGNIFICANT INVESTMENT IN FREEPORT WAS THE ESTABLISHMENT OF
THE BAHAMAS OIL REFINERY COMPANY IN 1960. RECENTLY THE
PETROCHEMICAL INDUSTRY, WHICH IS ONE OF FREEPORT'S MAJOR
INDUSTRIES, HAS SUFFERED AND SEVERAL COMPANIES HAVE CLOSED.

6. REFTEL DESCRIBES U.S. AGENCIES' SECURITY CONCERNS ABOUT
POSSIBLE SMUGGLING ATTEMPTS THROUGH THE TERMINAL. POST WILL
REQUEST VIA SEPTEL ASSISTANCE IN ADDRESSING THESE CONCERNS
NOW WHILE PORT DEVELOPMENT PLANS ARE STILL ON THE DRAWING
BOARD.

FORD##

EVENT BRIEF

Event :   Luncheon Hosted by Goldman Sachs

Date :   Sunday, October 5, 1997

Time :   11:30 am - 2:30 pm

Location :   Depart from Causeway Bay Typhoon Shelter

Participants :   Secretary Daley
Consul General Richard Boucher
Senior Commercial Officer David Katz
Tim Dattels and other Goldman Sachs Principals
Invited Guests, including:
- Gordon Wu, Chairman, Hopewell Holdings
- Raymond Kwok, Vice Chairman, Sun Hung Kai Properties
- Victor Fung, Chairman, Hong Kong Trade Development Council
- Ronnie Chan, Chairman, Asia Society; Chairman, Hang Lung Development
- Henry Cheng, Managing Director, New World Development
- Li Ka-shing, Chairman, Cheung Kong (Holdings) Ltd.
- Larry Yung, Chairman, CITIC Pacific
- Alasdair Morrison, Managing Director, Jardine Matheson
- Robert Kwok, Chairman, Kerry Properties
- Zhu Xiaohua, Chairman, China Everbright
- Mr. Duo, China Resources
- Canning Fok, Group Managing Director, Hutchison Whampoa

Scenario :   Goldman Sachs' boat ("Monkey's Uncle") will depart from the Causeway Bay Typhoon Shelter at 11:30 am. The boat will sail near the new airport site at Chek Lap Kok. Lunch will be served on board. The boat will return to the Causeway Bay Typhoon Shelter at approx. 2:45 pm.

Objectives :   Talk informally with a group of influential business people

Overview :   Casual Lunch

Press :   Closed

U.S. & FOREIGN COMMERCIAL SERVICE
American Consulate General Hong Kong
26 Garden Road
Central   Hong Kong

Tel. (852) 2521-1467   Fax (852) 2845-9800

Date	January 16, 1997
To	Richard Benson Commercial Attache U.S. Embassy Panama
From	David Katz SCO Hong Kong
Subject	Hutchison Group
Number of Page	1

Thank you for your Jan. 13 fax and the attached newspaper clipping.

As you know, journalists are sometimes misinformed on their reported stories. In this case, the article was incorrect in that China Resources Enterprises did not fully buy out HIT. China Resources Enterprises did, however, buy a 10% (TEN percent, NOT 100%) HIT stake (worth HK$3.5 billion) from its parent company (China Resources Holdings) in December 1996. Hutchison Whampoa Ltd. still owns 77.5% of HIT.

The Chairman of Hutchison Whampoa Ltd., Mr. Li Ka-shing, still has control over the group, having more than 44% ownership (through shares held by Cheung Kong Holdings and its subsidiaries). The rest of the stock is being held by the general public and a number of other tycoons in Hong Kong, including the Kadoorie family and Simon Murray and his family. While we are not lawyers, it is neither our understanding nor that of the business circles here that Hutchison Whampoa is "under the control of the Chinese Government". However, like most other tycoons in the territory, Li Ka-shing maintains friendly relationships with the PRC Government.

I hope the foregoing helps. Best regards.

STATEMENT OF

GENERAL CHARLES E. WILHELM, UNITED STATES MARINE CORPS

COMMANDER IN CHIEF, UNITED STATES SOUTHERN COMMAND

BEFORE THE SENATE ARMED SERVICES COMMITTEE

22 OCTOBER 1999

INTRODUCTION

Mr. Chairman and members of the committee, I am here at your request to address issues concerning the future security of the Panama Canal. As you know, the U.S. military presence in Panama and U.S. control of the Panama Canal end at noon on December 31st of this year. That reality raises legitimate questions about our future security relationship with Panama and our ability to respond effectively to known and unanticipated threats to the Panama Canal.

Let me begin with a quick update on our progress in implementing the Panama Canal Treaty of 1977. Using 1979 as the base year, we have withdrawn 95 percent of our troops (9,500) and have transferred to Panama 90 percent of the acreage (84,098 acres) and 6S percent of the buildings (3,160 buildings) formerly occupied by U.S. forces. In the context of the language of the treaty, we have met fully our obligations for cleanup of ranges. We turned over Fort Sherman and the Pina ranges on June 30th and Balboa West and the Empire ranges on July 28th. Together, these four ranges comprise 55,070 acres of land, to include firing, bombing, impact and maneuver areas. We transferred these four ranges to Panama only after removing over 880 metric tons of ordnance- and non-ordnance related scrap and after destroying 6,600 pieces of live ordnance.

Allow me to turn now to our future security relationship with Panama. U.S. Southern Command plans an assertive engagement effort to achieve shared U.S. and Panamanian security objectives. We will help the Government of Panama develop a national security strategy that will help them establish their own objectives and the means to achieve them. The latter will define the roles and missions of the Panamanian Public Forces (PPF).

Our engagement plan also addresses a current concern of Panama's leaders: national level command and control of the security forces. We will help Panama develop a national level command, control, communication, and intelligence (C3I) system to enhance government responsiveness to national emergencies. We will assist the PPF to develop expertise in emergency and crisis action planning, to modernize their equipment, and to professionalize their security forces. The desired end-state is an effective Panamanian national C3I system and a modernized

PPF capable of providing security for the Canal and playing an appropriate role in meeting common Panamanian and U.S. national security objectives.

THREATS TO THE CANAL

We are not aware of any current internal or external threats to the Panama Canal, and we have no evidence that it has been targeted by terrorists or foreign governments. That said, we believe that the Canal must always be regarded as a potential target for both conventional and unconventional forces given its importance to global commerce and for military transits.

The most likely threats to the Canal are internal and nonlethal. The potential for corruption and watershed mismanagement is real and could negatively impact Canal operations. Each ship transit (there are about 30 transits a day) requires 52 million gallons of fresh water. Deforestation of the Canal through clear-cutting, grazing, or development could threaten the watershed or lead to increased silting, ultimately jeopardizing Canal operations. Labor disputes and civil unrest in Panama could cause work stoppages or slowdowns, that would also adversely affect Canal operations.

Potential future external threats could include a hostile foreign power and/or transnational criminal organizations. Cuba and China have strong economic interests in Panama, but do not pose a threat to the security of the Canal at this time. Cuba operates businesses in Panama to generate hard currency as a means of circumventing the U.S. embargo. China maintains diplomatic relations with 18 countries in the U.S. Southern Command area of responsibility and maintains links with more than 200 commercial entities and joint-venture enterprises in Latin America and the Caribbean. Between 1988 and 1997, China quadrupled its level of investments in the region to $8.2 billion. In 1997, the Panama Port3 Company, a subsidiary of Hutchison Port Holdings (itself an international division of Hutchison Whampoa), negotiated and executed a 25-year lease with an option to renew for another 25 years to operate the Balboa and Cristobal port facilities at both ends of the Canal.

China's goals in Panama are to ensure unrestricted access to the markets and natural resources of Latin America, and to promote China as a potential political and economic alternative to the U.S. In my view, the impact of Chinese commercial interests in Panama is less a local threat to the Canal, and more a regional threat posed by expanding Chinese influence throughout Latin America.

Transnational crime, especially drug-trafficking organizations, pose a serious threat to the United States, Canada, and other countries of the hemisphere. While illegal commerce in drugs, arms, and aliens threatens the stability of all nations astride the numerous trafficking routes, the most serious threats are to Mexico and Colombia. Transnational crime in Panama will likely increase after the U.S. withdraws, but presently, there is no identified threat to Canal operations from transnational criminals.

Instability in Colombia poses a localized threat to Panama's sovereignty. The threat is greatest on Panama's eastern border within the Darien Province. For years, the Revolutionary

Armed Forces of Colombia (FARC) have used this province as a safe-haven, to rest and re-supply. The Panama National Police lacks the capability to oust the FARC and generally avoid confrontations. Localized violence occurs when armed paramilitary forces from Colombia pursue the FARC into Panama and terrorize local Panamanians accused of cooperation with the FARC. Other FARC supporters are scattered around Panama, but pose no identifiable or verifiable threat to Canal operations or to the Government of Panama.

CAPABILITIES AND PLANS TO RESPOND

Articles IV and V of the Permanent Neutrality and Efficient Operation of the Panama Canal Treaty declare the U.S. and Panama responsible for ensuring the permanent neutrality of the Panama Canal. In addition, The Chairman of the Joint Chiefs of Staff has assigned the mission of defending the Panama Canal to the U.S. Southern Command. We are prepared to act either unilaterally or jointly with the Panama Public Forces to fulfill these responsibilities.

The U.S. Southern Command recently completed FUERTES DEFENSAS, a three-phased, computer-assisted exercise to evaluate our ability to respond to a threat to the Panama Canal. This unilateral exercise assumed that no U.S. forces would be forward deployed in Panama. To enhance U.S. and Panamanian cooperation, future exercises will include participation by the PPF in all phases of planning and execution. To ensure future safe passage of high value transits through the Canal, we are examining new alternative approaches, all of which involve cooperation with the Panamanian Public Forces Maritime Service, their Coast Guard equivalent.

We are also in the final stages of revising our contingency plan for the defense of the Panama Canal. This revision calls for the establishment of a Joint Task Force using forces based in the U.S. We will continue to meet all U.S. obligations under the Treaties and ensure the permanent neutrality and safe operation of the Panama Canal.

CONCLUSION

The Government of Panama's capability to provide effective security for threats against the Canal will determine our future bilateral security relationship. Based on our on-going assessment of Panamanian security requirements, we strongly support. increased security assistance funding to modernize the PPF and to build a national command and control, communications, and intelligence system. We plan to intensify our engagement with the PPF to help them safeguard neutrality and security of the Canal. I appreciate your concern for the future security of the Panama Canal and your interest in our efforts to enhance bilateral relations with Panama, and the capability of its security forces to defend the Panama Canal.

SECRET//X1 UNCLASSIFIED

Intelligence Assessment

26 October 1999

Panama: People's Republic of China Interests and Activities (U)

(S) The Ports of Balboa (Pacific) and Cristobal (Atlantic) were leased for 25 years, with an option to exercise 25 years, to the Panama Ports Company (PPC). There is no direct ownership between the People's Republic of China (PRC), PPC or its parent company Hutchison Whampoa. ███████████████████████████████

(C) Summary: The PPC is a subsidiary of Hong Kong-based Hutchison Whampoa ████████████████████████

(C) Discussion: The PPC's contract includes tug boats operations, ship repair, and pilot services within ports facilities. Hutchison Whampoa also may plan to lease a limited portion of Rodman Naval station as well as some storage space at the reverted Albrook Air Station. Neither Hutchison nor PPC are involved directly with day-to-day operations of the Panama Canal at this time.

(S) Any potential threat posed by the presence of a pro-Chinese corporate entity in the Panama Canal zone is indirect. It is unlikely that PPC officials or employees would overtly sabotage or damage the canal on orders from Beijing, as it would be contrary to their own financial interests and would undoubtedly elicit an immediate response from the US and the international community. ████████████████████

SECRET//X1 UNCLASSIFIED

SECRET//X1

UNCLASSIFIED

(U) Hutchison Whampoa's owner, Hong Kong tycoon Li Ka-Shing, has extensive business ties in Beijing and has compelling financial reasons to maintain a good relationship with China's leadership.

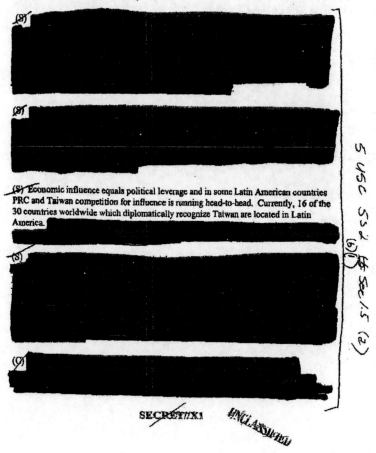

(S) Economic influence equals political leverage and in some Latin American countries PRC and Taiwan competition for influence is running head-to-head. Currently, 16 of the 30 countries worldwide which diplomatically recognize Taiwan are located in Latin America.

5 USC 552 ff Sec 1.5 (b)(1) (2)

SECRET//X1

UNCLASSIFIED

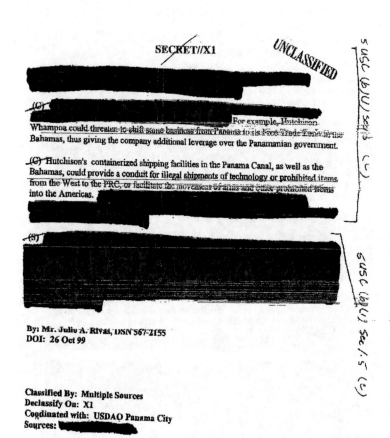

SECRET//X1   UNCLASSIFIED

(C)

For example, Hutchison
Whampoa could threaten to shift some business from Panama to its Free Trade Zone in the
Bahamas, thus giving the company additional leverage over the Panamanian government.

(C) Hutchison's containerized shipping facilities in the Panama Canal, as well as the
Bahamas, could provide a conduit for illegal shipments of technology or prohibited items
from the West to the PRC, or facilitate the movement of arms and other prohibited items
into the Americas.

(S)

By: Mr. Julio A. Rivas, DSN 567-2155
DOI: 26 Oct 99

Classified By: Multiple Sources
Declassify On: X1
Coordinated with: USDAO Panama City
Sources:

SECRET//X1   UNCLASSIFIED

UNCLAS   USDOC   PANAMA 03305

.CTION: FCS-2
INFO: DPO-0

DISTRIBUTION: FCS
CHARGE: FCS

VZCZCTRO243HKO140
PP RUEHHK
DE RUEHZP #3305 1871913
ZNR UUUUU ZZH
P 051913Z JUL 96
FM AMEMBASSY PANAMA
TO RUEHLO/AMEMBASSY LONDON PRIORITY 0126
RUEHBJ/AMEMBASSY BEIJING PRIORITY 0055
RUEHHK/AMCONSUL HONG KONG PRIORITY 0053
RUEHBH/AMEMBASSY NASSAU PRIORITY 0095
INFO RUEHC/SECSTATE WASHDC 5346
RUCPDOC/USDOC WASHDC
BT
UNCLAS PANAMA 003305

STATE FOR ARA/CEN/PAN

USDOC 3134/USFCS/OIO/WH/DPITKIN

USDOC FOR 4322/USFCS/IEP/OMCB/CBD/MGAISFORD

USDOC FOR 6000/TD/AC/ANN NGO

E.O. 12958: N/A
TAGS: BMGT, PM
SUBJECT: URGENT REQUEST FOR INFORMATION ON HUTCHISON
INTERNATIONAL TERMINALS

1. HUTCHISON INTERNATIONAL TERMINALS (HIT) REPRESENTED
TO BE A HONG KONG COMPANY AND A SUBSIDIARY OF A BRITISH
REGISTERED FIRM IS ONE OF THREE SHORT LIST BIDDERS FOR A
20 YEAR CONCESSION TO RUN THE PANAMANIAN ATLANTIC PORT OF
CRISTOBAL AND THE PANAMANIAN PACIFIC PORT OF BALBOA. THE
OTHER TWO BIDDERS ARE AMERICAN. THE CONCESSION COULD BE
AWARDED AS EARLY AS NEXT WEEK. THESE PORTS ARE CLOSE TO
THE ATLANTIC AND PACIFIC ENTRANCES TO THE PANAMA CANAL.
HIT IS ALSO SAID TO BE THE CONCESSION HOLDER FOR
FREEPORT, BAHAMAS.

2. EMBASSY PANAMA HAS RECEIVED INFORMATION TO THE EFFECT
THAT HIT IS CONTROLLED BY MAINLAND CHINESE PERHAPS
THROUGH A MACAO FRONT WHICH ALLEGEDLY RECENTLY INVESTED
$400 MILLION IN HIT. SUCH CONTROL WOULD HAVE SECURITY
IMPLICATIONS AND MIGHT AFFECT THE PANAMANIAN GOVERNMENT'S
VIEWS ON AWARDING THE PORT CONCESSIONS.

3. ADDRESSEE POSTS ARE REQUESTED TO SUPPLY FULLEST

UNCLAS   USDOC   PANAMA 03305

UNCLAS   USDOC   PANAMA 03305

.NFORMATION AVAILABLE ABOUT HIT OWNERSHIP LATEST TUESDAY JULY TENTH.

4. NASSAU IS ADDITIONALLY REQUESTED TO CONFIRM THAT HIT DOES HOLD A CONCESSION IN FREEPORT AND IF IT DOES TO DESCRIBE THE NATURE OF THE CONCESSION INCLUDING THE TYPE AND VOLUME OF CARGO HANDLED AND THE USUAL SOURCES AND DESTINATIONS FOR THIS CARGO. WE ARE TRYING TO ESTABLISH IF FREEPORT CONCESSION IS CONFLICT OF INTEREST WITH PANAMANIAN PORT CONCESSIONS.

(US&FCS-RFBENSON)HUGHES
BT
#3305

NNNN

8

MONEY FOR NOTHING

If they are greedy - lure them with goods.
Mei Yaochen - The Art of War

Documents from the files of Ron Brown confirm that President Clinton co-operated in the exchange of donations for trade trips with Ron Brown.

The documents were obtained from the U.S. Commerce Department using the Freedom of Information act. The previously with held files included letters which combine the son of a major communist Chinese party member, fund raising for the Chinese government, fundraising for the DNC, Chinese human rights, and trade trips.

The letters were written by Sanford Robertson, a California based banker and financier. The letters were sent directly to Ron Brown and President Clinton.

Robertson's letters show that both Clinton and Brown were informed of Robertson's donations to the DNC and of Robertson's request for a position on a Commerce trade mission to China in August 1994. Directly after the request Robertson was personally appointed by President Clinton under a "Presidential Business Development Mission" to accompany Brown to China.

Robertson personally wrote President Clinton a letter in November of 1994 thanking the President for "autographing the pictures taken in the cabinet room before Ron Brown's delegation to China".

Robertson noted that during the August 1994 China trip, Ron Brown "deftly navigated the human rights issues by obtaining an agreement on further talks" in a meeting with Li Peng, the Chinese Vice Minister.

Li Peng was a PRC major backer of joint economic projects, and well known for avoiding the human rights issue with American officials. Secretary Brown then, according to Robertson, "moved directly into the economic issues at hand, i.e. helping Chrysler, Sprint and others with their joint ventures".

Robertson also included a "P.S." to President Clinton at the end of his November letter. Other than trade, and future meetings to talk human rights, Robertson also clearly notes his money for Democratic Senator Dianne Feinstein.

"P.S.", Robertson wrote to President Clinton. "Bob Rubin came to our home on Thursday for a Dianne Feinstein dinner, which raised over $100,000 for her campaign. Bob, of course, turned out the financial community and

Silicon Valley".

The curious reference Robertson makes here is to Robert Rubin, then Assistant to the President for Economic Policy and manager of the White House National Economic Council (NEC). Rubin, according to Robertson, managed to turn out "the financial community and Silicon Valley" for a DNC fundraiser at Robertson's home. This fact alone points to the close working relationship between the White House, the DNC and Sanford Robertson.

Sanford "Sandy" Robertson had a long history of donations to the Democrats. Other documents in the hidden files kept by Brown include a 1995 article written by the NEW YORK POST. For some reason Brown kept the article hidden with the donation letters.

In 1995 Robertson admitted to the Post that the only reason he was select- ed for the China trade mission was because he "organized a group of CEOs" to support Clinton early in the 1992 election.

In fact, starting in 1993, Robertson and his investment company, Robertson Stephens & Co., donated about one million dollars to the DNC. One benefit of this financial relationship, according to Robertson's New York Post interview, was a spot on the August 1994 trade trip to China led by Ron Brown.

It is already known that one other major DNC donor was on the same August flight to China, Bernard Schwartz, the CEO of Loral aerospace. Loral and Schwartz are currently under investigation for illegal campaign donations to Clinton connected to a Loral missile technology transfer to China. Schwartz was the leading 1996 giver to Clinton and, like Robertson, has donated over a million dollars to the DNC.

Yet, Robertson also wrote two earlier letters to Ron Brown. One in April, 1994 - before the trip, and one in September 1994 - after the China trade mis- sion. These letters detail his direct involvement with the communist govern- ment.

In the April 1994 letter Robertson made his initial request to travel with Brown. Robertson wrote he represented a "medium sized" US company.

Robertson also reminded Brown of up coming money raising efforts for the DNC and of his efforts for DNC candidates.

"P.S." Robertson wrote to Brown. "It has been fund raising season out here for the Senate and we've had events at our home for Feinstein, Lieberman, and Cooper. I wish you were still head of the DNC for the December elections, but you are obviously doing a great job at Commerce."

In the same letter Robertson also noted for Brown of his influence in another political party. In April 1994 Robertson informed Brown of his suc- cessful effort to bribe a major Chinese Communist leader.

"Currently," wrote Robertson. "We are working on a joint venture with China's second largest pharmaceutical company... We have recently hired Bo Feng the son of Feng Zhijun the vice chairman of the China Democratic League and a member of the Standing Committee of the National People's Congress. It is anticipated that Bo Feng will open a Shanghai or Beijing office for us in the near future."

The world wide common practice of buying political influence by hiring the relatives of high party officials is not unknown even in the U.S. In fact, Ron Brown's son Michael Brown pled guilty to funneling illegal campaign dona- tions to the DNC for his father, Ron Brown. Michael got the money from Nora

Lum. Ms. Lum recently pled guilty to similar charges and is said to be cooperating with Federal Prosecutors.

Lum's company had been under investigation from the FBI since early in the 1992 Clinton campaign. Lum's company was also personally authorized to travel with Ron Brown by President Clinton under the "Presidential Business Development Mission" to China just like Robertson and Loral's Schwartz. Lum did not fly to China but Clinton offered a spot on the what Robertson described as an "oversubscribed" mission.

And what about Bo Feng, the son-of-a-high party official? Robertson's hired son-of-PRC ruler and new VP, wrote an article for FORBES in 1997, titled "Rousing the Sleeping Dragon".

The life of Bo Feng, it turns out, is quite different than what Sanford Robertson described. Bo Feng's stay in Silicon valley started in 1987. Bo was sponsored by an un-named "friend of the family" to come to America at the age of 18.

As a student Bo studied film, and worked in a sushi bar. In 1993 Bo claims "a lot of people in business were very interested in China". By early 1994 Bo was an executive VP for Robertson. Robertson hired Bo right out of community college at the ripe age of 24. According to the Forbes article, Bo toured China, investing American money from Robertson's firm into high tech PRC computer companies.

However, Bo claims in his 1997 Forbes article that father "was a professor at the Shanghai Institute of Railroad Technology".

This makes it sound like dad worked on the Chinese railroads or designed rail equipment. In contrast, according to Robertson's letter to Ron Brown, Bo's father, Feng Zhijun is a member of the Standing Committee of the People's Congress. This would make Bo's dad one of a few dozen ruling elite party members in China.

Thus, according to Robertson, Bo's father not only worked on the rail roads ... He ran the rail roads in China. Of course, father Feng's job would naturally include such mundane communist items such as working political prisoners on forced labor details, and moving People's Army troops in close co-ordination with PLA Generals.

Bo Feng also informed the Forbes reader of his other relatives as well. It seems that neither Bo nor his brother followed Father Feng's red party example by working the Chinese rail lines. In the article Bo Feng wrote that his brother "studied automatic missile control". In fact, Bo claims his brother "really is a rocket scientist"!

After the China mission Sanford Robertson also wrote a second letter to Ron Brown. This letter, written in September 1994, details what Robertson had gained from the China flight. "In one instance," wrote Robertson. "We have arranged a joint project with Shanghai International Securities, the largest investment banking firm in China."

Anyone investing in China should note that its stock market is run for the profit of the communist government. Because Chinese securities are normally denominated and traded in Chinese currencies, the investment value may be affected unfavorably by currency exchange rates.

In addition, there is less information publicly available about Chinese companies. The Chinese are not subject to accounting, auditing, and financial reporting standards and practices comparable to those in the US. Chinese brokerage commissions and other fees may also be higher than in the US.

China also has no requirements that money invested in a company has to be put into the "advertised" prime business. Thus, Chinese companies often invest American money in the local real estate market instead of their core "advertised" business. U.S. investors, for example, who thought they were buying stock in a bicycle company, found themselves funding high rise towers in downtown Shanghai.

Furthermore, legal remedies available to investors in China are more limited than those available with respect to investments in the US. In the case of securities issued by the Chinese government, they may be unable or unwilling to meet obligations on the securities in accordance with agreed terms. This raises the possibility of Chinese nationalization of U.S. investments that now total to over $180 billion dollars. In short: Buyer beware - this is a high risk investment.

Robertson's China funds invested in securities principally traded on the Chinese stock market. In return, Robertson usually took a percentage of the total fund's value in the form of broker fees and charges.

Win, loose or draw, Robertson got paid but the bigger the pot the more he acquired. Political instability, and diplomatic developments affected the value of Robertson's investments in China. Thus, issues such as "human rights" would affect Robertson's bottom line and had to be dealt with. Ron Brown calling for "future" US/Sino talks but doing nothing to anger the Chinese government clearly pleased Robertson and his CEO pals.

The Robertson deal with Shanghai International looked great on paper. Robertson brought American money into the Chinese market and Shanghai invested it.

Shanghai International was founded and run by 42 year old Guan Jinsheng, a Belgian educated son of peasants. Right after signing with Robertson - Guan boasted openly that his company would become the "Merrill Lynch" of China.

Within a year Guan was charged with illegally manipulating the Chinese market in treasury bonds. The communist Chinese government took the extraordinary step of voiding nine minutes of trades on the stock market because Shanghai International tried to push bond prices lower to cover over $100 million dollars in losses.

U.S. investors were not the only ones to loose. The Chinese stock market is also open to ordinary Chinese citizens. Many of them also lost life earnings in the Shanghai scandal. Again, this raises the relationship between the drop in Asian markets rippling into nearby countries and then into the western world. The result has already weakened other nations in Asia such as Indoneasia, Tawain, Malaysia and Korea.

Sandford Robertson's story does not end with simple trade trips and Shanghai stock deals. Vice President Al Gore said he did not violate the law by making phone calls for donations from the White House. One of those calls was supposed to be to Sandy Robertson.

According to Gore's call records of November 1995 the Vice President intended to call Robertson, a longtime Clinton backer, to seek a $100,000 donation. Robertson denies that Gore called him, nonetheless he gave $100,000 to the Democrats in January 1996, with $80,000 of soft money going to the DNC and $20,000 of hard money directly into the Clinton-Gore campaign.

Three months later Robertson's investment banking firm, Robertson Stephens & Co. raked in a financial advisors fee of $2 million for it's role in aiding the merger of two large computer security firms, RSA Data Security Inc., or RSA - the largest US encryption software company - and Security Dynamics Technologies Inc. or SDTI, shortly after RSA had obtained an exclusive deal to pursue encryption research with the People's Republic of China.

The merger of the two companies took place three months after an agreement was signed between James Bidzos, head of RSA, and the Chinese government for the purpose of performing joint research on encryption.

RSA is a leading-edge company in developing "public-key encryption" a type of strong encryption that allows the sender and the receiver to exchange messages without the need to meet beforehand and exchange keys. RSA's product is used by banking and financial institutions to send and verify transfers of funds and is considered the industry's standard means of funds verification.

Bidzos said in an electronic interview that the deal was a "memorandum of understanding," or MOU, with China's Laboratory of Information Security, or LOIS, and the Ministry of Foreign Trade and Economic Cooperation, or MOFTEC. Bidzos said the deal only applies to products that legally may be exported to China.

How important was this deal? According to an official of an RSA competitor, the MOU was a highly significant accomplishment for a US company. "The RSA MOU with China is an historic moment, akin to Linbergh crossing the Atlantic for the first time," said Rich Ankey, Vice President of Certco, a banking and finance information security firm based in New York City.

No other company, including Sun Microsystems, had this kind of agreement with the Chinese, according to Ankey, who added.

"There is no doubt that RSA has positioned itself on the inside track with the People's Republic of China, and the MOU certainly made RSA much more valuable to Security Dynamics."

Securities and Exchange Commission records show that before the merger RSA was worth at most $226 million, and that SDTI paid $285 million for RSA's stock. According to Bidzos, RSA was worth about $296 million at the time of the merger - a good profit by any standard.

For Robertson Stephen's role as broker of the merger, the firm was paid $2 million SEC records show. The merger was routinely approved by the Justice Department, according to Thomas Eddy, the Robertson, Stephens partner who advised SDTI on the merger.

True, Bidzos, who stood to gain a great deal from the China deal, donated nothing to the DNC. However, the following sequence of events is worth noting: According to SEC documents filed at the time of the merger, SDTI President Charles Stuckey discussed with Bidzos the possibility of merging their two companies in November 1995, just a month after Bidzos had made a preliminary visit to the People's Republic of China.

Within days of that meeting, Robertson's name was on Al Gore's call list. In late January of 1996, Robertson's $100,000 was received by the Democrats in Washington. A few days later, Bidzos signed the MOU with China; three months later SDTI merges with RSA to the mutual benefit of all parties.

Some lawmakers concerned about RSA's "joint-research" project wonder whether the Clinton administration was preaching strong control of encryption and practicing the opposite.

Rep. Curt Weldon, Pennsylvania Republican and Chairman of the House National Security subcommittee on Military Research and Development, is one.

"We have been working with the administration to slow the availability of selling encryption technology to developing countries like China," stated Weldon.

"If this [joint research] is the case, it is treason." Weldon said he was "dismayed that the administration was leading the effort to sell this kind of technology to an adversary." He also complained that if the "administration had sold out its own tough policy against encryption exports in exchange for campaign donations this could be grounds for impeachment."

RSA evidently received special attention at the highest levels in the Clinton administration. The Commerce Department never answered whether it had any active oversight of the RSA deal with LOIS. The department spokesman denied access to any answers, citing rules of protecting the proprietary interests of private businesses.

There isn't any evidence that Bidzos broke any rules simply by talking to the Chinese about future services. "The RSA export does not appear to require a license," says Cindy Cohn, a California based lawyer with McGashan & Sarrail who handles cases involving export rules.

"This simply is one of those gray areas in law that drives judges mad and frustrates honest businesses. These exports depend on bureaucrats who interpret broadly written regulations on an adhoc basis. There are no clear guidelines that can be applied equally to everyone. The bureaucracy can deny one export while allowing identical exports to go ahead. It is clearly a 'who-you-know' rather than a 'what-you-know' situation," she stated.

Robertson's warm relationship with the President undoubtedly was and is an asset. A self described lifelong Republican until switching parties in 1992 Robertson was one of the most generous contributors to Clinton and the DNC.

Although, Robertson denies he talked to Gore on the phone, he has backed Clinton since the 1992 campaign and has met both Clinton and Gore. In October 1992, Robertson held a fund-raising dinner party for Clinton, Gore and 70 Silicon Valley and high tech executives at his home in San Francisco.

The dinner raised $400,000. Robertson also lent $100,000 to Clinton's 1993 inaugural, according to a White House report of November 1996. Robertson stated that the latter figure was wrong and his gifts to the Inaugural totaled $8,400.

In his September 1994 letter to Brown, California financier Sanford Robertson thanked Ron Brown for "including me (Robertson) on the trip which was so much in demand and oversubscribed."

Indeed, Robertson had much to thank to Ron Brown for. Robertson's paid connections in Beijing, and Washington helped his business greatly. Robertson had previously noted to Brown in his April 1994 letter that he would "bring a medium sized growing business to your proposed traveling group".

Robertson sold his firm to Bank of America for over one billion dollars. China connections included.

Robertson is living proof that American campaign fund-raising has always been more of an art than a science. However, in 1996 the Democratic Party turned the political act of soliciting money into a criminal money-laundering scheme using Federal facilities and funding. One such operation included Ron Brown and the U.S. Commerce Department.

One document, obtained from the U.S. Commerce Department using the Freedom of Information Act, is the attendance list for a 1994 trade event sponsored by Counsel General Richard W. Mueller. The event was a dinner held in honor of Ron Brown at the "Peak" hotel in Hong Kong.

Attendees at the posh reception included DNC donors Robertson and Loral CEO Bernard Schwartz along with a host of other U.S. corporate executives. The DNC, of course, was also included with Loren Keith Stanton, the "Vice Chairman/Democrats Abroad", making the rounds among the rich, and famous.

The dinner at the "Peak" for Ron Brown also included the bankers for the Chinese Army. Top on the list was Robert Adams, the Governor of the American Chamber of Commerce and then the Executive Director of China International Trust and Investment Corporation (CITIC).

CITIC is the bank of the People's Liberation Army, providing financing for Chinese Army weapons sales and western technology purchases. CITIC serves as the chief investment arm of China's central government and holds ministry status on the Chinese State Council.

In February 1996, Brown arranged for the Chairman of CITIC, Wang Jun, to meet President Clinton. Wang Jun was not only chairman of CITIC but also President of Poly Technologies, a firm known to be an outlet for Chinese weapon exports. Wang Jun met with Ron Brown and DNC fundraiser Charlie "Yah-Lin" Trie prior to having coffee with Bill Clinton. Of course, coffee at the White House included a $50,000 donation from Charlie Trie to the DNC.

Yet, earlier in August of 1994, Charlie Trie also traveled to Beijing with Ron Brown. Trie may not have made the invitation list to the "Peak" in Hong Kong but according to then Commerce General Counsel Ginger Lew, Trie attended high-level meetings during the August 1994 trade mission to Beijing.

Trie is not listed as being invited nor listed as traveling with Brown. Yet, Ms. Lew, who did attend as part of the official U.S. delegation, testified that she saw Charlie Trie in Beijing.

Another U.S. Commerce economic event pushed heavily as a DNC fund-raising scheme was the 1994 Asia Pacific Economic Conference (APEC) in Jakarta, Indonesia. In late 1994, President Clinton and Ron Brown traveled to Jakarta and warmly embraced Indonesian dictator Suharto. Clinton's APEC embrace included a nice pay-off for both him and Suharto, called the Paiton power project, a Lippo sponsored coal burning electric plant in east Java.

However, limitations - legal or not - were not a DNC agenda item. Brown and Clinton did not limit themselves to just deals with dictators and Generals in the Indonesian Army during the APEC 1994 conference.

The official Commerce APEC advocacy report reads like a all-time hit list of the greatest DNC money-bags. Two of the honored (charged and convicted) attendees were Gene and Nora Lum from Dynamic Energy Resources.

Mr. and Mrs. Lum were convicted along with Ron Brown's son, Michael, for illegal campaign contributions, and are currently facing tax evasion charges.

Another attendee was Pauline Kanchanalak from Ban Chang International. John Huang solicited Kanchanalak, a business consultant from Thailand and a legal resident of the United States for donations. The DNC returned all of $253,000 she contributed because they thought that the money came from outside the United States.

Another 1994 APEC attendee was (again) Charlie "Yah-Lin" Trie from Diahatsu International Trading. Trie's old connections with Clinton and his friends inside the Chinese Army also allowed him to travel frequently to Brown sponsored events, including the August 1994 trade trip to China and the 1994 APEC Indonesia conference. For the APEC 1994 conference Charlie Trie also had a well-known Clinton supporter (and big dollar contributor) as his sponsor, DNC Arkansas fundraiser Martha Shoffner.

Other big DNC contributors invited to APEC 1994 include Mike Armstrong from GM Hughes, Gary Tooker of Motorola, Richard Bertsch from Metrosound, Noel Gould lawyer and Vice President of Samasonite Luggage, Richard Park of U.S. Woopon Company, Bill Johnson of Unisys, Adlai Stevenson from SCM (Hua Mei), David Sokol from California Energy, Edward Muller CEO of Mission Energy, Alice Young from the Kay Schuler Law firm, and even Alan Batkins from Kissinger Associates.

Curiously, the number one assignment for APEC '94 was not the sale of U.S. high tech goods or Indonesian energy resources. The number one priority for Ron Brown was the sale of U.S. weapons such as F-16 Fighting Falcon jet fighters to Indonesia. The Commerce Department documentation states "F-16 Fighter Aircraft Program ... Sale of 11 (ex-Pakistani) aircraft completed. Indonesia may purchase the remaining 17 Pakistani aircraft".

Brown convinced the Indonesian defense ministry to purchase U.S. built F-16 Fighting Falcons which were originally sold to Pakistan in 1992. The Falcon sale to Pakistan was canceled during the last days of the Bush administration because Pakistan had openly purchased nuclear weapons technology from China. The Chinese nuclear technology forced an embargo of U.S. arms sales to Pakistan, including the previously ordered F-16s.

In January 1994, Indonesia offered hard cold cash to buy eleven of the original order of twenty-eight Pakistani Falcons. Later that year, at the November 1994 APEC conference, Secretary Brown helped Indonesia realize they could get a great deal on the remaining seventeen Falcon jet fighters. Thus, Indonesia bought the remaining U.S. jets.

Supersonic jet fighters were not the only U.S. weapon for sale. The 1994 Brown advocacy document offered Indonesia the "HAWK Missile Program - Modernization" which upgraded their missiles to equal that deployed in the U.S. military. Indonesia at first sought advance pricing information on U.S. upgrades to their HAWK Surface to Air Missile (SAM) systems bought from Raytheon.

The Commerce notes covering the pending HAWK missile sale states "GOI (Government of Indonesia) has requested P&A (Price and Availability) data from the FMS (U.S. Foreign Military Sales) program and associated upgrades. Min/Finance (The Indonesian Ministry of Finance) has allocated money for this in FY (Fiscal Year) 97". Indonesia was so impressed with the U.S. built HAWK that they went ahead and dedicated funding from their 1997 budget to pay for the upgraded missiles.

The Indonesian HAWK missiles were upgraded by Raytheon but the Clinton campaign funding scandal ruined the Indonesian F-16 Falcon deal. Indonesia canceled the F-16 buy from Lockheed/Martin last year after political concerns were raised in the U.S. over Suharto's close relationship with Clinton. With the F-16 deal gone - Suharto had to do something. Thus, in 1996 he cut a low cost deal with Russia for thirty Sukhoi SU-27 (NATO codename "Flanker") jet fighters.

Nor was Indonesia the only interested party at APEC 1994 with a shopping list of U.S. jet fighters for Ron Brown. Malaysia also sought out the U.S. Secretary of Commerce to help arm their country. Another Brown document labeled "MALAYSIA SUMMARY OF ADVOCACY PROJECTS", dated 10/27/94, lists several interesting sale items for the Malaysian defense ministry including the F-18 Hornet jet fighter. The U.S. Hornets were included by Brown's Commerce Department under the aptly descriptive key word "DEAL".

Other advanced U.S. weapons sold to Malaysia included "patrol boats" from Bath Iron works , "Armored Personnel Carrier" made by United Defense company, and a "Command" and control secure communications system provided by LORAL. Brown even sold a U.S. made, "UAV" or Unmanned Aerial Vehicle - robot spy plane from an unnamed U.S. defense contractor.

Ron Brown was directly involved in arms transfers to Asia. The documents show that big buck foreign donors with a vested interest in buying U.S. weapons were also involved. At APEC 1994 the international arms trade was business-as-usual. The tasking of U.S. Commerce officials to push a massive arms build up in Asia says volumes about the Clinton administration.

Ron Brown wasn't just Secretary of Commerce - he was both the Secretary of war and a cash machine for the DNC.

Ron Brown was also a love machine. Ron Brown had a wide variety of lovers during his term as the Secretary of Commerce. The U.S. taxpayer funded many of Brown's sexual escapades directly with pay-offs, contracts and trade trips. Brown's lovers ranged from employees under him at the Commerce Department to outsiders wishing to cash in on the relationship.

One possible benefactor was Yla (pronounced "y-lah") Eason, President of OLMEC Toys. Eason eagerly cashed in on her relationship with Brown to make millions in the U.S. toy market. In 1994, Brown helped Eason to cut an exclusive deal with the Chinese Army to produce plastic dolls for sale in the U.S.

Yla Eason was a young single mother with striking features, who traveled frequently with Brown. In fact, she was a highly favored escort of Ron Brown. Eason traveled to China, Hong Kong and on the Commerce trade mission to South Africa with Ron Brown. Each mission was fully funded by the American taxpayer.

The Commerce Department picked Eason to serve as a speaking panelist at the 1995 BEM (Big Emerging Market) Conference in Washington. Some of her companions at these Brown sponsored events include other Democratic donors such as Bernard Schwartz, Sanford Robertson, Charlie Trie, John Huang, and Nora Lum.

In 1994, Eason took a Hong Kong cruise on board the luxury liner Pacific Princess - the "Love Boat" - with Brown. Eason and Brown sailed the midnight south pacific waters while attending a very posh and private party thrown by their Asian hosts.

Invitees to the "Love Boat" party included the President of the China CITIC bank. CITIC is part of the Chinese communist government and a firm linked to international arms traffic. Wang Jun, chairman of CITIC, is also President of Poly Technologies, a Chinese weapon maker and exporter. In 1996, Wang Jun met with Ron Brown and DNC fundraiser Charlie "Ya-Lin" Trie prior to meeting Bill Clinton and making a large contribution at a White House coffee/fundraiser.

In 1994, Brown took Eason to China. Eason met in Beijing with officials of the China National Toy Association (CNTA) at the personal arrangement of Ron Brown. The CNTA is actually a front for the People's Armed Police (PAP) and the Chinese Army (PLA). CNTA products are manufactured in Gulag like prison factories called Lao Gai.

Eason cut a deal with U.S. toy maker Hasbro to produce a line of "ethnically - correct" dolls in a Chinese Army prison factory. Hasbro, of course, is a donor to the Democratic National Committee.

Eason obtained the rights from Hasbro to the GI Joe plastic molds. Eason created the "Bronze Bombers"; a line of African American super-heroes, simply by painting the GI Joe doll faces black and charging $10 more. The "Bronze Bombers" were imported for sale in TOYS R US, KAYBEE Toys and Wal-Mart.

The rise and fall of Olmec Toys centers on trade deals with China, Ron Brown and Yla Eason. Eason created Olmec Toys in 1985 when "she couldn't find a black super hero for her son." At the peak of Olmec's operations, Eason claimed to make over $5 million in sales a year.

In 1998, Ms. Eason fled Virginia, and disappeared. Minority creditors filed in Court against Eason and seized the remaining Olmec inventory, including Eason's last toy creation - 1,600 Malcolm X dolls. As a result, Eason went into hiding after leaving $1.2 million in unpaid debts, and her company is out of business.

"OLMEC is another example of the kind of unscrupulous dealings that the Clinton administration has with China," stated Al Santoli, former national security advisor to Representative Dana Rohrabacher, R. Calif., in an exclusive interview from Capitol hill.

Before declaring bankruptcy in 1998, Olmec Toys was the largest U.S. manufacturer of Black and Hispanic dolls and action figures. Olmec coined the term "ethnically correct" in the American toy industry and served as a consultant to Hasbro, the world's largest toy company.

Olmec President and CEO Yla Eason, an MBA from Harvard and former journalist, received the 1997 Business Enterprise Award directly from President Clinton. Eason also traveled with Ron Brown to China, meeting with top Chinese officials in the People's Republic government.

Ms. Eason's relationship with China was not all that the official appearances made them out to be. The Clinton administration was forced by the Freedom of Information Act to reveal the details of Olmec meetings with top communist officials.

Eason met with the top trade official in China, Madam Wu Yi, the minister of Chinese Ministry of Foreign Trade and Economic Cooperation, MOFTEC, and sought meetings with the top Chinese representative for World Trade

Organization.

According to the newly declassified materials, some previously withheld by the Clinton administration, Ms. Eason met in Beijing with Mr. Zhang Qingpu, President of the China National Toy Association (CNTA) and the powerful MOFTEC trade minister Madam Wu Yi, at the personal arrangement of Ron Brown.

Ms. Eason's 1994 request to meet with top Chinese trade officials reflects directly on the leadership of the communist nation. According to Commerce Department documents, Ms. Eason sought a meeting with Long Yongtu, Chinese Vice Minister of trade and lead negotiator at the World Trade Organization. Long frequently appears in the western press to promote China trade. According to a recent CNN interview, Long pledged a wide range of market-opening measures aimed at further breaking down mainland trade barriers.

However, Long Yongtu is Vice Minister of MOFTEC, a Chinese government agency linked directly to shipments of advanced U.S. technology to the Chinese military. In 1996, American computer maker SUN Computer Corp. exported a super-computer directly to a Chinese Army nuclear weapons lab. According to the Cox report, the Chinese Ministry of Foreign Trade and Economic Cooperation (MOFTEC) explained that the actual buyer of the computer was the "Yuanwang Corporation" and that Sun was aware of "this corporation's PRC military ties."

In 1995, MOFTEC participated directly with the Chinese military in obtaining U.S. computer security and encryption technology. In October 1995, RSA/Security Dynamics sold computer security encryption technology to the Laboratory of Information Security (LOIS), an information warfare lab, under the control of China's Ministry of Trade and Economic Co-operation (MOFTEC) and the Chinese Army.

According to Al Santoli, former security advisor to Representative Dana Rohrabacher, R. Calif., MOFTEC is directly in business with the Chinese military. In a 1999 special congressional report, Santoli outlined how MOFTEC assisted Chinese military espionage operations by erecting front companies owned by the People's Liberation Army MID or Military Intelligence Department.

"China Resources Enterprise [CRE]... is the commercial arm of China's Ministry of Trade and Economic Co-operation [MOFTEC]," noted Santoli in his report.

"In its investigation into China's attempts to influence the 1996 U.S. presidential campaign, the U.S. Senate Government Affairs Committee identified CRE as a conduit for 'espionage - economic, political and military - for China.' Committee Chairman, Senator Fred Thompson said that CRE has 'geopolitical purposes. Kind of like a smiling tiger; it might look friendly, but its very dangerous.'"

Today, former defense advisor Santoli emphasized that U.S. trade with China is profitable - for the Chinese Army. The continued trade with China's military may look friendly but it is dangerous to U.S. national security.

"This company (OLMEC) and its bankruptcy is another example of the unimaginable wealth the Clinton administration says is in trade with China. With the only benefactors being the People's Liberation Army and communist regime, taking the money and funding a variety of activities including weapons," concluded Santoli.

Defense Department sources indicate that the "China National Toy Association" is actually under direct control of the communist State Council and the Chinese Army. According to the Defense Intelligence Agency, CNTA and all "China National" companies are directly owned by the Chinese military.

A recently declassified Defense Intelligence chart outlines the direct control of the "China National" group under the communist State Council, including China National Nuclear Corporation, China National Electronics and China National Machinery.

"While they are profit-oriented and are the key means for defense complex foreign exchange earning, they also are the primary conduits for acquisition of new and advanced technologies," notes the intelligence document.

U.S. Defense sources clearly document that the "China National" Corporations are totally owned and operated by the military, and they frequently produced consumer goods alongside of weapons. In addition, People's Armed Police business units are known to sell toys and manufactured goods using forced prison labor.

According to a declassified U.S. Defense Department report on the Chinese Army Defense industry "Official Chinese sources talk about more than 470 production lines producing civilian products. New civilian products range from airplanes, railroad cars, trucks, automobiles and spare parts to food, clothing, medicine, and, literally, the kitchen sink."

The 1994 Clinton administration documents show that Olmec had been working with a Chinese partner to "handle shipping, sourcing of products and manufacturing." Olmec was in China to "explore joint venture projects, especially with the mold machinery makers and toy manufacturers."

In 1994, Eason landed a deal with Chinese based Cogo Toys to manufacture modified 3 ¾ inch GI Joe dolls. One Commerce Department document noted, "Cogo Toys manufacturers Olmec's products in the orient. The relationship also establishes a line of credit for Olmec with Cogo Toys... the facility (in China) will be available for a delegation tour."

As a result of the Brown trade mission, Olmec was able to release a line of modified GI Joe dolls, the "Bronze Bombers", on American minority families in 1995.

"Originally fashioned after a Black Army unit from World War I and II, the Bombers are back," states the Olmec advertisement for the painted GI Joe dolls, aimed at directly minority mothers.

"These fully poseable 3 ¾" figures are now enforces of justice who assume identities of great kings of Africa. Each figure comes with a trading card and an action packed comic book. Average retail price is $3.99; recommended for ages 5 years and up."

Another document found in the personal files of Ron Brown noted that Ms. Eason landed the deal with Hasbro, including shelf space for her new idea at Wal-Mart, K-Mart, Toys-R-Us and Kay-Bee Toys using she borrowed from her mother.

"Creative mom, Yla Eason, created a $5 million business selling African American, Hispanic and Asian dolls with ethnically correct features. Her business, Olmec Toys, Inc. started with $60,000 borrowed from family," notes an article from Good Housekeeping, November 1996.

In a 1995 letter for Brown, Ms. Eason described how she secured a facility to assemble and sell the Gi-Joe dolls in a tax free zone in down town Richmond, Virginia.

"The office is 13,000 square feet which includes a warehouse facility," noted Eason in her letter to Brown.

"It is located in an enterprise zone not far from the Arthur Ashe Community Center. Richmond City Manager, Robert Bobb and his economic development group have been exceptional in helping us. Not only were we recruited as if were a fortune 500 company, we were able to take advantage of certain city and state funds as a result of locating in an enterprise zone."

Ms. Eason was reported to be "close" to the Commerce Secretary Ron Brown. This reporter attempted to contact Eason concerning allegations that she was one of Brown's lovers. In response, Ms. Eason promptly left Virginia. Eason was later charged in civil court with also leaving over a million dollars in bad debt with minority lenders such as the Consolidated Bank & Trust Company.

In 1999, all Olmec inventory and resources were sold, the facility in the Richmond "enterprise zone" was closed and creditors continued pursue Ms. Eason. The closing sale included 20,000 minority ethnic board games and Ms. Eason's last idea for the ethnic market, 1,600 Malcolm X dolls.

One recently declassified document reveals the personal relationship between the two. The document, a standard thank you letter from Ron Brown addressed to Eason, includes a curious hand-witten comment for Ms. Eason, "You are wonderful!" wrote Brown to Ms. Eason.

The rise and fall of Olmec is further mirrored in the American toy industry. Most of the blame falls upon the lucrative and expanding one-way toy trade with China and the massive U.S. deficit trade gap with China. The U.S. Commerce Department calculated that the U.S. toy makers lost 66,000 jobs in 1996 alone due to the trade deficit with China.

According to U.S. Commerce Department statistics, recent job losses to China fall hard on American minority workers. U.S. Commerce figures show that Women have been particularly hard hit, absorbing 54% of the total job lost despite being only 47% of the labor force. Blacks, Hispanics, and other minorities also experienced large job losses due to the trade with China.

"We have a thirty billion dollar trade deficit with China," stated Richard Trumka, Secretary-Treasurer of the AFL-CIO. "That translates into 800,000 jobs lost to China. They pay their people on average thirteen cents an hour. Worse, they use prison labor."

According to Chinese dissident Harry Wu, the Chinese police and Chinese Army run prison factories that produce a wide variety of goods, including Eason's "Bronze Bomber" line of dolls. Prisoners work from 12 to 16 hours a day, seven days a week, making highly volatile plastic products with no masks, no training and little ventilation. Statements provided by former prison camp guards to Mr. Wu show that torture and starvation is standard policy at Chinese prison factories.

There are several people who would like to find Yla Eason and get their money back. The minority creditors filed in Court against Eason, and seized the remaining Olmec inventory, including Eason's latest creation of ethnic genius - 10,000 Malcolm X dolls.

These dolls are the ethnically correct and politically incorrect toy story of the Clinton administration. The cover story is a successful businesswoman whose creations stirred pride in the African American community. The ugly facts are that she cheated African American parents with an Al Jolson like paint scheme. She sold toys made in a slave labor camp. Eason shafted her minority financial backers and is now on the run.

Brown had other intimate relationships outside Yla Eason. One confessed lover of Ron Brown is Nolanda Hill. Brown helped Ms. Hill establish TV and radio businesses, using minority set-asides provided by the Clinton administration.

Brown obtained financial backing for Hill who then purchased TV and radio stations under the pretense of minority access. Hill would later re-sell the stations for great profit, generally to the same financial backers locked out by the minority-based project. Brown and Hill are accused of splitting the profits.

Ms. Hill has testified under oath that Brown had some disturbing pillow talk after their passionate sex sessions. Brown confessed to her that the transfer of advanced U.S. military technology to China was treason.

Hill testified that Brown was scared and ordered by the White House to destroy documents. Brown informed her that Clinton advisors John Podesta and Leon Panetta ordered him to cover-up the high tech China exports by destroying evidence. Brown made these startling accusations just prior to his death in 1996.

Even today, the legacy of Ron Brown's sex for trade policy haunts the Clinton administration. Ron Brown was not the only Commerce employee with a lover on the side. John Huang allegedly stayed at his girlfriend's home in southern Maryland to avoid U.S. Marshals. The Marshals were attempting to serve Huang a subpoena to testify before Congress.

In 1997, Commerce legal counsel Hoyt Zia testified about his role in hiding John Huang from Federal authorities. Zia is a former Motorola employee who took a highly sensitive position under Ron Brown. Zia is currently in charge of super computer and other advanced exports at the Commerce Department. During Zia's last mission to Beijing in 1998, communist officials who denied access to inspect super computers previously sold to China rebuffed him.

During his deposition, Zia admitted that he called Huang several times at an unspecified location in Maryland. Zia refused to release his personal phone records despite the fact he agreed to do so under oath. The phone data reportedly shows the exact location of Huang's hideout and the name of his lover.

Zia openly admitted that he knew Huang was being sought by Federal law enforcement. Zia, himself a sworn officer of the Commerce Department, purposely withheld the location of Huang from Federal officials.

Zia admitted that Commerce officials had given him Huang's deposition before his own testimony. Zia confessed that he and Huang would frequently leave the Commerce Department and work at DNC headquarters raising money from the Asian-American community. Zia, however, refused to comment on what he and Huang did after these late night sessions of dialing for DNC dollars.

During his deposition, Zia denied that he had dated a former Commerce employee, who had taken a lobbying position with Iridium Corporation.

Iridium is a joint a satellite venture part owned by the Chinese Army and part owned by Motorola.

Zia smiled warmly during his deposition while denying that he and the Iridium lobbyist had sex. When the questioning grew detailed, Zia began to contradict himself and he confessed to keeping Huang's location secret.

Zia abruptly ended his deposition by walking out. Zia was clearly shaken by the questioning. Zia has since refused to submit any further testimony despite Court orders that he return.

Motorola officials refused an offer to comment on Zia or Iridium efforts to lobby him. Motorola refused to confirm or deny the alleged sexual affair between Zia and their Iridium lobbyist.

The use of sex in exchange for special trade deals is a disgusting and dirty tale. It is a Clinton legacy left for future historians to ponder but avoided by the Congress and the mainstream press. It involves money, toys and even national security, all the elements of a good spy novel or front-page expose.

Sex, sex and more sex. The mainstream media is fascinated with Bill Clinton's sordid little love affair with his child like employee, Monica Lewinsky. Yet, the evidence suggests that sex for favors was not only a common activity in the Clinton administration - sex for favors was a matter of national policy.

C433367
162-7

**ROBERTSON
STEPHENS &
COMPANY**

September 12, 1994

1994 SEP 23 P 1: 05

The Honorable Ronald H. Brown
Secretary of Commerce
U. S. Department of Commerce
Washington, D.C. 20230

Dear Ron,

Congratulations on your triumphant trip to China! Your salesmanship and diplomacy was valuable for the United States, and specifically for all of us involved in the trip.

Although my projects were less visible than the billion dollar contracts you were helping consummate, the trip was extremely worthwhile for our firm. By basking in the reflected glow of your trip we were able to facilitate projects in China and Hong Kong (as well as Japan).

In one instance, we have arranged a joint project with Shanghai International Securities, the largest investment banking firm in China, to underwrite a major company in China, as well as to exchange trainees between our firms.

I want to thank you for including me on the trip which was so much in demand and oversubscribed. It was very helpful to our firm and, I know we can make it helpful to medium-sized American businesses.

Congratulations again on a commercial and diplomatic triumph.

Very best regards,

Sincerely,

Sanford R. Robertson
Chairman

cc: Melissa A. Moss

555 CALIFORNIA STREET SAN FRANCISCO 94104 415-781-9700
INVESTMENT BANKERS   MEMBER OF ALL MAJOR EXCHANGES
A CALIFORNIA LIMITED PARTNERSHIP

180

C 428551

**ROBERTSON
STEPHENS &
COMPANY**

April 11, 1994

The Honorable Ron Brown
Secretary, Department of Commerce
14th Street between Constitution
    Avenue and E St., NW
Washington, DC 20230

Dear Ron,

I have read with great interest of your efforts in providing an economic balance to the current China MFN debate. The Wall Street Journal indicated that you have a trip of businessmen planned for August of this year. I would like to be considered a candidate for the trip.

Our involvement in the technology and pharmaceutical industries has meant an ever expanding involvement with both Japan and China over the past few years. Currently we are working on a joint venture with China's second-largest pharmaceutical company.

We have recently hired Bo Feng the son of Feng Zhijun, the vice chairman of the China Democratic League and a member of the Standing Committee of the National People's Congress. It is anticipated that Bo Feng will open a Shanghi or Bejing office for us in the near future to enhance the joint venture process with our current client base.

Thank you in advance for your consideration, as I think I might bring a medium sized growing business orientation to your proposed traveling group.

Very best regards,

Sincerely,

Sanford R. Robertson

P.S. It has been fund-raising season out here for the Senate and we've had events at our home for Feinstein, Lieberman, and Cooper. I wish you were still head of the DNC for the December elections, but you are obviously doing a great job at Commerce.

555 CALIFORNIA STREET SAN FRANCISCO 94104 415-781-9700
INVESTMENT BANKERS   MEMBER OF ALL MAJOR EXCHANGES
A CALIFORNIA LIMITED PARTNERSHIP

**ROBERTSON
STEPHENS &
COMPANY**

November 1, 1994

C-434415
162-8

President Bill Clinton
The White House
1600 Pennsylvania Avenue, NW
Washington, DC 20500-2000

Dear Mr. President,

Thank you for autographing the pictures taken in the cabinet room before Ron Brown's delegation to China. The trip seemed to be an economic and diplomatic triumph.

One of the highlights was observing Ron Brown in the way he represented the United States. His diplomatic skills were superb, particularly in the meeting with Li Peng. He deftly navigated the human rights issues by obtaining an agreement on further talks, and then moved directly into the economic issues at hand, i.e. helping Chrysler, Sprint and others with their joint ventures

The twenty-five CEOs were all very impressed with his diplomatic and commercial skills. We all hoped that you and your Administration could find increasing ways to utilize these abilities.

Thanks again for the great pictures.

Keep up the good work!

Sincerely

Sanford R. Robertson
Chairman

SRR/jh

P.S. - Bob Rubin came to our home on Thursday for a Dianne Feinstein dinner, which raised over $100,000 for her campaign. Bob, of course, turned out the financial community and Silicon Valley.

bcc: Ronald H. Brown, Secretary of Commerce
Melissa Moss

555 CALIFORNIA STREET SAN FRANCISCO 94104 415-781-9700
INVESTMENT BANKERS   MEMBER OF ALL MAJOR EXCHANGES
A CALIFORNIA LIMITED PARTNERSHIP

Olmec Toys
156 Fifth Avenue
Suite 231
New York, New York 10010

Yla Eason
President and Chief Executive Officer

Telephone: (212) 645-3660
Facsimile: (212) 645-6360

Biographical Information: Yla Eason, a former journalist, earned a master's in business administration from Harvard University in 1977, and her undergraduate degree from Fitchburg State College. In 1994, she received an honorary doctor of laws degree from Bloomfield College.

Corporate Profile: Olmec Toys is the largest U.S. manufacturer of Black and Hispanic dolls and action figures. It is also one of the oldest continuously operating minority-owned toy companies in America. Incorporated in 1985 and headquartered in New York, Olmec has 14 employees, 35 products, and approximately $3.5 million in sales. The company's sales have grown by 43 percent since 1992.

Olmec coined the term "ethnically correct" in the toy industry by creating toys that sculpted authentic features which represented correct ethnic characteristics. It also pioneered the concept of portraying ethnic doll and toy figures in different skin tones.

Olmec began its own agency service with a Chinese partner to handle shipping, sourcing of products, and manufacturing. The company has done business in China since 1985 and has shipped its products around the world from there. Olmec plans to announce the opening of an agency office in partnership with Cogn Toys of Kowloon, Hong Kong. Through this office, Olmec will handle its own distribution, shipping, and sourcing of products out of Asia.

Beginning in 1995, Olmec will market Asian baby and toddler dolls and hopes to promote these toys in China. Olmec hopes to find a distributor for its toys in China, and explore joint venture projects, especially with mold machinery makers and toy manufacturers.

奥麦克玩具公司
156 Fifth Avenue
Suite 231
New York, New York 10010

莉拉·伊森
董事长兼总经理

电话: (212) 645-3660
传真: (212) 645-6560

个人简介: 莉拉·伊森当过记者，毕业於费翠堡州立学院在
1977 年在哈佛大获得商业管理硕士学位，1994 年她获得布隆
赞尔学院的荣誉法学博士学位。

公司简介: 奥麦克玩具公司是美国最大的黑人玩具娃娃、南
美人玩具娃娃、及动作型人物玩具的制造厂商。该公司是少
数族裔人士开的玩具公司1是美国同类公司中连续营业时间
最长的公司之一。奥麦克玩具公司成立於1985 年。总部设在
纽约，有员工 14 人，35 种产品，销售额为550 万美元。
1992 年以来公司的销售额增加了 45%。

奥麦克公司通过，推出表现正确人种特微、容貌逼真的玩具
，在玩具业中创造了"从人种上说是对的"这一说法。该公司
还首先提出，用不同皮肤色彩来表现人种的玩具娃娃、和玩
具人物的思想。

奥麦克公司同一家中国公司合作，已经开始做自己的代理业
务，以处理运输、进货与制造业务。奥麦克公司自1985 年起
在中国做生意，并从中国把产品销往世界各地。奥麦克公
司计划与香港九龙可歌 (Cogo) 玩具公司合作，设立一个代办
处。奥麦克公司将通过这个办事处，处理其在亚洲以外地区
的批发、运输与进货业务。

从1995 年起，奥麦克公司将销售亚洲婴儿、和学步儿童玩具
娃娃，并希望将这些玩具推销到中国。奥麦克公司希望为其
玩具，在中国找到一家批发商，主要计划是希望与机器厂和
玩具厂建立合资企业。

DEFENSE TRADE ADVOCACY - INDONESIA

Project	Company	Sector	Estimated Value	Estimated U.S. Content	Status	Relevant Ministry
F-16 Fighter Aircraft Program	Lockheed-Martin	Defense			Sale of 11 (ex-Pakistani) aircraft just completed. Indonesia may purchase the remaining 17 Pakistani aircraft	MoD
HAWK Missile Program Modernization	Raytheon	Defense			GOI has requested P&A data for the FMS program and the associated upgrades. Min/Finance has allocated money for this in FY97	MoD

185

9

ENRON

Things pass for what they seem, not for what they are.
Balthasar Gracian - The Art of Worldly Wisdom

The attempt to paint the Enron bankruptcy as a Bush scandal includes a badly made-for-TV movie produced by CBS called "The Crooked E." The spin in the fictional world of Hollywood was that the Bush administration, wooed by Enron dollars, and helped the corrupt executives steal from the poor and working class heroes.

If you followed this spin, it was clear that Enron had no contact with the U.S. government prior to George W. Bush coming into office. According to CBS, Enron simply did not exist prior to George W. Bush.

Yet the CBS TV sit-com flopped like a dead fish when confronted by facts. Enron and Bill Clinton were the best of bedfellows in corruption.

The U.S Commerce Department has been forced to release over 5,000 pages of documents detailing the long list of corrupt deals, trips and government candy doled out to Enron by President Clinton.

The Bush administration did not want to release these documents but was forced by this reporter using the Freedom of Information Act.

For example, in 1999 Gov. Gray Davis of California led a $200,000 trade trip to Europe that was very high on the Enron list. Davis tripped on California taxpayer expense with his wife in ancient Greece, lobbying on behalf of Enron Wind for the "Greek Wind Project."

The project in Greece was so important that Davis also took his good friend, major DNC donor and Sacramento developer Angelo K. Tsakopoulos. Tsakopoulos and his family are million-dollar contributors to the Democratic National Committee or Democrat candidates including Davis, Bill Clinton, Al Gore and Hillary Clinton. Tsakopoulos also spent time as a guest in the White House Lincoln bedroom.

According to documents forced from the U.S. Commerce Department, Enron Wind noted that Davis and Tsakopoulos were tripping to Greece with some very unusual comments:

"Best man at my Greek wedding," noted one handwritten comment next to a Los Angeles Times article on Tsakopoulos attached to documents from the U.S. Embassy in Athens.

"Major Clinton donor - may be on Clinton trip to Greece."

Enron considered the trade trip so important that it also included a 22-

page briefing paper addressed to Gov. Davis detailing the "Greek Wind Project Permitting Issue." Interestingly, the same briefing paper made its way into the commercial section of the U.S. Embassy in Athens.

"An issue has arisen which seems to have some negative implications for follow-on investment in the renewable energy sector," states the Enron document.

"Namely on 4 August 1999, a decree was issued by the Ministry of Development which changes the procedure for obtaining future construction licenses for wind projects on the island of Crete and certain other islands. The decree would have a negative impact on a $30 million project Enron Wind was about to begin construction on in Crete, the Chronos (pronounced Honos) project."

The 1999 documents are part of a long string of heavy lobbying efforts that the Clinton administration carried out to convince the Greeks to buy Enron Wind products for Crete.

For example, a 1998 document prepared for the U.S. ambassador to Greece noted, "The company [Enron] was given an installation license last year, but construction was held up while an archeological study was performed. In the interim, the licenses lapsed and Enron's request for a renewal has not been answered."

"Enron should send more high-level visitors to Greece to underscore the importance of this market," states the 1998 memo to the U.S. ambassador to Greece.

Enron also pushed the limits inside the former Yugoslavia. Commerce Secretary Ron Brown worked on an Enron contract in Croatia just prior to his death in 1996. Brown's death did place the project on hold but only for a short period of time.

Enron executives flew to Croatia with Clinton Commerce Secretary Kantor after making a $100,000 donation to the DNC just days before the visit. As a result, Enron struck a deal with the Croatian government to build a power station and run it for 20 years - at a highly inflated price of nearly $200 million above market prices.

However, tapes of the Enron negotiations and Croatian officials show that the U.S. energy company had promised more than electricity at higher than normal cost. According to the Financial Times, Croatia hoped the Enron deal would secure political favors inside the Clinton administration, including a state visit to Washington and membership in the World Trade Organization - WTO.

In one reported meeting, Enron's head of international operations Joseph Sutton guaranteed that Enron would lobby President Clinton for Croatia's entry into the WTO, the NATO partnership for peace program and even NATO.

Stockholders and law enforcement officials should be very interested in the payments made by the energy giant to its foreign partners and White House patrons. Clearly, with promises of NATO membership, Enron felt its donations had bought top level White House influence.

In 1999, Enron Executive Vice President Terence Thorn wrote a personal letter of thanks to President Clinton, carrying out the promised support for Croatia.

"I have good news about an opportunity in a strategically important nation,

Croatia. Enron International through the direct involvement of President Franjo Tudjman has successfully concluded negotiations to build a 240 MW natural gas powered plant at Jertovec, Croatia," wrote Thorn to Clinton.

"Our people have come to know Croatia, its people and its President. Through our power project Croatia solidified those ties and welcomed the United States as its largest foreign investor. Croatia is also cooperating with NATO to bring peace to the Balkan region," wrote Thorn.

"President Tudjman's support and perseverance in having a United States company participate in Croatia's economy deserves to be recognized. He would welcome an invitation from you to come to the White House. I respectfully request President Tudjman be invited to visit you in the White House at the earliest possible time," concluded Thorn.

In 1995 Kenneth Lay, accompanied Secretary of Commerce Ronald Brown on the trade mission to India. In India, Enron signed a $400 million contract for a 2,000-megawatt power plant in Dabhol. Enron also won a contract to build a $920 million power plant on the West coast of India and a $1.1 billion contract for offshore gas and oil production.

The most infamous Enron project is the troubled Dabhol power plant in India. President Clinton highlighted Enron's problems with its planned $3 billion Dabhol power project in a short "FYI" note to his chief of staff Mack McLarty. McLarty worked with Enron and the U.S. ambassador in New Delhi to keep tabs on the Dabhol project.

Four days before India finally granted approval for the project, Enron donated $100,000 to the DNC. The donation made Dabhol and Enron top priorities in the Clinton White House.

One 1995 Commerce Department document outlined that Enron's Dabhol project was "currently experiencing major difficulties." The document noted that Dabhol had received "counterguarantess from the Central Government of India as a result of vigours USG (U.S. Government) advocacy efforts" resulting in a contract signing "witnessed by Secretary Brown during his January mission to India."

"Based on our most recent interventions (Secretary O'Leary meeting with Minister of Power Salve and the Embassy reporting), the Central Government is supportive of the project. Secretary Brown, Secretary O'Leary, State Under Secretary Spero and Commerce Assistant Secretary Raymond Vickery advocated vigorously over the last several months in support of the project with the Minister of Commerce, Chidambaram, Minister Salve and Chief Minister from Maharashtra Joshi, who, ironically just recently visited the United States to promote foreign investment in India."

The Clinton administration clearly documented its efforts on behalf of Enron, including those of the President himself. According to a March 2000 document titled "Prominent Major Projects in South India involving U.S. Firms", Clinton was still lobbying India for more Enron projects right up to his last months in office.

"The following is a list of project in South India for POTUS (President Of The United States) follow up," states the Commerce document.

"Enron plans to susstitute natural gas for coal for the Karnataka Power Corporation's proposed Vijayanagar 500 MW power project. Enron proposes to construct a pipeline from its gas terminal at Dabhol, Maharashtra to bring natural gas to central Karnataka," notes the March 2000 document for

Clinton.

"Advocacy support for this project requires subtle handling of the concerned local Karnataka government authorities, as it involves both project selling and escrow coverage. We will look for ways to continue to work with the Karnataka Power Corporation and the Power Secretary to support this project."

Enron's donations gave it exclusive access to Clinton administration support for deals inside communist China. One such project involved the direct intervention of the U.S. government with communist China to build the Songyu power plant and Liquid Natural Gas terminal located directly across from Taiwan.

According to U.S. Commerce Dept. documents, the Clinton administration successfully sought the approval of the Beijing government for the Songyu 2,000 mega watt power plant and for the Xiamen Liquid Natural Gas terminal in Fujian province.

"Project has support of City Gov't of Xiamen," states a 1999 Commerce Dept. advocacy document. "Support Enron and urge Chinese to approve project."

The twin gas projects inside China were worth nearly $2 billion to Enron. However, to the Clinton administration, a factor more important than money was how many Congressional districts in Texas were involved. According to the Commerce Dept. document, 18 Texas districts would be involved in the Chinese project.

Fiction writers documented the fall Enron as a scandal to be linked to President Bush. Yet, the U.S. Commerce Department has just released over 5,000 pages of real documents that detail the Enron scandal during the Clinton years.

The Commerce materials outline a long-standing and very close relationship between the Clinton administration and Enron. For example, in March 1999 U.S. Commerce Secretary William Daley's trade delegation to China produced several sweet business deals, including a special little gem for Enron.

Enron International China Pipeline, a wholly owned subsidiary of Enron Corp. of Houston Texas, signed a memorandum of understanding with China National Petroleum Corporation to jointly develop a natural gas pipeline.

"Enron International approached FCS (Foreign Commercial Service) Beijing for advocacy support for its joint venture to build a 4,000 km, $400 million natural gas pipeline from reserves in Sichuan Province to markets in and around Wuhan in eastern China," states an April 1999 Commerce document from Ivone Yang.

"CO Adams worked with Enron and USDOC's Advocacy Center to win the Chinese authorities blessing so that Enron International was able to sign a Memorandum of Understanding during Secretary Daley's visit to China in March 1999 with its partner, China National Petroleum Corporation (CNPC)," notes the Commerce Department memo.

The deal also sealed the first major U.S. energy effort with China National Petroleum. However, China National Petroleum already has great experience at building pipelines under hostile conditions. CNPC is a Chinese Army owned firm that currently operates an oil pipeline inside war torn areas of Sudan.

DECEPTION

According to an article published in Investor's Business Daily by John Berlau, "Chinese Oil Firm Listing on NYSE Faces Fight Due To Terrorist Links", CNPC operates an oil pipeline through the contested areas inside Sudan.

"Canada's Foreign Affairs Ministry recently found that the oil pipeline that CNPC is building with Sudan's government and others is 'exacerbating the conflict' that has already killed 2 million people," wrote Berlau. "Not only will the oil revenue go to fuel the war effort but Sudan's government is using the pipeline project's airstrip for bombing missions."

The work to help Enron even touched the king of "Green" - Vice President Al Gore. The Chinese deal with Enron has its roots with former Vice President Al Gore. In 1998, Gore wrote the Chinese leadership, urging them to sign lucrative contracts with Enron.

"In mid 1997, then State Development and Planning Commission (SDPC) Vice-Chairman Zeng Peiyan and the Secretary of Energy signed an Energy and Environment Cooperation initiative. Under that initiative, the two side have held two oil and gas forums and, last spring in Beijing, a national gas experts meeting," notes a 1998 Commerce Department document.

"The largest project to date in promoting natural gas use is the Guangdong Liquefied Natural Gas (LNG) terminal, to be constructed near Shenzhen... Several U.S. companies are actively pursing foreign partner status, including ExxonMobil, Enron and Chevron," noted the Commerce document.

"Vice President Gore recently wrote to Premier Zhu, expressing his hope that the Guangdong LNG project would become an example of successful U.S.-China clean energy cooperation," states the Commerce Department document.

In 1995, the Clinton-Gore effort to help Enron win deals crossed all bounds of decency by using humanitarian aid as leverage. The Clinton-Gore National Security Council and Vice President Gore strong-armed Mozambique so that Enron could obtain an exclusive deal using threats of aid cuts as leverage.

Enron failed to match the terms offered by South African firm Sasol for the giant Pande gas fields. However, Enron Corp.'s plan to develop Mozambique's Pande natural gas field was saved from cancellation by a blunt threat from Clinton Security Council head Anthony Lake to cut off future U.S. humanitarian aid to Mozambique.

When Mozambique threatened to cancel the Enron Pande gas deal, Lake promptly suspended a $135 million humanitarian aid payment. Lake also wrote a threatening letter directly to the Mozambican President.

"There is at the moment a debate of unprecedented intensity in Washington with regard to my government's overall budget, and particularly, funding for foreign assistance. Mr. President, we hope for a mutual effect on Africa on this debate. However, it will become increasingly difficult to defend such programs if some are able to argue that promising countries like Mozambique are not moving ahead rapidly to ensure economic growth through resources development," wrote Lake.

In the end, Mozambique caved, giving the exclusive deal to Enron over a South African firm. However, the only market for the Mozambique gas was a steel plant in South Africa. It would take two visits from VP Gore and Energy Secretary Hazel O'Leary to South Africa to convince the Pretoria government to buy the Enron deal.

O'Leary frequently included Enron officials on her trips to South Africa. In return, Enron donated money to a charity favored by the Energy Secretary. Enron donated an unknown sum of cash in O'Leary's name to a charity called "I Have a Dream" in late 1995.

Enron also dabbled in politics and legal systems of Mexico. For example, Mexican millionaire Carlos Gottfried Joy is well known to international circles as a butterfly enthusiast. According to the BBC, Gottfried recently met with Prince Charles to discuss the Mexican life of the Monarch butterfly.

However, in 1997 Gottfried had a serious legal problem at home. According to newly released documents from the U.S. Commerce Department, Gottfried's close relationship with both Enron and the Clinton administration got him out of jail. The documents were obtained using the Freedom of Information Act.

On December 17, 1997, Enron Wind CEO, Ken Karas, wrote Charles Brayshaw, the Charge d'Affairs U.S. Embassy in Mexico, a letter. In this letter Karas addressed his concerns about some legal problems with Enron's business partner Carlos Gottfried Joy.

"We are writing this letter to bring to your attention, and seek your assistance in connection with, what we believe to be the unjustified treatment of Mr. Carlos F. Gottfried Joy, whose company is the majority investor in a Mexican wind energy company in which we own an interest, by the state and municipal authorities of Zacatecas," wrote Karas.

"Since the early 1990's, we have endeavored to develop commercial wind power plants in Mexico and in fact own a minority interest in Fuerza-Eolica, a Mexican wind energy company. Mr. Gottfried's company, Grupo Fuerza, S.A., owns the majority interest in Fuerza-Eolica," noted Karas.

"Fuerza-Eolica is, and has been for some time, engaged in a commercial dispute with the State and Municipality of Zacatecas over a small, pilot wind energy project. The Municipality of Zacatecas commissioned the project in 1992, entered into a supply contract with Fuerza-Eolica and, in fact, made a down payment to Fuerza-Eolica of approximately US $1.5 million for the initial phase of the project," wrote Karas.

"Unfortunately, before turbines were shipped or other construction activities commenced in Zacatecas, the local government changed and the new administration summarily canceled the project," noted Karas.

"Some five years later and after several attempts by Fuerza-Eolica to work with Zacatecas to complete the project, Zacatecas has sued Fuerza-Eolica, demanding that it repay the loans owing to Banobras. We believe the demands are without merit and that the project would have been completed but for Zacatecas' decision to cancel it. To pressure Fuerza-Eolica, Zacatecas took the extraordinary step of arresting Mr. Gottfried, claiming that he defrauded Zacatecas. Mr. Gottfried is now out of jail on bail, set not coincidentally in the amount of the Banobras loan obligation,' wrote Karas.

"We have reviewed the activities of Fuerza-Eolica and have no reason to believe that Mr. Gottfried has engaged in any fraudulent conduct. At the same time, we find the conduct of Zacatecas, using its criminal powers to influence a commercial settlement, excessive. While of course we can not fully convey to you in this letter all of the facts surrounding this dispute, we would ask for an opportunity to more completely brief you on these events," noted Karas.

"We would also ask for your help in arranging a meeting with the appropriate Mexican authorities to address these issues and, importantly, to impress upon them that this is a commercial dispute and as such, the use of criminal process to influence the commercial outcome is not tolerable. With that assistance we are hopeful that the employees of Fuerza Eolica will not be subject to the type of criminal actions which has been used against Mr. Gottfried," concluded Karas.

Gottfried's criminal charges raised such concern to Enron officials that Adam Umanoff, Enron's Senior VP and General Counsel, forwarded a copy of Karas's letter to Jill Hinson at the U.S. embassy in Mexico City.

"Attached is a letter to Mr. Brayshaw from Ken Karas, my company's president, describing our recent unfortunate experience on a commercial matter in Mexico. I appreciate your offer to pass this letter on to the appropriate officials in our embassy. Please let the appropriate people know to contact me directly to discuss this matter," wrote Umanoff.

It is not unusual for U.S. embassy staff to contact foreign authorities when charges are filed in another nation against U.S. citizens. Enron, however, was asking the U.S. government to lobby Mexican officials on behalf of a Mexican citizen charged with illegal activity.

The problem of U.S. intervention in a Mexican criminal matter did not escape American embassy officers. Scribbled on top of the Enron fax cover page was a handwritten comment by an unnamed U.S. embassy official.

"I am meeting with Gottfried tomorrow. Would a letter such as is being requested represent 'pol(itical) pressure or interference'?" noted the U.S. embassy official.

Enron did not want pressure or interference. Enron wanted the Mexican contract to be paid. Thus, Enron's legal counsel Umanoff would go farther. On March 4, 1998 he wrote a long letter to Andrew Wylegala Commercial Attaché at the U.S. embassy.

"It was a pleasure meeting you on February 20. I especially appreciate your offer of assistance in connection with the difficulties being experienced by Fuerza Eclica and Carlos and Gustevo Gottfried. As a follow up to that meeting, I would like to request your specific assistance in connection with certain legal proceedings in Mexico. If the judges in these proceedings do in fact rule in accordance with law, we are optimistic that the 'criminal' complaints brought against various individuals will be set aside and the Zacatecas dispute can be properly resolved as a commercial dispute. As you know, one of our primary objectives in this dispute is to have it resolved in a commercial, not criminal, forum," wrote Umanoff.

"To give you some additional details, and as we discussed generally in our meeting, the Municipality of Zacatecas continues to pursue criminal proceedings against both Carlos and Gustavo Gottfried. Counsel for the Gottfrieds has initiated federal habeas corpus actions on behalf of the Gottfrieds which, as I understand it, are designed to protect the constitutional liberties of each of the Gottfrieds (in essence, to protect them from wrongful criminal prosecution). The habeas corptis action against Gustavo has been heard by Mrs. Avalina Merales Guzman, Second District Federal Criminal Judge in Mexico City. She is expected to rule on the action within the next week to ten days," noted Enron's Umanoff.

"The habeas corpus action for Carlos Gottfried is not scheduled to be heard until April and will be before Mr. Jose Rejugio Estrada Araujo, a Federal Judge in Zacatecas. The Gottfried's criminal counsel believes that if the federal judges hearing these actions rule on the merits and are not subject to any political pressure or interference they should find in the Gottfrieds' favor. Such a finding could result in the dismissal of the criminal case in Zacatecas," wrote Umanoff.

"Therefore, we would request the Embassy take whatever steps are allowed to encourage these judges to consider the cases in accordance with law. The Gottfrieds' counsel advises us that perhaps the most appropriate course would be for the Embassy to contact the Minister of the Interior, Lic. Francisco Labastida Ochoa to request his intervention with Minister Jose Vicente Aguinaco Aleman, the President of both the Supreme Court of Justice and the Judicature Counsel, as well as with Arturo Roman Gutierrez, the sitting Governor of Zacatecas, to request that the cases be ruled upon in strict accordance with law," noted Umanoff.

"Of course, as you mentioned in our meeting, there may be other appropriate avenues of communication between our Embassy and the Mexican authorities and we of course would appreciate whatever steps you might take to assist us in this matter," wrote Umanoff.

However, the best-laid plans of Key Lay often go Enron. In April 1998, the U.S. embassy's and Enron's attempt to influence the Mexican courts leaked out to the public. Enron's legal beagle Adam Umanoff wrote a letter to Andrew Wylegala at the U.S. embassy, trying to explain the leak.

"Thank you for your letter of March 30. It is encouraging that you have gotten a commitment from Mexican officials to look into the Zacatecas matter," noted Umanoff.

"I share, however, your frustration and concern over the apparent leak of Embassy correspondence to journalists in Mexico. As requested, we have looked further into the matter and have discovered the following. Ken Karas' December 17, 1997 letter to the Charge d'Affaires was in fact publicly disclosed by Carlos Gottfried's lawyers at a court hearing in Zacatecas. A copy of Carlos' March 31 fax to me describing the circumstance of this disclosure is attached. We were not aware of this disclosure until receiving Carlos' March 31 fax. This disclosure directly contravenes our working understanding with Carlos Gottfried and Fuerza Eolice concerning the confidentiality of our communications. Nevertheless, on behalf of our company, I apologize that this disclosure occurred," wrote Umanoff.

"As to the disclosure of the Charge's letter, we have not been able to identify the source of the 'leak.' It is apparent to me that we may never know how that letter became public," concluded Umanoff.

In the end, despite the leaks, the Clinton administration "interference" on behalf of Enron would succeed. In a final May 28, 1998 letter to Andy Wylegala at the U.S. embassy, Enron's legal top dog Adam Umanoff would write his thanks.

"With the recent positive news concerning the criminal proceedings in Zacatecas, we do not feel it appropriate to elevate any further the Zacatecas dispute," wrote Umanoff.

"Once again, thank you for your continued assistance in support of our activities in Mexico," concluded Umanoff.

DECEPTION

The newly released documents show that the Clinton administration worked for Enron in Mexico, China, Vietnam, South Africa, India, Brazil, Argentina, Mozambique, South Korea, Japan, Belgium, France, Russia, the Philippines, the West Bank and Uzbekistan.

Many former Clinton administration officials eventually went to work for Enron, including former White House counsel Jack Quinn, former Assistant Treasury Secretary Linda Robertson, former Chair of the Federal Energy Regulatory Commission Elizabeth Moler, and the former media adviser to Vice President Al Gore, Greg Simon.

Enron not only donated $100,000 to Clinton's 1993 inauguration but, according to the records, also added an additional $25,000 to the Clinton 1993 celebrations.

There are several direct connections between Enron and Bill Clinton. A major part of U.S. taxpayer financing for Enron's Indonesian projects was obtained through the EXPORT-IMPORT bank (EXIM).

Several of the Indonesian projects listed in Commerce documents note that EXIM head Ken Brody worked closely with Commerce Secretary Brown on the U.S. government financing. The EXIM bank under Brody financed over $4 billion dollars worth of gas deals for Enron.

Ken Brody is also a close friend of former Clinton Treasury Secretary Robert Rubin. Rubin worked with Brody during his years at the investment firm Goldman Sachs. Enron is listed as one of forty-four such companies in which Rubin had "significant contact" with during his years at Goldman Sachs.

Rubin would later call Bush administration Treasury officials in an effort to pressure the new administration to help Enron avoid bankruptcy.

A study by the Center for Public Integrity shows that 187 companies participated in 14 Clinton sponsored trade missions. Of those, 67 are known to have contributed money to the Democrats.

Between 1993 and 1994, 26 companies received support from the Overseas Private Investment Corp. and the Export-Import Bank totaling about $5 billion. According to the center's study, five corporations-Enron, U.S. West, GTE, McDonnell Douglas and Fluor-donated $563,000 to the Democrats and received at least $2.6 billion in contracts.

During the 1990s, Enron CEO Ken Lay personally contributed $11,000 to former President Bill Clinton for his two campaigns. In addition, Lay gave Vice President Al Gore $13,750 for his 2000 election campaign. During Clinton's eight years in office, the company and Lay contributed about $900,000 to the Democratic Party.

Former Enron officials said donation money was an important part of their strategy to win favor with the Gore campaign. In 1999 and 2000, the company gave $362,000 in soft-money donations to Democrats.

Enron donated $55,000 to the Democratic National Committee in 1997 and 1998. The donations were made at the same time Enron held meetings with Bill Clinton and Vice President Al Gore. Enron Corp. donated $420,000 to Democrats over a three-year period while heavily lobbying the Clinton administration to support the global warming treaty that would have dramatically increased the firm's sales of natural gas. Federal and confidential corporate records show that Enron obtained access to Clinton and Gore after donating thousands of dollars in soft money and PAC donations beginning in

1995.

In fact, the documented evidence shows that Enron did make it into the Clinton White House by special invitation. Senior Vice President Terrance H. Thorn had coffee with Bill Clinton on March 5, 1996.

Many of the other attendees of the Clinton White House coffee sessions also make up a long list of convicted criminals, arms dealers and bagmen for illegal DNC contributions.

It is little wonder that democrats are no longer anxious to follow the Enron corruption trail. Enron's documented "corruption, collusion and nepotism" started and ended with Bill Clinton.

The scandal that became Enron touched more than a few employees and stockholders. It corrupted nation after nation, spreading its wings as part of Bill Clinton's stained legacy.

Most Americans were not aware of Enron's dealings with a Chinese Army oil company engaged in an oil-for-blood in Sudan. The mass media neglected to inform the U.S. public about the cruel use of humanitarian aid by the Clinton administration that greased an Enron deal in Africa. The fiction writers who spin your news never mentioned the Enron donations to the DNC.

If you paid attention to any of the mainstream media outlets you can be certain that Enron never existed during the Clinton years.

C965559

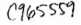

Enron Corp.
3776 Eye Street, N.W., Suite 800
Washington, D.C 20006
(202) 326-3360
Fax (202) 828-3377

April 20, 1999

The Honorable William J. Clinton
The President of the United States
The White House
1600 Pennsylvania Avenue, NW
Washington, DC 20500

Dear Mr. President:

It has been several months since we spoke about energy developments. In the interim, I accompanied Secretary of Commerce Bill Daley to Korea and China. In both countries Enron has either acquired energy assets or announced significant new projects.

I have some good news about an opportunity in a strategically important nation, Croatia. Enron International through the direct involvement of President Franjo Tudjman has successfully concluded negotiations to build a 240 MW natural gas powered plant at Jertovec, Croatia. This is the first such facility negotiated by an American energy company in Croatia. These negotiations were commenced with the assistance of former Commerce Secretary Ron Brown. The positive results are a lasting tribute to his service to the United States and his interest in Croatia.

Our people have come to know Croatia, its people and its President. Through our power project Croatia solidified those ties and welcomed the United States as its largest foreign investor. Croatia is also cooperating with NATO to bring peace to the Balkan region.

President Tudjman's support and perseverance in having a United States company participate in Croatia's economy deserves to be recognized. He would welcome an invitation from you to come to the White House. I respectfully request President Tudjman be invited to visit you in the White House at the earliest possible time.

I greatly appreciate your consideration of this request.

Sincerely,

Terence H. Thorn
Executive Vice President
International Government Relations
& Environmental Affairs
Enron International

Natural gas. Electricity. Endless possibilities.™

Briefing Paper

for Governor Gray Davis

Greek Wind Project Permitting Issue

Enron Wind Corp.
Tehachapi, California

IWECO, S.A.
an Enron Wind Corp. Company
Athens, Greece

Dr. James A. Walker
Managing Director

October, 1999

Davis--and Big Donors--Begin Trade Mission

By RONE TEMPEST, Times Assesment Bureau Chief

SACRAMENTO—California Gov. Gray Davis' first official overseas trip to Europe and the Middle East is billed by staff as a trade development mission.

But among the 20 prominent business and labor officials accompanying Davis on the two-week voyage, which begins today, are some of his most devoted supporters and generous campaign contributors, including several who donated more than $100,000 each to his election campaign last fall.

The Davis entourage, including his wife, Sharon, will visit England, Ireland, Scotland, Greece, Israel and Egypt. Highlights of the trip will include a meeting with British Prime Minister Tony Blair on Monday and an excursion to a water development project in the Sahara about 700 miles from Cairo on Oct. 28.

"The entire trip is about California business development," said spokesman Michael Bustamante, one of the more than two dozen staff and security people who will travel with Davis. Bustamante estimated that the trip will cost the state more than $200,000.

Private citizens traveling with the governor will pay their own costs, Bustamante said.

Tony Miller, a Sacramento attorney who is active in campaign finance reform, said the trip is also about rewarding those who contributed most heavily to Davis' election.

"Most of these people are major contributors to the Democratic Party," said Miller, a former acting California secretary of state. Among the major contributors accompanying the governor to some of the destinations are grocery store magnate Ron Burkle and workers' compensation insurance executive Stanley Zax. Burkle, chairman of the board of Ralphs grocery stores, spent $1.8 million on state political races last year, including the $335,000 he donated to the Davis campaign. Zax, whose insurance industry is heavily regulated by the state, gave $100,000 to the Davis campaign.

Another Davis supporter on the trip to Greece is Sacramento developer Angelo Tsakopoulos, whose family gave $150,000 last year, mostly to Democratic candidates.

Only one Davis Cabinet member, Trade and Commerce Secretary Lon Hatamiya, will travel with the governor.

Jerry Hallisey, a San Francisco attorney and influential fund-raiser for California Democratic politicians, will join Davis in London and Ireland. Hallisey, a former UC regent who serves on the California Transportation Commission, said his participation has public value for the state.

http://www.latimes.com/cgi-bin/print.cgi   10/10/2000

NOV 04 '99 01:27   +38 1 9963574   PAGE.19

198

Enron

Enron Wind Corp.

Handwritten note: JAH - I am meeting w/ Gottfried tomorrow. Would a letter such as is being requested represent "pol pressure or interference"?

TELEFAX

DATE.	March 4, 1998	NO. PAGES: 3	
		(including This Cover Page)	
TO:	Andrew Wylegala	FAX NO.:	011-525-207-8938
cc:	Tom White		713-645-8147
	Max Yzaguirre		713-853-9489
	Ken Karas		805-822-1168
FROM:	Adam Umanoff		
SUBJECT:	Fuerza Eolica/Zacatecas Dispute		

444 S. Flower Street, Suite 4340, Los Angeles, California 90071-2040 • Phone: 213-452-480 • Fax: 213-452-460 E-mail: AUMANOFF@enron.com • Web Address: http://www.enron.com

Kenneth C. Karas
Chairman and Chief Executive Officer

Enron Wind Corp.
P O Box 1910
Tehachapi, CA 93581
(805) 823-6720
Fax (805) 822-1269
kenkaras@compuserve.com
http://www.zond.com

December 17, 1997

Honorable Charles H. Brayshaw
Charge d'Affairs
United States Embassy
Paseo de la Reforma #315
Colonia Cuahtemoc
06500 Mexico, D.F.

Dear Mr. Brayshaw:

We are writing this letter to bring to your attention, and seek your assistance in connection with, what we believe to be the unjustified treatment of Mr. Carlos F. Gottfried Joy, whose company is the majority investor in a Mexican wind energy company in which we own an interest, by the state and municipal authorities of Zacatecas.

As you may know, we are the largest U.S. wind energy company. Based in California, our activities include the worldwide development of commercial wind power plants and the design, manufacture and sale of wind power generation equipment. We are a subsidiary of Enron Corp. which is headquartered in Houston, Texas. Enron Corp. is one of the world's largest integrated natural gas and electricity companies with assets of approximately $23 billion and 1996 revenues of $13 billion. Since the early 1990's, we have endeavored to develop commercial wind power plants in Mexico and in fact own a minority interest in Fuerza-Eolica, a Mexican wind energy company. Mr. Gottfried's company, Grupo Fuerza, S.A., owns the majority interest in Fuerza-Eolica.

Fuerza-Eolica is, and has been for some time, engaged in a commercial dispute with the State and Municipality of Zacatecas over a small, pilot wind energy project. The Municipality of Zacatecas commissioned the project in 1992, entered into a supply contract with Fuerza-Eolica and, in fact, made a down payment to Fuerza-Eolica of approximately US $1.5 million for the intitial phase of the project. Zacatecas financed this down payment with loans from Banobras. Under the supply contract, Fuerza-Eolica used the down payment to refurbish wind turbines and build other new components required for the project. The initial 10 wind turbines for the project were in fact refurbished in California, were inspected and approved in early 1993 by the Mexican Electric Research Institute, acting as the technical advisor to Zacatecas on

Natural gas. Electricity. Endless possibilities.

200

Enron

the project, and to this day remain in inventory in California. Unfortunately, before turbines were shipped or other construction activities commenced in Zacatecas, the local government changed and the new administration summarily canceled the project.

Some five years later and after several attempts by Fuerza-Eolica to work with Zacatecas to complete the project, Zacatecas has sued Fuerza-Eolica, demanding that it repay the loans owing to Banobras. We believe the demands are without merit and that the project would have been completed but for Zacatecas' decision to cancel it. To pressure Fuerza-Eolica, Zacatecas took the extraordinary step of arresting Mr. Gottfried, claiming that he defrauded Zacatecas. Mr. Gottfried is now out of jail on bail, set not coincidentally in the amount of the Banobras loan obligation.

We have reviewed the activities of Fuerza-Eolica and have no reason to believe that Mr. Gottfried has engaged in any fraudulent conduct. At the same time, we find the conduct of Zacatecas, using its criminal powers to influence a commercial settlement, excessive. While of course we can not fully convey to you in this letter all of the facts surrounding this dispute, we would ask for an opportunity to more completely brief you on these events. We would also ask for your help in arranging a meeting with the appropriate Mexican authorities to address these issues and, importantly, to impress upon them that this is a commercial dispute and as such, the use of criminal process to influence the commercial outcome is not tolerable. With that assistance we are hopeful that the employees of Fuerza Eolica will not be subject to the type of criminal actions which has been used against Mr.Gottfried.

Thank you for your attention to this matter and we look forward to speaking with you at your earliest convenience.

Sincerely,

cc: Mr. Thomas White
Mr. Mario Yzaguirre
Mr. Adam Umanoff

Natural gas. Electricity. Endless possibilities.

Adam S. Umanoff
Senior Vice President
and General Counsel

Enron Wind Corp.
444 South Flower Street, Suite 4545
Los Angeles, CA 90071-2046
(213) 452-6981
Fax (213) 452-6888
aumano@enron.com
http://www.enron.com

<u>VIA TELECOPY</u>

March 4, 1998

Mr. Andrew Wylegala
Commercial Attache
United States Embassy
Paseo de la Reforma No. 305
Colonia Cuahtemoc
06500 Mexico D.F.

    Re: <u>Fuerza Eolica/Zacatecas Dispute</u>

Dear Andy,

    It was a pleasure meeting you on February 20. I especially appreciate your offer of assistance in connection with the difficulties being experienced by Fuerza Eolica and Carlos and Gustavo Gottfried. As a followup to that meeting, I would like to request your specific assistance in connection with certain legal proceedings in Mexico. If the judges in these proceedings do in fact rule in accordance with law, we are optimistic that the "criminal" complaints brought against various individuals will be set aside and the Zacatecas dispute can be properly resolved as a commercial dispute. As you know, one of our primary objectives in this dispute is to have it resolved in a commercial, not criminal, forum.

    To give you some additional details, and as we discussed generally in our meeting, the Municipality of Zacatecas continues to pursue criminal proceedings against both Carlos and Gustavo Gottfried. Counsel for the Gottfrieds has initiated federal *habeas corpus* actions on behalf of the Gottfrieds which, as I understand it, are designed to protect the constitutional liberties of each of the Gottfrieds (in essence, to protect them from wrongful criminal prosecution). The *habeas corpus* action against Gustavo has been heard by Mrs. Avalina Morales Guzmen, Second District Federal Criminal Judge in Mexico City. She is expected to rule on the action within the next week to ten days. The *habeas corpus* action for Carlos

Enron

Gottfried is not scheduled to be heard until April and will be before Mr. Jose Refugio Estrada Araujo, a Federal Judge in Zacatecas. The Gottfried's criminal counsel believes that if the federal judges hearing these actions rule on the merits and are not subject to any political pressure or interference, they should find in the Gottfrieds' favor. Such a finding could result in the dismissal of the criminal case in Zacatecas.

Therefore, we would request the Embassy take whatever steps are allowed to encourage these judges to consider the cases in accordance with law. The Gottfrieds' counsel advises us that perhaps the most appropriate course would be for the Embassy to contact the Minister of the Interior, Lic. Francisco Labastida Ochoa to request his intervention with Minister Jose Vicente Aguinaco Aleman, the President of both the Supreme Court of Justice and the Judicature Counsel, as well as with Arturo Roman Gutierrez, the sitting Governor of Zacatecas, to request that the cases be ruled upon in strict accordance with law. Of course, as you mentioned in our meeting, there may be other appropriate avenues of communication between our Embassy and the Mexican authorities and we of course would appreciate whatever steps you might take to assist us in this matter.

If you need additional information or would like to discuss this further, please call. In the meantime, I will plan on calling you in the next several days to review the status of these matters. Once again, I greatly appreciate your assistance.

Very truly yours,

Adam S. Umanoff

ASU/mkc

cc: Tom White
     Max Yzaguirre
     Ken Karas

E:\MELAN E\WPDOCS\MEX CO\WYLEGA_A_.TR .wpd

203

New project

{Indonesia Power Letter}

(NOTE: This letter does not mention the Indonesia power projects covered by Rich or Ross: Paiton, Sibolga, nor the many geothermal projects covered by Les Garden, nor the Exxon Natuna project covered by Andy and Clyde, nor the Sumatra Pipeline project covered by Mike Miron/Ross Wright.)

Dear Minister XXXXX:

It has been a pleasure to meet and work with you this week both inside and outside the framework of the Asia Pacific Economic Council. Through the economic cooperation fostered by APEC, our two countries and all the participating APEC countries will undoubtedly benefit greatly from closer and more beneficial commercial and economic ties.

As you are aware, the sensational economic growth currently experienced in Indonesia is partially threatened by a power supply which is falling further and further behind surging power demand. Only through the ambitious power development plan that your ministry has initiated can Indonesia increase its generating capacity enough to sustain its globally beneficial economic expansion.

Several power projects which would effectively increase Indonesia's power production capability are being pursued by American companies. These companies offer the most advanced and efficient technologies, competitive price and financing packages, and reputations for excellence unchallenged throughout the world. I strongly encourage you to closely consider their bids.

Enron Power, a world-renowned private power developer, is in the final stages of negotiating two combined cycle, gas turbine power projects. The first, a 500 MW plant in East Java, should begin commercial power generation by the end of 1997 if it can promptly negotiate a gas supply Memorandum of Understanding with Pertamina. The other project, a smaller plant in East Kalimantan, also awaits a gas supply agreement.

Tondu Energy Systems, an independent power developer based in Texas, is striving to finalize agreements to construct a coal-fired power station in South Kalimantan. Tondu's project will provide cleaner power because of its clean-coal fuel.

General Atomics is competing with firms from China and Argentina to upgrade the nuclear research reactor in Bandung. Not only is General Atomics globally recognized as the leader in research reactor production, but it is particularly suited for this contract because it supplied the original TRIGA Mark II reactor.

Again, please allow me to express my pleasure at the remarkable progress all of our countries have made over the course of our meetings. Ideally, our meetings here will produce closer governmental ties as well as stronger private sector cooperation. To that end, I urge you to give full consideration to the proposals made by these and other U.S. companies.

Sincerely,

Ronald H. Brown

All in the Family

Selected U.S. firms' Indonesian power deals:

U.S. COMPANY (PROJECT)	SUHARTO REGIME PARTNER	CONTRACTED TARIFF (U.S. CENTS/ KWH)	STATUS
Mission Energy & General Electric (Paiton I)	Hashim Djojohadikusomo. Suharto's relative; Siti Hediati Prabowo. Suharto's daughter; Agus Kartasasmita, minister's brother	8.6[1]	Early 1999 startup
Unocal Corp. (Salak Geothermal)	Mohamad Hasan. former minister & Suharto family business partner[2]	Phase I. 8.47 Phase II. 4.9	On-line[3]
CalEnergy (Dieng Geothermal)	Retired Military Association	6.6[1]	In arbitration a completed
CalEnergy (Bali Geothermal)	Sigit Harjojudanto, Suharto's son	7.2	Postponed
El Paso Energy (Sengkang Gas-fired)	Siti Hardijanti Rukmana, Suharto's daughter	6.5	On-Line[3]
Enron Corp. (Pasuruan gas-fired)	Bambang Trihatmodjo, Suharto son	5.8	Postponed
Duke Energy Corp. (Cilicap)	Bambang Trihatmodjo. Suharto son	6.3	Postponed
Coastal Corp. (Palembang)	Martini Sulaiman, Suharto half-sister[2]	6.4	Postponed
Morrison Knudsen (Serang)	Sudwikatmono, Suharto cousin	6.0	Postponed

10

SIXTEEN CHARACTERS

A wise general strives to feed off the enemy.
Sun Tzu - The Art of War

The guiding policy for the Chinese military is the so called Chinese "16 Character Policy." Integrate the military with the civilian; integrate war with peace; give priority to weaponry; make goods for civilian use and use the profits thus generated to maintain the military (junmin jiehe, pingzhan jiehe, junpin yousizn, yimin yangjun).

The circular motion of the "16 Characters" is all too obvious. People's Liberation Army (PLA) businesses feed profit monies into the Chinese Army. The Chinese Army then uses the profit money to buy, borrow or steal advanced weapons. Some of the advanced weapons have civilian spin-offs that are then sold at profit by the PLA businesses, starting the cycle all over again.

The movement of money from commercial goods into weapons development by the Chinese Army is not without benefit for the leadership. A 1997 report sponsored by the Rand Corp. noted that Chinese Generals often took cuts or kickbacks from foreign deals for "Swiss bank accounts" and "luxury automobiles."

There is some logic to the leftist argument that the Chinese communists are corrupt enough to be bought. The Clinton China policy was based on the simple premise that the Chinese communists would reduce oppression once they were rewarded with "economic issues".

Yet, this policy has failed to reduce tensions between the U.S. and China. China continues to abuse its citizens, suppressing religious movements and punishing free speech with the death penalty. Instead of becoming more civilized, red China has threatened to invade Taiwan, and strike Los Angeles with nuclear weapons. The Chinese military continues to follow an aggressive stance by harassing un-armed U.S. surveillance flights over international waters and breaching the territorial air and sea space of U.S. allies in Asia.

The failure of the policy of trying to bribe China into submission was not limited to political disasters. Many of the "joint" business ventures have fallen apart, or worse, turned into fronts for the Chinese Army intelligence operations against America.

For example, a Chrysler "joint venture" cited as a glowing example of "diplomacy" was not with a civilian Chinese company but actually with the

206

Chinese Army.

"Despite almost a decade of relative success in producing both the Jeep Cherokee and a wholly locally produced military style jeep (the BJ2020 series), by 1995 Chrysler had pulled out of its bid to build a new minivan joint venture in Shanghai out of complete frustration," states a January 1999 U.S. Commerce Dept. report on technology transfers to China.

"Chrysler executives were expressly concerned over licit and illicit technology transfers," states the 1999 Commerce report. "Chinese officials were demanding more advanced technology than seemed appropriate or necessary to Chrysler."

The Chinese Army interest in advanced technology from Chrysler, then the maker of the U.S. Army M-1 tank, was in-line with the "16 Character" policy. However, they were also interested in profits.

"Chrysler's concerns were amplified when Chrysler CEO Robert Eton was made aware that knock-offs of Chrysler's Jeep Cherokee had been seen on the streets of Beijing. When complaining about this to Chinese officials, he reportedly was told that this (the ability to copy Chrysler's Jeep Cherokee) was a good sign of progress in China's auto industry, about which he should be pleased. Apparently, he was not, and Chrysler soon canceled plans to go ahead with the Shanghai plant."

Undisputed proof that the Chinese Army prefers Chrysler (knock-off) Jeeps, whether it's a Cherokee for the home or a BJ2020 "military" style Jeep for the office.

Bill Clinton understood the preference of the Chinese Army and he had the four wheel drive solution. Only the Lincoln bedroom innkeeper and booking agent for Air Force One could understand the corrupt needs of the red warlords.

According to a 1997 report on the Chinese Defense Industry by the Rand Corp., the Chinese communists "often reward themselves with large official and unofficial commissions... In the case of the ministry level receipts, these funds are believed to be used for a wide variety of legitimate and illegitimate purposes, ranging from modernization of industrial plants to the padding of the Swiss bank accounts of top ministry officials."

Doing business with the People's Liberation Army is very profitable for the corrupt. It is no surprise that the Chinese Army does its banking with the same firms who did Adolph Hitler's finances.

The Communist Chinese have come to accept Marxism and money. The curious mix of left wing politics and capitalist profits is not a new concept. The fall of old communism came during the 1980s with Premier Li Peng's order to "just go and make money."

Li Peng's order to go forth and raise money has given rise to a new fascism. The central party and singular power of the state are not threatened with the advent of consumer goods. Instead, the combination of capitalism and communism has made it easier for the west to invest massive amounts of funds inside China. The Generals profit, the Army profits and even the communist party profits.

However, the massive giant of over a billion people cannot match the economic output and standard of living earning by a few million on the tiny island-nation of Taiwan. China cannot match Taiwan even with the jewel of Hong Kong under its rule. Obviously, being able to choose which toothpaste to buy is not freedom.

The first to pay for the policy of loving the Beijing reds are the freedom loving Chinese, seeking to liberate themselves from the corrupt communist warlords. The anti-American fever that swept Beijing after the U.S. bombing of the Chinese embassy allowed the red masters to crack down on dissidents and divert attention from an ailing economy.

The nationalism also helps convince the masses that more weapons are needed to face down the American threat. The Chinese Army Second Artillery Corps has more nuclear weapons that all the other Asian nations combined.

No Asian nation can currently field an anti-missile system to stop a PRC nuclear tipped missile. While Korean, Japanese, Taiwanese and Philippine allies stood with America during the long years of the cold war, President Clinton abandoned our brave Asian allies to fend for themselves. The recent effort by the Bush administration to form joint anti-missile defenses with our Asian allies is a long overdue beginning. It will take years, however, to mend the torn fences.

And what benefit did the Chinese Army get from doing business with Clinton? According to the Rand Corp., "For those who oppose any subsidization of the PLA, there is thus ample evidence that profits from PLA-affiliated enterprises directly benefit the main-line forces of the Chinese military."

One clear benefit for China from U.S. technology and finance is the DF-31 missile. The new Dong Feng (EAST WIND) 31 missile performed flawlessly during its test flight series and it stands ready to be deployed. The DF-31 can reach any city in America and is armed with three nuclear warheads. The DF-31 has Clinton supplied guidance, nuclear warhead, nose cone and solid rocket engine technology.

The DF-31 is equipped with many technologies stolen or bought from America during Mr. Clinton's term. The DF-31 success was so spectacular that the PLA 2nd Artillery will deploy 20 missiles before the end of 2004. According to intelligence sources in the Pentagon, China will deploy over 1,000 nuclear tipped missiles in the next decade.

China pundits consider the PRC a nuclear pygmy and no threat to the United States. The Chinese currently fields no more than 20 long-range CSS missiles and their military forces are cramped by serious technology shortages. The total number of Chinese nuclear bombs, including short-range tactical weapons, is no more than 900. In comparison, the U.S. can field over 5,000 nuclear weapons.

Of course, no one has ever fought a nuclear war, and few of the pundits have studied such weapons in combat. The pundits are playing dangerous games with our lives. The DF-31 is better than the U.S. MX and Minuteman missiles. The DF-31 represents a decade of successful espionage against America.

Nuclear weapons do not require large numbers to be effective. The Chinese Army recently threatened to use neutron bombs on any U.S. Navy carrier that should stray too close to Taiwan. Chinese officials have already threatened to destroy Los Angeles if we help Taiwan resist an invasion. One new DF-31 missile could flatten L.A., San Francisco and San Diego.

The efforts by the Clinton administration to upgrade the Chinese nuclear arsenal are well documented. Commerce Secretary Ron Brown was an arms trader and his main customers were Chinese Generals. According to documents obtained from the U.S. Commerce Dept., Secretary Brown's three main clients were Chinese General Ding, General Shen and General Huai.

All three Generals were members of the Chinese Army Unit "COSTIND" (Commission on Science, Technology and Industry for National Defense). The official White House spin is that COSTIND was not a Chinese military unit but a "civilian" agency.

However, a November 1997 report written for the Commerce Dept. by "think-tank" company SAIC, noted that COSTIND was neither civilian nor engaged in purely commercial activities:

"COSTIND supervises virtually all of China's military research, development and production. It is a military organization, staffed largely by active duty officers... COSTIND also coordinates certain activities with the China National Nuclear Corporation (CNNC), which produces, stores, and controls all fissile material for civilian as well as military applications. COSTIND approves licenses for the use of nuclear materials for military purposes."

Clearly, COSTIND was a "military" unit and its mission is to kill. One COSTIND specialty is "fissile" materials for nuclear weapons. In 1995, the Vice Minister charged with COSTIND nuclear weapons development was General Huai Guomo. The same General Huai assisted in arranging the export of a SUN super-computer directly to a Chinese Army nuclear weapons lab.

General Huai Guomo was born in Zhejaing in 1932. Huai joined the Communist party in 1952 where he specialized in steel for the Chinese Army. Commerce Dept. documents show that General Huai then "became involved in the NUCLEAR INDUSTRY, joining the Second Ministry of Machine Building Industry as an engineer of its planning bureau... General Huai was promoted to COSTIND Deputy Director in spring 1988 and was made a Major General by the fall."

The Commerce documents show that General Huai visited "Washington, D.C., 26-19 March 1995 as part of the Sino-U.S. Joint Defense Conversion Commission/Chinese Air Traffic Control/Aviation Delegation."

However, General Huai's cover, the Sino-U.S. Joint Defense "Conversion" project was not an accurate translation. One document, a 1994 report written for the Commerce Dept. by the U.S. Army Defense Attaché to Beijing, contradicts this cover. The report states that the only "conversion" the Chinese Army was interested in was converting their old weapons into new ones:

"From a western perspective, what the Chinese call 'conversion' might better be called 'diversification'... New product lines are developed in separate areas while military production capability is retained. As a by-product of the defense conversion process, through acquisition of new technologies and manufacturing techniques, defense-related production will no doubt be enhanced to some extent. This will result in a more modern Chinese military," states the Commerce Department report.

In addition to modernizing the Chinese weaponry, according to the 1994 report, the Joint Defense Conversion might be better called a "cash cow" for the Chinese Army:

"Some of the monetary profits which accrue from defense conversion undoubtedly have found their way into the overall funds available for defense spending, whether officially listed as part of the budget of not. These additional funds naturally have given the military leadership greater options in how they spend the monies available... It cannot be denied that the portion of the Chinese defense industry that remains committed to military production has benefited, and will continue to benefit to some degree, from technology acquired through the defense conversion process. It is certain that some profits from defense conversion could be used to buy prohibited technology."

Additional Commerce documents show that in 1995 COSTIND General Huai met Secretary Ron Brown for the so-called "conversion" project and then toured the Energy Dept.

"Susan Tierney, Assistant Secretary for Policy, offered intro remarks," states a partially blacked out Commerce document.

"She noted that the DOE Secretary visited China last month and that cooperation with China is a high priority. She noted that DOE and the China State Planning Commission have similar goals in the following areas: 1) Science and technology development (especially in energy); 2) Funding of research (such as fusion and fission)."

Clearly, General Huai was interested in the atomic proposals. COSTIND, after all, does oversee the nuclear fission conducted by the Chinese Army.

General Huai asked several questions of his Energy Dept. hosts, mainly on how American capitalism worked. At the end of the meeting with DOE, Huai "indicated they would like to develop cooperation in the nuclear field."

In fact, COSTIND Chinese Army nuclear weapons engineers developed extensive "cooperation" with the U.S. nuclear weapon laboratories. In 1998, Bill Clinton invited Chinese Army spies and A-bomb scientists inside our weapons labs. Even after Chinese espionage was revealed to the public, Clinton continued to allow Chinese Army agents inside our nuclear weapons labs.

According to a 1998 Commerce Dept. document, titled "Laboratory to Laboratory Contacts", the China nuclear weapon exchange program "grew out of a request made in 1994 by State DAS Einhorn to DOE NN-40 Ken Luongo... The request called for contacts between scientists at the US DOE Weapons Labs (Sandia, Lawerence Livermore, Los Alamos) and their Chinese counterparts."

The 1998 Commerce document notes that the Chinese agents came "from the Chinese Academy of Engineering Physics (CAEP), whose oversight institution is COSTIND, and whose activities involve the weaponization of nuclear technology."

"Two Chinese scientists worked at LANL (Lawerence Livermore) and SNL (Sandia) to finalize the technical specifications of the project which will apply technologies to ensure physical protection and control of nuclear materials in a vault like room."

Translation: The Chinese Army can now protect its nuclear weapons in special bombproof underground vaults, designed with the official help of the Clinton Energy Dept.

One key point made by the Commerce 1998 nuclear documents is that the PLA warlords paid for the American technology. "There is no US funding of Chinese participation. The Chinese pay their own way on all of the joint projects."

U.S. weapons makers, hungry after the end of the long Cold War, awoke from starvation to face an equally hungry Chinese Army, seeking modern weapons. The red money not only fed the U.S. military-industrial complex but it also brought the Chinese Army out of hibernation.

"(Chinese) Defense conversion is a process that, in order to be successful, requires large foreign technological support and financial investment. China will continue to publicize its successes in this field and seek foreign assistance. Opportunities exist for the prudent investor... It is possible that American businesses could profit from the Chinese program," states a 1994 report written by Col. Dennis Blasko, then the U.S. military attaché to China.

Bill Clinton updated the PLA with U.S. military technology in exchange for hard cold cash. Thus, the so-called "conversion" of the Chinese Army was actually a paid "modernization."

The smell of money can overcome the wise, lull the vigilant to sleep, corrupt the wicked and tempt the weak. The red money also brought Democrat fundraisers like sharks to a fresh kill. The Chinese Generals carried the MAO credit card, accepted at all U.S. nuclear weapons labs.

However, not all Chinese business with the U.S. was in nuclear weapons. The Chinese Army was well known for its small arms production at low costs. This production was to pay off during the Clinton years.

How much business does the People's Liberation Army do in America? According to a Rand Corporation report forced from the U.S. Dept. of Commerce by a Federal lawsuit, the Chinese Army company called Poly Technologies made millions of dollars selling guns in America.

Poly Tech's prime U.S. subsidiary, PTK International of Atlanta Georgia, was run by Chinese princeling Baoping "Robert" Ma. The Rand report noted that the Poly Technologies businesses included "importation and distribution of semi-automatic rifles for the U.S. domestic market... Between 1987 and 1993 PTK sold more than US$200 million worth of these guns in the United States."

"Poly Technologies, Ltd., was founded in 1984, ostensibly as a subsidiary of CITIC (China International Trust and Investment Corporation), although it was later exposed to be the primary commercial arm of the PLA General Staff Department's Equipment Sub-Department. Throughout the 1980s, Poly sold hundreds of millions of dollars of largely surplus arms around the world, exporting to customers in Thailand, Burma, Iran, Pakistan, and the United States."

In 1994, Poly Tech took advantage of Clinton's executive order banning assault weapons or semi-automatic rifles. The 1994 Clinton ban on so-called "assault" rifles also included "surplus arms" imported from China.

"Loopholes allowed importers to bend the rules," states the Rand report. "Specifically, Congress exempted weapons in transit post hoc. The U.S. Treasury initially estimated this exemption would cover 12,000 weapons, but importers actually brought in 440,000."

The Rand report noted that Poly Technologies, a firm directly owned by the Chinese General staff, made great profits in America thanks to Bill Clinton and the 1994 Democrat controlled Congress. The so-called "Assault" weapon ban was, in reality, a financial windfall profit for the Chinese Army.

However, the affair between Bill Clinton and Beijing is far deeper than one sweetheart gun deal. Poly Technologies functioned inside the U.S. by hiding itself behind corporate camouflage of alias names and shells of bureaucratic paperwork. The Rand report noted that one such subsidiary of Poly Tech, a firm called "PTK International" was also involved in espionage.

"Poly's operations in the U.S. quickly diversified into a series of subsidiaries and holding companies. In 1988, (the) Poly Technologies 75% stake in PTK was transferred to Dynasty Holding Company, a wholly-owned U.S. subsidiary of Poly," states the Rand report.

"Dynasty handled all incoming and outgoing money for Poly, including management of all Poly investments in the U.S., and coordinated procurement of defense related materials with PTK and U.S. firms. Allegedly, Dynasty illegally shipped some of these materials, including advanced radar systems, minicomputers, and advanced communications equipment for use in the PLA UH-60 Blackhawk helicopters, to China under the guise of non-restricted merchandise."

The Rand Corporation report also noted that the Chinese Army CITIC bank is an "investment concern under China's governmental State Council." CITIC, according to the Rand Corporation "became identified with the PLA as a result of the scandal surrounding Wang Jun and his visit to the White House on 6 February 1996."

Another firm that received special attention inside the Clinton administration was China North Industries or Norinco. Norinco's role as arms maker for the PLA is well known. Norinco manufactures ballistic missiles, artillery, machine guns, tanks, lasers, radars, surface-to-air missiles, ammunition and land mines, to name a few.

Norinco also makes a wide variety of household products sold in retails stores in America. These products include tools, toys, bikes and ceramics.

The U.S. public knows little about how Norinco finances its arms production, however. The fundamental principles of Chinese strategy are embodied in two People's Liberation Army (PLA) terms for national defense. Junzhuanmin is the turning over of military resources to civilians for civilian use, and junmin jieje is the integration of the military and civilian.

Both terms refer to the combination of military and civilian resources such as airports, seaports, roads and communications.

However, Junzhuanmin and junmin jieje also translate into a conversion that is reversible, with each resource having a dual function - military and civilian. This twin-track policy has resulted in increased budgets for the Chinese army, advanced technology for modern weapons and a strengthening of the Chinese military-industrial complex.

According to a Commerce Department document on Chinese military defense industries, the PLA strategy is an economic war against America.

"[Chinese] Civilian resources should be transferable to military industries for weapons production," states the document, titled "Swords Into Market Shares," which was forced from the Clinton administration by a Freedom of Information lawsuit.

"This is not only to prepare for war, but also to use trading firms such as Norinco and China Great Wall Industry Corporation to acquire foreign technologies, such as electronics, for military as well as economic modernization."

The Bush administration imposed a two-year ban on imports from Chinese arms maker Norinco. According to U.S. defense intelligence sources, President Bush imposed the restrictions personally.

The move is welcomed in national security and human rights circles but viewed with great displeasure in the boardrooms of Wal-Mart and Kmart.

"The China Support Network (CSN) commends the Bush administration in taking this strong measure in imposing stiff economic sanctions on PLA-controlled Norinco," stated CSN spokesman David Chu.

CSN is an affiliation of human rights and national security experts who advocate a ban on all imports from China.

"CSN sees this as an important first step in checking the global ambitions of Communist China, which is not only hegemony in Asia, but around the world," noted Chu.

The Bush move to ban all imports from Norinco will hurt China. Norinco does an estimated $100 million in business in the West each year, selling everything from small arms to toys.

The low-cost Chinese products are a result of low-cost labor. In the labor market, PLA-owned Norinco does have an advantage over most U.S. corporations.

"The Communist Chinese are using tens of millions in thousands of Laogai slave concentration camps in Communist China to fuel this trade deficit, just as Nazi Germany did in WW II," stated David Chu of the China Support Network.

"They are using the hard currency from the trade deficits with America to buy the latest military weapons from Russia, such as the Sunburn cruise missile and the Shkval 'rocket' torpedoes - weapons primarily designed to kill U.S. aircraft carriers and submarines."

The Bush move is the first time in a decade that the U.S. has actually imposed such strict sanctions against a Chinese company. Norinco has had a long history of bad corporate behavior in the West.

Norinco frequently confronted the Clinton administration in a number of arms scandals, including attempts to sell Chinese-made machine guns to U.S. drug dealers.

While Norinco was very well known inside the Clinton White House, Clinton's front office for advanced military exports to China, the Commerce Department, claimed to know little about the multibillion-dollar arms giant.

In 1996, Clinton transferred export oversight to the inept and ill-equipped Commerce Department. President Clinton signed the executive order that ended 40 years of legislation designed to prevent war. The transfer also forced the paper trail for military exports to China to now end at the Commerce Department instead of at the Oval Office.

In 1997, after the transfer of authority by Clinton, Commerce Department officials in Beijing clearly stated they did not track Chinese army-owned companies. Thus, the only U.S. government agency with the legal authority to stop exports had no idea what to do.

"One of the largest PLA-affiliated firms is Norinco," states a 1997 e-mail from Commerce official Robert Bannerman in Beijing.

"Nothing is these databases indicated its affiliation. We do not maintain a formal FCS all-encompassing computer database of Chinese companies. ..."

According to a 1997 Rand Corporation report, Norinco plays a key role in the global arms market. In fact, the main reason why the Bush administration imposed the severe penalties on Norinco was for its unrestricted sales of ballistic missile technology to Iran.

It is a fact that Norinco sells its weapons to a wide variety of nations. In 1998, U.S. intelligence satellites tracked a Chinese freighter bound for Pakistan that contained a load of Norinco-made anti-tank missiles.

Information published in the Pakistan Observer on June 23, 1998, noted that China also transferred a large number of depleted uranium tank shells designed for the Pakistani armored forces. Norinco made the shells with help from the China National Nuclear Corp., which supplied the uranium.

Pakistan has recently upgraded its Type-59s with night vision, stabilized guns and laser range finders, and some have received a heavier 115 mm smooth-bore Chinese gun. Norinco supplied the new systems.

The Clinton administration even sought to help Norinco. According to Commerce Department documents, the Clinton administration approved the export of blade cutters and molds for a Norinco artillery-fuse production facility.

Another documented example of the Chinese arms efforts was made available in the Cox report. However, Rep. Chris Cox (R-CA) claimed that one third of the report never made it past the Clinton White House. The full report on Chinese espionage against America may never be made available to the public.

The Cox report did detail for the first time the long ignored sea leg of China's strategic arsenal. "The JL-2 (Julang 2, or Great Wave 2) is a submarine-launched version of the (Dong Feng, or East Wind) DF-31. It is believed to have an even longer range, and will be carried on the PLA Navy's Type 094-class submarine. Sixteen JL-2 missiles will be carried on each submarine."

What does the Great Wave 2 means to the U.S. homeland? The Cox report noted, "The JL-2's 7,500 mile range will allow it to be launched from the PRC's territorial waters and to strike targets throughout the United States."

On May 27, 1999, the South China Morning Post reported that the People's Liberation Navy (PLN) had begun preparations to test the Great Wave 2 (JL-2). PLN officials reported that the JL-2 is scheduled to be deployed on the nuclear submarine Xia by 2000. The sub launched missile is slated to carry a single 2.5 Megaton, thermonuclear warhead, or three 90 Kiloton warheads.

"If the JL-2 were to employ a shroud to protect its warhead as do the majority of submarine-launched ballistic missiles today," states the Cox report. "This would be the first use of a shroud or fairing on a PRC missile."

The JL-2 explains why the Chinese were so interested in American space contractor, Hughes, upgrading PLA rockets with "nose-cone" or "shroud" technology. The Cox report details Chinese Lt. General Shen Rougjun and his penetration of Hughes through his son, Shen Jun.

Two previously unreleased letters from Secretary of Defense William Perry also documented the close relationship between the Clinton administration and the Chinese Army. Federal Judge Robert Payne who ordered them to be released to the public in 1999 forced the letters from the U.S. Commerce Dept. One January 31, 1995 letter is addressed to Ron Brown and the other letter is addressed to Chinese General Ding Henggao.

"Dear Ron," wrote Perry in his 1995 letter to Secretary Brown. "I recently received a letter from General Ding Henggao, the Minister of the Chinese

Commission for Science Technology and Industry for National Defense (COSTIND). As you know, General Ding and I head the Sino-American Joint Defense Conversion Commission that was established during my visit to the PRC this past October (1994)."

"I am most appreciative, Ron," wrote Defense Secretary Perry. "Of the support that the Department of Commerce is providing for this effort. Unlike our defense conversion projects with Russia, Ukraine, and other states in the former Soviet Union, there are no funds earmarked for our activities with China. Hence, we need to rely on already established channels and create informal ones to accomplish the task at hand."

Perry's second letter of January 31, 1995 is addressed directly to General Ding Henggao. "Dear General Ding," wrote Perry. "I have asked our Secretary of Commerce, Mr. Ronald Brown, for the support of his Department to ensure U.S. businesses are apprised of the opportunities that have been offered."

"As you know, we have been working to develop a plan for air traffic control cooperation that meets the expectations of COSTIND, as well as the People's Liberation Army Air Force," wrote Perry to PLA General Ding. "I am confident that at the second meeting of the Joint Defense Conversion Commission, we will be able to receive reports detailing significant progress in all of our endeavors."

In fact, Perry wrote his letter to the Chinese spymaster with the warmest of affections reserved for an old friend. "Best wishes in the coming year," wrote Perry. "And I look forward to our next meeting."

The "informal channels" to "fund" the PLA operations required by Perry and the PLA placed Ron Brown in direct contact with Chinese military officers during the last few months of his life. According to the testimony of Brown confidant, Nolinda Hill, the Commerce Secretary openly worried that the deals with the PLA were bordering on treason and poised a threat to his life.

According to the GAO, the "air traffic control" that meets the expectations of "the People's Liberation Army Air Force" included a Presidential waiver from Bill Clinton. According to a June 1998 report to Congress, the GAO stated, "Waivers were also granted to permit the export of encryption equipment controlled on the Munitions List. One case involved a $4.3 million communications export to China's Air Force."

In addition, U.S. Global Positioning System (GPS) satellite navigation technology was also passed to the Chinese Air Force under the guise of commercial airline technology.

According to the GAO, "Since 1990, over $12 million in export licenses have been approved for Munitions List equipment designed for inclusion in civil products. These exports are not prohibited under U.S. sanctions and therefore do not require a presidential waiver. The majority of these exports involve navigational electronics used in commercial airliners operated in China."

Further evidence of the GPS transfer and its military impact is documented in a 1997 Rand Corp. report forced from the U.S. Commerce Dept. by a Federal lawsuit.

"The most troubling potential transfer to China is Rockwell's proposed joint venture deal with the Shanghai Broadcast Equipment Factory and the Shanghai Avionics Corporation, the latter of which is a key enterprise of the

Aviation Industries of China," states the 1997 Rand report.

"Rockwell Collins Navigation and Communications Equipment Company, Ltd. will design, develop, and build Global Positioning System (GPS) navigation receivers systems for the Chinese market. These components have serious dual-use applications, since the acquisition of reliable GPS data can enhance, to varying degrees, the capacity of militaries to field highly accurate cruise and ballistic missiles, such as those used to intimidate Taiwan during March 1996."

According to the Rand report, the GPS sale had great impact on Taiwan. "More accurate GPS systems would enhance the PLA's ability to carry out attacks against Taiwan's military and industrial facilities. Potentially reducing the ability of the Taiwanese military to defend itself against PRC coercive diplomacy."

"The use of GPS to enhance the accuracy of long-range Chinese cruise missiles, coupled with long-range sensors, would raise serious concerns for the U.S. Seventh Fleet in the Pacific," wrote the Rand Corp. "And possibly circumscribe their ability to provide an effective deterrent in a crisis over Taiwan."

FAA documents also show extensive briefings on GPS technology given to the PLAAF officers. One such document describes in English and Chinese the workings of the GPS "Space Segment" and the system's "Ground Control Segment" including the central control location in "Colorado." The document also details how GPS works using "triangulation from satellites" to "measure distances using the travel time of a radio signal" and "very accurate clocks."

Included in the detailed documents is a list of important political milestones, labeled "GPS-Related DOD/Civilian Cooperative Initiatives." According to the FAA, the major satellite navigation events include a Clinton "Presidential Decision Directive", dated March 29, 1996, and a "Vice President Gore" announcement of a GPS "modernization" on January 25, 1999.

The approved military technology sales to China clearly pose a significant threat to U.S. armed forces. Noteworthy, and under-reported in the mainstream press, is the transfer of American missile technology by the PRC to a number of other nations, including sold-fuel technology for Iran, and advanced guidance systems used in M-11 missiles sold to Pakistan and DF-15 missiles sold to Syria.

The PLAAF can use the equipment supplied by Clinton's waiver for offensive operations against U.S. forces in Asia. The next PLAAF bombs that fall will do so with great accuracy, due mainly to the efforts of General Ding and his puppets in Washington.

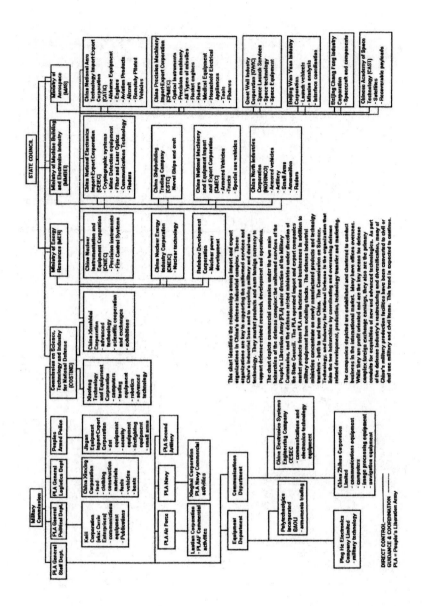

Defense Intelligence Reference Document

October 1995
PC-1921-57-95

China's Defense-Industrial Trading Organizations

Reference Aid

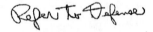

   **E066**

China's Defense-Industrial Trading Organizations

Key Judgments

This chart identifies the relationships among organizations engaged in import and export activities in China's defense-industrial complex. These organizations are key to supporting the uniformed services and China's industrial base and to acquiring military and dual-use technology. Defense-industrial organizations market products and services and earn foreign currency to support defense-related research, development, and operations. The activities of these organizations are crucial to modernizing the military and advancing the nation's economy.

The chart depicts commercial organizations under the two main hierarchies of the defense complex: the uniformed services of the People's Liberation Army (PLA) under the direction of the Military Commission and the defense-related and supporting industrial corporations and ministries under the direction of the State Council. In addition to selling military equipment from existing stocks, PLA-operated import and export organizations market services and products — many of them civil — from the large network of PLA-run factories and businesses. Defense-industrial corporations and ministries concentrate on newly manufactured products and technology transfers — both to and from China. A few of the larger defense production facilities and complexes have formed their own corporations in recent years and apparently are seeking to operate somewhat independently of national-level organizations. In general, industries operate through the organizations shown on the chart; because of space limitations, however, only selected corporations or their products or services are shown. The corporations have become more important and control research institutes and factories; formerly, government ministries organized along functional lines controlled research institutes, factories, and import-export corporations. The Commission of Science, Technology, and Industry for National Defense (COSTIND) is a key organization that links the two hierarchies by coordinating and overseeing defense-related development, production, technology transfer, and marketing.

Most of the organizations depicted are chartered to conduct business in the international market, and many have offices overseas. These profit-oriented organizations provide foreign exchange earnings to the defense-industrial complex; they also are primary conduits for new and advanced technologies acquired to improve weapons and civil products. The Chinese have restructured and diversified their defense industry, increasing the production of profit-earning civil products. Some defense plants now manufacture mainly civil or dual-use civil and defense-related products but also produce improved military equipment for the PLA and China's arms export customers. This trend is expected to continue.

Information Cutoff Date: 28 June 1995 PC-1921-57-95

U.S. COMMERCIAL TECHNOLOGY TRANSFERS TO THE PEOPLE'S REPUBLIC OF CHINA

Office of Strategic Industries and Economic Security
Bureau of Export Administration

and

DFI International

January 1999

The Chrysler Corporation

The Chrysler Corporation has been in China longer than most, beginning with the acquisition of their only joint venture, the Beijing Jeep Corporation in 1987. Despite almost a decade of relative success in producing both the Jeep Cherokee and a wholly locally produced military-style jeep (the BJ2020 series), by 1995 Chrysler had pulled out of its bid to build a new minivan joint venture enterprise in Shanghai out of complete frustration. According to press accounts, Chrysler executives were expressly concerned over licit and illicit technology transfers. Chinese officials were demanding more advanced technology than seemed appropriate or necessary to Chrysler.[23] Chrysler's concerns were amplified when Chrysler CEO Robert Eton was made aware that knock-offs of Chrysler's Jeep Cherokee had been seen on the streets of Beijing. When complaining about this to Chinese officials, he reportedly was told that this (the ability to copy Chrysler's Jeep Cherokee) was a good sign of progress in China's auto industry, about which he should be pleased.[24] Apparently he was not, and Chrysler soon canceled plans to go ahead with the Shanghai plant. According to interviews conducted for this study, given the experience in Beijing, Chrysler executives were made even more wary of the technology transfers, proposed licensing deal, and export quotas being requested as part of the Shanghai deal and decided that the risk was simply too great when it came to what was for Chrysler a relatively new car (the minivan) and, therefore, advanced technology.[25] Chrysler currently has no plans to expand its investment ventures in China.

"We should attach great importance to strengthening the army through technology, enhance research in defence-related science and technology, base the development of arms and other military equipment on our own strength, give priority to developing arms and equipment needed for defence operations under high-tech conditions and lay stress on developing new types of weapons and equipment" - Premier Li Peng, "Report on the Outline of the Ninth Five-Year Plan for National Economic and Social Development and the Long-Range Objectives to the Year 2010" (Delivered at the Fourth Session of the Eighth National People's Congress on March 5, 1996).

26   709

11

CLIPPER

*When you communicate a secret to someone, you make
yourself his slave.*
Balthasar Gracian - The Art of Worldly Wisdom

The Clinton administration engaged in a war on terrorism that was never designed to fight terrorists. The Clinton war was not against foreign terrorists or even domestic fanatics. The Clinton war was waged against the American public.

While many accuse the Bush administration of destroying America's privacy with the Patriot Act - the fact remains that nothing compares to the efforts of Bill and Hillary Clinton.

President Clinton engaged in a secret effort to bug America. No President worked harder to protect his personal privacy while attacking the privacy of Americans. The Clinton war against terrorism included invading the privacy of America's medical, financial and digital communications.

According to a TOP SECRET document obtained from the National Security Council (NSC) the Clinton secret project to bug America started in late 1992. The NSC documents detail secret meetings between top Bush administration officials and the Clinton transition team.

AT&T had developed new secure telephone technology that also blocked Federal wiretaps. The Bush administration presented a recommendation to the Clinton transition team that the Federal government secretly purchase the secure phones from AT&T in order to keep them out of the American public market.

In early 1993, President Clinton issued an executive order that authorized Janet Reno to secretly purchase the entire inventory of secure phones from AT&T. Ms. Reno purchased the secure phones using money confiscated from the war on drugs. Reno tasked Webster Hubbell, the former Whitewater partner of Hillary Clinton, to run the phone buy out from AT&T.

Hubbell arranged for a follow-up contract with AT&T to modify the secretly purchased secure telephones with a newly developed government chip. AT&T was paid to rip out the secure chip they developed for the telephones and replace it with the special chip that had a secret, Watergate style bug hidden in it at the micro level. The chip was called "Clipper."

In 1993, Webster Hubbell was personally charged by Janet Reno with a Top Secret project to tap America. Hubbell's initial task was to tap every phone in the U.S. government, starting with the Drug Enforcement Agency (DEA).

In February 1999, the Dept. of Justice was forced by the Freedom of Information Act (FOIA) to release the Hubbell files.

According to the Dept. of Justice, many of the Hubbell documents are being withheld for "national security" reasons. In addition, "fifteen" Hubbell documents remain in the hands of the FBI and NSA to be reviewed prior to any release.

According to the NSA, FBI and NSC, the Hubbell files are so sensitive that to release them today may result in charges of treason and perhaps the death penalty. The newly released Hubbell files are so secret that the National Security Agency (NSA), FBI, and National Security Council (NSC) blacked out even the code word classification level for "national security" reasons.

Furthermore, the Dept. of Justice was forced to admit that a 1993 letter from AT&T CEO Robert Allen to Hubbell was "destroyed pursuant to the records destruction schedules." This in itself is highly suspect because this author has obtained documents dating as far back as 1983 that were returned by the National Security Council (NSC) - over 10 years prior to the "destroyed" AT&T Hubbell letter.

Part of the secret project included re-fitting the purchased AT&T phones with a new chip called "Clipper" developed by the NSA at Ft. Meade, Maryland. This chip contained a secret "exploitable" feature allowing the government to tap the phone conversation with a special back door key.

The re-fitted Clipper phones were to be given to the DEA for their line agents to use. According to a 1993 classified White House email from George Tenet, "Ron Brown" insisted the Commerce Dept. be one of the "key holders" for all Clipper phones. Thus, the Dept. of Commerce and Ron Brown demanded direct access to tap any phone in America.

The Hubbell files show that in 1994 the soon-to-be-felon met with Vice President Gore, Ron Brown, NSA Director McConnell and White House power broker, John Podesta. The files show Hubbell met in late January 1994 at "the White House Situation Room" on secret Presidential orders such as "PDD-5" and "PRD-27". The 1994 secret meeting included details on the Clipper project and "Podesta Alternative Draft Legislation."

In 1993, the Clinton administration allowed a select set of civilians from AT&T and other companies to go inside the NSA to examine the Clipper chip in detail. The civilians obtained access to classified details under special clearances that swore them all to secrecy.

AT&T scientists were not the only civilians authorized to view the secrets of Clipper. The project also included the First Lady. Mrs. Clinton wanted every American to carry a Clipper chip. Mrs. Clinton's efforts to nationalize the medical industry included the Clipper chip in her health care legislation.

According to information obtained by the Freedom of Information act (FOIA), each American citizen was to be issued a national ID/health care card with a Clipper chip installed inside. In fact, one medical health care card manufacturer complained that including the special chip was too expensive.

A key part of the Clipper chip project was to install them into your planned national ID card and Hillary Clinton health care card. The intent would be for the Dept. of Justice to monitor health your health care providers for fraud and abuse. The result would be to monitor you.

According to a 1993 letter to the Commerce Dept. by Microcard, a U.S. smart card manufacturer, the high cost of Clipper sank the health care card proposal. Clipper, according to Microcard, was far "too expensive" at $25 per chip to be included into Mrs. Clinton's planned nationalization of U.S. health care.

Clearly, the First Lady and Hubbell were inside the top-secret world of Clipper. The selection of former Rose office associate Webster Hubbell and his repeated White House meetings on the National Health Care project with Mrs. Clinton shows the First Lady was aware of the chip and its secret exploitable feature.

In 1993, Vice President Gore and Attorney General Janet Reno were ordered to form an IWG or "interagency working group" in a SECRET White House memo. The sign off sheet on the secret memo specifically sought Gore and Reno's signature.

Included in the working group were White House Counsel Vince Foster, and convicted Whitewater figure Webster Hubbell.

When I first discovered that Vince Foster, Webb Hubbell, and Bernard Nussbaum attended a secret meeting on encryption at National Security Agency Headquarters I was stunned.

The first real details appeared when Washington Weekly forced the Clinton administration to reveal the attendance list of the secret meeting at Ft. Meade Maryland. White House spokesman Mark Fabaini had originally denied that Mr. Foster had anything to do with the highly secret intelligence agency but a freedom of information request (FOIA) by Washington Weekly proved that Mr. Foster did indeed attend a secret meeting in May of 1993.

This secret meeting is a snap shot of how the Clinton administration tried to apply some sort of policy to control the security of phones, faxes and computers. Technical minded folks call it "encryption". The magic art of turning real voice, fax or computer data into garbage and back again. To most this art of computer science seems more alchemy than reality. It is not turning gold into lead and back.

It is the high math equal of a football quarter back yelling secret "audible" plays to his team, a coded signal only those with the key can understand. It protects the trillions of dollars that pass through the Federal Reserve. It even protects your bank account. The battlefield on which encryption wars are fought is in cyberspace. One team invents software and hardware to defend. The other team uses software, and super computers to crack.

In an effort to debunk myths and legends from the conspiracy freaks I asked Admiral McConnell, former Director of the National Security Agency, about Foster and that meeting. His response:

"Foster had NO NO NO NO role in Clipper. He never went to NSA headquarters to meet on Clipper. The May 2, 1993 meeting at Ft. Meade is an annual event called 'Law Day'. It is a dog and pony show for the power elite. I doubt that Foster even knew what crypto meant. John Podesta was our contact inside the White House," stated McConnell.

VP Al Gore quickly went to work with the secret group of Clinton advisors and delivered a report to the President.

"Simply stated, the nexus of the long term problem is how can the government sustain its technical ability to accomplish electronic surveillance in a advanced telecommunications environment characterized by great technical diversity and many competing service providers (numbering over 1500, some potentially antagonistic) who have great economic and political leverage," states the TOP SECRET report prepared by Gore's Interagency Working Group.

"The solution to the access problem for future telecommunications requires that the vendor/manufacturing community translate the government's requirements into a fundamental system design criteria," noted the Gore report.

"The basic issue for resolution is a choice between accomplishing this objective by mandatory (i.e., statutory/regulatory) or voluntary means."

This chilling conclusion, that there is no choice but to be monitored by Big Brother is backed by several other documents. One such document released by the Justice Dept. is a March 1993 Justice Dept. memo from Stephen Colgate, Assistant Attorney General for Administration.

According to the Colgate memo, Vice President Al Gore was to chair a meeting with Hubbell, Reno, Commerce Secretary Ron Brown, and Leon Panetta in March 1993. The topic of the meeting was the "AT&T Telephone Security Device".

According to Colgate, AT&T had developed secure telephones the U.S. government could not tap. The Clinton administration secretly contracted with AT&T to keep the phones off the market. Colgate's memo noted that the administration was determined to prevent the American public from having a private phone conversation.

"AT&T has developed a Data Encryption Standard (DES) product for use on telephones to provide security for sensitive conversations," wrote Colgate. "The FBI, NSA and NSC want to purchase the first production run of these devices to prevent their proliferation. They are difficult to decipher and are a deterrent to wiretaps."

Buried in the Colgate memo is the first reference to government developed monitoring devices that would be required for all Americans. According to the March 1993 Colgate memo to Hubbell, "FBI, NSA and NSC want to push legislation which would require all government agencies and eventually everyone in the U.S. to use a new public-key based cryptography method."

In 1993, the "public-key" system referenced by Colgate had already been developed by the Federal government. The system, a special computer chip called "Clipper", provided the Federal government with an "exploitable feature" allowing a wiretap of any secure phone communications.

However, the only way to force "everyone in the U.S. to use" the new Clipper chip was to enact "legislation" which would require that it be manufactured into all phones, fax machines and computers.

There was a final solution to the problem. According to a Presidential Directive of April 1993 on the Clipper project, "Should (US) industry fail to fully assist the government in meeting its requirements within a reasonable period of time, the Attorney General will recommend legislation which would compel manufacturers to meet government requirements."

In April of 1994, Hubbell resigned from the Justice Department under allegations of fraud. By late June 1994, Lippo boss James Riady met with John Huang, Webster Hubbell and Bill Clinton during five days of White House visits. Early the next week, a Lippo unit paid Hubbell the first $100,000 of what is reported to be over a half million dollars.

In December 1994, Hubbell pled guilty to several felony charges relating to illegal billing in the Whitewater affair. Webster Hubbell also cited his Fifth Amendment rights to not testify before the Senate Congressional hearings. Two weeks after the Lippo money was given to Mr. Hubbell, John Huang got his job at the Commerce Department as Assistant Secretary. Huang's position determined technology transfers that went to places such as Indonesia and Communist China. Mr. Huang and his wife have both taken the Fifth Amendment and refused to testify at Senate Congressional hearings.

DNC fundraiser, former Lippo banker and secret cleared Commerce employee John Huang was briefed 37 times on encryption communications by the CIA while working at the Brown controlled Commerce Department. Immediately after each briefing, Huang would walk across the street to the Lippo/Stephens Group offices and make long distance phone calls and send faxes to points unknown.

Al Gore quickly embraced the Clipper chip and the concept of monitoring America at all costs. In 1994, Gore wrote a glowing letter supporting the Clipper chip and the government approved wiretap design.

According to Gore, "As we have done with the Clipper Chip, future key escrow schemes must contain safeguards to provide for key disclosures only under legal authorization and should have audit procedures to ensure the integrity of the system. Escrow holders should be strictly liable for releasing keys without legal authorization."

"We also want to assure users of key escrow encryption products that they will not be subject to unauthorized electronic surveillance," wrote Gore in his July 20, 1994 letter to Representative Maria Cantwell.

However, Gore did not tell the truth. In 1994, Federal officials were keenly aware that the Clipper chip design did not have safeguards against unauthorized surveillance. In fact, NASA turned down the Clipper project because the space agency knew of the flawed design.

In 1993, Benita A. Cooper, NASA Associate Administrator for Management Systems and Facilities, wrote "There is no way to prevent the NSA from routinely monitoring all (CLIPPER) encrypted traffic. Moreover, compromise of the NSA keys, such as in the Walker case, could compromise the entire (CLIPPER) system."

Please note, Ms. Cooper referred to Soviet spy John "Walker" who is serving life in prison for disclosing U.S. Navy secret codes. In 1993 Ms. Cooper did not know of Lippo, Huang, or Hubbell but her prophetic prediction was not so remarkable in retrospect.

Yet, Al Gore pressed ahead, continuing to support a flawed design, despite warnings that the design could "compromise" every computer in the U.S. A 1996 secret memo on a secret meeting of DCIA Deutch, FBI Director Freeh and Attorney General Janet Reno states, " Last summer, the Vice President agreed to explore public acceptance of a key escrow policy but did not rule out other approaches, although none seem viable at this point."

According to the 1996 report to V.P. Gore by then CIA Director Deutch, Ms. Reno proposed an all out Federal take-over of the computer security industry. The Justice Department, proposed "legislation that would ... ban the import and domestic manufacture, sale or distribution of encryption that does not have key recovery. Janet Reno and Louis Freeh are deeply concerned about the spread of encryption. Pervasive use of encryption destroys the effectiveness of wiretapping, which supplies much of the evidence used by FBI and Justice. They support tight controls, for domestic use."

In 1993 the Clipper "exploitable" feature was exposed to the public and the entire project fell into disfavor until it was officially canceled in 1996. Clipper violated the first rule of information warfare - secrecy. A secret back door (bug) must remain secret in order to be useful.

Declassified documents from the CIA and the U.S. State Department show that the Clinton administration considered sharing secret computer security code "keys" with foreign powers including China, Syria and Pakistan.

"Are Clipper devices likely to be permitted for importation and use in the host country?" asked a secret 1993 CIA cable addressed to the U.S. embassies in Beijing, Damascus and Islamabad.

"Would the host country demand joint key holding or exclusive rights to Clipper keys for law enforcement or intelligence purposes?"

"The U.S. intelligence community is concerned about the potentially profound impact on collection capabilities of the widespread foreign use of increasingly sophisticated encryption devices," states the secret CIA cable.

"Is there the possibility of cryptography 'race'?" asks the CIA cable.

The secret 1993 CIA cable is one of 69 documents released by the U.S. State Department on the secret Clipper chip project. The documents were forced from the State Department through the Freedom of Information Act.

In addition, the State Department refused to release 12 documents as classified "in the interest of national defense or foreign relations."

The newly released documents shows that the Clinton administration considered sharing secret Clipper surveillance keys with China and other hostile powers in order to monitor worldwide communications for "law enforcement" purposes.

However, during a 1997 interview, Adm. James McConnell, former director of the National Security Agency, confirmed that the Clinton administration gave the sophisticated key recovery surveillance technology to communist China in 1996.

McConnell noted that the advanced technology gives China the power to electronically lock out U.S. intelligence monitoring and lock in the Chinese population.

"Even if the Chinese use weak encryption the sheer volume of their communications will make it impossible for us to monitor. If China were to erect a public key infrastructure it will severely impact our intelligence gathering ability," stated McConnell.

He also stated that Clinton was aware that the advanced surveillance technology might be abused by hostile foreign powers.

"Can Key Recovery be used against dissidents and political opponents?" asked Adm. McConnell.

"In a word, YES," he concluded emphatically.

Yet, Clipper was never really canceled. Nor has the covert program to bug America stopped. The exposure of the Clinton bug-on-a-chip project did not end with its cancellation. The publicity only drove the effort back under-cover and back into the black world of "codeword" secrets and Clinton cronyism.

According to secret White House email sent by current CIA Director

George Tenet, "John Podesta" - then Deputy Executive Secretary to the President, was the top Clinton official on all policy matters concerning computers and encryption.

"We had a long meeting this morning in John Deutch's office on encryption which included, Admirals, McConnell, Studeman, John Podesta and other luminaries," wrote Tenet in December 1993.

Further evidence that John Podesta controlled computer policy is revealed in dozens of letters from top computer executives, all complaining about the Clipper project.

In the early 1990s, several U.S. computer CEOs formed a joint lobby organization called the CSPP or Computer Systems Policy Project. By 1994, Tony Podesta, the brother of John Podesta, ran the multi-million dollar corporate lobby effort through his firm, Podesta Associates, using his employee, Ken Kay, as the CSPP executive director.

In 1994, the CSPP association with Tony Podesta quickly paid off. Several CSPP members won exclusive trade deals through Clinton and Ron Brown. For example, CSPP computer CEO, James Treybig of Tandem, traveled with Ron Brown to China in August 1994. Treybig concluded an exclusive $150 million export of mission control computers for the Chinese Army Long March space rocket.

In June 1995, Ken Kay led the delegation of CSPP CEOs into a closed meeting inside the White House. In the 1995 White House closed meeting, the CEOs from AT&T, Apple, Compaq, Digital, HP, Unisys, Cray, Silicon Graphics, Tandem and others were sworn to secrecy. The CEOs could not talk under penalty of law.

Clinton used the same tactic employed with AT&T earlier in the Clipper project. The Clinton administration made top-secret designs and top-secret contracts available to the CSPP computer companies. In exchange for their cooperation and silence, the companies would be given lucrative export deals and access to even more advanced chip designs left over from the cold war days.

According to an official documentation from the CSPP, the computer companies were given several secret briefings on advanced encryption technology with back-door features. The CSPP refused to comment on whether any of these designs have made it into domestic production.

Yet, while it is true that CSPP members have thrived on high-tech exports authorized by the Clinton administration; it is also true that Clinton and Gore thrived on the millions of dollars in donations and soft money made available from CSPP members such as Apple, AT&T, Digital and Silicon Graphics.

For example, once inside the White House the CSPP CEOs were given a detailed briefing by a State Department expert on super-computers and nuclear weapons. Shortly after the meeting, CSPP member Silicon Graphics sold several super-computers to a Russian nuclear weapons lab under the pretenses of "civilian" uses. Silicon Graphics has never been prosecuted.

Nor is the Clinton cronyism hard to find. In response to a request for an interview, White House lawyers acknowledged that John Podesta did indeed have a conflict of interest problem with his brother Tony. According to White House Council, in 1997, President Clinton solved the Podesta problem by signing a legal waiver absolving John Podesta from any conflict of interest.

The White House has to date refused to show the legal waiver obtained by John Podesta. Nor have they explained why John Podesta felt it necessary to obtain a waiver in 1997 for actions he took in 1994 and 1995. Of course, a government waiver for possible criminal actions in the past is not a waiver but a pardon.

The CSPP Executive Director, Ken Kay, has also supplied evidence of corruption. Kay's lawyer, C. Boyden Gray, the former White House Council for George Bush, denied in writing that his client made thousands of dollars in donations to the DNC. Instead, according to Gray, his client only donated "$2,500", of which "$1,250" was returned to him by the DNC in the form of a "painting".

However, the claims made by Mr. Gray do not match with the official records from the Federal Election Commission. In fact, none of Kay's many donation records amount to $2,500 or $1,250.

The DNC refused to comment on Mr. Kay and has offered no explanation for the art deal. Neither Mr. Kay nor the DNC would comment on why the political party would give out valuable art. Neither Mr. Kay nor the DNC will acknowledge that the so-called "painting" in question is actually worth many times the claimed "$1,250" value.

C. Boyden Gray also claimed that the CSPP officials did not engage the administration in secret meetings in June of 1995 at the White House. When I offered Mr. Gray a copy of the official Commerce Department records showing the CSPP secret meeting in June 1995, he noted that he used the legal term "engage" and that the official CSPP classified briefings did not begin until November 1995.

Why the "legalese" from the former Bush lawyer? Is this client loyalty or protecting a dumb idea generated so long ago inside a Republican White House?

The CSPP documents show that a "Covert-Clipper" project is in operation today. The Covert-Clipper project has thrived in the dark, growing secretly behind closed doors, into American phones, computers and our lives. Domestic sales of the same secretly bugged products under Covert-Clipper will also allow domestic wiretaps on a scale that only Stalin would have dreamed of.

Perhaps the real truth is far worse than simple bi-partisan corruption. The concept was to bug computer and communications products being exported to China such as secure satellite communication systems. The project came to life under the guise of national security. Somewhere the concept to protect America expanded and became a project to monitor America. Uncle Sam became Big Brother.

The move to tighten domestic controls has so far failed. The Clipper chip was canceled in 1997 after wasting over a billion dollars. Yet, history often repeats itself, especially for those who refuse to learn from it. The FBI recently aroused much trouble in July by unveiling a new program called "carnivore". The FBI "carnivore" software is designed to monitor email by intercepting all mail at the Internet provider.

The FBI installed the carnivore software initially at several Internet providers with little requirements for legal authority. Testimony by software expert Matt Blaze revealed the FBI carnivore program might not be smart enough to recognize a target's email, thus false prosecutions are possible. In addition, the carnivore programs scoops up all data without regard to legal problems.

Carnivore is clearly open for abuse. While Federal law does provide for an audit trail to prevent abuse of carnivore data, the audit only occurs if there is a Federal prosecution. No prosecution - no audit trail. Data acquired by the FBI email tap could be accumulated on anyone without an audit.

The problems of privacy, email and government wiretapping are not unfamiliar to Vice President Al Gore. Al Gore lost a large portion of his official email and was unable to deliver them to investigators involved in the 1996 campaign finance probe.

The former Vice President has a darker side yet to be covered by the media. Al Gore knows much about the Federal government efforts to wiretap every home and office in America. He should. Al Gore led that effort to bug America since 1993. As part of the Clinton administration, Al Gore made the policy that endorsed the Clipper chip and created the FBI carnivore software program.

President Clinton waged an information war against America. Data accumulated by the Clinton White House took prisoners, destroyed lives and provided valuable bounty for criminals. The war was designed to limit freedoms and control political opponents.

The Clinton administration leaks of information are filled with terrible examples such as Kathleen Wiley and Monica Lewinsky. The most fertile ground for information exploited by Clinton was the data stored inside law enforcement computers such as the FBI.

The FBI's NCIC system (National Criminal Information Center) is a network of computers erected by the all states that is tied to a central FBI network. It is the Federal law enforcement Internet.

NCIC is a valuable tool to capture real criminals. NCIC was used to identify the vehicle in the first attack against the New York towers by Osama bin Laden. It was NCIC that tipped Oklahoma police to hold Timothy McVey as a possible suspect in the Oklahoma City bombing. NCIC is used to check your status whenever a local police officer pulls you over on the road.

However, this system also has a long history of abuse. NCIC was used by an ex-police officer to stalk and kill his battered wife. It has been used by drug gangs to identify and murder anti-narcotics undercover agents.

NCIC has also been used for political crimes. Each and every one of the over 900 files stolen by the Clinton White House started with a check of the FBI NCIC data base. According to the FBI, the Clinton White House inquired for information from the FBI on over 22,000 people during 1993 and 1994.

There is open evidence the FBI computers were abused by Clinton. In June 1996, Lisa Wetzl, former White House Intern under Craig Livingstone, testified during the Senate hearings that the very first task performed for White House reviews was a NCIC check.

In 1996, Howard Shapiro, then General Counsel for the FBI, went to the White House to recover some of the hundreds of files taken by Clinton operatives Craig Livingstone and Anthony Marceca. According Shaprio's deposition there was the following exchange:

"Q. The list of names were in two boxes is that correct?"

"A. Yes. The-the documents referred to in the list of names were in two boxes."

"Q. And the third box contained what kind of documents that you deter-

DECEPTION

mined were not FBI files?"

"A. For instance-and it would seem to comport with what's on this first page-various computer runs, various documents. It took us a while, and I'm-I'm not sure I was ever advised in detail what it was. I was advised that I didn't need to worry about it was because it wasn't FBI information. It was like NCIC computer checks and things like that."

The legal counsel for the FBI had no law enforcement experience. Mr. Shapiro did not know NCIC computer information is FBI property so he left the boxes of computer information at the White House. They were never been recovered.

In August 1996, I received a letter from the Dept. of Justice. Margaret R. Owens - Unit Chief Office of Public and Congressional Affairs. Ms. Owens wrote, "Unfortunately, the process of dealing with White House requests for file information was not managed as it should have been. You may be assured that all steps necessary to correct the deficiency have been taken and that the FBI will be more vigilant in the future."

However, the Clinton administration has little zeal for being "vigilant". There are no federal laws against government officials who abuse the NCIC system and President Clinton wants to keep it that way.

Government employees who are caught can be charged with a local misdemeanor at best. In response to this lack-of-teeth in the law, Senator Gregg (R-NH) proposed legislation in 1997 to make abuse of NCIC data files a felony. Clinton opposed Gregg's bill and had it defeated by Democrats in the Senate.

While giving his political operatives clear fields to run rampant inside Federal computer files, Clinton strived to accumulate more data for abuse. President Clinton made cynical use of the victims from the TWA-800 disaster to propose a whole new series of laws to combat terrorism, including expanding the FBI NCIC system to track the movements of every flying citizen.

According to the FBI and NTSB investigation, the TWA-800 crash was not caused by a terrorist bomb or enemy missile but by a faulty design in the central fuel tank.

Many more lives could be saved by hiring more FAA inspectors than by spending millions assuming that every flying citizen might be a "trans-national" terrorist. More lives can be saved with proper safety inspections made on the airplane than by inspecting the personal lives of the passengers boarding the plane.

The entire Clinton approach to law enforcement was designed to limit freedom and obtain more power for Federal forces. The "pro" law enforcement stance of the Democrat President silenced left-wing privacy advocates in the Democratic Party and drew the applause of traditional Republicans.

Privacy advocates and right wing police supporters should have learned that President Clinton made the policy not to fight crime but for pure political power. The only difference between a Communist police state and a Nazi police state is which boot - right or left - is on your neck. The Clinton compromise was both boots on your neck.

One way to justify a power grab was to issue studies supporting ideas that are alien to America. For example, the White House hired the Rand Corporation to do a study of transnational terror and information warfare.

232

Clipper

Somewhere in the study the brains at Rand forgot the Constitution.

The Rand report states, "An important factor is the traditional change in the government's role as one moves from national defense through public safety toward things that represent the public good. Clearly, the government's perceived role in this area will have to be balanced against public perceptions of the loss of civil liberties and the commercial sector's concern about unwarranted limits on its practices and markets."

The word from Rand... Capitalists, conservatives, constitutionalists and liberal privacy lovers beware. Your markets and civil liberties are at risk of being sacrificed in the name of the "public good".

The administration use of propaganda to dehumanize an imaginary domestic enemy of American citizens included issuing lies and fiction to itself. In 1993, the FBI issued a Top Secret report to President Clinton claiming that mass media computer security software could be used by criminals and terrorists to block Federal wiretaps.

The FBI linked every crime imaginable to the need to ban the mass media PC software. The FBI report noted that a child "snuff" film ring was prosecuted using phone wiretaps, implying that more children would be murdered on film unless computer security software was banned.

The FBI later told Congress the "snuff" story was false. No such ring existed. The Top Secret report was a fiction.

The FBI has claimed in public testimony that the Trade Tower bombers were caught using wiretaps of their phone. The fact is the terrorists were caught using an informant and a video camera hooked up inside their bomb factory. No wiretap information was produced at their trial.

The FBI has claimed to Congress that mobster John Gotti was prosecuted with wiretaps. The fact is no wiretaps were used in Gotti's trial because he never used the phone for business. The FBI caught Gotti with a radio-microphone bug placed inside his home.

The FBI has sought access to millions of phone lines, claiming a need to expand wire taps against domestic terrorists and criminals. The fact is the FBI has issued on average about a thousand wiretaps a year for the last ten years. None of the cases taken to prosecution involved violent terrorism crimes.

Meanwhile, Bill Clinton claimed to favor the privacy of the little people - such as Monica Lewinsky. The White House generated outrage over Linda Tripp and her tapes of Monica are so false as to be laughable. Political "Watergate" like break-ins and illegal third party taping of phone calls became the norm under Clinton.

For example, Democrat Congressman McDermott released a tape of House Speaker Gingrich talking to other Republicans taken from an illegally monitored cellular phone call. The Reno led Dept. of Justice did not prosecuted McDermott.

Nor is the war just between Democrat and Republican. Inner party fistfights are becoming more vicious than the traditional two party combat. For example, Senator Charles Robb had to dismiss two of his staff for illegally taping the phone calls of Democratic rival Governor Douglas Wilder. The subject of the Wilder phone taps was the hot relationship between the single black Governor and a rich white widow.

The victors and the vanquished litter the new information battlefield.

233

DECEPTION

Politicians in the 21st century who are not electronically literate will find them-selves on the backbench or out of office.

The modern world is full of computer tracking systems. Each of us creates an electronic image. You live in various databases or radio waves in the sky as you move about doing business and living in the modern world. The use of your own electronic emissions against you is a form of oppression. The intent is to deny your freedom and increase the power of a few.

We must choose not to be tagged, tracked and controlled like some horrific animal experiment. We can remain individuals in a collective modern democracy. Law and order can be maintained without having to compromise our liberty. Justice can be done to those who abuse the system.

We can free the world and ourselves or enslave it. Technology can increase liberties and markets but only if we want it to do so. It is up to us to choose the path to tomorrow, electronic freedom or digital slavery.

NSC CONTROL NO. *20756*

TOP SECRET

UNCLASSIFIED

Impacts of Telecommunications and Encryption Technology
on Law Enforcement and Intelligence Collection:
Assessment, Options, and Recommendations (C)

PARTIAL WORKING DRAFT

July 6, 1993

Partially Declassified/Released on 4/11/97
under provisions of E.O. 12958
by C. Van Tassel, National Security Council

F94-5

TOP SECRET

DDC # 84

SECRET

I. Introduction (U)

A. Purpose

This report has been prepared in accordance with Presidential Review Directive/NSC-27 (April 16, 1993) to: (FOUO)

1) broadly assess trends in telecommunications and encryption technology and their impact upon law enforcement and intelligence gathering; and (U)

2) evaluate the impact of the key escrow encryption technology initiative proposed in Presidential Decision Directive/NSC-5. (S)

PRD/NSC-27 directed that this policy review should, furthermore, include a full range of clear policy options and recommendations for dealing with these issues. (S)

B. Scope

This study addresses the impacts of two types of commercial technology, *encryption* and *advanced telecommunications*, on law enforcement and intelligence collection. The study also examines the Administration's key escrow encryption chip technology initiative. (U)

The use of other types of encryption (e.g. that used by foreign governments) is outside the scope of this study, except to the extent that commercially available products are employed. Additionally, U.S. government-developed cryptography to protect national security information is not within the purview of this study, with the exception of the key escrow encryption technology initiative which, while primarily developed for unclassified applications, may also be used to protect selected classified applications. (U)

C. Audience (U)

This report has been prepared for the President and the National Security Council by the Interagency Working Group established by the NSC pursuant to PRD/NSC-27. (C)

UNCLASSIFIED

- Consumer prices are higher by 0.3 percent; and, (U)

- Per capita personal income is lower by $77.22, measured in 1986 dollars. (U)

FBI Organized Crime Program Managers indicate the impedance or loss of court-ordered electronic surveillance would impair catastrophically Federal and state efforts to effectively investigate organized crime and would allow its damage to the U.S. economy to continue, if not become substantially greater. (U)

C. Narcotics and Dangerous Drugs (U)

The greatest use of electronic surveillance by law enforcement is in the Governments' war on drugs. Over two thirds (69%) of all Title III electronic surveillance is devoted to this serious national problem. Major drug trafficking organizations rely heavily on telecommunications to coordinate and carry out drug importation and distribution and to "launder" the billions of dollars in illegal drug proceeds. Accordingly, law enforcement focuses electronic surveillance on major drug importers, distributors, and money launderers. (U)

The U.S. Public Health Service has estimated the health, labor, and crime costs of drug abuse at $58.3 billion in 1988, exclusive of the value of the drugs themselves. A 1992 U.S. Department of Health and Human Services' study estimates the 1992 costs of drug abuse in the United States to be $168 billion or $675 per person. Approximately $40 billion dollars a year are spent by users to procure these drugs. (U)

The economic, societal, and personal harm of drug trafficking is also reflected in daily "drive-by shootings" in neighborhood streets; substantially increased crime such as thefts, robberies, and murders brought about by drug use; violent "turf battles" to control drug distribution; lost productivity; employee absence; extensive and expensive health care; as well as the legacy of a generation of drug dependant "crack" babies. (U)

Electronic surveillance is critical to intercepting the drug traffickers' "communications networks," identifying drug traffickers; and to dismantling national and international drug trafficking organizations. Further, information derived from electronic surveillance is essential in successfully prosecuting the executive levels of the drug trade, since national and international drug chieftains and local drug "kingpins" do not appear at the scene of drug buys or shipments. Without the use of electronic surveillance, the volume of drugs and drug-related violence and death would dramatically increase, and the ease and means of drug importation and distribution would be dramatically enhanced. (U)

D. Public Corruption and Governmental Fraud (U)

Integrity in government is a keystone to any democracy. Corruption and fraud can only flourish in secrecy. As a result, normal, overt investigative techniques are normally unavailing. Law enforcement thus finds electronic surveillance to be one of the few viable tools to effectively detect, investigate, and prosecute these crimes. (U)

Electronic surveillance evidence gathered in recent judicial corruption investigations directly led to the conviction of two Federal District Court Judges and, in another case, to the conviction, to date, of three Dade County, Florida state judges and six attorneys, for extortion and case-fixing. Electronic surveillance helped build a police corruption case against 30 Cleveland policemen and 17 others, which included extortion and protection for gambling and narcotics distribution. As a result, 46 of the 47 pled or were found guilty, with one acquittal. (U)

Electronic surveillance evidence in the "Ill-Wind" government fraud investigation was critical in the prosecution of the case, and it has had a tremendous impact subsequently on fraud and abuse within the defense contracting industry. The "Ill-Wind" investigation has resulted in 64 convictions (including high-level Department of Defense officials and eight corporations), sanctions against numerous contractors, and over a quarter of a billion dollars ($260,000,000)

EO 12956 14 1.5 (c)

UNCLASSIFIED

in fines, restitutions, and recoveries ordered. Evidence necessary to obtain these convictions, fines, recoveries, etc., would have been impossible to obtain without electronic surveillance. (U)

Billions of health care dollars are lost through fraud, and electronic surveillance now is being used aggressively to combat health care fraud. In 1993, electronic surveillance produced critical evidence in New York and Detroit cases involving widespread Medicare/Medicaid fraud carried out by numerous pharmacies and pharmacists. In New York, 79 individuals, including 58 pharmacists, were indicted; and, to date, 70 individuals have been convicted or pled guilty, with $10 million in forfeited assets. In Detroit, there have been 20 indictments and 16 convictions, to date, with $4 million in forfeitures expected to follow. The FBI estimates that the health care fraud in each of the foregoing cases alone ranged in the tens of millions of dollars. Cases currently under investigation using electronic surveillance are expected to result in a greater number of indictments and convictions. (U)

E. Terrorism (U)

A substantial number of terrorist bombings and murders have been prevented through the effective use of Title III and FISA electronic surveillance. Many of these terrorist acts, if not prevented, likely would have had grave national or international implications. Of particular note, the recent planned bombing of the United Nations, the New York Federal Building, and the Holland and Lincoln Tunnels by a radical terrorist group was thwarted by the use of electronic surveillance. Likewise, the bombing of a foreign consulate in the U.S. was prevented, and in another, a terrorist rocket attack by a foreign-based terrorist group against a U.S. ally was thwarted, saving scores of lives. (FOUO)

In 1986, the violent El Rukn Chicago street gang conspired to shoot down a commercial airliner within the United States with a stolen military rocket. This act was thwarted through electronic surveillance. The prevention of this terrorist act by the FBI was singularly attributable to the use of electronic surveillance -- but for the availability of this technique, a Pan Am 103 type disaster would have occurred on United States soil. (U)

In 1993, electronic surveillance contributed to the indictment of individuals in Abu Nidal on RICO charges of murder, conspiracy to commit murder, and conspiracy to bomb the Israeli Embassy in Washington, D.C. In 1990, foreign-based terrorists were prevented from acquiring a Stinger surface-to-air missile to be employed in a terrorist act wherein numerous people undoubtedly would have been killed. Also, in 1989, as a direct result of electronic surveillance in a terrorist-related matter, evidence was obtained which resulted in the conviction of two individuals for the brutal murder of their 16-year old daughter. (U)

Over the last decade numerous other terrorist-related cases have utilized electronic surveillance to: prevent a rocket attack against an FBI field office; prevent an attack on a nuclear power facility; solve several murders; identify the perpetrators of a $7,000,000 armed robbery; and solve and prevent several bombings by anti-Castro groups in Miami, Florida. (U)

F. Violent Crime (U)

Many violent crimes, including murder, have been solved and a significant number prevented by law enforcement's "real time" response and preventive actions taken based on conversations intercepted through electronic surveillance. (U)

• Use of court-ordered electronic surveillance regarding one of New York City's most violent Asian Organized Crime gangs prevented the gang from carrying out a "shoot out" with a rival Asian gang. Sixteen members of the group were later found guilty of murder, racketeering, kidnapping, home invasions, extortion, armed robbery, and bribery of a public official. (U)

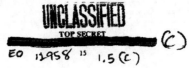

UNCLASSIFIED

TOP SECRET

(C)

EO 12958 15 1.5 (C)

Clipper

Office of the Deputy Assistant Attorney General   *Washington, D.C. 20530*

TOP SECRET

January 13, 1994

MEMORANDUM FOR THE ATTORNEY GENERAL

FROM: Mark M Richard
        Deputy Assistant Attorney General
        Criminal Division

SUBJECT: Discussion Paper: Advanced Telecommunications and
         Encryption

As you are aware, there will soon be a Principals Meeting on
Advanced Telecommunications and Encryption. Enclosed, at Tab A,
is a brief memorandum summarizing, and making recommendations on,
the Discussion Paper (Tab B) for discussion at that Meeting.
There are only two items genuinely at issue: (a) how to deal with
the advanced telecommunications (digital telephony) problem and
(b) what to do about export controls on encryption products.

The NSC-chaired Interagency Working Group on this issue will
meet at 1:00 on Tuesday the 18th to review and make final changes
to the Discussion Paper. At that time, it would be helpful for
agency representatives to be able to indicate their principals'
preferred options on those two points. [While I believe we are
all in agreement regarding the appropriate approach on the
digital telephony issue, we have not discussed the encryption
export matter in such detail.] Please advise me if you are able
to reach a tentative conclusion on the latter issue, and if we
may communicate that conclusion at Tuesday's meeting.

Enclosures
a/s

cc: Judge Hubbell
    Irv Nathan

TOP SECRET

b1, b3 per
NSA

Unclassified Upon Removal of Enclosures

239

U.S. Department of Justice

Washington, D.C. 20530

MEMORANDUM TO: **Webster L. Hubble**
                Assistant to the Attorney General

FROM: **Stephen R. Colgate**
                Assistant Attorney General
                for Administration

SUBJECT: **AT&T Telephone Security Device**

- The Vice President will chair a meeting Wednesday afternoon, March 31, 1993, with we believe the Attorney General, Secretary Brown, Leonard Panetta on the AT&T telephone security device.

- AT&T has developed a Data Encryption Standard (DES) product for use on telephones to provide security for sensitive conversations. The FBI, NSA and NSC want to purchase the first production run of these devices to prevent their proliferation. They are difficult to decipher and are a deterrent to wiretaps, an very important tool for the law enforcement community.

- Ultimately, FBI, NSA and NSC want to push legislation which would require all government agencies and eventually everyone in the U.S. to use a new public-key based cryptography method.

- Attached are recent relevant articles.

- Although the law enforcement issues are serious and real, there are other issues involved.

<u>Questions for the Attorney General to Ask</u>

- Ask if DES can be decrypted and if so, how long to do so?

- Ask if new encryption system can be decrypted and how long to do so?

- Ask why other firms will not build and market a DES based device and why <u>any one</u> would not buy DES based devices rather than ones based on the new standard without legislation outlawing DES?

- If encryption legislation passes, how will enforcement occur?

Attachments

240

Clipper

MEETING WITH DCI John Deutch, AG Janet Reno,
DAG Jamie Gorelick, and FBI Director Louis Freeh

DATE: Thursday, May 9, 1996
LOCATION: Justice, AG Reno's office
TIME: 4:30 - 5:30 p.m.

I. PURPOSE: Purportedly to receive a "status report" from the
DCI on recent discussions with the computer industry on the
Administration's encryption policy and to review a proposal the
DCI wants to present to industry next week on behalf of the
Administration on key escrow. If other economic agencies are not
in attendance (DoC has recommended NEC and OMB be invited), the
session will likely be used to try to convert you to the law
enforcement and intelligence communities point of view on the
encryption issue.

This meeting is in response to DoC's expressed concern about the
substance and tactics of the DCI's approach to industry.
Commerce believes that some near-term liberalization of
encryption export controls must be presented to industry, in
order to sell them on our longer-term Key Escrow proposal. While
admitting privately that export control relief will probably be
necessary at some point, the DCI rejected industry's demand in a
March industry meeting, angering industry and other agencies
(DoC, NEC, OMB, OSTP because of the lack of consultation).
Because of this treatment, industry is looking at our next
proposal to include a comprehensive response to their concerns --
including export control relief. Failure to respond to their
concerns will lead many of companies to oppose the
Administration's Key Escrow policy, thereby lessening the chance
of success and creating a significant political problem with the
high tech community. The political dimension of this issue has
grown since the May 2 announcement by Sen. Dole criticizing the
Clinton Administration's encryption policy and supporting a
bipartisan bill to limit U.S.G. control of encryption (see TAB
D).

II. BACKGROUND See attached material for background reading:

        Tab A -- DCI Deutch draft paper on Key Escrow procedures
          that he wants to give to industry next week;
        Tab B -- draft U.S.G. background paper on the encryption
          issue prepared by NIST;
        Tab C -- CSPP Paper
        Tab D -- Dole Press Release and San Francisco Examiner
          article
        TAB E -- 3/27/96 Memo to Secretary Brown

[NOTE: More complete background paper and talking points will be
provided at the Classified briefing on Wednesday afternoon.]

Recent Developments:

For the past several months, the Administration has been engaged in a dialogue ▮▮▮▮▮▮▮▮▮▮▮▮▮ to explore options on encryption export controls that both protects national security and law enforcement objectives, while allowing U.S. industry to maintain its competitive position. ▮▮▮▮▮▮ numerous working group meetings have taken place over the past five months, ▮▮▮▮▮ (b)(4)

▮▮▮▮▮▮▮▮▮ These efforts were side-tracked at a March meeting ▮▮▮▮▮▮▮ (see TAB E for a brief report to Secretary Brown on the session). ▮▮▮▮

▮▮▮▮▮▮▮▮▮▮▮▮▮ The Administration must agree internally on a bottom line on export controls and how to present it to industry within the next several weeks.

Brief Overview of Encryption Issue

Export controls on encryption have been a long-standing issue for exporters, the intelligence community (NSA), and domestic law enforcement. Efforts to maintain tight controls on encryption in the "Internet age" lack credibility, threaten to impose real costs on U.S. industry and its competitiveness, and are becoming a political embarrassment for the Administration.

NSA has been the lead agency in the government for encryption policy, although much of the debate has been driven by Justice and FBI domestic law enforcement concerns. Most encryption exports are controlled on the State Department's Munitions List (to the chagrin of exporters - our allies control encryption as a commercial good). State has de facto ceded much of its authority to NSA, which has tried to limit the spread of encryption through very tight export controls. Growing demand for encryption reflecting growth in electronic commerce (software and hardware) has led NSA to try to manage the spread of encryption overseas by promoting a "key escrow" policy, which involves a third party holding a "key" (the encrypting algorithm) that can be used to encrypt and decrypt messages and which could be accessed by government under certain defined conditions.

NSA proposed in 1993 that the Government be the third party to hold the keys. This was roundly rejected by industry and consumers. NSA has now accepted the idea of "Trusted Third Parties," such as banks or other fiduciary institutions, holding the keys, which is acceptable to many consumers. Access to a key would require a court order. Law enforcement agencies like this approach. As there could be many different key escrow encryption

systems; national and international standards would need to be
established to ensure sufficient commonality.

Janet Reno and Louis Freeh are deeply concerned about the spread
of encryption. Pervasive use of encryption destroys the
effectiveness of wiretapping, which supplies much of the evidence
used by FBI and Justice. They support tight controls, for
domestic use and exports. NSA is chiefly concerned with exports.
The Vice President chairs the senior group that set the
Administration's encryption policy; since February, 1994, it has
been supported by a working level group co-chaired by NSC and
OMB, composed of NSA, CIA, FBI, State, Commerce (BXA, NIST), and
Justice. Last summer, the Vice President agreed to explore
public acceptance of a key escrow policy but did not rule out
other approaches, although none seem viable at this point.

Before leaving for GSA, former Commerce Deputy Secretary Barram
served as the chief Administration liaison with industry for
encryption policy. In the past several months, DCI Deutch has
taken the lead in developing encryption policy ▓▓▓▓▓▓▓▓▓▓ (b)(4)
▓▓▓▓▓▓▓▓▓▓▓▓▓▓▓▓▓▓▓▓▓▓ He advocates a flexible approach to
key escrow, but resists (at least as an opening position) any
other export liberalizations, such as permitting longer
algorithms to be exported without a State license or excepting
additional sectors from restrictive treatment. Deutch has worked
closely with his UK counterpart to develop a common approach to
encryption policy for both exports and for electronic commerce.

The interagency working group met on April 25, 1996 to discuss
Deutch's paper. The Department of Commerce, NEC, and OMB
expressed the need for some liberalizations of export controls,
in the short term, in order to 'buy' industry into key escrow for
the long term. If consensus is not reached within the next week
at lower levels, the issue for Principals will be the tactical
question of when or what to give industry in terms of 'relief'
from current export controls. Economic agencies firmly believe
it would be a mistake to present industry with the key escrow
proposal without addressing liberalization of export controls.

Industry argues for decontrol of encryption, for moving it from
State to Commerce control; and for allowing DES (a powerful
encryption algorithm whose export is tightly controlled) to be
sold freely. The three industry sectors (hardware, software and
network services) do not always agree; hardware and network firms
are more amenable to key escrow; software firms oppose it
strongly, and are seeking legislation to achieve decontrol.
Some support Deutch's call for a "flexible key escrow only"
approach; most are undecided or opposed. The private sector has
begun pursuing a legislative strategy. Several Senators (Leahy,
Dole, Burns) and one House member (Goodlatte) have introduced
bills that, among other things, would significantly liberalize
export controls. The bills are unlikely to move, but their
presence, along with increasing industry public comments about

its unhappiness with the Administration's policy and the importance of this issue in California, is designed to pressure the Administration into modifying its policy. Lost in the debate, but not irrelevant, is the fact that it is virtually impossible to enforce export controls against them when they can be exported by phone and modem or in someone's pocket.

III. PARTICIPANTS -- (Principals only) Deputy of Central Intelligence John Deutch; Attorney General Janet Reno; Deputy Attorney General Jamie Gorelick; and FBI Director Louie Freeh

[Note: DoC has suggested the addition of NEC (Laura Tyson or Dan Tarullo) and OMB (Sally Katzen) -- other players with similar views to DoC, but CIA staff has resisted, characterizing this as a "status report", not a large decision meeting.

12

RED STAR IN THE SKY

Watch the light, stay on the heights.
Sun Zhu - The Art of War

To Bill Clinton, the term "Academy of Spaceflight Technology" would mean young students, working on peaceful science. Thus, helping these young students make their way into the cosmos was Bill Clinton's way of diverting swords into plowshares.

The western perception of "Academic" space work includes simulated shuttle flights, experiments for the NASA low/no cost science missions or even students building their own satellite. U.S. students from a number of universities have designed successful space experiments and many of these have flown on the Shuttle.

So, Clinton helping China with their space flight program was a very star trekie thing to do. In fact, Clinton planned to go to Beijing and announce major efforts by NASA and former U.S. "defense" contractors to help China reach for the stars.

After all ... We come in peace for all mankind, right?

Unfortunately, Bill Clinton's reach for the almighty campaign dollar extended directly into the Chinese Army.

Thus, space is not all flowers and doves of peace. In China, the "Shanghai Academy of Spaceflight Technology" is a major player in PRC's manned flight program. However, the Shanghai Academy also has taken on other projects one would consider a bit more challenging for the average student.

In December 1996, Shanghai Academy of Spaceflight Technology senior engineer Liu Xinamin revealed a project he and his students had been laboring on for over five years. His announcement came during a Beijing Arms show. Liu introduced the world to the Academy's best known young communist student achievement to date - the LY-60 air defense missile, designed to "process up to 40 targets, track 12 and distinguish the three that present the highest threat".

The LY-60 is a "hit-to-kill" interceptor missile, with a maximum speed of 1,165 Knots, designed to destroy aircraft, cruise missiles and helicopters. It is 15 feet long, 10 inches in diameter with a single solid propellant motor and can maneuver up to 7 gs.

Liu said the LY-60 had been under development for five to six years and completed testing in 1996. The Academy designed anti-air missile is current-ly being deployed by the People's Liberation Army and has been exported to the middle east.

The Chinese "Spaceflight" academy does do other things (other than design and build weapons). For example, China plans to orbit two cos-monaunts. The Shanghai Academy of Spaceflight Technology has con-tributed their expertise to the mission of manned space flight.

There is no question that exports of U.S. made computers, electronics and software are critical to the Chinese Army's efforts to reach for the stars. Chinese space engineers openly admit that the People's Liberation Army is using U.S. made software and computers to improve its ballistic missile force.

Cheng Qifeng, an engineer at the Shaanxi Engine Design Institute in Xian, admitted that PLA engineers are using EDS Unigraphics CAD/CAM comput-er-aided design software to help improve rocket engines for both space and ballistic missile applications.

Cheng made the statements during the recent Beijing Asia-Pacific confer-ence on multilateral space cooperation.

"We chose Unigraphics software as the core software of our liquid rocket engine CAD/CAM system," stated Cheng.

Cheng noted that the PLA had made improvements on turbo pump, oxy-gen pressure pumps, fuel pumps and gas generator hardware "using hybrid modeling technology supplied by Unigraphics software" running on UNIX and Windows NT workstations.

The Chinese Army runs all space activities from its brand new mission control facility located 30 miles northwest of Beijing. The control center is packed with U.S. made computers supplied during the Clinton administration.

In 2002, China orbited its Shenzhou spacecraft. According to Aviation Week and Space Technology, two days after the Shenzhou launch, NASA Administrator Sean O'Keefe told a forum in Washington that he and Deputy Secretary of State Richard Armitage are spending "a lot of time" exploring whether and how to bring China into closer co-operation with the U.S. in space.

China has previously sought to join the U.S. led International Space Station (ISS) as a partner. According to Luan Enjie, director of the China National Space Administration, the space station "is not a true international program" without Chinese participation.

"We want more frequent communication with entreperneurs, engineers and enterprises in the U.S. so that we can have extensive cooperation in the future," stated Luan during a November 2001 interview published by Aviation Week and Space Technology.

However, the People's Liberation Army runs virtually all of China's space efforts. Chinese President Jiang Zemin appeared at the Shenzhou launch dressed in an Army uniform, underscoring the military significance of the PLA manned program.

The Long March 2F vehicle lifted off at 10:15 p.m. Beijing time. At launch, the combined launcher and spacecraft weighed 1 million lb.

The Shenzhou orbital module is reported to have carried a piggyback satellite that was released later in the flight. This is the first time a Shenzhou has carried an additional satellite. The Chinese have not disclosed the satel-lite's mission.

According to the official Chinese news agency Xinhau, President Jiang sent a message of congratulations on the successful return of the Shenzhou spacecraft.

Jiang reportedly sent the message in a telephone call to PLA General Cao Gangchuan, head of the General Armaments Department of the Chinese People's Liberation Army, a member of the Central Military Commission (CMC) and chief director of the national manned spacecraft program.

"I believe that this is the first time that General Cao has been identified as 'chief director of the national manned spacecraft program.' As GAD (General Armaments Department) head, he oversees the collection of, and development of all PLA technology and weapons," stated Richard Fisher, a senior fellow at the Jamestown Foundation.

"As an ISS partner, would General Cao be feted all over like the equal of the NASA Director? One must at least consider the possibility that all ISS information the PLA can get will go straight into their military space programs," said Fisher.

China is now officially seeking to join the U.S. led International Space Station (ISS) as a partner. European sources reportedly support a role for China in the space station program.

According to Luan Enjie, director of the China National Space Administration, the space station "is not a true international program" without Chinese participation.

"My hope is that the U.S. can treat us as friends," said Luan.

However, U.S. defense analysts are opposed to any Chinese Army participation in the ISS program because of weapon sales and human rights policies.

"Anything the U.S. does to help the Chinese space-launch program is also helping the Chinese ICBM program," stated Michael Waller of the Center for Security Policy.

"Haven't we learned yet from September 11 that we shouldn't be looking away from-let alone helping-the bad guys?" said Waller.

"China has nothing of scientific value to add to the international space station. Even if it did, it is not in the interests of the United States to allow the regime in Beijing to exercise any leverage whatsoever in the U.S. space program," noted Waller.

"Whoever controls space can control our way of life," said Waller. "Our financial, economic, political, social, and military systems depend on our nation's control of space and space-based satellites because of our total dependence on satellite communications. The U.S. should do everything it can to limit the PRC's ability to move into space."

According to Aviation Week, the new U.S./PRC space cooperation could also play into the possible loosening of U.S. aerospace export restrictions that have prevented the commercial Chinese launch of U.S.-built communications satellites and European satellites containing U.S. parts. Several U.S. space industry sources noted that the export restrictions have hurt both the Chinese and American communications satellite sales.

Richard Fisher, a Senior Fellow at the Jamestown Foundation, agreed, also noting that China should not be allowed on the space station project.

"The Europeans are now beginning a real push to get China on the ISS and if Russia joins this push it could get rough," stated Fisher.

"All of this means that it is in the Administration's best interest to give an emphatic NO as soon as possible to dispel this issue now," said Fisher.

"Allowing China onto the International Space Station would be a mistake at this time. The ISS is about many things but it is also about the countries that use it living in peace with each other," noted Fisher.

"As long as China is preparing for a war against Taiwan-that would include fighting U.S. forces as well-there is no good reason to give China access to the bounty of technology that would come via access to the ISS. Whether they get on the ISS or not, China is committed to building its own space station. Getting on the ISS would result in an immediate transfer of technology and knowledge that China will pour into its own station program."

"PRC reports also note the Shenzhou 3 launched its own small satellite. This could be a possible nano-sat prototype that could serve a number of military purposes including ASAT (Anti-Satellite) missions. In addition, the orbital module remains in orbit, performing many functions including 'earth observation'," stated Richard Fisher.

"For a number of years the Europeans have been trying to sell China manned space technologies and they are pushing to get China into the ISS. One might imagine that U.S. companies would like to follow suit," noted Fisher.

In addition, the open publication of possible new links to China via the International Space Station brought a swift reaction on Capitol Hill. One Congressional source demanded and received an official explanation for the statements from NASA.

"Over the last 4 years, at the request of the U.S. Department of State, NASA has informed all interested Chinese entities including the Chinese National Space Agency and the Chinese National Remote Sensing Center that a prerequisite for any potential new cooperation between NASA and China, would be China's adherence to the Missile Technology Control Regime (MTCR) guidelines and annex, and adoption of export control policies consistent with the MTCR," states an official response from NASA dated April 3 to the Congressional inquiries.

"Further, that once MTCR issues are resolved, NASA would be interested in renewing a dialog with China in areas of potential cooperation. This USG (U.S. Government) position was reiterated to the Chinese Government by Embassy Beijing in bilateral discussions conducted in November 2001," noted the NASA response.

Congressional sources noted that the proposal being floated by NASA administrator O'Keefe and State Dept. Undersecretary Armitage are not and have never been official policy. NASA officials, backed by White House policy, will not bring up nor support any Chinese participation in the International Space Station.

"By his own admission O'Keefe has yet to determine whether or not he'll be able to keep the promises NASA has made to our current partners, so it's premature for him to start looking for additional players," noted one source inside Capitol Hill.

According to the official April NASA response, "under the International Space Station agreements (ISS), it is possible for non-Partners to participate in ISS program through an ISS Partner."

"However, all other Partners must be notified and give their consensus prior to the non-Partner's participation in the program. Non-Partner participation could occur through contribution of hardware to the ISS or through collaborative research. The ISS international partners are currently not discussing any plans to pursue Chinese participation in this program," noted the official NASA response.

"The only purpose I could see in putting forth such a proposal is intelligence gathering for us," said Douglas Brown of the Nathan Hale Institute.

"Maybe something to dangle in front of them and to initiate some preliminary activities that would be useful for us but the idea of letting them in the ISS as full partners sounds like John Huang is now sending faxes from State. What's next? Co-piloting our recon planes?" asked Brown.

"The statements made by Jiang Zemin and General Cao surrounding the Shenzhou 3 launch were much more Klingon Empire than Kennedyesque. They very clearly link the manned space program to the PLA's military ambitions," stated the Jamestown Foundation's Richard Fisher.

"I'm all for space exploration cooperation with China but not before we create some peace on Earth, like on the Taiwan Strait and concerning China's missile and nuclear proliferation. The minimal 1970s level strategic framework that preceded space cooperation with the Soviet Union does not exist between the U.S. and the PRC. A strategic framework that promotes peaceful behavior on Earth should precede attempts at peaceful cooperation in space," concluded Fisher.

The Chinese Army multi-billion dollar Shenzhou manned mission illustrates the new aggressive space effort by China. China is currently training a dozen astronauts for the first flight.

The 17,000-lb. Shenzhou vehicle resembles a Russia Soyuz spacecraft but is larger and equipped with two sets of solar panels. China tested unmanned versions of the Shenzhou twice, the first in November 1999 and the second test in January 2001.

In 2003, China joined an elite club of world powers with its launch of the manned Shenzhou spacecraft - code-named Project 921. However, the Chinese manned space program is neither a civilian effort nor peaceful.

The Chinese manned space program is under the complete and direct control of the People's Liberation Army (PLA). The Shenzhou missions are part of an overall space program under the personal command of PLA general Li Jinai. Gen. Li is a senior member of the Central Military Commission and head of the General Armaments Department of the PLA. Li was trained in Russia and has played a major role in the Chinese army's strategic nuclear weapons modernization program.

Li has a vested interest in seeing Project 921 succeed. The Long March missiles, deployed as part of China's nuclear arsenal, are interchangeable with the rockets powering the Shenzhou manned space program.

The fact that the Chinese army is running Project 921 comes as no surprise to many defense analysts, who contend that the Shenzhou spacecraft was designed for war. While the spacecraft was slated to carry one Chinese astronaut, its primary cargo was a high-resolution camera for military space-based reconnaissance.

"China is pursuing a manned space program for two key reasons. First and most important is its political payoff for the Chinese Communist Party, which shows that amid all China's raging crises that the Party can still rally the nation," stated Richard Fisher, a senior fellow at the Center for Security Policy.

"Second, but just as important, is that the manned space program serves to justify a far more expansive military-civil space program and the expensive investment in a large technical infrastructure that it requires," noted Fisher.

The new Chinese military space effort has also raised more than just international security questions. China has reportedly spent billions of dollars on its military manned space mission while ignoring crushing poverty, inadequate education and poor health care for its people.

"The Chinese government has a large amount of hard currency. They could use the money for education because millions of people in China do not have an opportunity to go to school. They could use it for health care to prevent epidemics and disease.

Instead, they are spending it on aerospace," stated Harry Wu, a prominent human rights advocate and executive director of the Laogai Research Foundation.

"The U.S.-China trade generates billions of dollars in profits. The Chinese government is using this profit not for schools or hospitals. They are spending it for aerospace. This is exactly the same kind of national spending priority that the Soviet Union engaged in. The space launch is not for the Chinese people. It is so that China can become the world's Communist superpower," concluded Wu.

"Should China's manned space program meet with success, and soon [progress] to manned space stations as is expected, it is inevitable that there will be increasing calls in the U.S. and Europe to expand space cooperation with China. This would be unwise as long as China remains a key proliferator of weapons of mass destruction, serves as North Korea's main protector, and prepares for war against democratic Taiwan. Better there be peace with China on Earth before cooperation in space that could aid its military-space ambitions," concluded Richard Fisher.

"A nasty new slave labor tyrant that pays his mortgage from slave labor just moved into the space neighborhood and he didn't move in for the view," stated a senior Canadian intelligence source.

"Its time for a neighborhood watch program."

China also recently signed a deal with Alcatel of France for a new 5-ton DFH-4 communications satellite. In addition, China is developing 15 new space satellites and has started two new joint space ventures with Iran and Pakistan.

The massive civil space build-up in China is mirrored by the Chinese Army, which is currently upgrading its space-based assets as well. The new military space program includes reconnaissance, navigation, weather and communications satellites designed specifically to support PLA combat operations.

Despite the propaganda from Beijing, the ambitious Chinese space program is designed for war. The Chinese army launch of a Long March 2D rocket on Nov. 3 2003 carried an FSW-18 photo-image reconnaissance satellite into orbit. The PLA space launch was the third in less than a month, indicating an upsurge in Chinese military capability.

According to the official Chinese press organ, Xinhau, the FSW-18 satellite is carrying "scientific research, land surveying, mapping and other scientific experiments." The Chinese press reports that the satellite is also carrying samples of seeds that are to be irradiated in space in the hopes that they will produce better crops.

The only seeds onboard FSW-18 are the seeds of war. The FSW-18 was actually a People's Liberation Army (PLA) military film photographic satellite. The FSW-18 photographed U.S. and allied military targets in Korea, Okinawa, Japan, Taiwan, Afghanistan and Iraq.

The FSW-18 satellite remained in orbit for two weeks taking pictures of U.S. military sites and then returned the film to China by a remote-controlled re-entry capsule. The Chinese military certainly shared the space images with its allies, including North Korea. In fact, North Korea needs the images in order to re-target long-range SCUD and No Dong missiles against recently re-deployed U.S. forces in South Korea.

Pyongyang also will be very interested in the firing positions of new long-range South Korean missiles recently moved to the DMZ, which divides the two nations. The South Korean Tactical Missile System Block 1A missiles have a range of 186 miles.

The recoverable FSW-18 spacecraft joined the Shenzhou V orbit module that remained in space after the recent Chinese manned mission. The unmanned Shenzhou V spacecraft is equipped with two high-resolution digital infrared cameras.

The Shenzhou orbit module is currently imaging cities and military installations inside the United States. The images will provide target-mapping data for the Chinese army's long-range nuclear missile force.

Unlike the film recovery system on the FSW-18 spacecraft, the Shenzhou images are returned to earth by encrypted digital radio signals.

Ironically, the Chinese army is all too familiar with satellite image processing and encrypted satellite communications technology, thanks mainly to the United States.

U.S. Dept. of Commerce documents show the Chinese satellite "remote sensing center" was supplied with "world class remote sensing data acquisition, processing, archive and distribution" equipment. The state-of-the-art satellite equipment was provided by Hughes Corp.

According to the 1997 Commerce Department report, the Clinton administration also gave the Chinese "fine images of rural China and Beijing as well as Siberian port cities, Seoul and Kadena Air Force Base on Okinawa."

In 1997, U.S. Commerce Department officials at the American Embassy in Beijing wrote that the Chinese obtained satellite images in order to "help demonstrate that Tibet has enough arable land to feed itself."

The heartfelt concern for Tibet by the communist government is a touching piece of propaganda. However, the Chinese were not the only ones seeking high-resolution U.S. space photographs.

According to the same 1997 document, Commerce officials "were told that two North Koreans visited the station some time ago but did not buy any [satellite] imagery. The North Koreans do not have any significant earth resources satellite utilization capability."

The current Shenzhou secure image transmissions of U.S. target cities are a direct result of the U.S. high-tech sales to the Chinese army.

Exports of encrypted satellite communications technology was de-controlled by President Clinton in 1996, removing the State and Defense departments' oversight of such high-tech exports.

The Clinton executive order was supported by the CEOs of Lockheed, Loral and Hughes, and it allowed China to purchase sophisticated encryption for its military satellite systems. According to a Hughes document sent in March 1995 to Clinton National Security Advisor Anthony Lake, satellite encryption "has no military significance."

The Hughes document concluded that control over the export of a wide range of advanced U.S. satellite technology should be moved to the Commerce Department. The U.S. technology sent by Clinton to China included the entire list of items sought by Hughes: anti-jam capability, advanced antennas, cross links, baseband processing, encryption devices, radiation hardening, and perigee kick motors.

In fact, the CEOs of Hughes, Loral and Lockheed co-wrote a letter to Bill Clinton in October 1995 expressing their desire that the president "transfer all responsibility for commercial satellite export licensing to the Commerce Department."

The 1995 letter, signed by C. Michael Armstrong of Hughes, Bernard Schwartz of Loral and Daniel Tellep of Lockheed, states that "we understand you may soon be issuing an Executive Order intended to make further improvements to the process for reviewing export license applications."

"During a recent meeting involving Vice President Gore and representatives of the satellite industry discussing national/global information infrastructure, this was one of several issues raised. We clearly appreciate your administration's strong commitment to reforming the U.S. export control system, but we respectfully request your personal support for establishing the Commerce Department's jurisdiction over the export of all commercial communications satellites," states the letter from the three CEOs.

Further documentation obtained from the Defense Department shows that China has launched a massive and expensive laser weapons build-up. The new Chinese weapons include anti-cruise missile, anti-satellite and lasers designed to instantly "blind" soldiers on the battlefield. China has already deployed the blinding laser and is currently offering the man portable unit for export.

According to the documents, Chinese laser technology is being run by Li Hui, the Director of the Beijing Institute of Remote Sensing Equipment. The Defense Department document noted that the Chinese "Institute of Remote Sensing" is actually a front for Army missile guidance design laboratories. The Institute of Remote Sensing is "a developer of optical precision and photoelectric guidance systems for surface-to-air missiles". Director Li Hui recently stated that "laser technology as the only effective means to counter cruise missiles."

Recent translations of PLA documentation shows the Chinese Army has accelerated development of beam weapons. Red Chinese Army doctrine states laser weapons will be used for "active jamming of electro-optics, blinding combatants and damaging sensors, causing laser guided weapons to deviate from their true targets and target destruction."

The newly declassified Defense Department documentation describes in detail the use of high-speed computers with a powerful new laser, controlled through "fast-steering mirrors." The new laser uses "piezoelectric" actuators that flex very thin mirrors at high speeds to "compensate for beam wander caused by device jitter and atmospheric turbulence."

The system allows the laser to focus a powerful light beam over long distances. An air defense version of the new PLA laser is estimated to be able to deliver over 10,000 watts of output power on a target up up to 500 miles away.

According to the Defense document, China will deploy an even more powerful ground-based laser by the year 2000. The new laser requires a "4 meter (M) diameter beam director mirror for an antisatellite mission. The Nanjing Astronomical Instrument Research Center... is currently producing a 4.3 M (meter) diameter mirror for the Beijing Observatory. This mirror is scheduled to be installed in the year 2000."

In addition, the U.S. Naval Institute Proceedings magazine has revealed that China is also offering a blinding laser weapon for export. The January 1999 issue of Proceedings noted the Chinese are now offering their ZM-87 battlefield laser on the open market.

The ZM-87 is a "dazzler" system, designed to disable night-vision equipment and to instantly blind combatants on the battlefield. Several international treaties ban lasers that blind. The ZM-87 resembles a conventional machine gun on a tripod mount with a separate power unit and sighting system.

The U.S. military, starved by Clinton budgets into a shell of its former self, have only recently started counter-measures against the PLA laser program. U.S. armed forces have deployed some simple protective glasses to shield soldiers from lasers. However, American pilots rely on aging night-vision equipment that cannot deal with the intense light-beam threat.

Furthermore, the current U.S. missile inventory relies on 1970s microchip technology with a fraction of the speed, resistance to radiation and capability of those in their PLA counter-parts. The American military relies on a satellite communications system that is rapidly degrading into useless junk.

According to the GAO, the current U.S. military satellite network is already not capable of supporting a major war and will fail within the next 5 years. Again, the Clinton administration starved U.S. military space-based assets with budget shortfalls and planned upgrades moved years into the future.

In contrast, the Communist Chinese espionage success penetrating America is best illustrated by the sudden and rapid advance of PLA weapons during Bill Clinton's Presidency. China has taken a great leap forward from the frail force of ex-Soviet 1950s, vacuum tube driven, left-overs, deployed in December 1992.

Current PLA weapons such as the SU-30 strike fighter, the C.802 cruise missile, the DF-15 mobile, tactical-ballistic missile and the Hong-7 supersonic bomber, all use state-of-the-art, radiation-hardened, microchips. These advanced weapons communicate directly with PLA troops using state-of-the-art, radiation-hardened, global satellite communication systems.

The successful effort by China to obtain details on U.S. microchip technology included both espionage, and sabotage. The red intelligence windfall freed the Chinese Army to finance new weapons such as lasers while it modernized using advanced American technology. The legacy that President Clinton will leave for the next century is a modern Chinese Army equipped for global war.

For example, the People's Liberation Army Air Force (PLAAF) unveiled its long-anticipated fourth-generation combat jet. Despite being touted as the first indigenous fighter, the J-10 is filled with a combination of technologies either bought or stolen from America.

The Chengdu J-10 advanced combat fighter is clearly a product of years of military cooperation between Israel and China, taking much of its design from the now defunct U.S.-Israeli Lavi project.

The exact amount of Israeli support for the J-10 project is debatable; however, there is overwhelming evidence that much of the new jet fighter's design comes from the joint U.S.-Israeli project from the 1980s.

Externally, the J-10 appears to be almost an exact copy of the Israeli/U.S.-designed Lavi fighter. The aircraft is a single-seat, multi-role, delta-canard fighter design equipped with a digital fly-by-wire system for control.

Chinese engineers, working with Russian counterparts, modified the aircraft to be powered by a single Saturn Lyuika Al-31 power plant. The new power plant, more powerful that the U.S.-made engine designed for the Lavi, gives the J-10 a higher top speed and longer-range performance.

In addition, China has added several features that were directly reverse-engineered from a U.S.-made F-16 Falcon jet fighter provided to Beijing by Pakistan.

The Pakistani F-16, sold to Islamabad during the 1980s, was given to the PLAAF as part of a secret military trade deal between Pakistan and China. In return for the U.S.-made F-16 jet, Pakistan received a deep discount on the purchase of Chinese-made M-11 ballistic missiles.

The new Chinese J-10 supersonic fighter is designed to take on and defeat U.S.-built F-16 and F-18 fighters that make up the bulk of American airpower. Western sources estimate that Chengdu will manufacture over 1,000 of the delta-winged fighters to replace aging MiG-21 and MiG-19 fighter designs that currently make up the vast majority of China's air force.

Western intelligence sources noted that China has been flying about a half-dozen J-10 prototypes for at least two years, and the fighter is not slated to join the PLAAF until 2007. Prototypes of the J-10 that have been seen were armed with the PL-9 air-to-air missile, a Chinese copy of the Israeli Rafael Python 3.

Exactly what kind of radar the new J-10 will be equipped with, however, is still under debate. The new fighter was thought to be equipped with a version of the Israeli-made Elbit ELM-2021 radar system, which can track multiple aerial targets simultaneously.

Russian sources now indicate the J-10 will be equipped with a version of the Phazotron Zhemchoung radar, which has both an air-to-air and air-to-ground targeting capability. The new Russian-made radar system for the J-10 will complement existing N-001 radars supplied to the PLAAF for its Sukhoi SU-30MK twin-seat strike fighter.

The Xian FBC-1 was publicly displayed for the first time during Air Show China '98 in Zhuhai. Although the Communist party has declared the FBC-1 to be the first true all-Chinese modern bomber - it is true they had a little help in the conception of their bomber from friends in the west.

The FBC-1 is a twin engine, swept-wing, super-sonic two seat, all weather attack bomber, equipped with American GPS bombing - navigation and powered by licensed copies of the British Rolls Royce Spey engine. The all weather FBC-1 GPS bombing system will eventually be upgraded with Chinese made Synthetic Aperture Radar (SAR) and an infra-red night vision pod.

Chinese engineers bragged that the FBC-1 was designed with CAD (computer aided design) techniques on U.S. built super computers. The computers were provided through the China Flight Test Establishment at Xian University.

The aircraft that flew past the airshow is similar in design to the Anglo-French Jaguar attack jet. The FBC-1 displayed was obviously repainted from Chinese Navy camouflage to the brighter colors of China's Test Flight Establishment.

Some western analysts speculated the FBC-1 will be equipped with a Chinese copy of the Russian, supersonic anti-ship, Zvezda Kh-31 missile and fielded against U.S. carrier task forces. However, NATO observers at the air show noted the Russian Kh-31 is made of titanium and unlikely to be copied by the Chinese. According to NATO, the FBC-1 will be equipped as a costal bomber and armed with the Chinese made C.802 cruise missile to deal with surface ships.

The bomber/missile combination is likely to be marketed as a package to foreign buyers. The FBC-1 may be exported to North Korea, Pakistan and Iran. Iran is viewed as the first likely customer. Iran has already purchased large numbers of C.802 cruise missiles and must replace aging U.S. made F-4 Phantom jets that are the bulk of the IAF anti-ship units.

There are no current export customers for the FBC-1 but the People's Liberation Army Air Force (PLAAF) has an order for up to 72 bombers, designated the FH-7, or "HONG" - 7, using a Maoist slogan for domestic tradition.

China has been somewhat more successful in exporting advanced ballistic missile technology. The communist leaders in Beijing have taken every opportunity to export missile and nuclear warfare equipment to such nations as Iran, Pakistan and Iraq.

The entire Pakistani atomic arsenal was built from scratch with the direct assistance of the Chinese military, including advanced nuclear warhead designs from PLA labs and nuclear tipped missiles directly out of the Chinese Army inventory.

The National Intelligence Estimate, a threat analysis published by the CIA, noted that Beijing has "enabled emerging missile states to accelerate development timelines for their existing programs" and sold "turnkey systems to gain previously non-existent capabilities - in the case of the Chinese sale of the M-11 short-range ballistic missile to Pakistan."

In 2001, the U.S. lodged sanctions against the China Metallurgical Equipment Corp. after it continued to ship missile parts to Pakistan, violating Beijing's sixth promise to stop such exports. It should not surprise you to find that the People's Liberation Army owns China Metallurgical.

Pakistan has conducted numerous tests of its improved "Shaheen" medium-range ballistic missile. The Shaheen is widely known to be a copy of the Chinese made M-11 (Dong Feng 11) surface-to-surface missile.

During the 1990s, China exported M-11 missiles and ballistic missile technology to Pakistan. The new missile test prove that Chinese and Pakistani missile engineers have improved the M-11 missile from its original 186-mile range to a range of over 500 miles.

"The 'Shaheen-I' - also known as the 'Hatf-3' - is one of three defined variants of Pakistan's 'Shaheen' class of rockets," stated Ilan Berman, Vice President for Policy at the American Foreign Policy Council.

"Conservative estimates place the range of the missile, which is a copy of the Chinese 'M-11,' at approximately 300 kilometers. However, unofficial reports dating back to 1999 have cited the missile - which is the subject of continued intensive development by Pakistan - as having an expanded range of 800 kilometers," noted Berman.

"Multiple news reports from the most recent October 5th test of the 'Shaheen' list the missile as having an 800-kilometer range. If true, this news is confirmation that Pakistan - with help from both North Korea and China - is substantially expanding the range of its missile arsenal," said Berman.

"With Chinese assistance, Pakistan is making significant strides in its ballistic missile programs. Projects like the 'Shaheen' medium-range missile - modeled after PRC weaponry - are expanding the threat posed by Pakistan to India, its neighbor and regional rival. This is significant, because it is likely to spark growing instability in South Asia as New Delhi moves to counter the growing threat posed by Islamabad's missile arsenal," concluded Berman.

Russian sources also accused Beijing of helping Pakistan's missile program. According to ITAR/TASS, Moscow's main government information agency, a Russian missile expert stated that China is directly responsible for the rapid Pakistani missile development.

"Islamabad is trying to persuade the world that Ghauri and Shaheen are national designs, yet there is information that nearly all missile systems of Pakistan are precise copies of North Korean and Chinese analogues," states the Russian report.

"Despite the official statements of Pakistan that it is not developing intercontinental missiles, some of Pakistan's leading scientists have confirmed the readiness of the national defense industry to start the production of such weapons as need be," noted a Russian missile expert quoted by the ITAR/TASS news agency.

"The test launch of a ballistic missile in Pakistan shows that South Asia remains the most dangerous area from the point of view of a possible nuclear conflict," noted the Russian report.

In contrast to the current administration, President Clinton imposed sanctions against China for the missile transfers to Pakistan for only four months. Instead, according to documents obtained by the Freedom of Information Act, the Clinton administration decided to relax export controls on space technology, enabling U.S. companies such as Loral and Hughes to obtain satellite contracts with China.

"Last August (1993), the U.S. imposed sanctions on China for an M-11 missile-related transfer to Pakistan. On January 7, 1994 it was decided that communications satellites licensed by the State Department are covered by the sanctions law, export licenses for communications satellites licensed by the Department of Commerce may be approved. Two such export licenses for communications satellites were recently approved by the Department of Commerce."

The news that China and Pakistan have improved the M-11 missile directly impacts on Beijing's future conflict with Taiwan. The Chinese People's Liberation Army Second Artillery Corps is known to have as many as 400 M-11 type missiles deployed across from Taiwan. The improved version of the M-11 could threaten any U.S. efforts to re-enforce Taiwan during a crisis and the missile could be targeted far beyond Taiwan to attack U.S. aircraft carriers.

The news that Beijing and Islamabad have improved the M-11 missile comes directly after China announced that it would conduct lives tests of the Dong Feng 31 (DF-31) missiles in the next few weeks. Unlike the M-11, the DF-31 missile is capable of reaching the United States and has a range of over 7,000 miles. The DF-31 is armed with advanced, lightweight, Hydrogen bomb technology stolen from U.S. nuclear weapons labs.

In addition, the announced DF-31 missile tests come on the heels of several missile launches by Beijing in late August. On August 28, the Chinese Army conducted a successful launch of its Dong Feng 4 (DF-4) missile from a site in southern China. The DF-4 is known to carry a large H-bomb warhead over 4,000 miles.

The DF-4 missile currently equips two units of the Chinese Second Artilery Corps, unit 80305 and unit 80306. The 80305 unit is based in Huaihau, Hunan province, with its DF-4 missiles aimed at the U.S. military base in Guam. The 80306 unit is based in Xining, Qinghai province, and its missiles are aimed at targets inside India.

"There is no indication whatsoever that China has halted or cut back its weapons of mass destruction programs," stated Al Santoli, national security advisor to Rep. Dana Rohrabacher, R. CA.

"Equally troubling, the Chinese government has recently made military training mandatory for all high school and college students, under the combined control of the Ministry of Education and the Ministry of Defense. These types of national policies should set off alarm bells in neighboring countries and in the West, that despite efforts to integrate China into the world economy, Beijing continues to pursue belligerent military/political goals," said Santoli.

Chinese exports to Pakistan have increased the threat of war between rivals Pakistan and India. The ongoing series of missile tests are only a small sample of the tensions between the two nuclear-armed South Asian neighbors.

India said it conducted two tests of its short-range "Akash" surface-to-air missile without fanfare. Indian Defense Minister George Fernandes defended the missile tests, blaming China for the growing tension between India and Pakistan.

"China is not only economically stronger, but has conducted nuclear tests much before us. They are also well armed. Pakistan's arrogance is because of China's backing," stated Fernandes.

"To tackle the situation today we must have the same strength that our neighbors have," noted Fernandes, referring to the military might of China.

Both India and Pakistan have over 1 million soldiers deployed along their tense border and each nation is armed with dozens of nuclear tipped missiles. The Asian nations have fought two major wars and are currently locked in a dispute over the contested Kashmir region.

Defense sources are also concerned because China has sold germ warfare equipment to Iran. In Jan. 1997, Madeleine Albright confirmed during a Senate hearing that China had shipped biological warfare equipment to Iran.

The concern is that Iran may have passed germ warfare technology to terrorist groups such as Hamas and Hezbollah that have carried out recent suicide attacks in Israel. U.S. intelligence sources refused to confirm or deny that China may be the original source of recent Anthrax attacks in the United States.

In 1997, the Clinton administration refused to identify the specific Chinese company that made the germ warfare shipments to Iran. The Clinton administration also refused to impose sanctions required by export laws against China.

Instead, documentation obtained using the Freedom of Information Act shows that in 1997 Clinton officials approved super-computer exports to a known Chinese germ warfare lab without an end use inspection.

In December 1997, U.S. Commerce officials sought permission to inspect Xian Jiatong University prior to the export of a high performance computer made by Digital Corp. American inspectors wanted to verify that the Chinese university would not use the computer for germ warfare research.

However, all efforts to inspect the site were denied by the communist Chinese government. The Clinton administration approved the super-computer sale despite Beijing's refusal to allow inspections.

Xian Jiatong University is a known center for Chinese Army biological and chemical warfare research. The Xian Jiatong sale is the only reported U.S. super-computer export associated with Chinese biological and chemical warfare.

Pentagon sources are convinced that the Chinese Army is now using the U.S. made super-computer to develop a chemical cluster "bomblet" munitions to arm missiles and bombers. A bomblet warhead can disperse hundreds of miniature germ filled grenades over a vast area instead of a single large warhead, which would infect a smaller target zone.

In addition, convicted China-Gate figure Charlie "Yah Lin" Trie confirmed that he helped China obtain germ warfare technology from the west. during a March 2000 Congressional hearing

"If they don't get it from me, they get it from someone else," testified Trie. "They gonna get it."

According to his testimony, Trie received thousands of dollars in commissions from the Chinese by arranging a deal with a Swiss biological equipment manufacturer.

The Trie led deal allowed China to obtain a 500-liter fermenting machine used to cultivate microorganisms, viruses or biotoxins. The institute in China that received the fermenting machine is based in Xian, near the known Chinese germ warfare lab.

PLA front companies continued to provide camouflage for Beijing as it attempted to export more advanced weapons to Iraq. For example, the harmless sounding Shandong Arts and Craft Company is in fact a front for Chinese missile proliferation. In 2001, the firm acted as a cover for a PLA military delegation to Iraq seeking to sell advanced long-range missile technology to Saddam Hussein.

The Chinese Army is preparing to wage war against the United States. A recently declassified Chinese military document states that China will first conduct a "Vietnam" like conventional war against America and then eventually fight a nuclear war against the U.S. homeland.

The document was recently translated by an American intelligence agency. The Chinese Army Central Command sent the orders to all the regional garrisons and Army Corps headquarters.

According to the August 1999 policy document published by the People's Liberation Army Office of The Central Military Command, China is "willing to sustain major losses of our armed forces" in exchange for large losses of U.S. military personnel.

"If the U.S. forces lose thousands or hundreds of men under our powerful strikes, the anti-war sentiment within their country will force the U.S. government to take the same path as they did in Viet Nam," states the Chinese Army document.

Titled "Watching Closely for Changes in Relationships with Taiwan and Enhancing Awareness of Military Leadership of Current Situation", the Chinese Army strategy document also describes a chilling scenario of nuclear war with America:

"In comparison with the U.S. nuclear arsenal, our disadvantage is mainly numeric, which in real wars the qualitative gap will be reflected only as different requirement of strategic theory. In terms of deterrence, there is not any difference in practical value. So far we have built up the capability for the second and third nuclear strikes and are fairly confident in fighting a nuclear war. The PCC (communist Party Central Committee) has decided to pass though formal channels this message to the top leaders in the U.S."

The Chinese Army command document also noted that recent U.S. combat experience couldn't be compared to a future war with the massive People's Liberation Army. China is capable of massive millions of troops and has well over 5,000 aircraft that could be thrown into a battle over Taiwan. In addition, the Chinese military noted they had a clear edge in fighting a tactical nuclear war with American forces in the Pacific region.

"In terms of air defense," noted the Chinese Army document "it is impossible for the U.S. Air Force to enjoy the kind of dominance which they maintained in Iraq or Yugoslavia."

"It can be safely expected that once the U.S. launches an attack, the front line of U.S. forces and their supporting bases will be exposed within the range of our effective strikes. After the first strategic strike, the U.S. forces will be faced with weaponry and logistic problems, providing us with opportunities for major offensives and win large battles."

According the Chinese military, "Unlike Iraq and Yugoslavia, China is not only a big country, but also possesses a nuclear arsenal that has long since been incorporated into state warfare system and play a real role in our national defense."

"During the last crisis across the Taiwan Straits, the U.S. tried to blackmail us with their aircraft carrier(s), but when their spy satellites confirmed that our four nuclear submarines which used to be stationed at Lushun Harbor had disappeared, those politicians addicted to the Taiwan card could not imagine how worried their military commander were."

The Chinese military command also outlined its plan for a quick victory by using over-whelming numbers in a massive assault against Taiwan.

"Taiwan occupies only a small area. Although the quality of its equipment is not too bad, its quantity is limited. It is obvious that after the first fatal strike, the Taiwan forces have no way to organise effective resistance. Under such circumstances, we will be able to control Taiwan before the U.S. intervention and the concentrate our forces to fight the U.S. Based on this scenario, it is impossible for the U.S. to force us to fight on two fronts when it tries to protect Taiwan."

The Chinese Army document also noted that the Chinese diplomatic front has started in the "war" with America. According to the military, recent Chinese diplomatic efforts successfully lined up a solid wall of support from the other Asian powers, allowing the Chinese Army to move forces south in preparation for an invasion of Taiwan.

"Internationally, President Jiang Zemin, will go to Biskek in late September to attend the five-country meeting, including China, Russia, Kyrgzstan, Kazakstan and Tajikstan. The meeting will sum up and expand cooperations in the field of security and reach agreements on reduction of armed forces stationed along the borders and establishment of military trust."

"The above efforts will not only eliminate security concerns along our rear by reducing the traditional pressure along our northeast and northwest border, and increase the proportion of forces which can be moved to the southeast coastal regions, but also serve to ensure our exchanges with the outside world by land routes during the war."

The China apologists in the United States assure us that the communist state is not a threat, that it is a peaceful nation prepared to take its place in the world. Their simplistic view of Chinese history omits the past 40 years of confrontation with America.

They refuse to see Beijing's growing inventory of advanced missiles, warships, and planes. They ignore years of espionage and covert political influence through contributions to U.S. political campaigns. They continue to seek appeasement despite the overwhelming evidence of missile and nuclear weapon proliferation.

In the next 40 years, China will attempt to take its place among the world's super-powers. China's growing arsenal of advanced weapons will enable it to do so in a forceful and violent manner. It is time that we recognize what the People's Liberation Army already knows - that America is their number one target.

OFFICIAL CHINESE ARMY ORDERS

The following document was obtained from sources inside the Chinese People's Liberation Army.

Confidential***

Document of Office of the Central Military Commission (OCMC) OCMC Serial No. [1999] 65

OCMC Notice on Forwarding the Document "Watching Closely for Changes in the Relationships with Taiwan and Enhancing the Awareness by Military Leadership of the Current Situation"

All Regional Garrisons, All General Departments Affiliated to the Central Military Commission (CMC), All Arms and Services, All Corps Headquarters, All Provincial Garrisons, and All Prefecture Garrisons:

Attached please find the document "Watching Closely for Changes in the Relationships with Taiwan and Enhancing the Awareness by Military Leadership of the Current Situation," which has been drafted by the General Political Department approved by the CMC Conference to be distributed down to the commanders at the division level. Please read carefully and implement seriously.

Office of the Central Military Commission of the Communist Party of China August 10, 1999

(Seal of the CMC)

Watching Closely for Changes in Relationships with Taiwan and Enhancing Awareness of Military Leadership of Current Situation

As soon as Li Denghui put forth the "two country theory," which aimed at splitting our motherland, the ranks and files of our armed forces were filled with indignation. At all levels within our armed forces, seminars, discussions, presentations, and symposiums were held to condemn Li Denghui's evil intention of splitting the motherland in open disregard of the national interests. The CMC has, on behalf of the armed forces, made a solemn commitment to the Party and the Country that "we shall not sit idle while allowing one inch of territory to be split away from the map of our motherland," which conviction is obviously based on solid political ground given the above-mentioned militant zeal of "opposing split, committed to reunification." Such a sentiment has provided a precious opportunity to promote political goals within our armed forces. The current priority of our political work is: holding high the great banner of Deng Xiaoping Theory, unifying closely around the Party's Central Committee with Comrade Jiang Zemin as its core, implementing the "Requirements" adopted at the Expanded Emergency Meeting of the CMC and "OCMC Notice on the Current Situation," further exposing and criticizing the "two country theory," taking advantage of the strong determination of opposing the split and high emotions of nationalism and incorporate them into daily training, and ensuring that in carrying out the Party and the country's great strategy of reunifying the motherland, the people's army always retains firm and correct political goals, fully-charged patriotism, constant battle alert, and staunch and conquering-all operational capacity so as to make new contributions to the motherland.

With this focus, high-ranking commanders in non-combat as well as combat positions should be well aware of the following issues so as to better understand the strategic decisions made by the Party's Central Committee and be well-prepared for the war in their units based on the rapidly-changing relationships with Taiwan.

1. To Fully Recognize the Subjective and Objective Factors Which Necessitate the Reunification of the Motherland

To resolve Taiwan issue and achieve reunification is a matter of uttermost importance which reflects the intentions of the three generations of leaders of our country. in view of the overall world pattern as well as rapidly-changing domestic and international situations, to achieve the reunification in the foreseeable future has become a most important task facing the Party and the country and specific measures must be taken from now on. In this regard, all members of our armed forces must deepen their understanding of the following points.

(1) Historical mission. National independence and reunification has remained the sole purpose of China's revolutionary movement throughout this century, including both the old democratic revolution led by Mr. Sun Yah-sen and the new democratic revolution led by our Party, both having attracted countless people of aspiration and integrity. The Northern Expedition and the War against Japan represented cooperations on different occasions between the Nationalist Party and the Communist Party and were based on the above goal. From this perspective, the reunification which our Party and country are committed to achieve represents the ultimate aspiration and interests of the Chinese nation throughout the current century. In terms of historical mission, the cause of reunification is based on past efforts and constitutes an issue of nationalism which goes beyond political parties and beliefs and represents the interests of all the Chinese people, including the people of Taiwan.

(2) Taiwan issue has resulted from the Civil War and has never ceased to be an internal affair. The founding of the People's Republic of China in 1949 symbolized the decisive victory of the revolutionary cause of the Chinese people on the Mainland. Because of the international and domestic situations at that time, Taiwan issue was temporarily shelved. However, since both sides accepted the political concept of one China, Taiwan issue was never internationalized. During the Korean War, when the Seventh Fleet moved into Taiwan, our government raised serious protests against the United States and pointed out that such a move had constituted an invasion, thereby clearly defining Taiwan issue as China's internal affair, which demonstrated a high degree of political sensitivity. After half a century's delay, the Chinese government's sovereignty over Taiwan has not changed; as a continuation of history, the substance of the Civil War has not changed, either. If military actions constitutes the sole means to achieve reunification of the motherland, we must not concentrate on one point at the expense of the other.

(3) We must create a complete image of a big country. Judging by the various elements which make up a big country, our country is certainly a big country. In the five thousand years of outstanding civilization, our country has commanded a predominant position in the whole world. After the founding of the People's Republic of China, particularly after the reform and opening to the outside world, our country has not only stood up politically, but achieved remarkable progress in economy and strength. As a result, our country was able to regain its sovereignty over Hong Kong and Macao without resorting to war, which not only washed away the national humiliation since the Opium War, but also set the first example of ending the colonial rule with peaceful means in the world history. However, as long as Taiwan has not returned to the motherland, the unified image will remain incomplete, which is not only an emotional trauma for the Chinese people, but an issue involving the dignity of our country; it should not be neglected. If the fifty-year delay has been caused by historical background and various constraints, the situation today points exactly to the opposite — it is now possible to accomplish the great cause of reunification from whatever perspective.

(4) The damage to our country's interests and dignity. In the international political struggle, Taiwan issue has long since become a trump card by the anti-China forces and deteriorated into a malicious tumor that hinder the development of our motherland. Playing the Taiwan card and using it to contain China is a manifestation of the old cold-war thinking in the new international arena and an important means of opposing China by a handful of politicians in the US Congress who cling desperately to the cold-war thinking. In terms of social system, it is expressed as anti-communist thinking; in terms of outlook, it is revealed as naked racial discrimination. In view of this situation, to resolve Taiwan issue and achieve the reunification as soon as possible not only involves our sovereignty and national dignity, but also directly relates to our country's development and important strategy in opposing world hegemonism.

(5) An obstacle to diplomatic relations. With regard to international affairs, Taiwan issue is the biggest obstacle when it comes to implementing the principles of equality and mutual benefits. In recent years, the Taiwan authorities have been engaged in money diplomacy, capitalizing on the economic difficulties of a number of small and weak countries and using money as baits to induce and infiltrate some countries which have had long-standing relationships with our country. As a result, we had to put in some efforts to counter such moves, not only giving diplomacy a greater-than-normal political weight, but also introducing unstable elements into the conventional reciprocity in international relations to seriously interfere with normal diplomatic affairs. On the other hand, because of Taiwan issue, when it comes to territorial disputes and effective protection of the interests of overseas Chinese, we have to consider many different factors and engage in trade offs. Consequently, some countries refuse to behave properly; on the contrary, they use their intermittent relations with Taiwan as bargaining chips when dealing with us, seriously harming the interests and reputation of our country.

(6) Taiwan issue directly affects the solidarity of different nationalities within our country and constitutes the most serious hidden problem that could endanger the very existence of the Chinese nation. Ever since he came to power, Li Denghui has devoted himself to changing the one-nation principle followed by the previous leadership of the Nationalist Party and gradually turned Taiwan into a testing ground for splitting the motherland while colluding with the Dalai Lama and other traitors. The potential damage which could be caused by Li Denghui's "seven-block theory" in terms of instigating minority nationalities to split away from the motherland should not be underestimated. If Taiwan issue were to drag on, Taiwan would not only set an example for the handful of splittists among minority nationalities, but also become a base for splitting activities, in which case the whole nation would have to pay a heavy price.

Commanders at all levels should enhance their understanding of the position adopted by the Party's Central Committee in regard to the reunification and carry out, at the same time of patriotic education, a wave of politically-oriented military exercises aimed at opposing splittism and promoting reunification so as to raise the political consciousness of all commanders and soldiers up to a level required by war.

2. Dialectical Relationship Between Taking Initiative and Timing in Resolving Taiwan Issue

The principle followed by the Party's Central Committee (PCC) towards Taiwan issue is clear, namely, to continue to seek peaceful reunification under "one country, two systems." However, to prevent the splittists within Taiwan and international anti-China forces from splitting Taiwan away from the motherland, PCC has also stated that we would not give up the option of using military power. We have defined the latter in three different aspects, combining strategy and initiative. In view of the fact that the Taiwan authorities deliberately confused the nature of the dialogue between the two sides and avoided progress in reunification, the leaders of our country have on different occasions since the beginning of this year stated the principle that Taiwan issue would not be allowed to drag on indefinitely, which reflected the basic attitude of our Party and country in regard to the time frame and brought the reunification issue from front strategy to the phase of implementation in a stable and methodical manner, greatly enhancing the morale of the Party, the armed forces, and the people. This is a concrete example that our Party and country are capable of taking initiatives in achieving reunification; it is also an important symbol that the core of the leadership of our Party and country have reached political success and maturity.

Based on the current situation, Li Denghui has pushed the relationships between the two sides into a dead end with his "two-country theory" and therefore stuck his foot across our bottom line, actually providing us with solid grounds for achieving reunification using military power. On the other hand, in citing historical evidence, depicting the current status quo, and disguising the "two-country theory" as an effort to seek reciprocity, Li Denghui and his followers also revealed their inner weakness, providing us with solid grounds as to timing. The meaning of timing is not limited to military operations, it also involves our strategic principle of seeking reunification through peaceful means. This is the main purpose of the General Political Department in distributing this document in accordance with the spirit of the CMC Conference. Commanders at all levels must come to a unified view in the following aspects.

(1) Considering long-term interests, peaceful reunification is still the best option, which not only will ensure for the moment the safety and well-being of the Taiwan people, but is a practical solution which will be beneficial to the long-term stability of our country. First of all, because of the propaganda by the Taiwan authorities, ordinary people in Taiwan tend to have views very different from ours. If we opted for non-peaceful means, such differences will manifest themselves in various ways even after the reunification and cause instabilities. "Peaceful reunification and one country, two system" has reflected our Party's practical stance in the past decades and combined both possibilities. First and foremost, peace is emphasized. We must realize that in the foreseeable future peaceful reunification will be most beneficial to our country's development, prosperity, and lasting stability and is therefore a well-advised decision.

Taking a glance across the world, all the contentions and wars taking place in various countries after the cold war have derived from two aspects: nationality and religion. In comparison, the role of ideology has been reduced. People on both sides of the Taiwan Straits are of the same race and share common ancestors, so there exists no social genes giving rise to animosities and hostilities based on nationality or religion. Moreover, the "one country, two system" principle has provided a common ground for resolving the differences in social system. In particular, we have been persistently following a policy of reform and opening to the outside world, which not only represents the interests of all nationalities on the mainland, but also reflects and incorporates the best interests of the Taiwan people in the long run. Under this overall prerequisite, the "two-country theory" put forward by Li Denghui has posed a serious challenge to peaceful reunification, totally wiping out the ground for the dialogue between both sides. However, does this mean the end of peaceful efforts? We should wait for the PCC to make the decision.

(2) Li Denghui and his followers make up only a handful of people, who cannot represent the people in Taiwan in theory or in reality. Although many people in Taiwan are willing to keep the status quo, this only reflects their political short-sightedness caused by lack of understanding of the motherland's mainland and does not represent their interests and true wishes. The willful wrongdoing of Li Denghui has led to heightened tension between the two sides; if a war breaks out, the first victims will be the Taiwan people. In this sense, when Li Denghui, in an attempt to split the motherland, marketed his own illegitimate idea under the disguise of public opinion despite the risk of provoking a war, he not only openly betrayed the Chinese nation, but went against the best interests of the Taiwan people. No matter how the situation evolves in future, what awaits Li Denghui will be a solemn trial by the people.

However, we must realize that Li Denghui's days are numbered. His poor performance may serve to poison the relationships between the two sides, but will never change the fact that Taiwan is part of China. Nor will it prevent the overall trend that Taiwan will return to the arms of the motherland within a certain period of time. Based on such facts, although the Taiwan Straits crisis resulted from Li Denghui's behavior has increased the possibility of a military solution, we have to consider post-Li Taiwan political situation so as to decide on the best timing and correctly evaluate the political future of Taiwan on which the means of reunification rests.

(3) Deciding on the best timing as far as foreign relations are concerned. Internationally, the many obstacles to the resolution of Taiwan issue have been put in by the United States, while Japan has a complicated attitude towards our handling of Taiwan issue, but because of historical and geographical reasons, Japan does not have the right to comment. EU has ideas different from those of the U.S. and strategically focuses on Europe, so they do not have direct interests in Taiwan issue. In recent years, the relationships between EU and our country have been developing smoothly, and therefore it is very unlikely that EU will fight a full-scale war with us simply because of the United States. In fact, none of the U.S., Japan, and West Europe has given up the one-China position. The "two-country theory" by Li Denghui was to them a source of trouble rather than a gift. Even from the standing point of the U.S., Li Denghui's behavior has long since crossed the bottom line of the Sino-US dialogue on Taiwan, which will make it think twice before intervention. When deciding on the timing, we must take into account the above factors and use diplomatic leverage to minimize international resistance.

(4) The factor of deterrence. Based on strategic considerations, the CMC has decided to disclose, when appropriate, some information on strategic weaponry so

that the U.S. will exercise some caution in decision-making and be aware that it would have to pay a price if it decided to intervene in a military conflict. The purpose is to prevent the U.S. from being deeply involved even if a war becomes unavoidable so that the losses on both sides of the Taiwan straits will be minimized throughout the war. The main point is deterrence, which is the test for a peaceful solution. The test is within the strategic scope of taking initiative and promoting good timing.

Based on the international situation as well as realities on both sides of the Straits, Li Denghui obviously misjudged the situation when he threw out the "two-country theory" shortly before the end of his office in an attempt to destroy the well-established exchange channels and internationalize Taiwan issue. Ostensibly, he underestimated our determination and capability; in reality, he was blackmailing with foreign forces behind him in total disregard of the safety of the Taiwan people. In substance, his behavior constituted a sharp contrast to our concern for the safety and best interests of the Taiwan people while seeking reunification. To stay well-informed, be ready to take initiative, and grasp the best opportunity within our predetermined limits represent in a nutshell our high sense of responsibility for the Chinese nation.

3. Enhancing the Awareness Within Our Armed Forces of the Increased Possibility for A Military Solution and Certainty of Winning the War Should It Break Out

The Sino-US relations are currently at a low ebb. However, in terms of mutual efforts to improve the bilateral relations, it should be pointed out that the US government is relatively more active. The U.S. believes that it has responsibilities for all the affairs in the world, but such a philosophy must find expressions in international cooperations, particularly among big countries. China is a big country and therefore the US government could never afford to neglect the existence of China in handling international affairs ever since the establishment of diplomatic relationships between the two countries. Such a trend has been strengthened after the disintegration of the Soviet Union. During the cold war, the United States and the Soviet Union were engaged in confrontation under the surface of detente. However, in carrying out exchanges with the U.S., we have followed the principle of mutual benefit and equality and aimed at maintenance of regional stability, which reflects normal bilateral relations. The Chinese government has its own principles in handling domestic and international affairs and will never be at the beckon and call of another country. Because of such an attitude, when disagreements arose between the two countries, some US politicians would nail China down to the position of the former Soviet Union through exaggeration and turn China into a potential opponent of the U.S..

Pointing fingers at China based on the US social system and human rights standards is but an excuse, and the substance is to implement the hegemonism which would never prevail. In containing China, the U.S. has only one tangible means, which is Taiwan issue. In fact, both Jiang Jingguo and Li Denghui were presented with a historical opportunity to make contributions to the reunification of the motherland and could have become a hero in the Chinese history, because only by peaceful reunification can the strength of our nation remain intact: externally, to avoid fighting a war against the U.S. while internally, to grasp the opportunity to develop and achieve prosperity. Jiang Jingguo belonged to the second generation of the Nationalist-Communist dispute and was seriously constrained by his family background. Therefore, apart from sticking to the one-China concept, he failed to make due contributions to the reunification, which is historically regrettable. Although Li Denghui did not carry a similar historical burden, he was filled with animosity towards the Chinese nation, which gave rise to the instability in the relations between both sides of the Taiwan Straits and ultimately led to the current situation under which a military solution has to be considered. Li's behavior obviously caters to the taste of some anti-China US politicians, but when military actions become a must, neither Li Denghui nor those short-sighted anti-China US politicians will be able to control the outcome. Based on the long-term interests and current strength of our country and our armed forces, the question that we have to consider is not Taiwan's capability to defend itself or what kind of war will be fought if the U.S. intervenes, but our tactics and timing, with regard to which we provide you with the following points of reference.

(1) The impact on economic development. Taking into account of possible intervention by the U.S. and based on the development strategy of our country, it is better to fight now than future — the earlier, the better. The reason being that, if worst comes to worst, we will gain control of Taiwan before full deployment of the US troops. In this case, the only thing the U.S. can do is fighting a war with the purpose of retaliation, which will be similar to the Gulf War against Iraq or the recent bombing of Yugoslavia as far as its operational objective is considered, namely, to first attack from the sky and the sea our coastal military targets, and then attack our vital civil facilities so as to force us to accept its terms like Iraq and Yugoslavia. This is of course wishful thinking. However, before completely destroying the attacking enemy forces from the sea and their auxiliary bases which together constitute a threat to us, even if we successfully carry out interception and control the sky, our military and civil facilities will still incur some damages. The damages will be more extensive if the war cannot be ended within a short period of time and the U.S. launch the second and third strategic strikes, which will take a toll on the economic development of our country. If the above scenario cannot be avoided, an early war will delay the success of our reform whereas a later war will jeopardize the full achievement of the reform.

(2) The balance of strategic weaponry. From the perspective of winning a large-scale modern war with defense as the main purpose but involving local offensives, an early war has another advantage over a later war; namely, not counting the risk of a nuclear war, our conventional forces compare favorably with those of the U.S.. From a purely technical point of view, the US armed forces indeed have no match in the world, which characteristic constitutes the fundamental strength and framework of the U.S. in fighting a war. However, what we are talking about above is the whole

US military organization with its formal forces at the core, and the gigantic power also includes its advanced and powerful weaponry as well as its capability for nuclear strikes. Based on its structure, in times of strategic necessity, one third of its joint combat forces can be assembled and deployed for overseas operations within a short period of time, but this capability is limited to strategic flexibility. It may constitute a great deterrence to small military powers such as Iraq and Yugoslavia, but has no tactical advantage whatsoever in fighting against us, because we are close to home while they will be exhausted by the arduous expedition. When both sides rely mainly on missile strikes based on electronic confrontation, we evidently enjoy superiority in terms of the number of short-range and middle-range missiles.

So far the strategic superiority of the US joint forces has not been tested in a war against a big country. In contrast, using the Vietnamese War as an example, our forces do have the experience of fighting the US forces under modern warfare conditions. In that war, the Chinese forces were mainly responsible for air defense and accumulated a whole set of experience in this regard. Things have changed significantly since then, but the most telling changes should have occurred to our forces in terms of personnel qualifications and weaponry, which are well-tuned to meet the requirements of modern warfare. In terms of air defense, it is impossible for the US air force to enjoy the kind of dominance which they maintained in Iraq or Yugoslavia. Considering the morale of our forces and the nature of the war, and also considering the fact that the performance of the missiles on both sides is basically at the same level as well as the fact that both our defense and offense, which are the two major types of operation that can be imagined, will be carried out from our territory, the strategic superiority which can be claimed by the U.S. is close to zero. It does not even enjoy a sure advantage in terms of the foreseeable scale of war and the hi-tech content which can be applied to combat. It can be safely expected that once the U.S. launches an attack, the front line of the US forces and their supporting bases will be exposed within the range of our effective strikes. After the first strategic strike, the US forces will be faced with weaponry and Logistic problems, providing us with opportunities for major offensives and win large battles.

(3) Reaction to and preparation for escalation of war. Basically, we do not foresee a nuclear war between China and the U.S., for two basic facts will prevent it. First, it is against the US interests to fight a nuclear war against China simply for Li Denghui and his followers. On this point the anti-China US politicians will have to respect public opinion within the U.S.. Our principle is "willing to sustain major losses of our armed forces to defend even just one square inch of land." If the US forces lose thousands or hundreds of men under our powerful strikes, the anti-war sentiment within the their country will force the US government to take the same path as they did in Viet Nam.

Unlike Iraq and Yugoslavia, China is not only a big country, but also possesses a nuclear arsenal that has long since been incorporated into state warfare system and played a real role in our national defense. During last crisis across the Taiwan

Straits, the U.S. tried to blackmail us with their aircraft carrier(s), but when their spy satellites confirmed that our four nuclear submarines which used to be stationed at Lushun Harbor had disappeared, those politicians addicted to the Taiwan card could not imagine how worried their military commanders were. In comparison with the US nuclear arsenal, our disadvantage is mainly numeric, while in real wars the qualitative gap will be reflected only as different requirements of strategic theory. In terms of deterrence, there is not any difference in practical value. So far we have built up the capability for the second and the third nuclear strikes and are fairly confident in fighting a nuclear war. The PCC has decided to pass through formal channels this message to the top leaders of the U.S.. This is one of the concrete measures that we will take to prevent the escalation of war in the spirit of being responsible.

However, conceptually we are fully prepared for a prolonged warfare. Judging by each's domestic situation, it is the U.S. that will not be able to keep up for long. Historically, China has experience prolonged warfare against foreign invasion, and the People's Liberation Army (PLA) has the ability to safeguard the peaceful production activities by the people of all nationalities in China during the war. We do not want to fight a prolonged war, but this is because our country's basic principle is preserving peace and developing economy, not because we are afraid. Prolonged warfare will work to our advantage and enable us to defeat the enemy, which will be one of our strategic options to win the war under extreme circumstances.

(4) The basic principle of military operation against Taiwan. Our operational planning has been receiving extensive attention, not just from the U.S.; some friendly countries have also inquired about our intentions on various occasions. Foreign news media have published speculations on this topic, too. Since these speculations were based on research done by experts and specialized institutions, they did score some points. However, strategic perspectives can only be valuable when matched with battle operations and tactics. The key factor that has caused the West's lack of understanding of the capability of our armed forces to fight a modern war is bias and prejudice. The quality and level of their studies have not changed much since the early 1980s. For instance, some US studies questioned the capability of our armed forces to resolve Taiwan issue. The method employed in such studies is typical of studies on positional warfare under modern conditions.

Since Li Denghui came to power, Taiwan's military equipment has been updated, basically completing the generation change of the combat arms. However, how much this has enhanced the combat power of the Taiwan forces is yet to be seen, because the Taiwan forces do not have any combat experience and will not be able to stand the test of a large-scale war, which is a fatal weakness. For many years, Taiwan's defense system and war planning have not gone beyond the operational procedures of so-called "air superiority, sea superiority, and resistance to landing" and therefore will not be able to react accurately to the basic warfare model of instant, large-scale, and fully-extended operations. In particular, geographically

Taiwan occupies only a small area. Although the quality of its equipment is not too bad, its quantity is limited. It is obvious that after the first fatal strike, the Taiwan forces have no way to organize effective resistance. Under such circumstances, we will be able to control Taiwan before the US intervention and then concentrate our forces to fight the U.S.. Based on this scenario, it is impossible for the U.S. to force us to fight on two fronts when it tries to protect Taiwan.

4. To Fully Understand the PCC's Preparation for Resolution of Taiwan Issue

Taiwan issue is China's internal affair, and to resolve Taiwan issue and achieve reunification of the motherland is purely a concern of the Chinese government and the Chinese people. On this issue we will not take orders from anyone, nor do we allow anyone to point their fingers at us. Li Denghui's reliance on foreign forces shows that he does not understand the determination and capability of the Chinese government and the PLA in resolving Taiwan issue; it also shows that he does not care about the best interests of the Taiwan people. Before we take necessary reactions to Li and his followers motherland-splitting conduct, he will continue to create an atmosphere for splitting in answer to the call of a handful of anti-China US politicians and in an attempt to manipulate political trends in Taiwan, further poisoning the relationships between the two sides across the Straits. This will surely cause concern and discontent of neighboring countries and regions and objectively benefit us by working against the public opinion.

First of all, to effectively reduce the rampant arrogance of Li Denghui and Taiwan's splitting forces represented by him and to adapt our armed forces to cross-the-Straits operations, the CMC has decided, in accordance with the directions of the PCC, to carry out, based on combat phases, a series of large-scale of military exercises in both southeast coastal and inland regions from now on through early September. In comparison with the exercises in 1996, the PCC has not only made specific requirements as to the scale and the degree of combat likeness, but also clearly identified the target of these exercises, namely Taiwan's splitting forces represented by Li Denghui. These exercises will serve both as a warning to the Taiwan authorities and as a notice to the world of our current policy towards Taiwan. The timing for these exercises has been decided on by the PCC in consideration of the overall Taiwan policy, taking into account both internal and external as well as military and political factors. These exercises constitute a specific step and an important part of the current campaign waged by the Chinese people against the splitting under the leadership of our Party and government.

Internationally, President Jiang Zemin will go to Biskek in late September to attend the five-country summit meeting, including China, Russia, Kyrgyzstan, Kazakstan, and Tajikstan. The meeting will sum up and expand cooperations in the field of security and reach agreements on reduction of armed forces stationed along the borders and establishment of military trust. During the meeting, President Jiang Zemin will hold bilateral talks with President Yeltsin on political and military exchange and cooperation in face of challenges posed by new interventions out of hegemonism in international affairs. The above efforts will not only eliminate security concerns in the rear by reducing the traditional pressure along our northeast and northwest borders, and increase the proportion of forces which can be moved to the southeast coastal regions, but also serve to ensure our exchanges with the outside world by land routes during the war. This is an important strategic decision to maintain social stability and normal exchanges with other countries in case we are forced to fight a full-scale war against the U.S.. Such a decision represents a concrete expression of the PCC's determination to resolve Taiwan issue.

Apart from the above summit meeting, President Jiang Zemin will also make state visits to Thailand, Australia, and New Zealand in early September. He will meet with Clinton in mid-September to officially inform the U.S. of Chinese government's position on Taiwan issue. To complement the above visits, other Party and state leaders will also meet, either at home or abroad, leaders of a number of countries to manifest the Chinese government's determination to preserve sovereignty and territorial integrity and reunify the nation. These final efforts will promote the understanding of our position among countries throughout the world.

Domestically, our Party and government have intensified the effort to clean out corruption, taking organizational and administrative measures to preserve the outstanding tradition of the Party, to strengthen the relationships between Party cadres and ordinary people, and to alleviate popular discontent. At the ideological front, we grasped the opportunity and outlawed "Falun Gong," rooting out the biggest tightly-organized counterrevolutionary religious group with a platform and plans since the founding of our country and eliminating unstable factors in domestic politics. This measure has not only safeguarded the predominant position of materialism in the field of ideology, but also provided practical support for our armed forces to prepare for the war.

It must be pointed out that when we were dealing with "Falun Gong," we had to bear on one hand pressure from the so-called human-rights-ism, on the other hand, the Sino-US relations were at a low ebb because of conflict in Yugoslavia; moreover, Li Denghui threw out his "two-country theory" and caused Taiwan issue to take an abrupt turn. Given all these factors, we had to consider carefully the timing and the strategy. In fact, the determination with which our Party and state did away with "Falun Gong" reflected the overall evaluation of all the above factors. To outlaw "Falun Gong" was a pre-emptive measure aimed at the ultimate resolution of Taiwan issue, not only eliminating domestic trouble, but paving the way for the reunification as well. Negative international reaction has proven to be limited, and the protest from the U.S. was particularly pale and powerless, fully demonstrating that our Party has the ability and courage to gain advantage in complicated domestic and international struggles.

Between now and the end of the year, we will celebrate two grand occasions: the 50th anniversary of the founding of the People's Republic of China and resumption of sovereignty over Macao. To properly handle these two big events will have great impact on the resolution of Taiwan issue. The National Day celebrations should focus on the splendid achievements of the 50 years. According to the directions of the PCC, the PLA shall play the predominant role in the celebrations and the development of our armed forces shall be a reflection of accomplishments in all walks of life, which shall be displayed through a large-scale review of armed forces to our people of all nationalities and the people around the world. At the review, a number of advanced equipment and strategic weapons will be revealed to the outside world. Internally, this will enhance the morale of our people of all nationalities and inspire patriotism; externally, this will make clear to the world that we do have the capability to defend our country and promote reunification. Such a move constitutes an important link in our overall strategy on Taiwan.

On December 20, with the resolution of Macao issue, the humiliation that the Chinese people have been subjected to for more than a century will be washed away and a new chapter of the ultimate reunification of the motherland will begin. The smooth transition of Macao shows that we have surmounted yet another hurdle along the path of reunification and Taiwan issue has entered a substantive phase. This is also a premeditated decision made by the PCC. Although Li Denghui's splitting tricks have increased the possibility of a military solution and forced us to advance our timetable, they did not have any effect on our overall plan as far as priority is concerned. Our principle is seeking a peaceful solution and not resorting to military actions until the last moment. When this principle has been trampled upon and military actions become the only means to achieve reunification, we will not hesitate to carry out the historic mission that embodies the wishes of several generations. We will accomplish with our own hands the eternal cause of the reunification of the motherland.

For our Party and government as well as the people of China, including the people of Taiwan, Taiwan issue is the last issue before the achievement of the complete reunification of the motherland. Peaceful and gradual reunification are not only in the best interests of the people on both sides of the Taiwan Straits, but also in the long-term interests of the Chinese nation. This reasonable solution was first proposed by our Party based on the changes in domestic and international situations. At present, the foundation of a peaceful dialogue between two sides has been destroyed and the possibility for military actions has been greatly increased. Even so, we still strive to bring about a peaceful solution, which option shall remain valid until the last moment.

Every commander and soldier in our armed forces shall keep in mind the expectations of our Party and our people, attach great importance to political orientation, science, and skills that will stand the tests, strive to acquire modern military expertise under the guidance of Deng Xiaoping Theory, unwaveringly follow the leadership of the PCC with Comrade Jiang Zemin as its core, play the all-conquering role of the Great Wall of iron and steel, and make new contributions to our national defense and reunification of the motherland under the new historical conditions.

General Political Department of the People's Liberation Army August 1, 1999

DECEPTION

INDEX

DECEPTION